Listeners Guide to Musical Understanding

Fourth Edition

Listeners Guide to Musical Understanding

Leon Dallin
California State University
Long Beach

Wm. C. Brown Company Publishers
Dubuque, Iowa

Cover:
Emilio Pettoruti
The Quintet
Used by permission of San Francisco Museum of Modern Art, Gift of Dr. Grace L. Morley.

Consulting Editor
Frederick W. Westphal
California State University, Sacramento

Library of Congress Catalog Card Number: 76–11296

ISBN 0–697–03437–2

Third Printing, 1978

Printed in the United States of America

TO LYNN—

Who did much more than "only stand and wait."

Contents

Part II—THE FORMS OF MUSIC

Part III—THE PERIODS AND STYLES OF MUSIC

Colorplates

Figures

Tables

Preface

LISTENERS GUIDE to Musical Understanding is designed as a textbook for introductory music courses for general students at the college level. Its purpose is to increase the student's enjoyment and knowledge of music and to cultivate the art of intelligent and perceptive listening. No prior training or experience in music is assumed. Technical terminology is kept to a minimum while a working vocabulary of common and essential terms is developed. The book deals with music itself, not with such peripheral matters as biographical anecdotes or pictorial allusions.

A survey conducted on representative campuses revealed that a high percentage of students enrolled in introductory music classes lacked a functional knowledge of music notation and that even those who played an instrument could not readily comprehend abstract examples of printed music. Music notation, therefore, does not appear in the body of the text. An Appendix of Musical Examples is printed at the back of the book for the convenience of teachers and those students who find it helpful, but the ability to read music is not essential for listening pleasure or for comprehension of this text.

The listening material suggested for each unit of study is described objectively. In selecting the examples, four criteria were considered: musical value, appeal, suitability, and availability. Dates are given for each composer and work to place them in the proper time frame and historical perspective. The specified examples or equivalents can be found in most institutional record collections. Except as noted, the composers and works are listed in the current *Schwann-1 Record & Tape Guide* or in the semiannual *Schwann-2* supplement. Some examples appear in more than one section of the book to encourage repeated hearings. A stereo LP record album specially prepared to accompany the LISTENERS GUIDE contains more than 70 examples illustrating the principal materials, mediums, forms, periods, styles, and composers of music. These examples are keyed to the text and serve multiple functions.

Listening to the examples included in the record album and/or a representative selection from those cited in the text assures a balanced and varied exposure to music in a wide range of styles, but the intent is not to prescribe an inflexible listening program. When listening examples are omitted or substitute examples are used, or the book is read without interspersed listening, the material relating to specific examples (separated from the body of the text and set in different type) can be skipped without detracting from the continuity or completeness of the general information.

The amount and kind of listening can be adapted to the available time, resources, and facilities. It can be done in and out of the classroom, individually and in groups, and from commercial recordings or specially prepared tapes. More listening examples are listed than can ordinarily be heard in a typical course for the following reasons: (1) to suggest a wide range of listening experiences, (2) to provide alternate selections when all are not available, (3) to allow latitude for individual preferences, (4) to include adequate material for more comprehensive courses, and (5) to provide multiple examples for teachers who prefer to use excerpts. Performance times are given as an aid in planning classroom listening and outside assignments. The timings (in minutes:seconds) are accurate for a specific recording and approximate for other performances. Elapsed time is also used as an aid in the perception of musical form.

The organization of the book, starting with the materials of music (Part I), makes it possible to begin the course with music that is immediately appealing and for students to focus their attention initially on elements which they can perceive without difficulty. In Part II the forms of music are discussed, and descriptive outlines provided for the listening examples enable students to follow the various plans of musical organization without recourse to notation. The periods and styles of music are introduced chronologically in Part III, but the preceding sections contain extensive background information pertaining to style. The relative emphasis on each area of study and the order of presentation can be adjusted to individual requirements. Modern music, which sometimes receives short shrift, is abundantly represented throughout the book and is the subject of special chapters, as are folk and popular music, jazz, and the music of other cultures.

The information presented in the text combined with the recommended listening stimulates the formation of broad and discriminating musical tastes. With its emphasis on general principles that can be remembered and listening experiences that can be relished, the LISTENERS GUIDE launches readers on a program of enduring pleasure and personal enrichment.

Introduction

1

Music has been an integral part of man's culture since the dawn of civilization. Human beings have used rhythms and pitches for expressive purposes throughout recorded history and for thousands of years before. There is speculation that primitive music even antedates speech. Through the ages music has figured prominently in a wide range of human activities —in man's rituals, religions, ceremonies, and amusements.

There is no completely satisfactory explanation for the universality of music. It is not essential for life, yet life without it is unimaginable. It does not provide basic requirements or satisfy obvious instincts, but it has flourished with all peoples in all times and places.

Developing an appreciation of music and the arts is more important now than ever before. Modern efficiency is making more leisure time available. If it is to be utilized for more abundant living, worthwhile and enduring sources of pleasure must be cultivated. One of the most rewarding is music, and unlike many recreational activities, it is accessible throughout one's lifetime.

As a starting point, everyone likes some kind of music. The purposes of systematic listening and study are to heighten the pleasure derived from the music one already likes and to develop one's ability to appreciate additional types and styles of music. This book pursues both objectives, the relative emphasis depending upon one's perspective and previous exposure to music. Reading the book should prove of value in achieving the twin goals of greater understanding and broader taste, but reading alone assures but little progress. The reading must be followed by listening. A perusal of a travel folder is no substitute for a trip, and reading about music is no substitute for hearing it. Music must be given an opportunity to speak for itself.

For practical reasons, most of the listening will be done by means of recordings. Modern recording and playback equipment has reached an unprecedented degree of perfection. Still, there is an elusive quality in a live performance that a microphone cannot capture. More important, the empathy between performers and audiences is possible only in the concert hall. Recordings are a wonderful convenience and provide repeated hearings on demand, but only in live performance situations is the full impact of the listening experience achieved. Record listening should be supplemented by concert attendance whenever possible. The performances do not have to be by professionals. Living presence compensates for the technical limitations of students and amateurs.

The electronic age has revolutionized the listening habits of the world's peoples. Gone is the time when music was available only to the privileged and on special occasions. Gone is the time when audiences were limited to the capacity of a concert hall and when sound could be preserved only as long as an instrument continued to vibrate. The treasures of music now await the entire population at the turn of a dial or the push of a button. The inventions which make this possible are so much a part of 20th-century life it is difficult to realize that they have come into general use within the memory of senior citizens.

Sound recording has not been enlisted exclusively in the cause of art. It also serves the purposes of commerce and industry. Our ears are bombarded with sounds from loudspeakers while we shop, eat, work, and travel. Neither music nor advertising has been quite the same since the advent of the singing commercial, and now that music's efficacy in increasing production has been recognized, it competes regularly with the din of factories. When we seek diversion, music is generally in the background, if not in the foreground. We are engulfed in sound during our waking hours. In this situation a distinction must be made between *hearing* and *listening*.

A person hears music playing in the background but listens to the person with whom he is speaking. A person hears a room full of people talking but listens to one conversation. The ears and mind are capable of concentrating on one sound source to the exclusion of others. This is attentive listening, the first requirement if one is to appreciate music. Persons whose exposure to music is limited to random encounters in the course of other activities are bypassing opportunities for pleasure every day.

In the chain of musical expression there are three mutually dependent links—the composer, the performer, and the listener. Composers and performers are among the most ardent listeners, and it is not uncommon for musicians to be active in all three roles. Most people, however, are content to be listeners most of the time. Just to learn the craft of the composer or to acquire the technical proficiency of an artist performer requires years of arduous study and hours of daily practice, not to mention talent. Fortunately, the pathway to becoming a perceptive listener is considerably less demanding. Only the inclination and a modest amount of conditioning, which consists of listening to worthwhile music, are required. Appreciation inevitably follows sufficient acquaintance with good music. The process is hastened perhaps by acquiring knowledge about music, but most important is a judicious selection of listening experiences.

Music which has only transient appeal, which is already assimilated in our culture, or which functions primarily on a subconscious level will receive only passing notice in this study. The field is thus limited to music of enduring value which has achieved or which merits wide recognition and which sustains interest under scrutiny. Musical works which qualify are legion. The problem is not one of finding worthy examples but of making choices from the infinite possibilities. Limitations of time and space suggest a search for prototypes in various forms and styles and for various mediums which will serve as touchstones to the vast treasury of music.

To open the doors to this treasury, it is not necessary to study the rudiments of music or to play an instrument. These activities provide a source of pleasure and accomplishment for some, but for others they are sheer drudgery. If a person has outgrown his youthful enthusiasm for such things and has reached maturity without coping with them, chances are he never will. Fortunately, this is no barrier to the joy of music listening. If one has a particular interest in music fundamentals or in learning to play an instrument, that is another matter, but it is going the long way if the objective is to become an informed listener. There are more direct and pleasant routes.

One such course is charted here. It consists mostly of listening—listening to sounds of inherent beauty organized with consumate skill and brought to life by incomparable artists. Lest the impression be created that there is nothing to do but to bathe in sound, it must be understood that concentration and attentive listening are required. Specific features of the music must be sought out, learned, remembered, and recognized. Music, even a familiar piece, becomes more understandable and more meaningful in the process. There may be no obvious logic for liking music, but there is high correlation between preferences and the amount and sort of listening. It follows naturally that the person with the broadest and most extensive experience possesses the greatest potential for enjoyment. It is never too late, or too early, to begin acquiring this experience.

The Materials of Music

1

Characteristics of Sound

2

Objects which vibrate when energy is applied to them set the surrounding air in motion. The air transmits the vibrations, and human ears perceive as sound vibrating frequencies between approximately 20 and 20,000 per second, the limits varying somewhat with individuals and circumstances.

Three conditions are necessary for sound: (1) a *source,* (2) a *medium of transmission,* and (3) a *receiver.* Any object capable of causing the air molecules to vibrate in the appropriate frequency range can serve as a source of sound. The medium of transmission between the sound source and the receiver is normally the air, but water and solids also transmit sound vibrations. The ear serves as the receiver, responding to the vibrations and sending impulses to the brain which are interpreted as sound. Microphones and recording devices are receivers only in the sense that they detect and store vibrations for subsequent reproduction.

The main characteristics of sound are *pitch, loudness, color,* and *duration.*

Pitch

The first characteristic of sound is *pitch.* Pitch is directly related to the vibrating frequency of the sound source: the faster the rate of vibration, the higher the pitch; the slower the rate of vibration, the lower the pitch.

To experience the perception of pitch differences, listen to several notes played at random on the piano starting toward the left end of the keyboard and progressing toward the right end. Differences in pitch will be apparent to all who have normal hearing. The keys of the piano produce notes of graduated frequency and pitch from slow and low on the left to fast and high on the right.

When tuned to standard U.S. pitch (A = 440), the lowest note on the piano has a frequency of 27½ vibrations per second. The white key third from the right end of the piano keyboard produces a note with a frequency 128 times greater, 3520 vibrations per second. The frequency of the highest note on the piano is over 4000. Even so, the perceived pitches of the piano and all musical instruments fall in the middle and lower portions of the audible range. If the rate of vibration of the lowest note on the piano were halved, it would be below the audible range, but the frequency of the highest note could be doubled twice and still be heard by a young person. The ability to hear high pitches declines with age.

Now listen to the sounds produced alternately by two adjacent keys on the piano, from a white key to a black key or vice versa if they are next to each other. Adjacent keys on the piano produce the smallest pitch difference used consistently and systematically in the music of our culture. Nearly everyone can hear the difference and can tell whether the second tone was higher or lower in pitch than the first. Pitch perception this acute is essential for the complete comprehension of music. Actually, most people can distinguish between pitches with much less difference, especially in the middle register. Recognizing small differences in pitch is easiest in the middle registers, somewhat more difficult in the high and low registers.

Faulty pitch discrimination can often be improved with a few minutes of drill. It is not that the ability to hear pitches actually improves so much as that one learns what to listen for and how to interpret what he hears. The results of such drill can be measured and general pitch acuity determined by playing pairs of notes, one after the other, in different registers of the piano and with varying distances between them. Students indicate whether the second note is higher or lower than the first. With a few minutes of practice, the percentage of individuals who cannot make a perfect score will be relatively small.

A distinguishing characteristic between tones and noises is the presence or absence of pitch. Musical sounds are produced by regular vibrations at a constant rate and have a definite pitch. Noises are produced by erratic vibrations with variable frequencies and have no precise pitch, though they can be classified generally as high or low. Some sounds combine elements of tone and noise, and sounds acoustically classified as noise are utilized in certain avant-garde musical styles.

Loudness

The second characteristic of sound is *loudness.* The perception of loudness is the subjective reaction to intensity. The intensity or energy of a sound is related to the area and the amount of displacement in the vibrating body producing it. Other factors being equal, a large vibrating surface produces a louder sound than a small one, and wide fluctuations produce louder sounds than narrow ones. The perceived sound, however, is also affected by the medium of transmission and the distance from the source. Since air is the normal medium of transmission it may be regarded as constant. Loudness is roughly inversely proportional to the square of the distance from the source of the sound.

Musical instruments are designed to take advantage of the physical properties of sound in the matter of loudness. A string of the length and diameter used on a violin vibrating by itself would be barely audible. The body of the instrument increases the area of vibrating surface and amplifies the tone. A sound board in pianos serves the same purpose. Also, the amount of displacement in the vibrating surface of most instruments can be regulated by performers by striking, blowing, bowing, or plucking with more or less force, providing a wide range of dynamic levels.

The human ear has amazing adaptability to variations in loudness. It can detect the faintest whisper or rustle of leaves and yet is capable of withstanding the shock of thunder and cannons. Composers take full advantage of this ability and explore dynamic ranges approaching both extremes. A unit of sound representing the smallest change the ear can discern is called a *decibel.* The sound produced by an orchestra playing full force is approximately 100 decibels. In other words, the ear can detect 100 graduations of loudness between the threshold of sound and the volume of the full orchestra.

Tone Color

Musicians use a word of French origin, *timbre,* for the third characteristic of sound, but *tone color* and *tone quality* convey the same meaning and are easier to remember and pronounce. Color is the tonal characteristic which enables one to distinguish the sounds of the various instruments. The tones produced by each instrument contain, in addition to the fundamental frequency heard as the pitch, a distinctive pattern of higher frequencies. These higher frequencies, present in most sounds and all musical tones, are *overtones.* Overtones are the coloring components in sounds which make it possible to identify their sources. Though overtones under normal conditions are too weak in relation to the fundamental to be heard as pitches, a simple experiment will make some of the more prominent ones in a piano tone audible.

Select any white key in the lower part of the piano. Starting with the selected key, count up eight white keys. Those familiar with music will recognize this as an octave. Depress the second key without playing it, and hold it down. Now strike the first key sharply, and release it immediately. The pitch of the second key will sound faintly but audibly. The pitch of the second key can be verified by playing it. This experiment will work under favorable conditions (in a quiet room with a well-tuned piano) with the twelfth, fifteenth, and seventeenth white keys above the selected key. Attentive listeners may be able to hear the pitches of these keys depressed singly or in combinations concurrently with the pitch of the first key if it is held down until its tone begins to fade. In this way the overtones are amplified but are heard in conjunction with the predominant fundamental tone, as they are normally.

The effect of overtones on tone quality can be demonstrated by comparing the sound of a modern high fidelity record player with that of an old or inexpensive model or the sound of a new stereo record with that of an old 78 rpm record. Similar effects can be obtained by reducing the high frequencies with the treble control or a filter. In each instance the difference in the perceived sound is due primarily to the relative presence or absence of the high frequencies of the overtones. High fidelity sound reproduction is possible now that the complex problems of reproducing the frequencies of the entire audible range have been solved, and recorded sound at its best recreates to a remarkable degree the vivid color and beauty of live sound.

Instruments and voices produce several overtones of varying intensity extending into the upper limits of the audible range. In distinguishing the sounds of the various instruments and individual voices, the ear detects minute differences in sound waves, including those differences caused by overtones. To duplicate this feat in the laboratory requires an array of complicated equipment. The aural capabilities are utilized to the fullest, but not taxed, in detecting the subtle differences by which the sources of sound are identified.

Still finer shadings of quality distinguish the tone of a concert artist from a beginner and the tone of a Stradivarius violin from a factory production model. Musicians readily differentiate between the tone of a valuable instrument and a cheap one and between the tone of a professional player and a young student. Discrimination of this sort requires experience and an adequate basis for comparison but no special ability.

Composers consciously exploit the myriad tone qualities at their disposal, and no small part of the music listener's delight derives from the exquisite coloring of musical sounds.

Duration

The fourth attribute of sound is *duration*. Sounds may be long or short, lasting from a small fraction of a second to many seconds. All instruments can play short notes, but there are practical limitations on the duration of tones. Wind instruments and voices can sustain tones only for the duration of one breath; string instruments for the length of one bow. A piano can sustain a tone only as long as the string continues to vibrate from the initial impetus imparted to it by the hammer. The piano tone is loudest at the moment of impact, and from that instant it diminishes constantly to the vanishing point. Tones in the lower register of the piano with a loud start can be heard for several seconds. Those in the upper register are audible for a much shorter period. Of all the instruments, only organs can sustain tones indefinitely.

Musicians develop skills in breathing, blowing, bowing, and fingering which enable them to create the illusion of almost continuous sound. At least listeners are rarely aware of the physical limitations imposed on duration.

Factors other than pitch, loudness, color, and duration influence how tones are perceived. Especially important is the way a tone begins and ends. *Attack* and *decay* are the terms for the initial and terminal phases of a tone. The attack may be sudden and explosive, as it tends to be when a piano key or a percussion instrument is struck, or the sound may reach its peak intensity more gradually, as it does typically when a string is bowed. Tones normally fade at the end, but the fading may be gradual or abrupt. Each sound source has characteristic attack and decay patterns which contribute to its identity. When tones are heard in succession as in a melody, they are attacked and released, joined and separated in a manner deemed appropriate by the performer. The terms used to describe the total effect are *phrasing* and *articulation*. All of the essential attributes of musical sound can be more or less accurately represented in musical notation.

Notation

A reasonably precise system of notation has evolved through the ages for the characteristics of sound. It serves as a means of communication between composers and performers and as a method of preserving the music of previous generations. Modern notation dates back to about 1600, and musicologists can read and transcribe the music manuscripts of much earlier periods.

Composers can designate any pitch or combination of pitches by means of note symbols placed in relation to an arrangement of five lines enclosing four spaces following a sign. These devices tell the performer which note or notes to play on his instrument, and since each note has by agreement a certain frequency, the specified pitches can be realized with absolute precision.

The notation of loudness is less exact. A set of signs, really abbreviations of Italian terms, indicate relative degrees of loudness from very loud to very soft, or in extreme cases from very, very loud to very, very soft. Appropriate signs indicating the degree of loudness or softness plus certain additional signs indicating gradual or sudden changes from one to the other are given at strategic places in written music. Performers must exercise judgment in the interpretation of these signs since they are only relative.

When composers specify a particular instrument, they are designating tone color. They hope, of course, for a gifted performer playing an adequate instrument. In addition, composers may include in the notation special instructions regarding the type of tone or style of playing desired. They may also indicate the use of devices which affect the tone color, such as *mutes*.

Modifications in the shape of note symbols are used to show relative duration. The same symbols denote duration by their shape and pitch by their location. Though only relative values are established by the shapes of the symbols, this may be supplemented by an indication of how many units of a specified type will occur in a minute. This gives the notation of duration an absolute value which otherwise is lacking.

Being able to read and write music or the lack of this ability has very little to do with the listening process for either musicians or nonmusicians. Often nonmusicians think they are missing something when they hear a concert or a recording because they cannot read music. They may suspect that the ability to read music makes sounds more meaningful. Such is not the case. If musicians get more out of hearing music than others, it is because they have learned to listen better, not because they read music. They do not sit in a concert visualizing the symbols for the music they are hearing. They couldn't if they tried, and even to attempt it would reduce rather than enhance their pleasure. One who reads language but not music has only to compare his reaction while watching a play or movie to recognize the validity of this statement.

You will not need to read music or even program notes to appreciate the voluptuous beauty of the following example. Listen for the broad sweep and infinite variety of its musical sounds from soft to loud, low to high, transparent to full, and somber to brilliant.

Maurice Ravel: *Daphnis and Chloé, Suite no. 2* (1911)
(1875–1937)

1. Daybreak 5:25
2. Pantomine 6:00
3. General Dance 4:35

The great Russian impresario, Diaghilev, commissioned Ravel to compose music for a ballet. *Daphnis and Chloé,* from which this suite is taken, was the result. For sheer beauty of musical sound this work is without peer. It exploits the full dynamic range of the orchestra from the soft rustle of the opening to the thundering climax of the end. It uses the full pitch range of the orchestra from the top register of the high-pitched instruments to the bottom register of the low-pitched instruments.

Supplementary Material

Science in the Orchestra, 3 sound films, British Information Services (available from McGraw-Hill)

1. Hearing the Orchestra 13:00
   The nature of sound and its transmission. The structure and mechanism of the ear.
2. Exploring the Instruments 14:00
   How different pitches are produced and the range of various instruments.
3. Looking at Sounds 12:00
   Demonstration of harmonic components (overtones) by means of an audiospectrometer.

The Science of Musical Sounds, sound film, Academy Films 11:00
Explores the basic principles of sound production using three types of musical instruments: harp, flute, and xylophone.

The Science of Sound, 2–12″ LP's, Folkways 6007 (abridged version 6136)
Recordings produced by the Bell Telephone Laboratories describing and demonstrating the phenomena of sound, including how we hear, frequency, pitch, intensity, loudness, fundamentals and overtones, and quality.

The Sounds of Music, sound film, Coronet 11:00
Characteristics of musical sound and principles of amplitude and frequency. Illustrations using string, wind, and percussion instruments.

Sources of Musical Sound

3

The first source of musical sound was the human body. It possessed an ideal sound source in the vocal cords, and the body could also produce sounds by stamping, clapping, and slapping. In prehistoric times these innate sources were augmented by external devices, and the development of instruments began.

Instruments expand the dimensions of sound. They can produce sounds which are louder and both higher and lower than those possible with the body unassisted. They add to the available tone colors and make possible the playing of combined pitches by a single performer. Some instruments contribute agility and others sustaining power to the sound resources.

The sounds of music are produced by the voice, by bowing, blowing, striking, and plucking an assortment of instruments, and by electronic devices. Keyboard instruments couple one of these basic sound producing processes with a keyboard mechanism. The functions of instruments are to provide a responsive source of sound, a means of amplifying that sound, and ways of controlling its pitch, duration, and loudness. Modern instruments in the hands of adroit performers attain these objectives to a high degree, but for warmth, intimacy and immediacy of appeal the human voice remains supreme. The sound sources of concert music are described and pictured in the following pages, and the suggested listening provides an introduction to the great music created for each voice and instrument.

Voices

Voices are classified according to range, sex, and somewhat according to quality. From high to low the basic classifications are: *soprano, alto, tenor,* and *bass.* Soprano and alto designate respectively high and low female and unchanged male voices. Tenor and bass designate high and low changed male voices. Observe that the range of a high, mature male voice still is lower than that of a low female or unchanged voice. The compass of any voice is limited, but the span from the top of the highest soprano voice to the bottom of the lowest bass voice is about four octaves (compared with a piano range of a little over seven octaves).

The terms *soprano, alto, tenor,* and *bass* are applied not only to voices and singers but to the parts they sing in ensembles and to corresponding parts in instrumental music.

The most ordinary range for a woman's voice lies between that of soprano and alto. This intermediate voice is called *mezzo-soprano.* The parallel male voice with a range between that of tenor and bass is known as *baritone.* These, together with the four previously named, constitute the six usual voice types. Further distinctions are made, primarily in operatic music, on the basis of style and quality.

SOPRANO voices are subdivided into *coloratura, lyric, dramatic,* and *mezzo.* Coloratura sopranos have unusually high voices and specialize in performing music *colored* by ornamentation, runs, and rapid passages requiring great agility. In operas, the heroine's role often calls for a coloratura soprano. Lyric sopranos concentrate on beauty of sound rather than extreme range or power. Their literature demands a light vocal quality and a melodious, flowing style. A lyric soprano voice is ideal for many art songs and for leading parts in light operas and musical comedies. Arias in grand operas, too, may require lyric soprano style and quality. Dramatic soprano is the appellation for sopranos with powerful voices and pronounced histrionic ability. Operatic roles portraying intense emotions are assigned to dramatic sopranos, and only sopranos of this type can cope with the heavy orchestral accompaniments and emotional demands of Wagnerian music drama. Mezzo-soprano voices lack both the brilliance of the higher soprano voices and the richness of the lower alto voices. Since more women's voices fall in this category than any other, supreme vocal quality and musicianship are essential for mezzo-sopranos who make a career of singing. *Carmen* is one of the few operas with the leading role assigned to a mezzo-soprano, but many supporting parts in operas are sung by mezzo-sopranos.

Various types of soprano voices are illustrated in the following selections.

LEO DELIBES: *Lakmé,* opera (1883)
(1836–1891) Act II. Bell Song 5:10

Lakmé, the beautiful daughter of a Hindu priest, sings this coloratura aria at a religious festival attended by British soldiers, including her lover, Gerald.

GIUSEPPE VERDI: *La Traviata,* opera (1853)
(1813–1901) Act I. Sempre libera (Always Free) 3:50

La Traviata is based on Dumas's *Camille.* The coloratura heroine sings of a life of freedom and pleasure in this brilliant aria.

HEITOR VILLA–LOBOS: *Bachianas Brasileiras no. 5* (1938)
(1887–1959) 1. Cantilena 6:50

Composed "in memory of Bach," this song for lyric soprano and eight cellos evokes the nocturnal beauties of nature.

(Also record side 8 bands 2–4)[1]

GEORGES BIZET: *Carmen,* opera (1875)
(1838–1875) Act III. Micaela's Air 4:25

In this lyric aria Micaela brings Don José news of his mother and pleads with him to leave the gypsy, Carmen, and return home.

RICHARD WAGNER: *Tristan and Isolde,* music drama (1865)
(1813–1883) Act III. Liebestod (Love Death) 7:20

This dramatic lament is Isolde's last utterance before she is reunited with Tristan in death.

(Also record side 2 band 1)[1]

GIACOMO PUCCINI: *Tosca,* opera (1900)
(1858–1924) Act II. Vissi d'arte (I lived only for art) 3:02

Tosca, in this dramatic aria, sings of her life unselfishly devoted to art and love.

(Record side 6 band 4)

GEORGES BIZET: *Carmen,* opera (1875)
(1838–1875) Act I. Habanera 4:00
Act I. Seguidilla 3:50
Act II. Gypsy Song 3:45

---

1. The "also" in a record reference indicates an optional example in the *Listeners Guide* record album which serves the same function as the example described and which may be used to supplement or to replace it.

Carmen, a mezzo-soprano in the title role, sings the taunting *Habanera* as she begins her flirtation with Don José, a soldier. She tempts him with the prospect of a rendezvous in the seductive *Seguidilla*. The *Gypsy Song* is sung by Carmen for the entertainment of her merrymaking friends at the inn of Lillas Pastia.

Voice classifications beyond the basic types are determined more by the particular selection being sung than by the voice. The literatures are not mutually exclusive, and the repertoire of most singers includes songs of various types. Singers for obvious reasons choose numbers which show their voices to advantage, but many are equally at home in two or more styles.

ALTO and CONTRALTO are used synonymously, though contralto sometimes seems to carry the connotation of a particularly deep alto voice. There is no distinction between them in the literature. It exploits the low tones of the female voice. The quality, typically and in the following examples, is rich, resonant, dark, and "throaty."

G. F. HANDEL: *Messiah*, oratorio (1742)
(1685–1759) 9. O thou that tellest good tidings 4:57

This, *He shall feed his flock*, and *He was despised* are the three arias for alto (or contralto) in Handel's immortal *Messiah*.

(Record side 2 band 6)

GUSTAV MAHLER: *Das Lied von der Erde (Song of the Earth)* (1908)
(1860–1911) 4. Von der Schoenheit (Of Beauty) 6:40

The Song of the Earth is really a symphony for orchestra with two solo voices, alto and tenor, which alternate in its six movements. The texts are free translations of Chinese poems contemplating aspects of earthly existence.

TENOR voices, like soprano voices, sometimes are classified according to type. *Robusto* (robust), *lyric*, *dramatic*, and *heroic* are adjectives commonly attached to tenors. *Tenor robusto* is the type with tremendous power in the upper register featured in Italian opera. This is the type of voice to which most young tenors aspire. *Lyric* tenors, also referred to as "Irish" tenors, are the counterpart of lyric sopranos. Their voices possess the same qualities, and they sing the same type of music, ofttimes the same songs. *Dramatic* and *heroic* tenors have much in common with robust tenors, but the terms are associated with German opera. These tenors often begin their careers as high baritones and through training and practice add to their natural range the high tones necessary to sing tenor roles.

The following examples, without specific designations, illustrate various types of tenor voices.

RUGGIERO LEONCAVALLO: *I Pagliacci* (*Punchinello*), opera (1892)
(1858–1919) Act I. Vesti la giubba 2:30
(On with the play)

Having learned of his wife's infidelity, the tenor Canio sings this anguished aria as he prepares for the performance of a comedy.

GIUSEPPE VERDI: *Rigoletto,* opera (1851)
(1813–1901) Act IV. La donna è mobile 2:11
(Woman is fickle)

The Duke, portrayed by a tenor, sings of women but reveals his own fickleness in this rollicking aria.

(Record side 5 band 11)

GEORGES BIZET: *Carmen,* opera (1875)
(1838–1875) Act II. Flower Song 3:15

Don José discloses a flower preserved from his first meeting with Carmen and sings of his devotion in this tenor aria.

W. A. MOZART: *Don Giovanni* (*Don Juan*), opera (1787)
(1756–1791) Act I. Dalla sua pace 3:50
(On her all joy dependeth)
Act II. Il mio tesoro (To my beloved) 4:10

In the second of these arias, the tenor executes florid passages similar to those associated with coloratura sopranos. It was replaced by the first when the tenor engaged for the Vienna performance found the original too difficult. Both love songs are included in modern scores and performances.

RICHARD WAGNER: *Die Meistersinger* (*The Mastersingers*), opera (1868)
(1813–1883) Act. III. Prize Song 5:45

The *Prize Song* with which Walther wins the song contest and the hand of Eva figures prominently in the *Prelude* to the opera and is also heard in Act II.

BARITONES, like mezzo-sopranos, are in competition with the most prevalent voice type of their sex. They cannot hope to impress audiences with extremes of range or feats of brilliance. They compensate with solid production and skillful interpretation. The designation is not customary in choral music, but operatic parts are entrusted to baritone voices.

GEORGES BIZET: *Carmen,* opera (1875)
(1838–1875) Act II. Toreador Song 4:25

This rousing song about the glory of the bull ring is sung by the baritone, Escamillo, to an entranced group, including the impressionable Carmen.

(Also record side 5 band 3)

RUGGIERO LEONCAVALLO: *I Pagliacci* (*Punchinello*), opera (1892)
(1858–1919) Prologue 7:45

Tonio, a baritone playing the role of a clown, slips through the closed curtain and explains in song that the play to be presented is based upon life and that the players are real people, not mere actors on a stage.

BASS is the general term for all low male voices. Subdivisions, as with other voices, are predicated more upon the role or selection being sung than upon the characteristics of the voice. A bass singer especially proud of his low notes may advertise himself as a *basso profondo.* One who claims a range encompassing that of bass and baritone combined (or who lacks extremes of either) may adopt the title of *bass-baritone.* A bass specializing in a lyric style will be known as a *basso cantante,* and one associated with comic roles will be known as a *basso buffo.*

W. A. MOZART: *The Magic Flute,* opera (1791)
(1756–1791) Act II. In diesen heiligen Hallen 4:19
(Within these sacred halls)

In this aria the bass, High Priest Sarastro, consoles the despairing Pamina and assures her that Prince Tamino will soon be free to marry her. When the opera is sung in Italian, this aria is known as *Qui sdegno non s'accende.**

*(Record side 4 band 1)

MODEST MUSSORGSKY: *Boris Godounov,* opera (1874)
(1839–1881) Act I. Prayer of Boris 3:00
Act IV. Monologue 5:00

Immediately following his coronation as Tsar of Russia, Boris, a bass, prays for mercy and guidance in his reign. In the *Monologue* the dying Boris bids his son farewell and gives him advice as successor to the throne.

W. A. MOZART: *Don Giovanni (Don Juan)*, opera (1787)
(1756–1791) Act I. Madamina (Catalog Aria) 5:00

In this humorous bass aria, Leporello, Don Giovanni's manservant, recites a catalog of his master's conquests—640 in Italy, 231 in Germany, 100 in France, 91 in Turkey, and in Spain 1003!

The practice of publishers, for reasons more pecuniary than artistic, to issue songs with piano accompaniments in high, medium, and low versions fosters the interchange of literature between voice types and between male and female voices. Because of this, all of the foregoing examples were drawn from extended works with orchestral accompaniments, mainly operas. The singers in operatic roles must perform the parts as they are written to be in agreement with the orchestra and the other singers. Furthermore, the full potential of any given voice type will be exploited in the part of a leading character. Singers are selected for operatic roles on the basis of having a voice that fits the part, and they concentrate their efforts on a limited number of roles for which their voices are best suited. Successful composers of opera are aware of the special abilities and problems of singers and as a rule provide them with ample opportunities for vocal display and, after strenuous scenes, a chance to recuperate.

The human voice as a musical medium has one exclusive attribute. It is the only source of musical sound that can convey a message or tell a story.

Instruments Played by Bowing

One method of producing a tone is to draw coarse hair dusted with rosin across a taut string. The hair is fastened at each end to a stick originally curved in the manner of an archer's bow but now bent in the opposite direction. The name, however, is retained. The hair is obtained from horses' manes and tails, and most of it comes from Russia. The sticks are made of Brazilwood, and the best comes from the state of Pernambuco in Brazil. The venerable bow has gone the way of many modern products, and synthetics are sometimes substituted now for both the hair and the wood. Fittings attached to the stick hold the hair (or synthetic) straight and smooth and make the tension adjustable. The act of drawing the bow over the strings is *bowing,* and instruments played by bowing are *string instruments.*

Modern bowed instruments are the product of a long period of evolution which culminated with the perfection of the violin family around 1600. They all have four strings with one end tied firmly to a tailpiece and the other wrapped around a peg that is turned to adjust the tuning. Near the fixed end the strings pass over a bridge which transmits the vibration of the strings to the body of the instrument. The body serves as a resonating chamber which amplifies the sound of the vibrating strings to useful levels. Its distinctive shape resulted partially from experiments leading to the perfection of its resonating characteristics, but the indentation at the middle of each side was a practical concession which permits the bow to function on the outside strings. Protruding from the body of the instrument is a narrow neck which accommodates the left hand of the player and allows his fingers easy access to the strings. Length, tension, and diameter determine the pitch of the open strings. Pitch changes are made by depressing the strings against the fingerboard with the fingers. Variations in loudness, tone quality, and style are made by applying the bow to the strings in different ways. Slight variations in tone quality also can be made by a motion of the hand stopping the strings known as *vibrato*. Vibrato affects the pitch slightly but not audibly. It appears as a shaking motion of the hand. Another tone modification is obtained by inhibiting the vibration of the bridge with a small device of wood, metal, plastic, or rubber called a *mute*.

The four bowed string instruments arranged from the highest pitched and smallest to the lowest pitched and largest are: *violin, viola, cello* (also called *violoncello*), and *bass* (also called *string bass, contrabass,* and *double bass*). The strings are the most versatile instruments. Together they have a pitch range almost as wide as that of the piano. They are equally at home in rapid pyrotechnics and slow, sustained melodies. They are capable of great expressiveness and brittle wit. It is small wonder that they are both the prima donnas and the workhorses of every instrumental ensemble from which they are not excluded.

The VIOLIN is the most brilliant and agile of the string family. This is partially because its relatively short, thin strings respond instantaneously to the slightest pressure of the bow, and partially because its small size allows a very efficient technique of stopping the strings with the fingers of the left hand. The instrument is held in a horizontal position under the chin, and the bow is drawn at right angles to the string by the right hand and arm. Violins are the sopranos of the string section and more often than not play the melody, but they are just as effective in a variety of supporting roles. Cataloging their capabilities is impossible, but the suggested listening gives an impression of their versatility.

NICCOLO PAGANINI: *Caprices, op. 1*
(1782–1840) 24. Theme and variations 4:27

Paganini was the greatest violinist of his age. With him the tradition of the virtuoso performer began. His 24 *Caprices* for unaccompanied violin exploit every facet of violin technique, including some features he originated. Publication of most of his compositions was withheld during his lifetime to preserve his secrets.

(Record side 5 band 1. Theme p. 381)

FIGURE 1. *Violin and Viola*

EDOUARD LALO: *Symphonie Espagnole, op. 21* (1875)
(1823–1892) 1. Allegro non troppo 7:30

The title notwithstanding, this is a concerto for violin and orchestra. It is a brilliant display vehicle in the Spanish idiom with strikingly varied writing for the solo instrument.

(Also record side 2 band 4)

The VIOLA is the alto member of the string family. Violas are slightly larger than violins, but not enough to be immediately apparent to the casual observer except by comparison. They are played in the same manner as violins. Their range is lower, more so than the difference in size would indicate. The ideal ratio of string length to pitch is compromised somewhat to keep the instrument within practical dimensions for under-the-chin playing. Heavier strings less tightly strung compensate for the reduced length in producing the desired pitch. These adjustments contribute to the distinctive tone quality of the viola which tends to be more somber than the violin and a bit nasal. Listening is suggested which provides direct comparison with the violin, with which the viola is most easily confused.

BELA BARTOK: *Concerto for Viola* (1945)
(1881–1945) 2. Adagio religioso 5:15
3. Allegro vivace 4:20

The *Adagio* with its typically somber viola style and quality is followed without interruption by the *Allegro* demonstrating the agility of which the instrument is capable. The high register of the viola, used at times in this and other solo works, is less common in orchestral writing.

W. A. MOZART: *Duo no. 2 in B-flat,*[2] *K.424*[3] (1783)
(1756–1791) 3. Andante con variazioni 7:45

This duo for violin and viola provides an ideal means of comparing the tone quality of the two instruments, especially when a theme stated by one instrument is imitated immediately by the other.

The CELLO has the same basic shape as the violin and the viola, but it is much larger. It is held between the player's knees and is supported by an end pin resting on the floor. This playing position, which is upside down in comparison with the violin and viola, and the cello's greater size necessitate different fingering and bowing techniques. The highest open string on the cello is tuned just one step higher than the lowest open string on the violin, but a cellist can play many notes in the violin range. Violins and cellos have essentially the same ratio of size to pitch, so a cello in its high register can be mistaken for a violin. The low register is rich, sonorous, and distinctive. The cello is the tenor of the string family, but in ensembles two parts are often taken by violins, and the cellos are moved down to the bass.

J. S. BACH: *Suite no. 4 in E-flat for Cello, S.1010*[4]
(1685–1750) 2. Allemande 2:55

This suite for cello unaccompanied is one of six Bach wrote in the years 1717–1723. The characteristic middle and low registers of the cello are heard in the *Allemande.*

---

2. Keys unless otherwise indicated are major.
3. The works of Mozart are identified by K. numbers. These numbers relate to the order of the works in a chronological catalog of Mozart's compositions compiled by Dr. Ludwig Koechel in 1862.
4. The identifying numbers for Bach works are from the thematic catalog compiled by Wolfgang Schmieder.

FIGURE 2. *Cello and Bass*

JOSEPH HAYDN:	*Concerto in D for Cello, op. 101* (1783)		
(1732–1809)	2.	Adagio	5:30
	3.	Rondo: Allegro	5:00

These two movements of the concerto, in contrasting tempos and styles, demonstrate the extreme registers of the cello and some of the intricate figurations playable on string instruments.

The DOUBLE BASS, STRING BASS, CONTRABASS, or simply the BASS is the largest of the string family. It is so large the player stands or perches on a high stool beside it, and the full weight of the instrument is borne by an end pin resting on the floor. The lowest bass string is as heavy as a small rope, and its pitch is almost as low as the lowest note on a piano. The other strings are only slightly smaller, and considerable energy must be imparted by the bow to set them in motion. Strong fingers are essential to stop them for the different pitches. Notes higher than the lowest violin pitch are possible but rare on the bass. The normal bass range overlaps the lower cello range and reaches into that of the viola. The tone of a single bass tends to be fuzzy and lacking in focus. This effect is reduced with a group of basses, but even so they seldom are used in a solo capacity or unsupported by other instruments.

CAMILLE SAINT-SAENS: *Carnival of the Animals* (1886)
(1835–1921) 5. The Elephant 1:35

This is one of the few instances in which the orchestral string basses play the principal melody unassisted.

Instruments Played by Blowing

A number of instruments with quite different shapes, sounds, and mechanisms are played by blowing. Instruments played by blowing are *wind instruments*, and their sound is produced by a vibrating column of air. At one time wind instruments could be divided conveniently on the basis of the material from which they were made—wood and brass. The terms *woodwind* and *brass*, derived from this division, are still used to classify instruments, though metal is now substituted for wood in the manufacture of some "woodwind" instruments.

The sound of all wind instruments stems from a vibrating column of air, but the means of setting the air in motion varies. In playing brass instruments the lips, activated by the breath, become vibrating membranes, and in contact with mouthpieces of assorted sizes and shapes they energize the air inside the instruments. The lips, breath, and mouth function rather differently in producing sound in woodwind instruments. A stream of air issuing from the lips strikes the edge of a hole in flutes and piccolos and produces the sound in the same way sound is produced blowing over the top of a small bottle. With clarinets and saxophones a thin, finely shaped piece of cane called a *reed* is the primary source of vibration. The reed is firmly attached to the mouthpiece at one end. The other, parallel with the tip of the mouthpiece, is inserted between the lips. Air passing between the reed and the mouthpiece causes the reed to vibrate. The reeds of oboes and bassoons consist of two pieces of cane bound together as double reeds with just enough space between them at the center for the passage of air. The free end of the double reed is inserted between the lips, and both halves vibrate when air is forced between them.

A distinction also can be made between woodwinds and brasses on the basis of their mechanisms. The woodwinds have several holes located along the instrument which are opened and closed by the fingers or by keys and pads activated by the fingers. The pattern of open and closed holes in conjunction with the manner of blowing determines the pitch. There are alternate fingerings for some notes, but most patterns produce only one pitch.

The mechanism of the brass instruments is most clearly illustrated by the trombone. The trombone has a slide which can be extended or shortened to change the length of the tubing through which the air passes. The principle is the same for the other brass instruments, but changes in tube length are accomplished by valves. Each valve is connected to a different length of tubing through which the air passes when the valve is depressed. Otherwise this tubing is bypassed. The air takes the longest route through the horn when the valves are all down and the shortest way when they are all up. Various combinations of three valves suffice for all the pitches on the instrument. The fourth valve with which some brass instruments are equipped serves either to improve the intonation or to change the key of the instrument. Several pitches are obtained with each valve combination by altering the manner of blowing and the formation of the lips. *Embouchure* is the term used to describe the formation of the lips and the placement of the tongue in relation to the mouthpiece of wind instruments.

The tone of brass instruments, like that of strings (but not woodwinds) can be modified by mutes. Mutes for brass instruments made of various materials and in assorted shapes and sizes are inserted in the bell, that is, in the flared open end of the instrument. All have the effect of reducing and muffling the tone, the exact quality depending upon the construction and material. Unlike the other brass instruments, French horns are shaped so the player can insert his hand in the bell of the instrument. French horns are usually muted or *stopped* with the hand rather than with a mechanical device. *Stopped* notes on the horn sound delicate and far away when they are soft, brassy when they are loud and accented.

In Table 1 instruments listed in the first column are most common and widely used. Those in the second column are essentially a larger or smaller version of a basic instrument on the same line in the first column. Instruments in the third column are either further modifications of basic instruments or special purpose instruments used mostly in bands and/or popular music.

Instruments on the same line in Table 1 generally are constructed and their music written in a manner which enables a player to transfer technique from one to another with minimum difficulty. For example, a flute player with a modest amount of practice can play a piccolo or an alto flute. Likewise, a person who plays any one of the clarinets can readily adapt his technique to the others. The same relationship exists between all the saxophones, between oboe and English horn, and so on.

TABLE 1
WIND INSTRUMENTS

	Basic Orchestra	*Large Orchestra*	*Band and/or Popular*
WOODWIND			
APERTURE:	Flute	Piccolo	Alto flute
SINGLE REED:	Clarinet	Bass clarinet	E-flat clarinet Alto clarinet Contrabass clarinet
			Saxophones Alto Tenor Baritone
DOUBLE REED:	Oboe Bassoon	English horn Contrabassoon	
BRASS			
VALVE:	Trumpet		Cornet Fluegel horn
	French Horn Tuba		Sousaphone Baritone (Euphonium)
SLIDE:	Trombone	Bass trombone	

The FLUTE is the soprano of the woodwind family. It is held parallel to the floor extending to the player's right in a position permitting him to blow over an opening near the left end of the instrument. Ancestors of the flute were made of wood, but now flutes are made of silver alloy with an occasional specimen of gold or platinum. The flute is very agile and often serves to spin a delicate filigree in the orchestral fabric. The tone is breathy and sensuous in the lower register, clear and bright in the upper register.

FIGURE 3. *Flute and Piccolo*

FIGURE 4. *Clarinet and Bass Clarinet*

Claude Debussy: *Syrinx* (1912) 2:35
(1862–1918)

Syrinx is another name for panpipes, an instrument presumably invented by Pan, Greek god of woods and shepherds. This miniature for flute alone reveals the characteristic beauty of the flute tone.

Edgard Varèse: *Density 21.5* (1935) *4:13*
(1883–1965)

Density 21.5 was written for Georges Barrère who owned a custom-made platinum flute. The density of platinum is 21.5. The writing for the flute is not typical, but the extreme registers are well displayed.

The Piccolo is a miniature flute about half the size of its counterpart. It is the highest pitched orchestral instrument, reaching within one step of the highest note of the piano. Its low register is thin and of limited usefulness. Its special purpose is to double at a higher level lines appearing in other instruments, particularly the flute. In its upper register the piccolo has a sparkling tone which becomes shrill and piercing when it is played loudly.

John Philip Sousa: *Stars and Stripes Forever* (1897) 3:13
(1854–1932)

The piccolo is featured on a high, decorative melodic line in the second half of this march (on RCA LSC 2569).

P. I. Tchaikovsky: *Nutcracker Suite, op. 71a* (1882)
(1840–1893) 6. Chinese Dance 1:00

In this dance the piccolo is employed in the most usual way, playing the same melody as the flute an octave higher.

The Clarinet has a wide practical compass with distinctive colorings in its low, middle, and high registers. The low register is rich and mellow. The middle register has a neutral quality which blends well with other instruments and lends itself to accompanying parts and filling in harmonies, though it is also used for solos. The higher register becomes progressively more penetrating and, except with expert players, pinched at the top.

C. M. von Weber: *Concertino for Clarinet, op. 26* (1805) 8:15
(1786–1826)

Weber exploits the clarinet in all of the traditional ways in this *Small Concerto* for solo clarinet and orchestra.

Igor Stravinsky: *Three Pieces for Clarinet* (1918)
(1882–1971)

1.	M.M. = 52	2:00
2.	M.M. = 168	2:40
3.	M.M. = 160	1:35

The contrasting qualities of the different registers of the clarinet are evident in these unaccompanied pieces for the instrument. The M.M. numbers indicate the rate of speed at which each piece is to be played.

The Bass Clarinet extends the clarinet sound into the bass range. A comparative newcomer in the musical world, it has found favor for its velvety low register. It is often added to the bass line, occasionally appears in brief solo passages.

The Saxophones are too familiar both by sight and sound to require detailed discussion. They are hybrids fusing a single reed (like a clarinet) with a metal body (like the brasses) in a conical shape (like an oboe). The saxophones are the only widely used instruments which can be attributed to one individual. They were developed by Adolphe Sax of Brussels about 1840. The *alto, tenor,* and *baritone* saxophones are the most familiar because of their use in dance bands, but a complete family of saxophones is manufactured. Any recording of a large dance band will demonstrate the sound of a saxophone section. Saxophones are responsible for much of the fullness in dance, marching, and concert bands. In the suggested listening the saxophone is featured as a solo instrument.

Jacques Ibert: *Concertino da Camera for Saxophone* (1935)
(1890–1962)

2.	Larghetto	3:50
3.	Animato molto	4:00

This *Little Chamber Concerto* for alto saxophone and orchestra illustrates the legitimate saxophone tone quality and style associated with concert music, as opposed to the more familiar saxophone sound heard in jazz and popular music.

George Gershwin: *I Got Rhythm* (1930) 4:55
(1898–1937)

In all probability more jazz improvisation has been based on Gershwin's *I Got Rhythm* than on any other song. The version suggested to illustrate jazz saxophone sound is the one recorded in 1945 by Don Byas, tenor saxophone, and Slam Stewart, bass, on Atlantic SC–310 and on side 7 band 4 of the *Smithsonian Collection of Classic Jazz.*

The Oboe, with its double reed, has a more reedy sound and plaintive quality than the flute, clarinet, or saxophone, and it is less dexterous.

FIGURE 5. *Alto Saxophone, Tenor Saxophone, and Baritone Saxophone*

The oboe is associated with simple, pastoral melodies, but it is only slightly less versatile than the other members of the woodwind family. Its lowest note is about the same as that of a flute, but a flute can play higher. In ensembles the oboes customarily play between the flutes and the clarinets, which exceed the oboe range both top and bottom.

W. A. MOZART: *Quartet in F for Oboe & Strings, K.370* (1781)
(1756–1791) 2. Adagio 3:45

This quartet for oboe, violin, viola, and cello treats the oboe as a solo instrument accompanied by the three strings. The writing for oboe in this slow movement is fairly typical, unlike the preceding and following fast movements which make extreme technical demands on the oboist.

G. P. TELEMANN: *Sonata in C minor for Oboe & Harpsichord*
(1681–1767) 5. Grave 1:00
6. Allegro cantabile 1:20

These movements of Telemann's sonata—one slow and sustained, the other fast and sprightly—show the oboe in contrasting moods.

ENGLISH HORN is a misnomer if there ever was one. The instrument is neither English nor a horn. The origin of the name is shrouded in mystery. There are many theories but few facts. The English horn is an oversized and lower-pitched oboe which emphasizes the reedy and plaintive qualities of that instrument. Except in its lowest register the English horn is difficult to distinguish from an oboe.

JEAN SIBELIUS: *The Swan of Tuonela* (1893) 6:50
(1865–1957)

Tuonela, the land of death in Finnish mythology, is surrounded by a broad, black river upon which floats a swan. The quality of the English horn is admirably suited for this somber tone painting.

The BASSOON plays in the same pitch range as the cello, and they frequently are used together in orchestral music. The bassoonist in an orchestra or band is much busier than is generally suspected, because his part is so often hidden in the background. When the bassoon is used prominently, it is often cast in the role of comedian because of the dry, raucous tone of which it is capable. It is equally at home in lyric melodies and is more flexible than its awkward size and shape would suggest.

FIGURE 6. *Oboe and English Horn*

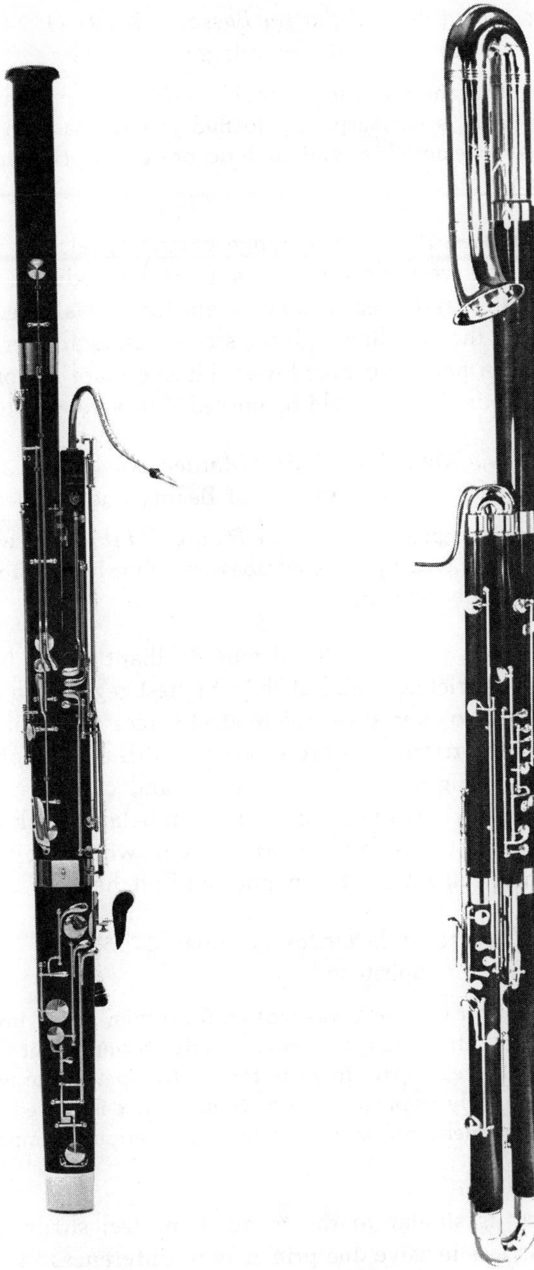

FIGURE 7. *Bassoon and Contrabassoon*

W. A. Mozart: *Concerto in B-flat for Bassoon, K.191* (1774)
(1756–1791) 2. Andante ma adagio 4:50

Mozart wrote many concertos, probably more than any other great composer, so it is not surprising to find one for bassoon among them. This movement is essentially lyric, one of the styles in which the bassoon excels.

The Contrabassoon, with a range extending almost as low as a piano, supplies the very bottom notes to the woodwind section. Its lugubrious sound is rarely heard alone except for special effects. Its usual function is to play the bass line with the string basses and/or tuba and to double the bassoon part an octave lower. Listeners are seldom conscious of the contrabassoon, but it would be missed if it were not there.

Maurice Ravel: *Ma Mere l'Oye Suite (Mother Goose)* (1912)
(1875–1937) 4. Conversations of Beauty and the Beast 4:15

This movement depicts the fairy tale *Beauty and the Beast* with the beast aptly portrayed by the contrabassoon, first heard about one minute after the beginning.

The Trumpet is the highest and most brilliant of the brass instruments. Formerly restricted in all but their highest register to fanfare-like figures and inclined to overpower the modest forces of the other sections of the orchestra, the trumpets were reserved (with a few notable exceptions) for rhythmic figures, sustained tones, and climaxes. Mechanical improvements and orchestral resources more in balance with their power now enable trumpets to display the versatility of which they are capable and to utilize their full range of dynamics and pitches.

Joseph Haydn: *Concerto in E-flat for Trumpet* (1796)
(1732–1809) 3. Spiritoso 4:45

Haydn's *Trumpet Concerto* was written for a then newly invented keyed trumpet rather than for a modern valve trumpet, but the key mechanism allowed Haydn to write for the trumpet in the modern manner. This early trumpet masterpiece nowadays is played on the standard instrument and is learned by every serious trumpet student.

The Cornet is similar to the trumpet in size, shape, range, and sound. Its tone is less incisive due primarily to differences in the internal shape of its mouthpiece. Trumpets are the rule in orchestra and dance bands. Cornets are used, often in conjunction with trumpets, in concert and marching bands and sometimes in jazz groups. Louis Armstrong plays cornet on the Bessie Smith recording of Handy's *St. Louis Blues*

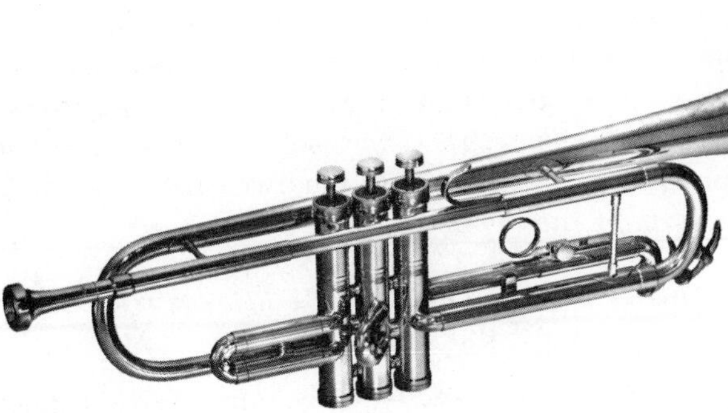

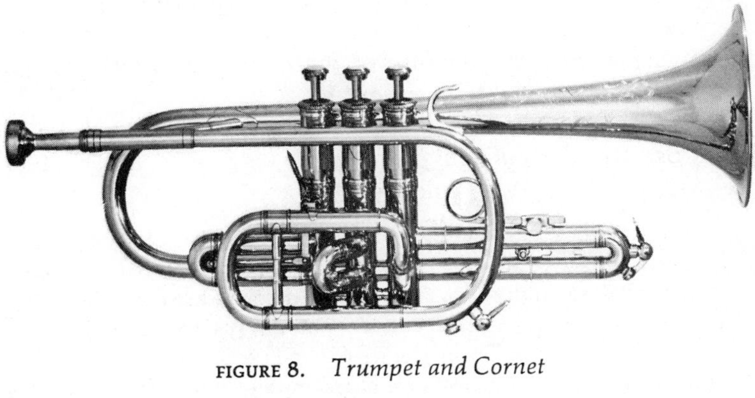

FIGURE 8. *Trumpet and Cornet*

(record side 9 band 2). Stravinsky includes a cornet in some of his best-known works. The original version of *Petrouchka* (1911) has a solo for the cornet in Scene Three (the music for the ballerina's entrance and waltz). In the revised version (1947), this solo is given to a trumpet, demonstrating the interchangeability of the two instruments. Cornet is specified in the score of the *Soldier's Tale.*

IGOR STRAVINSKY: *Histoire du Soldat (Soldier's Tale)* (1918)
(1882–1971) Part 2. Royal March 2:45

The cornet is used prominently and typically in this march. Do not confuse it with the trombone, clarinet, or bassoon which also have solo passages.

FLUEGEL HORNS, used in the New Don Ellis Band, are difficult to distinguish from cornets by sight or sound, though their bore is somewhat larger and their tone somewhat mellower.

The FRENCH HORN, more often called simply the HORN, is a noble instrument with enough power to dominate an orchestra and enough control to blend with a delicate string passage. The horn has by far the widest range of the brass instruments, going almost as high as a trumpet and lower than a trombone. It is an important member of the brass section and an adjunct to the woodwind section, frequently serving as a link between the two. It is a magnificent solo instrument and an admirable accompanying instrument. Because of the horn's versatility, composers and arrangers are tempted to overwork it.

BENJAMIN BRITTEN: *Serenade for Tenor, Horn, & Strings, op. 31* (1943)
(1913–) 1. Prologue 1:20
5. Hymn 2:00

The *Prologue,* which returns as the *Epilogue,* is played without using the valves on the horn. The pitches thus produced are those of the natural overtone series and do not always correspond with conventional tunings. The extremes of the French horn range, from its highest note to its lowest, are heard in the course of the *Hymn.*

RICHARD STRAUSS: *Concerto no. 1 in E-flat for Horn, op. 11* (1884)
(1864–1949) 3. Rondo: Allegro 4:50

Richard Strauss' father was a horn player, so Richard had ample opportunity to hear the instrument. He obviously was well acquainted with its capabilities when he wrote this concerto at the age of twenty. The solo part was so difficult, however, his father declined to play the premiere.

The TUBA provides the foundation for the brass section and indeed

FIGURE 9. *French Horn*

for the whole orchestra. Its normal function is to reinforce the bass line in loud passages. In the standard orchestra and band literature the tuba practically never has a solo, or even an exposed part. This situation is dramatized in Kleinsinger's whimsical *Tubby the Tuba.* The work is intended for children, but adults are not immune to its charm.

GEORGE KLEINSINGER: *Tubby the Tuba* (1945) 11:45
(1914–)

> The narrator describes the plight of *Tubby the Tuba,* and typical sounds of the tuba and several other instruments are illustrated before Tubby finds a melody he can play. Victor Jory is the narrator on Columbia record CL 671.

WILLIAM KRAFT: *Encounters II* (1966) 6:00
(1923–)

> This is an avant-garde piece for unaccompanied tuba which exploits the extreme range and extraordinary sound effects possible on the instrument in the hands of a virtuoso performer.

SOUSAPHONES are portable, bass, brass instruments named for John Philip Sousa, the March King. Designed for ease of carrying, they take the place of the tubas in marching bands and sometimes in concert bands. The circular shape and forward-facing bell are familiar sights in football halftime shows.

FIGURE 10. *Tuba and Sousaphone*

FIGURE 11. *Trombone and Bass Trombone*

BARITONE horns are closely related to trombones in range and sound but are shaped like a small tuba and have valves. EUPHONIUMS are similar instruments. Baritones and euphoniums are band instruments exclusively.

TROMBONES and BASS TROMBONES are the only instruments with slides. The two types of trombones can play the same music for the most part, and in their middle registers their tones are indistinguishable. The ordinary trombone plays with greater ease in the high register. The bass trombone tone has a little more body, and the instrument is equipped with an attachment activated by a valve which extends the range down four tones.

PAUL HINDEMITH: *Sonata for Trombone* (1941) 10:15
(1895–1963)

> This sonata is in one movement but four distinct sections, any one of which effectively demonstrates the tone quality and characteristics of the trombone.

Instruments Played by Striking

Instruments played by striking are *percussion* instruments. There are two types of percussion instruments—those producing definite pitches and those producing indefinite pitches.

The TIMPANI, also called KETTLEDRUMS (but not by musicians), are the most useful and used of the percussion instruments. They consist of a kettle-shaped, metal body over which a head is stretched. The heads formerly were made of calfskin, but in recent years plastic heads have been introduced. At least two timpani are used. The most common sizes are 25 inches and 28 inches in diameter. Large orchestras also have available a smaller one 23 inches in diameter and a larger one 30 inches in diameter. Several pitches can be played on each one. The range is determined by the size and the precise pitch by the tension on the head. The tension is adjusted by hand screws around the rim and by a pedal mechanism. Timpani are played by two felt-headed sticks, one held in either hand. Notes can be sustained by a rapid alternate striking by the sticks, called a *roll*. Timpani are capable of a wide dynamic range by varying the force with which they are struck and of some change of quality by varying the hardness of the stick heads and the location of the striking. A special effect possible only with pedal-equipped timpani is gliding from one pitch to another while the tone is sounding.

A GLOCKENSPIEL is a set of metal bars of different sizes each one of which produces a specific pitch when struck with a hard mallet. The pitch is very high, the quality clear and metallic. A BELL-LYRA is a portable version of the glockenspiel with a lyre-shaped frame. This adaptation of the instrument is a familiar sight in marching bands.

TABLE 2
PERCUSSION INSTRUMENTS

DEFINITE PITCH	
Frequently used:	*Infrequently used:*
Timpani (kettledrums)	Glockenspiel (orchestra bells)
	Xylophone
	Tubular bells (chimes)
	Vibraphone (vibraharp, vibes)
INDEFINITE PITCH	
Frequently used:	*Infrequently used:*
Snare drum (side drum)	Tenor drum
Bass drum	Tambourine
Cymbals	Gong (tam-tam)
Triangle	Castanets
	Wood block
	Temple blocks
	Claves
	Maracas
	Whip (slapstick)
	Ratchet
	Tom-tom
	etc.

A XYLOPHONE is similar to a glockenspiel except that its bars are made of wood, it is larger, and its pitch is lower.

TUBULAR BELLS, also called CHIMES, are long, metal tubes open on one end and closed on the other. They are made in complete sets, but each tube is individually suspended on a rack. Bell parts often have but few pitches, and sometimes only the tubes actually required are hung on the rack. When struck with a wooden mallet on the corner of the closed end, the tubular bells produce a sound similar to that of real bells.

THE DRUMS are round, wooden frames of various depths and diameters covered on both ends by skin or plastic heads. Tension on the heads is adjustable within limits, but no precise pitches result. Drums are struck with assorted sticks and beaters. The SNARE DRUM is the smallest. Its name stems from the metal bands or *snares* stretched across the bottom head which create a rattling sound. When the snares are released, a snare drum sounds more like a tom-tom. SIDE DRUM is another name for snare drum. The BASS DRUM is the largest drum. The TENOR DRUM is a less

FIGURE 12. *Percussion Instruments*

frequently used, medium-sized drum. Similar medium-sized drums used in military and marching bands are sometimes given specialized names.

CYMBALS are large, plate-shaped instruments of finely wrought brass. They are played in two ways. Holding one in each hand, the player strikes them together in a *crash*, or one cymbal is *suspended* and struck with beaters.

A TRIANGLE is made from a metal rod bent into a triangular shape. It is struck with a smaller metal rod to produce a light, bell-like sound. A ringing effect is produced by rapid strokes with the beater alternately hitting one side of the triangle and then another near the corner.

The infrequently used percussion instruments are employed for special and exotic effects. In addition to those listed in Table 2, any object which emits a sound when struck can be used as a percussion instrument. Some idea of the possibilities can be had from the instrumentation listed for the first suggested listening example, *Ionization*.

EDGARD VARÈSE: *Ionization* (1931) 4:50
(1883–1965)

> The score of this work calls for 13 performers, each playing two or more of the following instruments: crash cymbals, suspended cymbal, bass drum (three sizes), side drum, snare drum, military drum, string drum (lion roar), gong, tam-tam, (three sizes), bongos, claves, güiro, maracas, castanets, tambourine, siren (high and low), Chinese (temple) blocks, sleigh bells, cow bells, tubular chimes (bells), glockenspiel, anvil (high and low), slapstick, triangle, and piano. Both snare and side drums are specified, also gong and tam-tams, though the terms are usually synonymous.

Bela Bartok: *Sonata for Two Pianos & Percussion* (1937)
(1881–1945) 3. Allegro non troppo 6:45

Bartok creates distinctive effects by imaginative use of conventional percussion instruments in this sonata. The instruments in order of their appearance are: pianos, xylophone, timpani, cymbal crash (very soft), triangle, side (snare) drum without snares, bass drum, side drum with snares, and suspended cymbal with soft-headed stick.

These are concentrated examples of percussion. In normal instrumental ensembles the percussion element is used more sparingly owing to the limited and highly specialized nature of the percussion sound.

Instruments Played by Plucking

There are several kinds of plucked string instruments, but the Harp is the only orchestral instrument played exclusively by plucking. The strings of a harp, strung in an elaborately beautiful frame, produce the same pitches as the white keys of a piano when the pedals around the base of the instrument are in the middle position. The pitches of the various strings are raised or lowered a semitone by moving the corresponding pedal up or down a notch. *Glissando* is a characteristic harp effect in which the player's fingers are drawn rapidly over the strings sounding all of pitches between specified limits in rapid succession.

Maurice Ravel: *Introduction and Allegro* (1906) 10:35
(1875–1937)

This work for harp accompanied by 2 violins, viola, cello, flute, and clarinet includes brilliant writing for the harp.

P. I. Tchaikovsky: *Nutcracker Suite, op. 71a* (1892)
(1840–1893) 8. Waltz of the Flowers 6:25

The introduction to this waltz contains one of the most famous harp passages in the orchestral literature.

Though the usual way of producing the tone on violins, violas, cellos, and basses is by bowing, tones can also be produced on these instruments by plucking the strings or *pizzicato,* as it is called. The string instruments are played pizzicato exclusively in the following symphonic movement.

FIGURE 13. *Harp*

P. I. TCHAIKOVSKY: *Symphony no. 4 in F minor, op. 36* (1878)
(1840–1893) 3. Scherzo: Allegro 4:55

The entire string section of the orchestra is heard playing pizzicato in the first part of this movement and again after the middle part played by the wind instruments.

The most popular plucked instrument is GUITAR. Only the piano is played by more people. Guitars come in two basic types, acoustic and electric. The tone of acoustic guitars, used for Spanish, classical, and folk music, is resonated by the body of the instrument like the orchestral string instruments. The tone of electric guitars, used in jazz and popular music, is amplified electronically. Some electric guitars differ from acoustic guitars in shape and design, but others are merely acoustic guitars with a pickup unit installed under the strings and connected to an amplifier. Selections are suggested to illustrate both types of guitars and the music associated with them.

HEITOR VILLA-LOBOS: *Five Preludes for Guitar* (1940)
(1887–1959) No. 2 in E: Andantino 3:08

Villa-Lobos, one of the most prolific and original composers of the 20th century, composed more than 2000 pieces permeated with folk influences of his native Brazil. He played cello and guitar and wrote extensively for both instruments. The recording by Narciso Yepes is played on an acoustic guitar.

(Also record side 10 band 8)

KURT WEILL: *Mack the Knife* (1928) 3:49
(1900–1950)

Mack the Knife from Weill's *Three Penny Opera* has established itself as a standard pop tune and, as such, a suitable basis for jazz improvisation. A superb rendition by Barney Kessel (guitar), Shelly Manne (drums), and Ray Brown (bass) recorded just after they swept the jazz polls for the third consecutive year is included in the album *Poll Winners Three!* (Contemporary S7576). The guitar is electric; the bass is plucked.

Keyboard Instruments

The coupling of a keyboard mechanism with a sound-producing medium is documented in a type of organ found in ancient Greece before 250 B.C. In this and all subsequent keyboard instruments the purpose of the keyboard is to activate the sound-producing force and to facilitate the striking, blowing, plucking, or electronic response that actually generates the sound. The keys proper neither vibrate nor directly cause vibration.

FIGURE 14. *Gibson acoustic guitar Model J-10 and electric guitar Model SG-1.*

A long evolutionary period was required to bring the keyboard to its definitive form, and several predecessors of the modern instruments became obsolete in the process. Of the various prototypes, four basic keyboard instruments survive: the piano (more properly the pianoforte), pipe and reed organs, the celesta, and the harpsichord, an instrument which flourished 1600–1800 and is now enjoying a revival. To these must now be added electronic organs and the new electronic music synthesizers which utilize a keyboard mechanism in their circuitry.

Striking a piano key activates a felt hammer which in turn strikes a string or strings to produce the sound. The celesta action is essentially the same except that a hard hammer strikes a metal bar. Depressing a pipe organ key opens a valve allowing air to blow through a tone-producing pipe. With a reed organ or harmonium the air blows over a metal tongue which is set in motion to produce the sound. Harpsichord keys are connected with a mechanism which plucks the string in response to a downward motion of the key. Of the instruments with keyboards, only electronic organs and synthesizers produce sounds in a way not found in other instruments.

The PIANO is used in more combinations and in more different ways than any other instrument. It is a stellar solo instrument; it is used to accompany solo voices and choruses, solo instruments and ensembles; it is combined with other instruments in sonatas and chamber music; it is included in symphony orchestras and dance bands; it serves as a teaching aid in public schools; it is found in homes, churches, club rooms, and bars. Because it is so fundamental to the study of music, all serious music students learn to play it.

The hammers in the piano mechanism fall back instantly after striking the strings, leaving them free to vibrate until arrested by dampers. Dampers drop on the strings stopping the vibration when the keys are released unless restrained by the action of a pedal. Depressing the right pedal lifts all of the dampers allowing the strings to vibrate after the keys are released. The left pedal reduces the amount of tone. Grand pianos have an extra pedal in the center which sustains the sound only of keys which are down at the time the pedal is applied.

Ordinary piano sounds are too well known to require illustration, but 20th-century composers have elicited many new effects from this familiar source. Henry Cowell and John Cage were pioneers in the exploration of new piano resources. In performing Cowell's *Banshee* the lid of a grand piano is raised, and the sounds are produced directly on the strings by scratching, plucking, striking, and stroking them in various ways.

HENRY COWELL: *The Banshee* (1925) 2:40
(1897–1965)

> A banshee is a female spirit in Gaelic folklore whose wailing forebodes a death in the family. The eerie sounds of Cowell's *Banshee* can be heard on Composers Recording CRI-109 and on Folkways 6160.

A different genre of special piano effects is exploited in Cage's numerous works for *prepared piano,* which he is credited with inventing in 1938. The preparations, specified for each work, consist of applying such things as screws, bolts, nuts, strips of rubber, and weather stripping to the strings in ways that drastically alter the sound even when the notation and manner of playing are conventional, as they are for his *Bacchanale.*

John Cage: *Bacchanale* (1938) 9:00
(1912–)

> Cage studied for a time with Cowell and was exposed to new piano sounds early in his career. *Bacchanale* and several other Cage pieces for prepared piano are included in Columbia album M2S 819.

The Pipe Organ is the most imposing of instruments. Large models have four keyboards or *manuals,* each similar in appearance to that of a piano. They have, in addition, a pedalboard with a size and location which permits playing with the toes and heels. All the keys are connected mechanically, pneumatically, or electrically to thousands of pipes of various shapes and materials ranging in size from smaller than a pencil to larger than a stovepipe. Each type has a distinctive sound. The player selects the desired tone quality and to an extent the pitch by means of *stops* located above the keyboards. Air under pressure formerly coming from manually operated bellows but now usually from electric blowers is supplied to all the pipes. Depressing a key activates a valve allowing air to flow into the pipes selected by the stops and causing the pipe to sound its note. The organ has a tremendous range both in volume and pitch.

Large organs are not mass produced, and hardly any two are identical. Smaller organs are more inclined toward standardization, having only two manuals and lesser numbers of pipes and stops, but they are completely adequate to play most of the organ literature. For those acquainted with the organ only in the restrained atmosphere of a religious service, the resources of the full organ may come as a revelation. The two works suggested for listening, the first church music and the second a concert piece, reveal the broad spectrum of color and dynamics available on the majestic pipe organ.

J. S. Bach: *Schübler Chorale Prelude no. 1, S.645** (1746) 4:37
(1685–1750) (*Wachet auf, ruft uns die Stimme*)

Toccata and Fugue in D minor, S.565 (1717) 9:15

> Bach was equally at home playing and writing for the organ and composing sacred and secular music. These works representing the

early and late periods of his career are proof of his lifetime devotion to the instrument.

*(Record side 2 band 5. Chorale melody p. 382)

Electronic organs attempt with varying degrees of success to simulate the sounds of pipe organs. The blowers and pipes of pipe organs are replaced by electrical circuits and speakers in electronic organs. They are no match for the full resources of a large pipe organ but they have the advantages of economy and compactness, which make them practical for small churches and large cocktail lounges.

The CELESTA is most easily described as a keyboard glockenspiel. A cabinet supports a small piano-like keyboard and encloses a series of metal bars which sound when struck by hammers connected to the keys. Because of the keyboard, greater dexterity is possible and multiple notes are easier on a celesta than on a glockenspiel. The celesta is a regular member of symphony orchestras where it is grouped with the percussion instruments.

P. I. TCHAIKOVSKY: *Nutcracker Suite, op. 71a* (1892)
(1840–1893) 4. Dance of the Sugarplum Fairy 1:45

This is the first orchestral composition to include the celesta. The tinkling of the celesta solo is placed in sharp relief by the velvety low tones of the bass clarinet.

The HARPSICHORD, supplanted by the piano, all but disappeared from the musical scene though much of the keyboard music written prior to 1800 was intended for it. Musicologists interested in the authentic reproduction of early music sparked a move to take harpsichords out of museums and into recording studios and concert halls. This movement led not only to a reevaluation of the music but of the instrument itself. Contemporary composers have been stimulated to write for harpsichord, and it has even made a tentative debut in popular music and in radio and television commercials and background music.

In appearance the harpsichord is like a small, angular, grand piano. The keyboard is shorter, and traditionally the black-and-white color of the keys is reversed in relation to the piano. The harpsichord tone is produced by an intricate mechanism which plucks a string when a key is struck. Unlike a piano, hitting a key harder or softer does not influence the tone. This is done by modifying the bite of the plucking device with a pedal. The old instruments are very fragile, but modern ones are relatively sturdy and durable. In some, nylon is used in place of leather or crow quills for the plectra, and steel frames are used in place of wood.

DOMENICO SCARLATTI: *Sonata in C, L.454*[5] (1753) 1:46
(1685–1757)

Scarlatti sonatas, unlike those of later periods, are in one concise movement. This one is typical of the more than 500 sonatas Scarlatti composed for harpischord.

(Record side 2 band 7)

MANUEL DE FALLA: *Concerto for Harpsichord* (1926)
(1876–1946) 1. Allegro 3:10

Though this work is called a concerto, it requires only five players (violin, oboe, flute, clarinet, and cello) other than the harpischord soloist. It utilizes the antique instrument in a thoroughly contemporary idiom.

Electronic Instruments

Composers and performers today have at their disposal a vast array of electronic instruments and devices—audio oscillators, tone generators, filters, modulators, equalizers, sequencers, and reverberation units—that were virtually unknown in musical circles a generation ago. Tones of any desired pitch, duration, loudness, and quality can be synthesized electronically, and the sounds from any source, including conventional instruments, can be modified beyond recognition. Many of the electronic devices now used to generate and modify sounds could be found in scientific laboratories and in broadcast and recording studios long before anyone thought of using them to make music. When the electronic components useful in the production and control of sound were assembled in integrated systems, ELECTRONIC MUSIC SYNTHESIZERS were born. The development of synthesizers opened up a whole new world of sound resources. Two of the numerous makes and models of synthesizers now on the market are shown in Figure 15.

Though the more sophisticated synthesizers are capable of imitating the sounds and playing the music of conventional instruments, their primary function is to produce tone qualities and effects that are uniquely electronic. The following example illustrates the use of a synthesizer to reproduce a piece written for organ in standard music notation. The pitches and rhythms of this 18th-century piece are realized precisely. Only the tone quality is changed.

---

5. Scarlatti harpsichord works are identified by numbers from the complete edition of Allesandro Longo.

(a)

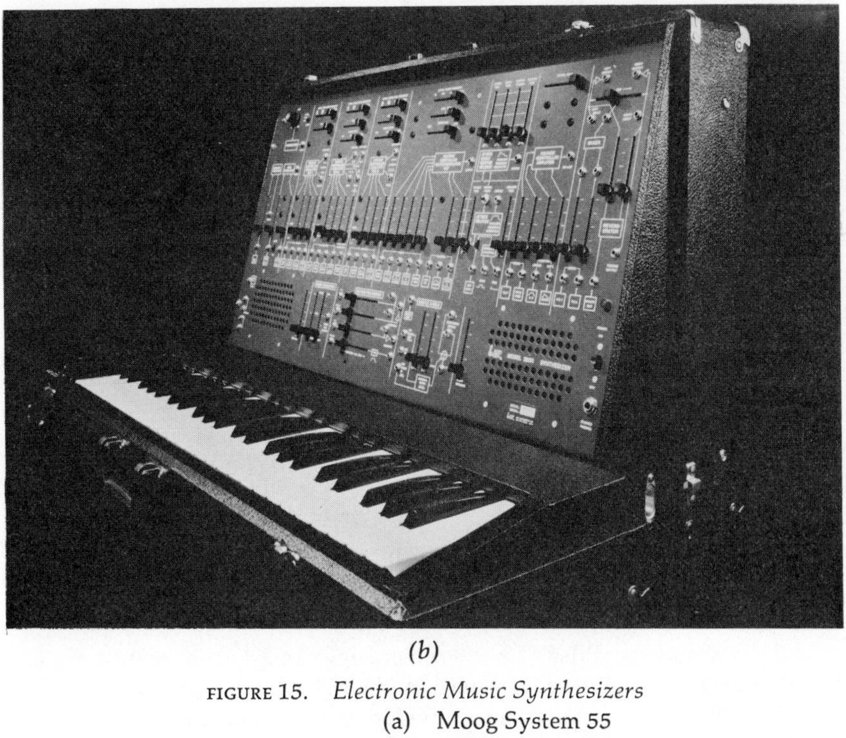

(b)

FIGURE 15. *Electronic Music Synthesizers*
(a) Moog System 55
(b) ARP Model 2600

J. S. Bach: *Switched-On Bach*
(1685–1750) Chorale Prelude *Wachet auf* 3:37

The complete recording (Columbia MS–7194) contains ten Bach selections "realized and performed" by Walter Carlos with the assistance of Benjamin Folkman on a Moog electronic music synthesizer. Compare this electronic rendition of Bach's *Schübler Chorale Prelude no. 1* (Wachet auf, ruft uns die Stimme) with the traditional version for organ cited on pages 50 and 180. (Record side 2 band 5. Chorale melody p. 382)

Synthesizers are adaptable to any musical idiom. The electronic version of the Bach chorale prelude just cited illustrates one style. Examples of avant-garde electronic music and additional information about synthesizers are given in Chapter 23. Synthesizers are also providing refreshing new sounds in the popular music field. The versatility of synthesizers is dramatically illustrated by comparing the *Switched-on Bach* music with that in the album *The Age of Electronicus* (Command 946–S), which includes an electronic version of the popular song *Alfie*. The sound source in both instances was a Moog synthesizer.

Burt Bacharach: *Alfie* (1966) 3:38
(1928–)

Common practice in popular music is for performers to make special arrangements of the music they perform. The arrangements and performances are often as distinctive as the composition and contribute as much to its success. This recording (Command 946–S) is Dick Hyman's arrangement of *Alfie* for Moog synthesizer.

Each of the foregoing examples features the specified voice or instrument in a complete work or self-contained excerpt. The suggested listening, therefore, introduces not only the various voices and instruments but some of the masterpieces of music created for them. For a more concise introduction to the instruments, the following recordings and the one film are recommended.

Benjamin Britten: *Young Person's Guide to the Orchestra, op. 34* (1946)
(1913–) 18:00

In this work, subtitled *Variations and Fugue on a Theme of Purcell* (1659–1695), the theme is played by the full orchestra and the four sections of the orchestra in turn before the variations begin. Then each instrument of the orchestra is spotlighted in a variation and again in the fugue. Some recordings, including the one in the *Listeners Guide* album, have narration naming and describing the instruments before they are heard. Though intended for young people, this composition provides a marvelous introduction to the instruments for initiates of all ages.

(Record side 7 band 2)

Additional Examples

Instruments of the Orchestra, film version of Benjamin Britten's *Young Person's Guide to the Orchestra,* produced by the British Ministry of Education and available from Contemporary/McGraw-Hill Textfilms.
Instruments of the Orchestra, Capital HBZ–21002.
Instruments of the Orchestra, RCA Victor LES–6000.
Instruments of the Orchestra, Vanguard VRS–1017/8.
The Orchestra and Its Instruments, Folkways 3602.

Additional experience in recognizing instruments, individually and in various combinations, is provided by the examples suggested for listening in the following chapter on mediums.

TABLE 3
RANGES OF VOICES AND INSTRUMENTS

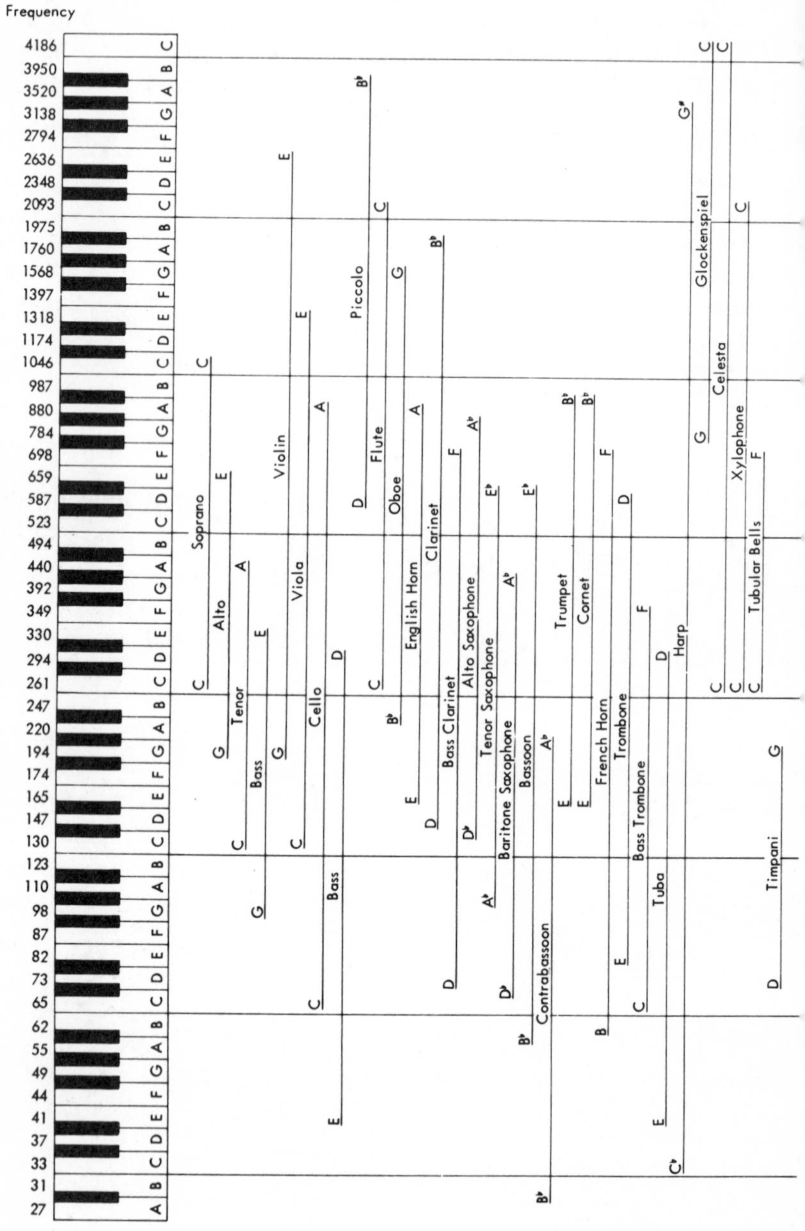

Mediums

4

The voices and instruments surveyed in the previous chapter make music in many combinations. There are no restrictions on the types or numbers used together, and at one time or another music probably has been written for almost every conceivable group. Certain combinations by virtue of special qualifications are most prevalent. These are the common mediums of music.

Solo

Solo, literally, means alone. In music it is used both in its literal sense and in the sense of a piece or passage for one predominant instrument or voice with accompaniment. Unaccompanied solos are occasionally written for other instruments, but the only one which regularly appears by itself is the piano. The piano is adaptable to old music and new, to brief character pieces and extended major works. Because of the wealth of literature, the abundance of competent performers, and the availability of instruments, the piano undoubtedly is heard more than any other instrument or combination of instruments.

SERGEI RACHMANINOFF: *Fantasy Pieces, op. 3* (1892)
(1873–1943) 2. Prelude in C-sharp minor 4:00

Piano solo: piano alone.

(Also record side 6 band 5)[1]

1. See fn. p. 16.

Used in the sense of a piece for an instrument or voice with accompaniment, solo usually is modified by the name of the instrument or voice performing the solo part. It is generally safe to assume that the accompaniment unless otherwise indicated is played by the piano. Thus, a *vocal solo* or a *soprano solo* is a song for voice and piano; a *violin solo* is a piece for violin and piano, and so on.

Independent songs for solo voice and piano are called *art songs* or *lieder* (from the German word for songs). Composers using German texts produced a vast treasury of such songs during the 19th century. Franz Schubert (1797–1828) is credited with originating the form. Robert Shumann (1810–1856), Johannes Brahms (1833–1897), and Richard Strauss (1864–1949) contributed substantially to it. The foregoing composed extensively for other mediums, but the reputation of Hugo Wolf is based primarily upon his production of lieder.

HUGO WOLF: *Mörike Lieder* (1888)
(1860–1903) 19. Verborgenheit (Secrecy) 2:15

Art song or lied (singular of lieder): voice and piano.

(Also record side 5 band 7)

Instrumental solos with piano accompaniment are a common medium of musical expression. The solo literature is especially plentiful for instruments like the violin which are heard in solo recitals. Many concert artists add to their laurels by composing and arranging music for their own instrument. Sarasate was known primarily as a violinist during his lifetime, but his fame is perpetuated by his compositions.

PABLO DE SARASATE: *Introduction and Tarantella, op. 43* 4:40
(1844–1908)

Violin solo: violin and piano.

Instrumental solos accompanied by orchestra most often fall in the concerto category. In a *piano concerto* the piano is elevated to the solo role, and the accompaniment is provided by the orchestra. The amount of orchestral participation in the presentation and working out of thematic ideas varies considerably from one concerto to another. The primary function of the orchestra in some is to provide background for the solo. Others are virtually symphonies with one predominant instrument. The following example is between these extremes.

EDVARD GRIEG

EDVARD GRIEG: *Piano Concerto in A minor, op. 16* (1868)
(1843–1907) 1. Allegro molto moderato 12:20

Piano concerto: solo piano and orchestra.

(Also record side 7 band 1)

Chamber Music

Chamber music is the general designation for instrumental ensemble music performed with one player on a part. Since there is only one player for each part in the music, the number of players is never large. A word indicating the number of players or parts (e.g., *duo* or *duet, trio, quartet, quintet, sextet, septet, octet,* or *nonet*) is often included in the title of chamber works. Music for more than nine players usually does not qualify as chamber music, and most chamber music is for groups of two to five players. Musical interest is distributed, more or less equally, between the parts. There is no soloist or leader, and opportunities for displaying individual virtuosity are purely incidental.

Duos or *duets* for two melody instruments are abundant in the teaching literature, but only a few are programed. The following example is one of the exceptions. The Bartok *Duos* are progressively arranged teaching pieces using 20th-century devices. Their musical value makes them an effective source of recital material.

BELA BARTOK: *Duos (44) for Two Violins* (1931)
(1881–1945) 44. Ardeliana 1:50

Duo: two violins.

A *sonata* is an extended work in three or four movements for one or two instruments. Sonatas for two instruments, usually a melody instrument and piano, conform to the basic definition given for chamber music, but they are not always included in the classification. This is because the solo-accompaniment relationship between the two instruments in some sonatas is inconsistent with the ideals of chamber music. Sonatas in which the primary function of the piano is to provide an accompaniment for the melody instrument perhaps belong in the solo category, but many are perfectly valid examples of chamber music.

Though sonatas have been composed for piano in combination with virtually every instrument, including another piano, those for violin and piano are most numerous. Both instruments may be named in identifying sonatas, or the piano may be taken for granted in sonatas as it is in solos. The chamber music classification of the following example and similar sonatas is substantiated by the absence of superficial technical display and by the participation of both instruments in the presentation of the musical ideas.

CESAR FRANCK: *Violin Sonata in A* (1886)
(1822–1890) 4. Allegretto poco mosso 6:05

Violin sonata: violin and piano.

(Record side 6 band 1)

A *trio* may comprise any three instruments, but the only combinations standardized to any degree are the *string trio,* consisting of violin, viola, and cello, and the *piano trio,* consisting of violin, cello, and piano. The piano trio is the only combination of three instruments for which a large and significant body of literature exists.

FELIX MENDELSSOHN: *Piano Trio no. 1 in D minor, op. 49* (1839)
(1809–1847) 1. Molto allegro ed agitato 7:45

Piano trio: violin, cello, and piano.

The dearth of music for three instruments contrasts with the abundance of music for four. Any combination of four instruments constitutes a *quartet,* but the most usual combination consists of two violins, viola, and cello, the instrumentation of a *string quartet.*

The string quartet is an ideal medium, and practically every composer since Haydn (1732–1809) has written for it. This combination of instruments provides the composer a perfectly balanced, homogeneous medium with a wide range of pitches and dynamic levels. The sounds of a string quartet can be sonorous one moment and ethereal the next. If power and brilliance are limited, clarity and intimacy compensate. String players regard the quartet as the ultimate musical medium, and string quartets are what they play for their own satisfaction. The next example is one of the many masterpieces in the string quartet literature.

L. VAN BEETHOVEN: *String Quartet no. 16 in F, op. 135* (1826)
(1770–1827)

1.	Allegretto	6:30
2.	Vivace	3:05

String quartet: 2 violins, viola, and cello.
Beethoven wrote string quartets in each period of his creative life and devoted his last years to this form. This quartet is his final opus.

(Also record side 3 band 5)

The plentiful literature for string quartet is balanced by a bounteous array of stellar performers. Renowned string quartets tour and record regularly and, by playing as a unit through many seasons, achieve perfection as ensembles. University faculty, student, and amateur string quartets, in addition, are numerous and often excellent. The literature and the performing groups are sources of reciprocal stimulation. String quartets are organized to perform the existing literature, and the active performing groups are a constant incentive for composers to write still more for them.

The instrumentation of the string quartet is accepted as the norm, and deviations from this combination are reflected in the designations for works and the groups required to play them. For example, a *piano quartet* consists of a violin, viola, cello, and piano, not four pianos as the name might imply. An *oboe quartet* consists of oboe, violin, viola, and cello. The name in each case is derived from the instrument which replaces one of the violins in the string quartet instrumentation. The piano quartet, particularly, is a standard and frequently heard ensemble. Several quartet combinations of three string instruments and one wind have been used effectively, but no combination of four instruments challenges the supremacy of the string quartet as a medium of musical expression.

Quartets of woodwind and brass instruments are also possible, though less common than those involving string instruments. The usual makeup of a *woodwind quartet* is flute, oboe, clarinet, and bassoon. There are several likely combinations of four brass instruments. *A brass quartet* can consist of two trumpets, and two trombones; two trumpets, horn, and trombone; trumpet, horn, trombone, and tuba, or any group of four brass instruments, including those with cornets and baritones. Many brass quartet compositions can be played by more than one combination of instruments. Woodwind and brass quartets are not the perfect chamber music mediums that string quartets are. The tone quality of the various woodwind instruments is lacking in homogeneity, and the brass instruments by nature are less suited to the performance of intimate music.

A *quintet* often consists of a string quartet augmented by one additional instrument, in which case it is identified by the name of the added instrument. A *viola quintet* is a string quartet with an extra viola. A *cello quintet* is a string quartet with an extra cello, and a *clarinet quintet* is a string quartet plus clarinet. The most popular addition to the basic instrumentation of the string quartet is the piano, resulting in the *piano quintet*.

ROBERT SCHUMANN: *Piano Quintet in E-flat, op. 44* (1842)		
(1810–1856)	1. Allegro brillante	9:00

Piano quintet: 2 violins, viola, cello, and piano.

Woodwind quintet is a curious but usual way of referring to a group of four woodwind instruments and one brass. In the interest of accuracy the name is sometimes shortened to *wind quintet*. Both names apply to a group consisting of flute, oboe, clarinet, bassoon, and horn. This combination lacks the warmth of a string quintet and the power of a piano quintet, but it has greater diversity of tone color than either. Wind quintet music tends to be witty and clever rather than emotional or profound. Contemporary composers have found the medium attractive, and many have composed effectively for it.

JACQUES IBERT: *Trois Pièces Brèves (Three Short Pieces)* (1930)		
(1890–1962)	1. Allegro	2:25
	2. Andante	1:20
	3. Assez lent—Allegro scherzando	3:00

Woodwind quintet: flute, oboe, clarinet, horn, and bassoon.

Chamber music has been written for groups of six (sextet), seven (septet), eight (octet), and nine (nonet) players. There is no standard instrumentation beyond the quintet, and the literature is not extensive. Isolated chamber works exist for larger ensembles, but the tendency with larger groups is to depart from the chamber music concept and to use more than one player on a part.

Vocal music is ordinarily excluded, by definition and custom, from the chamber music category. However, *madrigals* are a type of vocal ensemble music intended for performance (but not usually performed) with one on a part, which qualifies them for consideration in this context. Madrigals of the most prevalent type are secular works for four to six voices, with five most usual. Four-part madrigals are for soprano, alto, tenor, and bass. Five-part madrigals usually call for an additional soprano; six-part madrigals for these five and another tenor. Madrigal writing flourished in Italy and England during the 16th and 17th centuries, and the name has been revived by contemporary composers.

Orlandus Lassus: *Matona mia cara (Matona, my dear)* (1550) 2:45
(1532–1594)

(Record side 1 band 10)

Thomas Morley: *My bonny lass she smileth* (1595) 1:45
(1557–1602)

(Record side 1 band 11)

Madrigals: 2 sopranos, alto, tenor, and bass.

The performances of jazz combos are chamber music of a sort, startling as the idea may seem to purists. The small combos improvise intimate jazz with one player on a part. Emphasis is on group performance, but each member has opportunities to be in the spotlight. Classic chamber music designations—trio, quartet, quintet, and sextet—are common. The instrumentation in a combo is completely flexible, but the elements of melody, harmony, and rhythm must be represented. A recording of any small combo or Dixieland group will serve to illustrate this new style of chamber music.

Choirs

A *choir* is a group devoted to the singing of sacred music. A *choir* is also a group of instruments belonging to the same family. It is used here in both senses, though an instrumental choir within an orchestra or a band is usually called a *section*.

Vocal choirs have been an important adjunct to worship since the time people learned to sing together, and the magnificent sound of numerous voices did not go unnoticed by composers of secular music. Composers of both sacred and secular music have written copiously for voices since the beginning of the Renaissance. The enormous quantity of music for voices is in sharp contrast to the relatively meager amount for individual instrumental choirs. Choral music is normally written for soprano, alto, tenor, and bass voices. Each of these can be divided when the music requires more than four parts. Technically, a choir sings sacred music and a chorus secular music, but the distinction is not always observed. Church music was formerly for unaccompanied voices, and *a cappella* (meaning "for the chapel") is now a general designation for unaccompanied vocal music and the groups that perform it.

G. P. da Palestrina: *Pope Marcellus Mass* (1555)
(1525–1594) Kyrie 3:47

(Record side 1 band 9)

Randall Thompson: *Alleluia* (1940) 4:15
(1899–)

A cappella choir: sopranos, altos, tenors, and basses.

Of the instrumental choirs, the string choir is the most versatile. It becomes the string section in an orchestra and a string orchestra when it performs independently. It includes all of the bowed instruments—several of each. Music for strings is normally written in five parts, two for violins and one each for violas, cellos, and basses. The cellos and basses at times play the same part, reducing the number to four. Oftentimes one or more of the five is divided to accommodate additional melodic lines or to provide fuller harmonies. Though the instrumentation of a string orchestra adds only basses to that of a string quartet, the larger number of players and the possibility of dividing the parts affects the style of writing and noticeably alters the tone quality. Tchaikovsky's *Serenade* would not be mistaken for a string quartet nor would the composer have written precisely the same way for the smaller ensemble.

P. I. Tchaikovsky: *Serenade in C, op. 48* (1880)
(1840–1893) 2. Waltz 3:40

String orchestra: 1st violins, 2nd violins, violas, cellos, and basses.

Many passages in the symphonic literature are assigned exclusively to the woodwind section, but the woodwind choir is rarely, if ever, used independently. The Strauss *Serenade* will serve to illustrate the sound of the woodwind choir, though its score includes, in addition to a full complement of woodwinds, four horns.

Richard Strauss: *Serenade in E-flat, op. 7* (1881) 9:10
(1864–1949)

Thirteen winds: 2 flutes, 2 oboes, 2 clarinets, 2 bassoons, a contrabassoon, and 4 horns.

The brass section of an orchestra consists of trumpets, horns, trombones, and tuba. All of these instruments are heard in the following work, but the numbers are not the same as would be found in an orchestra.

GIOVANNI GABRIELI: *Canzona Septimi Toni* 4:05
(1551–1612)

Modern instruments differ from those on which this music was played originally, so in recorded performances the instrumentation varies. The instruments heard in the New York Brass Ensemble version (Counterpoint CPT–5503) are: 4 trumpets, 2 horns, trombone, bass trombone, and tuba.

The remaining section of the orchestra is the percussion section. It is not customary to refer to it as a choir, perhaps because the number of players is small or perhaps because so few of its instruments produce definite pitches. At one time it might have been because percussion instruments were only heard in orchestras and bands, but this is no longer the case. Percussion ensembles are springing up all over the country, and music is being composed for them to play. The percussion instruments seem to have a special appeal for contemporary composers.

CARLOS CHAVEZ: *Toccata for Percussion Instruments* (1942)
(1899–)

1. Allegro, sempre giusto 4:35
2. Largo 3:40
3. Allegro un poco marciale 3:10

Percussion ensemble: large and small Indian drums, side (snare) drums, tenor drums, bass drum, timpani, large and small gongs, glockenspiel, xylophone, suspended cymbals, chimes, claves, and maracas—6 players.

Band

Woodwind, brass, and percussion sections are combined in a band. The instrumentation in bands is not uniform. They are student groups predominantly, and their makeup is influenced in some cases and determined in others by the availability of players and instruments. Bands vary in size from fewer than 28 members, the normal complement of a military band, to well over one hundred. There is no typical band, but the Eastman Wind Ensemble, widely known for its recordings, gives some idea of the usual instrumentation and proportions.

FIGURE 16. *Eastman Symphonic Wind Ensemble, Frederick Fennell Conducting*

EASTMAN WIND ENSEMBLE INSTRUMENTATION

Woodwind

Piccolo
Flutes (2)
(Alto flute)
Oboes (2)
English horn
Bassoons (2)
Contrabassoon
E-flat clarinet
Clarinets (8)
Alto clarinet
Bass clarinet
Alto saxophones (2)
Tenor saxophone
Baritone saxophone

Brass

Cornets (3)
Trumpets (2)
French horns (4)
Euphoniums (baritones) (2)
Trombones (3)
Tubas (2)
—String bass (not a brass instrument, but used in conjunction with the tubas)

Percussion

5 players (available for any percussion required by the score; normally includes timpani, snare or tenor drum, and bass drum)

The alto flute is available only if the piccolo player or one of the flute players shifts to that instrument. Other players also double, providing flexibility in the instrumentation. Harp, piano, organ, harpsichord, solo string instruments, and chorus are added as required for special works.

RALPH VAUGHAN WILLIAMS: *Toccata Marziale* (1924) 6:30
(1872–1958)

The Eastman Wind Ensemble performance of *Toccata Marziale* is on Mercury recordings 75011 and 75028.

(Also record side 6 band 3)

In marching bands instruments like oboes, bassoons, and tubas that are ineffective outside or are difficult to carry are eliminated, and the brass, saxophone, and drum forces are augmented. The participation of marching bands in parades and football half-time shows has won them an exalted position in the realm of entertainment. Concert bands in recent years have been recognized by composers and audiences as a significant new medium deserving serious attention.

Dance Band

The larger dance bands have three distinct sections.

Reed: saxophones, sometimes clarinets
Brass: trumpets and trombones
Rhythm: piano, string bass, drums, sometimes guitar

Striving for an individual style, a name band plays special arrangements exclusively, making a unique instrumentation both feasible and desirable. This concept is the exact opposite of that prevailing in symphonic literature. Symphonic composers do their own orchestration, and every orchestra plays the same version.

Reed sections have a minimum of four saxophones—2 altos, tenor, and baritone—often more. Most saxophone players also play clarinet, so the arranger has at his disposal four or more players to divide between saxophones and clarinets as he wishes. The distribution is not necessarily the same for all selections.

Brass sections vary from three trumpets and two or three trombones to as many as five of each, with the numbers approximately equal. The lowest trombone part is usually written for bass trombone.

The rhythm section provides the steady, underlying beat that renders the intricate rhythms of the other sections meaningful and makes the music danceable. Rhythm players, if they use music, read from parts containing chord symbols rather than complete notation, and they improvise on the harmonic framework indicated by the symbols. The drummer is surrounded by an impressive assortment of percussion instruments, known collectively as *traps*, which make him virtually a one-man band. The bass drum and a cymbal device are played with the feet, leaving both hands free for the snare drum and other instruments.

A dance band constituted along these lines is capable of both subtlety and power. To achieve maximum sonority arrangers write an independent part for each player and distribute the notes so that each chord is complete in all three sections of the band. This style of writing and this type of band were in vogue during the *swing* era of the 30s and 40s. Legendary figures of that generation—Glenn Miller, Benny Goodman, the Dorsey brothers, and Artie Shaw, to name a few—can still be heard on reissues of their recordings, like the following.

Cole Porter: *Begin the Beguine* (1938) 3:15
(1892–1964)

> The 1938 recording of this number by Artie Shaw and His Orchestra has been reissued in a current album *This Is the Big Band Era* (RCA VPM–6043). In addition to Artie Shaw on clarinet, the instruments are: 4 saxophones, 3 trumpets, 3 trombones, guitar, bass, piano, and drums.

(Also record side 9 band 4)

The big band sound has been revived by the stage bands currently popular in high schools and colleges. The big band instrumentation is sometimes augmented to include strings and other symphonic instruments. Paul Whiteman, Duke Ellington, and Stan Kenton in turn have evoked favorable, even enthusiastic responses with innovations which combined symphonic and jazz elements, but their pioneering efforts have not yet led to enduring traditions.

Orchestra

An orchestra consists of four sections: woodwind, brass, percussion, and string. The string section, which distinguishes orchestras from bands, is always the largest. The instrumentation of symphony orchestras, having evolved gradually over an extended period, tends to be relatively stable. Therefore, the approximate distribution of instruments for orchestras of various sizes can be tabulated. The major professional orchestras have resources beyond those listed on the table, and extras are available for special requirements.

The seating plan of orchestras varies. The conductor stands front and center on the stage with the orchestra spread in a fan shape around his central position. First violins are always on his left. The concertmaster, who leads the section and functions somewhat as an assistant conductor, is at the head of the first violins on the outside. The second violins may be next to the first violins, or they may be at the front of the stage opposite the first violins. Prevailing practice is to keep all of the violins together and to place the violas and the cellos on the conductor's right. The cellos may be on the outside and the violas on the inside, or vice versa. The string basses are at the side of the stage behind the cellos. The woodwinds are in front of the conductor. The French horns are usually between the woodwinds and the rest of the brass instruments. The trumpets, trombones, and tuba form a semicircle with the percussion section at the rear of the stage. Figure 17 shows the seating plan of the Philadelphia Orchestra.

Orchestral works composed during the second half of the 18th century typically are scored for a classic orchestra—pairs of flutes, oboes, sometimes clarinets, bassoons, horns, trumpets, timpani, and a modest body of strings. The full orchestra which became standard during the next century routinely included clarinets; the number of horns was increased to four; trombones and later tuba were added along with an extra percussion player or two and strings to balance. Since the late 19th century, composers have had available and have created works utilizing the full resources of the large orchestra shown in Table 4, where the instrumentation of the various orchestras is given for comparison. Isolated works have been written for still larger, gigantic orchestras, but practical considerations inhibit the use of extras beyond the standard large orchestra. The expansion which occurred during the last century and the first part of this one seems to have run its course. The three examples suggested for listening are scored for representative classic, full, and large orchestras.

W. A. MOZART: *Symphony no. 35 in D, K.385, "Haffner"* (1782)
(1756–1791) 1. Allegro con spirito 7:59

Classic orchestra: 2 flutes, 2 oboes, 2 clarinets, 2 bassoons, 2 horns, 2 trumpets, timpani, and strings.

(Record side 3 band 1)

L. VAN BEETHOVEN: *Leonore Overture no. 3, op. 72a* (1806) 12:10
(1770–1827)

Full orchestra: 2 flutes, 2 oboes, 2 clarinets, 2 bassoons, 4 horns, 2 trumpets, 3 trombones, timpani, and strings.
Beethoven composed four overtures for his only opera, known first as *Leonore* but subsequently as *Fidelio*. The exact purpose and chronology of the overtures have been the subject of much speculation. This one is a revision of the one written for the first performance of the opera in 1805.

(Also record side 8 band 5)

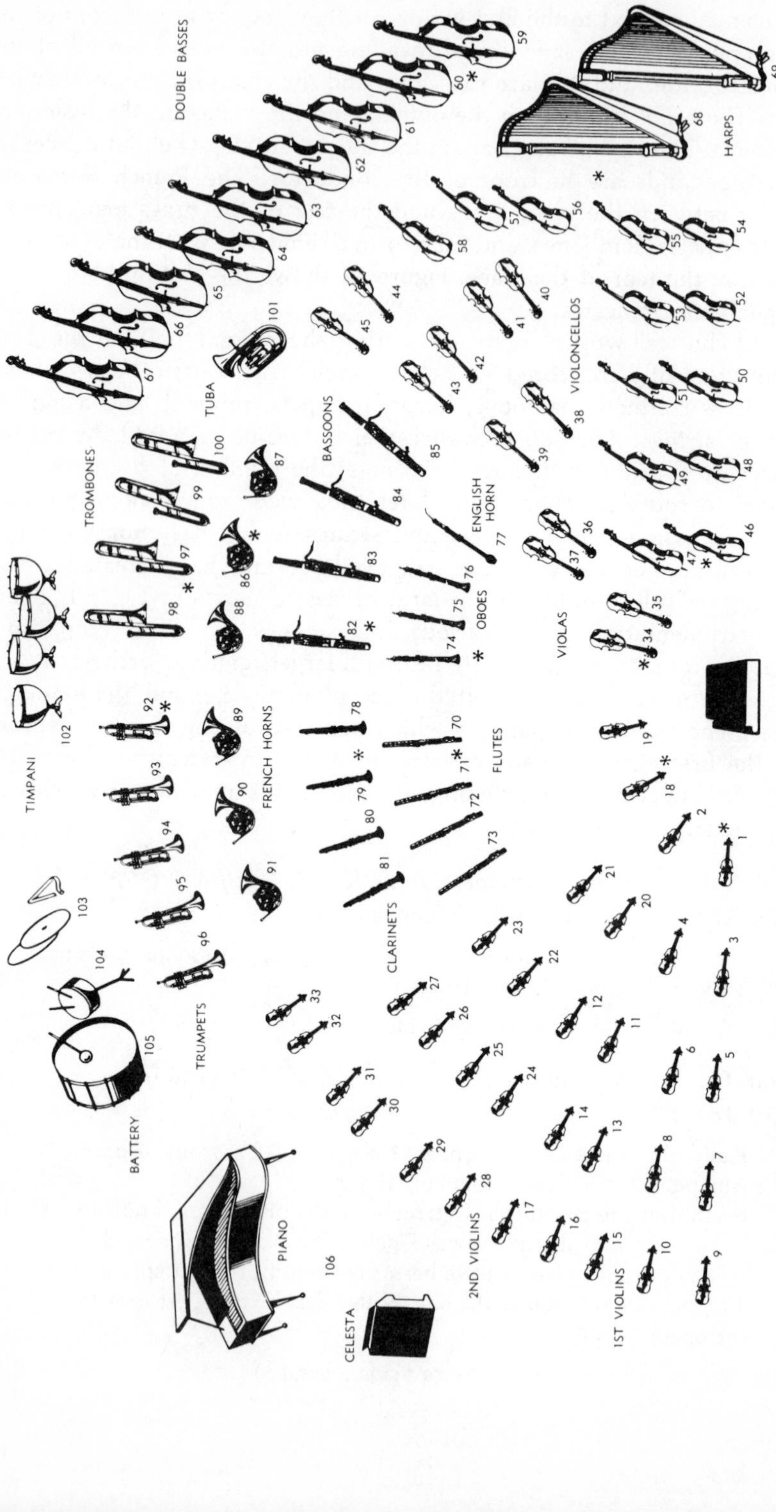

FIGURE 17. *Seating Plan, Philadelphia Orchestra, Eugene Ormandy, Music Director*

Table 4
DISTRIBUTION OF INSTRUMENTS IN THE ORCHESTRA

	Classic Orchestra	*Full Orchestra*	*Large Orchestra*
WOODWIND			
Piccolo			1
Flute	2	2	2–3
Oboe	2	2	2–3
English horn			1
Clarinet	(2)	2	2–4
Bass clarinet			1
Bassoon	2	2	2–3
Contrabassoon			1
Total	6(8)	8	12–17
BRASS			
French horn	2	4	4–8
Trumpet	2	2–3	3–5
Trombone		3	3–4
Tuba		1	1
Total	4	10–11	11–18
PERCUSSION	1	3	4
HARP AND PIANO		1	2–3
STRING			
1st Violin	4–8	8–12	14–18
2nd Violin	4–6	6–10	10–16
Viola	2–4	4–8	8–12
Cello	2–4	4–8	8–12
Bass	2–4	4–6	8–10
Total	14–26	26–44	48–68
Grand total	25–39	48–67	77–110

Samuel Barber: *Symphony no. 1 in One Movement, op. 9* (1936) 18:30
(1910–)

Large orchestra: 2 flutes, piccolo, 2 oboes, English horn, 2 clarinets, bass clarinet, 2 bassoons, contrabassoon, 4 horns, 3 trumpets, 3 trombones, tuba, timpani, percussion, harp, and strings. (Page of orchestral score showing all instruments except harp, p. 369)

(Also record side 6 band 2)

While the instrumentation of the Barber symphony is the largest that can be regarded as standard, much larger orchestras are called for on occasion. Stravinsky's ballet *The Rite of Spring* (see Chapter 5) is

FIGURE 18. *The New York Philharmonic with Pierre Boulez, Music Director, in Avery Fisher Hall.*

FIGURE 19. *Zubin Mehta, Music Director of the Los Angeles Philharmonic*

scored for 3 flutes, piccolo, alto flute, 4 oboes, English horn, 4 clarinets, bass clarinet, 4 bassoons, contrabassoon, 8 horns, 5 trumpets, 3 trombones, 2 tubas, timpani (2 players), percussion, and strings. Schoenberg originally scored his *Five Pieces for Orchestra, op. 16* for woodwinds in 4s and 6 horns, but his subsequent revision, significantly, is for a standard, large orchestra. Additions to the woodwind and brass sections necessitate augmentation of the string section in proportion for balance. The added cost and difficulty of performing works for extraordinarily large orchestras restrict performances, a fact which composers must ponder before embarking on such projects.

Combined Groups

The orchestra is combined with voices in operas, oratorios, and cantatas. Some masses are for chorus and orchestra, and a few symphonies include voices. The combination of instruments and voices adds the vocal qualities and the capability of expressing a text to the already luxuriant sound spectrum of the orchestra. Luciano Berio's *Sinfonia* is a surrealistic collage of quotations both literary and musical, which obviously require both vocal and instrumental resources for realization. In the first performance and on the only recording to date the vocal parts are performed by the Swingle Singers and the orchestral parts by the New York Philharmonic.

Luciano Berio: *Sinfonia* (1968)
(1925–) Section III 12:21

Large orchestra and vocal ensemble.

Hector Berlioz was an extremist in an age of extremes, so it is not surprising that one of his compositions is of gargantuan proportions. His *Requiem* is scored for an enormous orchestra, a chorus to match, a section of timpani, and 4 brass choirs. To hear a live performance of this work is a memorable experience. Only a fraction of its magnitude can be captured on a recording, but its overpowering splendor is still apparent.

Hector Berlioz: *Requiem (Grande Messe des Morts), op. 5* (1837)
(1803–1869) 2. Dies irae 12:30

Chorus, orchestra, and 4 brass choirs.
The 4 brass choirs enter in the *Tuba mirum* section, about 6 minutes after the beginning of the *Dies irae*.

The Elements of Music

5

Individual sounds of varying pitch, loudness, color, and duration are combined simultaneously and in series to form the elements of music. The elements are not isolated in ordinary listening, but considering them separately facilitates study.

Rhythm and Meter

The most primitive element of music is *rhythm*. A dictionary defines rhythm as measured motion, the regular rise and fall of sounds, a symmetrical and regularly recurrent grouping of tones according to accent and time value. *Meter* is defined as systematically arranged and measured rhythm, the aspect of rhythm concerned with the division of music into measures consisting of a uniform number of beats or time units. Rhythm and meter are slightly different but closely related aspects of the same element. In musical parlance, meter refers to the basic, underlying pulse —the fixed pattern of strong and weak beats to which one responds physically in marching, dancing, or in tapping the toe. Rhythm, properly, means the organized interplay of varied note values, including durations both longer and shorter than the beat. In practice, no such precision of usage is observed. The terms rhythm and meter are sometimes used interchangeably, and rhythm commonly is used to denote all aspects of duration, stress, grouping, and time value. No attempt to refine current terminology is made here.

Rhythm, unlike the other elements of music, can exist independently. Any sound, including noise, can establish rhythm. It is present in speech. Motion can be rhythmic, but rhythm usually implies organized sound. The sound of heels clicking on the pavement as a person walks creates a rhythmic pattern. The steps measure identical units of time, and these units are grouped in pairs by the alternation of left and right. The measured motion of walking has a direct counterpart in the rhythm of a march.

John Philip Sousa: *Hands Across the Sea* (1899) 2:50
(1854–1932)

> This is one of Sousa's many stirring marches. Observe how easy it is to feel the pulse of this piece, as it is in all true marches. Tap your toe or wave your hand in time with the music as this or some similar march is played.

(Record side 6 band 3)

The pulse of music is called the *beat*. With certain types of music, marches among them, responding physically to the beat is almost a reflex action. When the beat is more obscure, tapping or clapping with it focuses attention on the rhythm and aids in sensing the beat.

Some instruments play with the beat, some faster than the beat, and some slower than the beat. In other words, music is made up of notes longer, shorter, and with the same duration as the beat. This does not disturb the perception of the beat or the regular pattern of the underlying rhythm. Quicker notes are heard in groups comprising beats, and slower notes are heard as combinations of beats. The drums and certain lower pitched instruments usually mark the beat in marches.

Musicians sometimes count with the beats as a teaching device. The counting for a march goes *ONE-two, ONE-two*. The beats in a march are alternately accented and unaccented. *ONE* coincides with the accented beats and *two* with the unaccented beats. The complete pattern, an accented beat plus an unaccented beat, constitutes a *measure* or a *bar* of music. In the interest of accuracy, it should be stated that marches also are written with a four-beat pattern, *ONE-two-three-four*. It simplifies the discussion to consider all march rhythms as two-beat patterns for the moment.

Listen to other traditional marches and compare their rhythm with that of some concert marches for band such as Barber's *Commando March*. The beat in concert marches is not always as clear and regular as it is in street and military marches. It is common practice to adapt march and dance rhythms for use in concert music. Essential characteristics are preserved, but the music is not necessarily suitable for marching or dancing.

Samuel Barber: *Commando March* (1943) 3:05
(1910–)

Stylized march rhythms also appear in works for orchestra and piano.

Serge Prokofiev: *Love for Three Oranges Suite, op. 33–bis* (1925)
(1891–1953) 3. March 1:40

Frederic Chopin: *Piano Sonata no. 2 in B-flat minor, op. 35* (1839)
(1810–1849) 3. Funeral March: Lento 7:30

These two works illustrate opposite poles of the march concept. The first is fast and gay; the second slow and somber. One must probe beneath the surface to detect the common rhythmic source indicated by the titles.

The *ONE-two* beat pattern found in marches also provides the rhythmic basis for much dance music. Like marches, dances are written in measures of four beats as well as in measures of two. The same steps are appropriate with either, and the sound is not affected noticeably by the difference in notation.

The *ONE-two* beat pattern is only one of numerous possibilities. Waltzes, for example, have a *ONE-two-three* rhythmic background. The lilting, supple rhythm of waltzes contrasts sharply with the angular, straightforward rhythm of marches. The traditional *oomp-pah-pah* waltz accompaniment highlights the waltz rhythm with the accented first beat in the low register and the unaccented second and third beats in a higher register. This figure establishes the rhythmic pattern and continues as an accompaniment for the melody in the following example, as it does in most waltzes.

Johann Strauss: *The Blue Danube, op. 314* (1867) 9:50
(1825–1899)

The nearly 500 works of Strauss include several operettas, but he is best known as a composer of waltzes. They were conceived as dance music but endure as concert music. This waltz, one of his most famous, is not a simple dance tune, but a series of sophisticated melodies elaborately scored for full orchestra. An introduction in another rhythm precedes the waltz proper, and in concert performances the strict tempo of the dance is not preserved.

Just as march rhythms are found in music not intended for marching, waltz rhythms are found in music not intended for dancing. In the

JOHANN STRAUSS

following example the name and the rhythm pattern of the waltz have been retained, but other connections with the dance have been severed.

FREDERIC CHOPIN: *Waltz in D-flat, op. 64 no. 1, "Minute"* (1846) 1:25
(1810–1849)

> The familiar name of this delightful miniature suggests that it should be played in 60 seconds. Double that time is more realistic for most piano students, and the piece would still be too fast for dancing. Listeners hearing it played in the usual way tend to hear the beats in groups and the measure rather than the beat as the rhythmic unit. Concentrating on the typical waltz pattern of the accompaniment instead of the melody makes the waltz rhythm easier to detect.

The rhythmic element is prominent and uncomplicated in marches and waltzes, so they make a logical point of departure for the study of rhythm and meter. The basic two-beat and three-beat patterns underlying the rhythm of marches and waltzes, respectively, are also found in music far removed from parades and ballrooms. Music of widely divergent types may share a common rhythmic background. The rhythmic element in concert music is usually less obvious than in march and dance music, but in most instances the beats and groupings are readily perceptible. Try tapping and counting with the beats as you listen to the following examples illustrating various rhythms and meters.

W. A. Mozart: *The Marriage of Figaro Overture* (1786) 4:00
(1756–1791)

The rhythm of this dazzling piece has the same underlying *ONE-two* pattern as a march, but the style and character are totally different. This overture is frequently heard in symphony concerts apart from the opera.

Franz Schubert: *Symphony no. 8 in B minor, "Unfinished"* (1822)
(1797–1828) 1. Allegro moderato 11:10

This movement has a *ONE-two-three* rhythmic background, like a waltz. Conceivably one could dance to it, but the idea would hardly suggest itself. The innate beauty of the symphony and romantic legends about its "unfinished" state have combined to make it Schubert's best known orchestral composition. It consists of only two movements, instead of the customary four, but his untimely death at the age of thirty-one does not account for this fact. He lived six years after he presented the score of the two existing movements to a music society as a condition of membership. During this time he wrote another very large symphony (no. 9 in C).

Regular, recurrent patterns of two beats or three beats underlie the rhythm of most music. In a two-beat pattern the first beat is accented and the second unaccented. In a three-beat pattern the first beat is accented and the second and third are unaccented. These are the basic beat patterns. Each basic pattern may constitute a *measure* of music. Two or more basic patterns are combined in larger measures. A measure of four beats, for example, consists of two groups of two beats. The first of the four beats receives a primary accent. The third receives a lesser, secondary accent, and the second and fourth beats are unaccented. This, at least, is the theory learned by young musicians. From the standpoint of the listener, the distinction is not always clear. The amount of accent is purely relative, and it is not always possible or even desirable in performance to exaggerate the difference between the stresses to the point where the primary and secondary accents are readily distinguishable. As a result, many marches are written in four-beat measures rather than in two-beat measures. When a march has a four-beat pattern, the left foot comes alternately with the first and third beats of the measure, the right foot with the second and fourth, but no one is disturbed by it. The same is true of dance music, which is written both ways.

It must be noted that the possibility of confusion exists only for the listener. Musical notation is explicit, and conductors are meticulous about making appropriate gestures, the ones which players expect for a given notation, though such subtleties are lost in radio and recorded performances.

The following example is written in measures of four beats. The rhythmic element is pronounced, and no difficulty will be experienced in locating the march-like beat. Distinguish if you can not only between accented and unaccented beats but between primary and secondary accents. Once you have located the primary accent, count with the rhythm *ONE-two-three-four.* A certain sensitivity is required to differentiate between qualities of accent, but a reasonable degree of accuracy can be achieved by careful listening when performers are punctilious in their rendition. The distinction between two-beat measures and four-beat measures is not so much a fact to be observed as a suggestion to be sensed.

P. I. Tchaikovsky: *Symphony no. 6 in B minor, op. 74 "Pathetique"* (1893)
(1840–1893) 3. Allegro molto vivace 9:35

From a standpoint of the written measure, the next example is the same as the previous one, but the effect is totally different. The notated beat of the Bach *Air* is so slow that what is written as a half beat is usually felt as the rhythmic unit. In effect this creates measures with a total of eight beats. Eight-beat measures quite logically can be heard as two four-beat measures or even as four two-beat measures. The possible dichotomy between the sound and the notation of rhythm is apparent, but only the former is of importance to the listener.

J. S. Bach: *Suite no. 3 in D for Orchestra, S.1068* (1730)
(1685–1750) 2. Air 5:30

> The bass line moves in a persistent rhythm, treading along in notes of equal duration. Over this soars one of the most inspired melodies in music. The unswerving rhythmic regularity of the bass provides an effective foil for the sustained, singing melody.

Just as rhythmic groups of two beats are combined in four- and eight-beat measures, rhythmic groups of three beats are combined in six-, nine-, and twelve-beat measures. In measures with six beats, the first receives the primary accent as always. The fourth receives the secondary accent, and beats two, three, five, and six are unaccented. The possibility of confusion between the primary and secondary accents and consequently between three-beat measures and six-beat measures is apparent. It is reassuring to note that appreciation is not seriously impaired by such minor discrepancies in perception and that professional musicians are not infallible in this regard. The following example is written in measures of six beats, but at least parts of it can be heard just as readily in independent groups of three.

W. A. MOZART: *Symphony no. 40 in G minor, K.550* (1788)
(1756–1791) 2. Andante 7:50

> The first note of a composition is not necessarily the first beat of a measure. Many works begin, as this one does, with a fraction of a measure. When the first measure of a piece is incomplete, the first note or group of notes is unaccented, and the first primary accent comes at the beginning of the first complete measure. This particular movement commences on the sixth beat of the measure. The second note of the melody comes on the first beat of a measure. See how long you can follow the six-beat pattern of the underlying rhythm. Later in the movement there is a theme which is almost waltz-like, but the written measures still have six beats.

In measures with nine beats, the first receives the primary rhythmic accent, the fourth and seventh secondary accents. The remainder are unaccented. This is the rhythmic foundation of the following example.

L. VAN BEETHOVEN: *String Quartet no. 1 in F, op. 18 no. 1* (1800)
(1770–1827) 2. Adagio affettuoso ed appasionata 10:00

> The pulse and pattern of the underlying rhythm are established by the accompanying instruments before the melody enters. The beat is slow and the motion stately, but as the work progresses, splashes of rapid notes appear against a throbbing background. The rhythm should continue in the imagination during momentary periods of silence in the music, called *rests*.

Measures of twelve beats are the most extended that are commonly used. The primary accent falls on the first beat of the measure, secondary accents on the first of each succeeding group of three beats. The following example from *L'Estro Armonico* has twelve-beat measures.

ANTONIO VIVALDI: *Concerto Grosso, op. 3 no. 11 in D minor* (1712)
(1678–1741) 2. Largo e spiccato 3:15

> Except for a brief passage at the beginning and again at the end, the motion of the accompanying instruments coincides exactly with the beat. This accompaniment consists of repeated notes of equal duration with four groups of three in each measure. Concentrating on the accompaniment orients the listener and the performer rhythmically, but the interest and beauty of this work lie in its incomparable melody.

The underlying rhythmic pulses of music basically may be grouped and divided into duple and triple patterns. These basic duple and triple patterns and combinations of them in measures of four, six, eight, nine, and twelve beats constitute the conventional metric units of familiar music. Conceivably six- and twelve-beat measures can result from combinations of either two- or three-beat patterns, but usually they are derived from three-pulse groups. The rhythmic possibilities of measures with five, seven, ten, and eleven beats and asymmetric divisions were not exploited until recent times. These possibilities open new vistas for composers and listeners alike. Tchaikovsky was one of the first to use five-beat measures in a symphonic composition.

P. I. Tchaikovsky: *Symphony no. 6 in B minor, op. 74* (1893)
(1840–1893) 2. Allegro con grazia 7:15

The five-beat rhythmic pattern of this music may not feel quite as comfortable as the more usual patterns, but one soon becomes accustomed to its regular, though asymmetric groupings. Five-beat measures usually are heard as a group of two followed by a group of three or vice versa. The unequal length of the groups and the irregular spacing of the accents produces an effect quite unlike that of symmetric rhythms.

Asymmetric divisions of a more complex genre are found in the works of many contemporary composers, among them Bela Bartok. This feature appears not only in his major orchestral and chamber works but also in small pieces for one and two instruments. The latter provide ideal examples as they both are concise and varied.

Bela Bartok: *Mikrokosmos* (1926–1937)
(1881–1945) Six Dances in Bulgarian Rhythm

148.	4 + 2 + 3	1:50
149.	2 + 2 + 3	1:10
150.	2 + 3	1:20
151.	3 + 2 + 3	1:25
152.	2 + 2 + 2 + 3	1:13
153.	3 + 3 + 2	1:40

Each of the dances makes use of a different asymmetric meter. The beats within measures are grouped as shown. The pace in some is too fast for individual units to be discerned, but the effect of the irregularity is unmistakable. The fact that these rhythms are derived from Bulgarian folk music suggests that they perhaps are newer to us than to some other peoples. These six dances are the last of a group of progressively graded piano pieces. The total collection, published in six volumes, is a virtual encyclopedia of contemporary devices.

It is only a short step from the use of asymmetric meters to the abandonment of fixed rhythmic patterns. The constant patterns and regular accents which regulated the rhythmic flow in music of the past are no longer universal. Many works of this century have irregular accents defining unpredictable groupings of beats and notes. The old sense of rhythmic stability and security is replaced by a sense of freedom and excitement. Symmetric rhythms, while still used, can no longer be taken for granted. Contemporary composers have added a new dimension to rhythm and have used it with skill and imagination. As a result, rhythm has been elevated from a role of subservience, a mere handmaiden of melody and harmony, to that of an equal in the hierarchy of musical elements. One of the first to grasp the potential of rhythm for attracting attention and sustaining interest and to feature it in extended passages was Igor Stravinsky.

IGOR STRAVINSKY: *Symphony in Three Movements* (1945)
(1882–1971) I. ♩ = 160 (𝅗𝅥 = 80) 9:45

Stravinsky provides no clue to the style of this movement but only specifies the number of beats per minute as shown. The fact that he gives the rate for two units, one twice as fast as the other, suggests that either may be taken as the beat. Considering the shorter of the two time units (160 per minute) as the beat, measures of 4, 3, 2, 6, 5, 1, and 1½ occur in that order. Irregular measures and shifting accents figure conspicuously in the rhythmic plan of the work. In some passages almost every measure has a different duration than its neighbors. In others the measures are fairly constant, but accents occur in unexpected places. Sometimes there is silence where an accent is anticipated. All of this adds up to rhythm which is as complex and high-tensioned as the age in which it was composed. Its intricacies are a challenge to performers and listeners alike. Many are attracted to this music immediately. Others have to learn to like it, but very few are tempted to sleep through it.

(Also record side 8 band 1)[1]

Accents and obvious rhythmic groupings are not mandatory in music. Notes can be played and sung without perceptible accents or divisions, though this possibility is largely ignored. The tendency to

1. See fn. p. 16.

organize sounds in groups seems to be innate. It emerges spontaneously in the writing of composers and in the playing and singing of performers. Listeners are inclined to attach significance to the slightest hint of stress or division and to organize sounds into patterns even while none are intended. Furthermore, it is impossible in traditional notation to avoid suggestions of division. Bar lines, originally introduced as an aid to reading, are drawn between measures, and they have an acquired rhythmic significance which musicians are trained to observe. It is difficult for them to overcome this conditioning in the few passages where it is not appropriate. The net result is that few passages and fewer performances are lacking in stresses and groupings, but stresses should not be regarded as perpetual necessities. No music exists without flow and motion, but the obvious type of accent and grouping heard in marches and dances diminishes to the vanishing point at the opposite end of the rhythmic spectrum. The notation of many avant-garde compositions is lacking in bar lines and conventional metric groupings. Rhythmic relationships are sometimes specified using new notational devices, and sometimes they are left to the discretion of the performer or to chance. Principles of rhythm must be redefined and listening habits reoriented to accommodate the revolutionary rhythmic concepts in the new music of recent years.

At the beginning of each piece of conventional music and wherever changes in the rhythmic framework occur, there is a *time signature,* also called a *meter signature.* The time signature most often consists of two Arabic numerals, one written above the other in the manner of a fraction. The lower number shows which note symbol is used to represent the beat. The upper number indicates the number of beats in each measure of the music. The measures are marked in musical notation by vertical lines called *bar lines.* Vestiges of an older system of rhythmic notation persist in two time signatures which have a symbol in place of the two numbers. A large "C" is the equivalent of a 4/4 time signature, and the same symbol with a vertical line through it is the equivalent of a 2/2 time signature.

Conductors, with their right hand or a baton, describe stylized patterns in the air appropriate to the various time signatures. Each conductor makes personalized modifications in the designs, but sufficient uniformity is preserved to make the beats intelligible to players. A stroke straight down directly in front of the conductor is used for the first beat of each measure. For this reason, the first beat of a measure is referred to as the *downbeat.* If there are two beats in the measure, the second is indicated by an upward motion roughly parallel with that of the downbeat. A three-beat pattern approximates the shape of a triangle—down, right, and up to the point of origin. The conductor's beat for four-beat measures is down, left, right, and up. The motion for six-beat measures is down, left, left, right, right, and up. Unaccented beats at the end of measures come on the up stroke of the conductor's beat and are referred to as *upbeats*. Measures with more than six beats usually are conducted with motions following one of the contours mentioned, with subdivisions as necessary. When the beats are too fast to be conducted individually, one gesture is used for a group of beats. Conversely, when the notated beat is very slow, it may be divided and conducted with two or three motions.

What aspects of rhythm should listeners be able to discern? Distinguishing between two-beat and three-beat patterns presents no formidable problem. Recognizing combinations of basic groups is more difficult, and infallibility cannot be expected. However, attentive listeners will be aware of extended measures in the more obvious examples. Sensitivity to shifting accents, to changes of meter, and to the absence of rhythmic stresses should be cultivated. Rhythm is the foundation of the musical edifice. The realm of listening experience is extended by an awareness of its patterns and functions.

Tempo

Tempo refers to the rate of speed in music. In 1816 Johann Maelzel constructed a device using the pendulum principle capable of marking units of time, and hence the tempo of music, with absolute precision. Called a *metronome,* it could be set to swing and tick at any selected rate in a range exceeding the requirements of practical music. Metronome markings are expressed in terms of the number of units per minute. The marking M.M. = 60 indicates 60 rhythmic units per minute or one per second. Often a note symbol is used in place of the abbreviation M.M. Thus ♩ = 72 indicates 72 quarter notes (the symbol shown) in a minute or that one quarter note has a duration of 1/72 of a minute, 5/6 of a second.

Beethoven was intrigued by the possibilities of the metronome, and he provided his symphonies with metronome markings. Contemporary composers are more inclined to use metronome markings than were composers of the period immediately following its invention. Perhaps composers object to the mechanical nature of the metronome, for they continue to use Italian terms introduced early in the 17th century as tempo indications. These terms lack the precision of metronome markings, but they convey implications of style as well as of pace. Combining Italian words with metronome markings is a common practice which secures the advantages of both.

Tempo indications would be of no particular concern to the listener except that they are used to designate the various movements of multimovement works and sometimes figure in the titles of compositions. This makes familiarity with at least the more common ones desirable. Arranged from the slowest to the fastest with approximate English equivalents, they are:

Largo: broad, large
Lento: slow
Adagio: comfortable, easy
Andante: going along, walking
Moderato: moderate
Allegro: cheerful
Vivace: lively, quick
Presto: very fast, rapid

Derivative forms of these terms provide shades of meaning. *Larghetto*, a diminutive form of *Largo* indicates a tempo slightly less slow. *Allegretto*, a diminutive form of *Allegro*, indicates a tempo slightly less fast. There is disagreement on the interpretation of *Andantino*, the diminutive form of *Andante*. Some regard *Andante* as a slow tempo and *Andantino* as somewhat faster. Others class *Andante* as a fast tempo and consequently consider *Andantino* to be a little slower. No less a personage than Beethoven was puzzled by this question. Though the precise meaning of *Andantino* is in doubt, the confusion about its significance establishes the fact that *Andante* falls at the center of the scale of tempos and on the dividing line between those classified as fast and those classified as slow. *Prestissimo* is a superlative form of *Presto* meaning extremely fast. Diminutive and superlative forms of other terms also are used.

To provide more explicit and descriptive directions, tempo indications are modified with additional Italian words and phrases such as:

Agitato: agitated
Animato: animated
Appassionato: passionately
Assai: very
Cantabile: singing
Con brio: with spirit
Con fuoco: with fire
Con moto: with motion
E or *ed*: and
Espressivo: expressively
Grazioso: with grace
Ma: but
Maestoso: majestically
Marcato: marked
Molto: very, much
Non: not
Non troppo: not too much
Piu: more
Poco: little
Sostenuto: sustained

Many combinations of these and other terms are used in identifying the examples. See the glossary for additional definitions.

In addition to the words and phrases for rates of speed, there are indications for gradual and sudden changes, both faster and slower. Listeners should be alert to changes of pace, a significant means of musical expression.

Composers from time to time abandon Italian terminology in favor of the vernacular, but this practice has not become general. It is more prevalent now than formerly, but it has two disadvantages. Italian words and phrases through long usage have developed connotations difficult or awkward to express in other languages, and musical terms in Italian are more universally understood than any other.

There are no absolute limits on musical pace, but practical considerations regulate extremes. Sustaining accuracy in extremely slow tempos is difficult. Equally difficult is conducting, counting, and playing extremely fast tempos. Tempos related to the physiological rhythm of the heartbeat seem most natural. These encompass rates between approximately 60 and 80 per minute. Tempos outside these limits are perceived as slow or fast. The tendency is to divide or combine units to bring them within this range, though the points at which this occurs vary with individuals, both performers and listeners.

Tempo is a major factor in setting the mood of music, and it is a prime source of variety. Contrast of tempo is sought between sections of larger works, between movements of multimovement works, and between selections on programs. The usual order of tempos in a four movement symphony is: fast—slow—moderate or moderately fast—fast, the last usually faster than the first. There are, of course, many modifications of and exceptions to this plan. A typical sequence of tempos is illustrated in Mozart's *Haffner Symphony*.

W. A. Mozart: *Symphony no. 35 in D, K.385, "Haffner"* (1782)
(1756–1791)

1.	Allegro con spirito	7:59
2.	Andante	4:25
3.	Menuetto	3:05
4.	Presto	3:34

This symphony was written in honor of Siegmund Haffner, the son of Salzburg's mayor, at the time he was elevated to the nobility. No tempo indication is given for the minuet (*menuetto* in Italian), a practice of the period that leads to diverse interpretations. Originally a rustic dance, the minuet made its way into the French court and thence into concert music. The dance was characterized by grace and dignity, but the minuets in symphonies are often played in a sprightly style. The most usual tempo marking, when one is given, is *Allegretto*.

(Record side 3 bands 1–4)

The thirteen brief pieces comprising Schumann's *Scenes from Childhood* provide an interesting study in tempo. Each editor (and performer) has different ideas regarding their interpretation. The tempo markings in two editions are given for comparison. The Italian tempo indications are from the G. Schirmer edition. They must have been added by the editor, Harold Bauer, because they do not appear in other editions. The metronome marks immediately following the Italian terms are also from the Schirmer edition. The metronome marks in parentheses are from the Kalmus edition "edited according to manuscripts and from her personal recollections by Clara Schumann," a famous pianist and wife of the composer. The metronome markings for numbers 9 and 12 in the two editions are for different note values, as shown. Comparable metronome marks would be 56 for number 9 in the Schirmer edition and 40 for number 12 in the Kalmus edition. English translations of the original German titles are from the Schirmer edition.

ROBERT SCHUMANN: *Scenes from Childhood (Kinderscenen), op. 15* (1838)
(1810–1856)

1.	About Strange Lands and People			1:30
	Andante	♩ = 72	(♩ = 108)	
2.	Curious Story			1:00
	Allegro giojoso	♩ = 132	(♩ = 132)	
3.	Blindman's Buff			:35
	Allegro scherzando	♩ = 116	(♩ = 120)	
4.	Pleading Child			:50
	Moderato	♩ = 60	(♩ = 88)	
5.	Perfectly Contented			:35
	Allegro moderato	♩ = 84	(♩ = 72)	
6.	Important Event			1:00
	Allegro marziale	♩ = 120	(♩ = 120)	
7.	Reverie (Traumerei)			2:10
	Adagio espressivo	♩ = 56	(♩ = 80)	
8.	At the Fireside			:45
	Allegretto grazioso	♩ = 104	(♩ = 108)	
9.	The Knight of the Rocking Horse			:40
	Allegro con brio	♩ = 176	(𝅗𝅥. = 76)	
10.	Almost too Serious			1:10
	Moderato, poco rubato	♪ = 100	(♪ = 104)	
11.	Frightening			1:30
	Poco allegro	♩ = 96	(♩ = 108)	
12.	Child Falling Asleep			1:25
	Lento non troppo	♩ = 44	(♪ = 80)	
13.	The Poet Speaks			1:30
	Adagio espressivo	♩ = 88	(♩ = 92)	

It is interesting to compare the tempos of recorded performances of the *Scenes from Childhood* with those given by the two editors. This can be done by counting the beats with the music for 10 or 15 seconds and then multiplying the total by 6 or 4 to give the number of beats in a minute. The procedure is complicated somewhat by occasional deviations indicated by the composer from the regular tempo and by liberties taken by artists in their interpretation of the music without which performances would seem mechanical and uninteresting. Total performance time provides another basis for tempo comparisons, since slower tempos result in longer performance times and faster tempos in shorter performance times.

Unless a composer gives a metronome marking, he merely suggests an approximate tempo, and no two conductors or players will give identical interpretations. Some performers choose to ignore even precise directions. Fast, brilliant tempos are favored by some while others are partial to slower, more deliberate paces. Both schools of thought have many partisans, and tempo is a frequent subject of debate among musicians.

Melody

Melody is that inscrutable, magical element of music that captures the imagination and lingers in the memory to be recalled, hummed, and whistled long after words and accompaniments have been forgotten. Melody and music are almost synonymous. It is strange, therefore, that countless textbooks are devoted to harmony, counterpoint, and form but few to melody. One reason may be that dissecting and analyzing melodies is not very illuminating. Melody, perhaps more than the other elements of music, is dictated by inspiration and appreciated by instinct. Some questions about melody, however, can be posed and answered objectively.

What is a melody? How are melodies conceived? What are the characteristics of a good one? How are melodies recognized and remembered? These are questions inquisitive listeners might ask. The first is the easiest to answer.

A melody is a succession of musical tones conveying an impression of continuity—a series of pitches arranged in a logical sequence. Random sounds are not perceived as melodies, nor are tones unduly separated in time, register, or color. As usually construed, melodies have definite points of beginning and ending, the latter attended by a sense of completion. The proportions of individual melodies are modest, and most compositions have more than one. Extended works have many, though probably only a few of them are remembered vividly. An essential art of composition is to delineate separate melodies without disturbing the flow and continuity of the whole.

Most melodies are played or sung in their entirety by the same instrument, voice, or group. This is not mandatory, but it is suggested by the requirement of continuity. It also serves the purpose of making the melody easier to follow. Exceptions to this occur in repetitions after a melody is familiar. Then various instruments may share a single statement for variety. In orchestral compositions, contrasting melodies usually are assigned to different instruments.

The principal melody more often than not is higher in pitch than the accompaniment and secondary melodies. This, however, is something which changes with the period, the style, and the form. Occasionally the main melody is assigned to the bottom or middle of the musical texture. At other times melodic interest is divided between all the parts. Composers and performers subtly direct the listener's attention to the most important melodic line when it departs from its accustomed position. This is done by making it louder, faster, slower, or different in color from the background.

The exact mechanism by which a person is able to remember and recognize hundreds of different tunes is a mystery, but musical memory is not much different from any other. It is aided by repetition and association. It improves with use and retains best that which it finds most pleasant. Musical memory and musical enjoyment are closely linked. There is satisfaction in hearing familiar melodies and in anticipating well-known strains. Extending the scope of one's listening experience to include both more and better music develops the musical memory and in the process broadens the foundations of musical enjoyment. The full potentials of memory and appreciation are realized when music one initially finds intriguing is heard repeatedly under agreeable circumstances.

Remembering melodies, like remembering words, names, addresses, and telephone numbers, requires the ability to recognize familiar arrangements of a limited number of components—twelve tones in the case of music. Melodies are nothing more than distinctive arrangements of notes selected from the twelve available. Few melodies make use of all of them. More important than the selection and order of tones in melodic recognition is contour. Melodic contour results from the interplay of pitches and durations.

A graph of the melodic contour of *Who Is Sylvia* is given as an aid in visualizing that aspect of melody. Follow it during the performance. The melody is heard three times with different words.

Franz Schubert: *Who Is Sylvia, op. 106 no. 4* (1826) 2:42
(1797–1828)

Observe the balance between ascending and descending motion and between conjunct and disjunct movement. Notice also the distribution of high and low points in the line. Small rhythm and pitch patterns, which are repeated literally and varied, provide unifying elements. Schubert demonstrates infallible intuition in achieving these desirable melodic characteristics.

(Record side 5 band 3. Notation p. 370)

Knowing that a composer draws his material from a fundamental stockpile of twelve notes and that his melodies can be represented by graphs may make composing sound like fitting pieces of a jigsaw puzzle into suitable patterns of up and down, long and short. This obviously is not the case. What about inspiration? Its role is not as decisive as popular legends would lead one to think. Composers do not experience a powerful emotion and dash wild-eyed to the piano to create, spontaneously, an immortal masterpiece. In reality the creative process is much less romantic and more arduous, but not a mechanical or perfunctory task.

Composition begins with an idea—call it inspiration if you will. Ideas may come out of the blue, but far more often inspiration strikes the composer while he is pursuing it, pencil in hand. Each composer develops a personal approach to composition, but with most the initial germ is born in the mind without recourse to any instrument. The idea is abstract, conceived mentally, but immediately it is translated into symbols and perhaps into sounds as well. Most often the initial idea for a composition is a motive or a melody, occasionally a rhythm, a chord, or a harmonic progression. A unique fragment envisaged in a flash may contain the seed of an entire symphony, but infinite skill, patience, and imagination are required to bring it to fruition. This is the craft of the composer.

If inspiration dictates any aspect of music, it is melody, but even the most inspired melody rarely springs from the composer's mind full blown and perfect. More often initial melodic conceptions require reworking and polishing. When a composer applies technique to his inspiration, he strives for those melodic characteristics illustrated in the Schubert example: balance between unity and variety and between high and low points. His own artistic instinct serves as the sole arbitrator of what constitutes *balance*, and his success or failure as a composer depends in large measure upon his ability to make such decisions in a manner acceptable to discerning audiences. Immortal masterpieces and rejected manuscripts are made from the same raw material.

The dividing line between good and bad melodies, like that between good and bad music generally, is blurred by subjective judgments. Beauty and ugliness, order and chaos, and the like are not states of being but reflections of personal opinion. Such opinions are supported more by emotional convictions than by logic, and logic at best is not easily brought

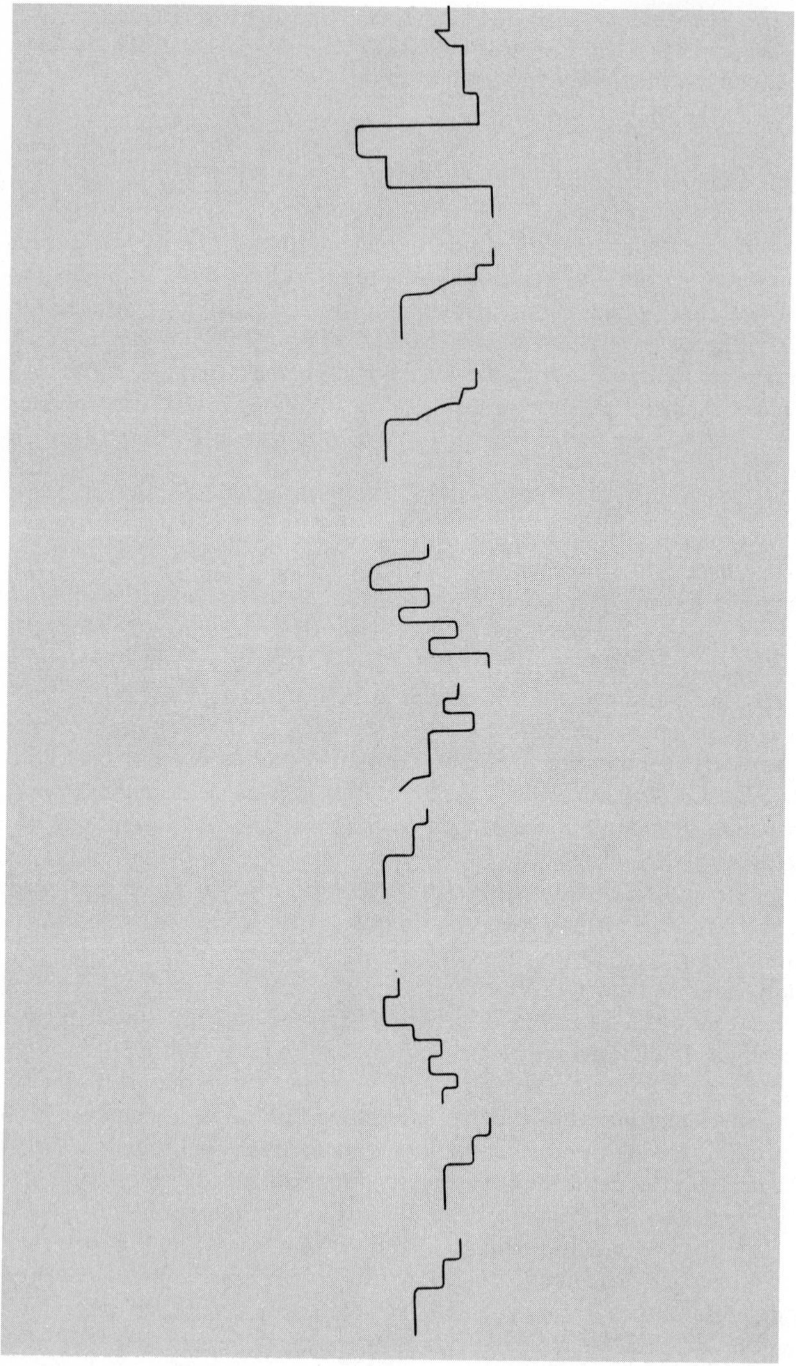

FIGURE 20. *Melodic Contour Graph: Who Is Sylvia* (Notation p. 370)

to bear upon aesthetic matters. The result is that great disparity exists in melodic and musical preferences, in likes and dislikes. This is not only inevitable, but essential. Except for differences in taste, there would be only one kind of music, and what could be more dreary? The vitality of the art is in a large measure a product of its diversity, but the diverse melodic styles illustrated will not prove equally attractive to everyone. Personal inclinations as well as differences in conditioning dictate otherwise. The appeal of some melodies is immediate and almost universal, but the taste for others, like the taste for green olives, must be acquired.

A melody, as most listeners would define the term, is a lyric, flowing, and song-like series of musical tones. Melodies of this sort are found in the music of all periods. Romantic composers added to these qualities their own special kind of sensuous emotion to write soaring melodies of breath-taking beauty and grace. Though Sibelius lived and composed well into the present century, he was a great melodist in the romantic tradition. His music is imbued with lyricism and copiously supplied with singing and singable melodies.

JEAN SIBELIUS: *Violin Concerto in D minor, op. 47* (1903)
(1865–1957) 2. Adagio di molto 8:30

> The only concerto by Sibelius was for the instrument he played, the violin. His intimate knowledge of the instrument undoubtedly stimulated his rare melodic gift as he conceived this movement. The solo violin at times leaves the principal melodic material to the orchestra and spins a delicate filligree around it.

In the late 18th century, melodies typically were also lyric, flowing, and song-like, but they were inclined toward classic simplicity, clarity, and purity rather than sensuousness. Melodies of this type are more akin to folk songs. They are expressive, but the emotions they express are subdued and restrained. They are more elegant than dramatic, more charming than poignant. The melodies of Haydn, Mozart, and their contemporaries fall into this category.

W. A. MOZART: *Clarinet Concerto in A, K.622* (1791)
(1756–1791) 1. Allegro 12:50

> The availability of the fabulous clarinetist, Anton Stadler, induced Mozart to write several works involving clarinet, including this, one of his most significant instrumental compositions.

Another type of melody, instrumental in character but found also in vocal music, is active and athletic rather than lyric. Insistent rhythms bordering on perpetual motion progress mostly along scale lines, relieved by skips along chord lines. The supple curves of the styles previously illustrated are supplanted by rugged and vigorous contours. Melodies of this type are characteristic of the early 18th century and appear frequently in the works of Bach and Handel.

J. S. BACH: *Magnificat in D, S.243* (1723)
(1685–1750) 7. Deposuit 2:00

This aria for tenor aptly illustrates the bustling, continuous melodic motion typical in fast movements, both instrumental and vocal, of the period. The text of the song is, "He hath put down the mighty from their thrones and hath exalted the lowly."

Twentieth-century composers have been energetic in expanding melodic concepts beyond the types illustrated thus far. Singable melodies are no longer considered essential. Melodies with wide ranges, angular leaps, and disjunct contours are in vogue. Contemporary rhythmic and harmonic resources have exerted strong pressures on melodic designs. The combined effect of these influences has altered recent melodic invention to the point where modern music is accused of being tuneless by some schooled exclusively in the old traditions. A blanket indictment is not justified, though isolated pieces of evidence can be cited to support it. Modern melodies depart radically from traditional means, but their objectives remain the same. The intent of contemporary composers is to achieve greater interest and expressiveness by abolishing arbitrary restrictions and exploiting new freedoms. They may at times sacrifice ordered regularity, tonal stability, the clarity, the simplicity, and the sensuousness of the previous melodic styles in their quest for melodic materials more suitable to their requirements, but they are still striving for successions of musical sounds conveying impressions of continuity and logic. The old ways of achieving these ends have not been entirely discarded, but many new ones have been added. The melodies of Hindemith's *Kleine Kammermusik* are certainly recognizable as melodies, yet they have a thoroughly contemporary flavor. They are capricious, brittle, and fresh.

PAUL HINDEMITH: *Kleine Kammermusik, op. 24 no. 2* (1922)
(1895–1963)

1. Lustig (Merry) 2:30
2. Walzer (Waltz) 2:00
3. Ruhig und einfach (Quiet and simple) 4:45
4. Schnelle (Quick) :45
5. Sehr lebhaft (Very lively) 3:00

The mocking humor in this gay and witty piece is not to be taken too seriously. The clever melodies sparkle, with no pretensions of profundity. Not until the third movement is there a hint of traditional melodic lyricism.

Harmony

Different pitches sounding together produce *harmony*. The smallest elements of harmony are *intervals*, which consist of two tones. The harmonic effect of an interval depends upon the relationship between the vibrating frequencies of the two tones comprising it. In general, simple ratios are more harmonious; complex ratios more discordant. The Table of Intervals, Table 5, shows the intervals above C in relation to the piano keyboard and lists them in order of complexity. The ratios are only approximate because of minor discrepancies between the natural ratios and modern tuning. The descriptive terms given for the quality of the intervals are purely subjective.

To hear the effect of all the intervals, find the note C near the center of the piano keyboard (see Table 5), and play each interval, progressing from the smallest to the largest. Then play the intervals in order of complexity, as they are listed at the bottom of the Table of Intervals. After this, you may wish to substitute your own descriptive terms for those given.

Intervals are classified as consonant or dissonant. Those with the simple vibrating ratios, up to and including the minor sixth (5:8), are consonant. The remaining intervals are dissonant, some more so than others. There is a tendency to regard consonant intervals as pleasant and dissonant intervals as unpleasant. This is unfortunate. No musical sound or combination of sounds is intrinsically unpleasant. A more valid association can be made between dissonance and tension and between consonance and repose. Dissonance generates tension which is relieved by consonance. This is analogous to the conflict in a novel produced by problems which are resolved at the end. Consonances and happy endings are meaningful artistically only in terms of the dissonances and conflicts that precede them. Dissonant intervals and chords should not be regarded as distasteful but as the harmonic elements which render consonant intervals and chords imperative. The interaction of consonance and dissonance in the composer's matrix gives substance and direction to his musical thought.

The various intervals provide several shades of consonance and dissonance. The range of consonance and dissonance is expanded to infinity when the number of tones sounding together and the relationships between them are unrestricted. The music of different styles and periods operates on entirely different harmonic planes. Just as drama runs the gamut of human emotions from the comparative tranquillity of

Table 5
TABLE OF INTERVALS

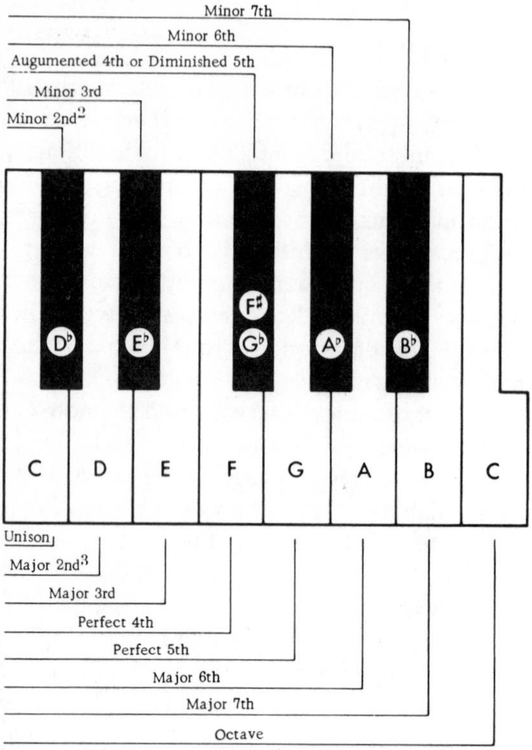

Notes	*Interval*	*Ratio*	*Description*
C-C	Unison	1:1	amplifies sound only
C-C	Octave	1:2	white, transparent
C-G	Fifth, perfect	2:3	barren, open, hollow
C-F	Fourth, perfect	3:4	barren, open, hollow
C-E	Third, major	4:5	clear, bright
C-E♭	Third, minor	5:6	somber, dark
C-A	Sixth, major	3:5	clear, bright
C-A♭	Sixth, minor	5:8	somber, dark
C-D	Second, major	8:9	mildly discordant, rough
C-B♭	Seventh, minor	9:16	mildly discordant, rough
C-B	Seventh, major	8:15	sharply discordant, harsh
C-D♭	Second, minor	15:16	sharply discordant, harsh
C-F♯	Fourth, augmented	17:24	strident, unstable
C-G♭	Fifth, diminished		
	(different ways of notating the same relationship)		

2. Or *half step* or *semitone*.
3. Or *whole step* or *whole tone*.

Arcadian idylls to the intensity of Greek tragedies and the horror of explicit violence, music explores the extremes from purest consonance and complete repose to ear-shattering dissonance and electrifying tension. Any harmonic sound can be meaningful and appropriate in the proper frame of reference.

Most harmonies contain three or more tones. Three or more tones sounding together make a *chord*. The foundation structures of harmony are three-note chords built from alternate notes of a scale, C-E-G for example, called *triads*. The three notes of a triad may be arranged in any order and doubled in various octaves without causing the triad to lose its identity, but every detail of order, spacing, doubling, and scoring modifies the sound somewhat. A triad may be constructed on any note, and each one has a distinctive quality and function in relation to the others.

Clear examples of unadulterated triad harmony are not plentiful. During the period when triad harmonies were used exclusively, all of the parts in the prevailing style were conceived melodically, not harmonically. The melodies combined to form triads at strategic points, but between these points notes not belonging to the triad were used. Also, one part sometimes arrived at its triad note slightly after or before the other parts. In listening to such music the ear is attracted to the melodic lines by their independent rhythms, and the harmonic foundation governing the melodic movement goes unnoticed. The following example is typical. Only triad harmonies are used, but this fact is obscured by the motion of the lines except at the end of phrases and sections.

G. P. DA PALESTRINA: *Pope Marcellus Mass* (1555)
(1525–1594) Kyrie 3:47

Triads were the only chord structures acknowledged by Palestrina and his contemporaries, but other notes occur melodically as the voices move from one triad tone to another. The triad harmonies are most apparent in the final section of this example.

(Record side 1 band 9)

The harmonic materials of music are never static, and it was inevitable that additions to triad structures would be made almost as soon as composers started to think of music in terms of chords and chord progressions rather than in terms of combined melodies. Four-note chords constructed in the same way as triads, from alternate scale tones, began to make tentative appearances early in the 17th century. If the numbers 1-3-5 are used to represent triad formations, the numbers 1-3-5-7 would represent the components of these four-note chords, called *seventh chords,* a seventh being the interval between 1 and 7. Seventh chords were assimilated gradually into the harmonic vocabulary during the 17th and 18th centuries but never threatened the supremacy of the triads. The bulk of music now performed was written during the period when triads and seventh chords were the accepted chord structures. This period encompasses the greatest names in music—Bach, Haydn, Mozart, Beethoven—and the most universally appreciated music, but the suggested example is drawn from a lesser composer, Rameau, who codified the principles of traditional harmony.

J. P. Rameau: *Les Indes Galantes (The Gallant Indies)* (1735)
(1683–1764) Act II: Clair flambeau du monde (Bright torch of the world) 4:30

> This aria, besides illustrating triad harmonies with occasional seventh chords, shows evidence of Rameau's systematic use of chords to accompany one predominant melody. Rameau is remembered primarily as a theorist rather than as a composer, but the dramatic works of this contemporary of Bach aroused the highest enthusiasm when they were presented on the French stage during his lifetime. *Les Indes Galantes* combined elements of ballet and opera in an elaborate, costumed spectacle with dancing, singing, and staging, but very little plot, a format not unknown on Broadway and in Hollywood.

In some works composed during the second half of the 19th century, seventh chords displaced triads as the most prevalent chord structure. Concurrently, a predilection for chromaticism (that is, the use of the five tones not included in the scale or key of the piece) emerged. Extensive use of seventh chords and chromatic (color) notes led to highly colorful and expressive harmony. Richard Wagner pioneered this trend. Criticized as an undisciplined radical by some of his contemporaries, he now is acclaimed as one of the great innovators in the history of music.

Richard Wagner: *Tristan and Isolde,* music drama (1865)
(1813–1883) Prelude 10:45

> Nowhere are Wagner's revolutionary harmonic ideas employed more effectively than in his Prelude to *Tristan and Isolde.* After more than a century, this music is unsurpassed for sheer sensuousness, and the harmonies still have an aura of strangeness. The first performance must have been astounding.

Adding another note, the second note above the seventh, to a seventh chord produces a *ninth chord.* Ninth chords are both too rich and too cumbersome for a steady diet, but they contribute added spice to the musical fare. Claude Debussy exploited ninth chord sonorities around the turn of the century. Later, jazz composers and arrangers discovered these sounds and soon put a blight on them by excessive use.

CLAUDE DEBUSSY: *Nocturnes* (1899)
(1862–1918) 2. Fêtes (Festivals) 5:45

> Ninth chords are used freely, but by no means incessantly, in this atmospheric work. Debussy's tone painting is devoted more to conveying impressions than details, but his depiction of a procession, first approaching and then departing, is unmistakable.

Continuing the process of building chords from alternate scale tones beyond the ninth produces *eleventh chords* and *thirteenth chords*. Eleventh chords are fairly common, especially in popular songs of the Broadway musical variety. Thirteenth chords, which contain all of the notes of a seventh-tone scale, are somewhat less useful and less used. One hesitates to suggest a specific selection from the popular field, because most of them are short-lived. Almost any sophisticated arrangement of a popular song will provide examples of this type of harmony. Gershwin's *Rhapsody in Blue* is a more enduring work in a similar vein.

GEORGE GERSHWIN: *Rhapsody in Blue* (1924) 16:10
(1898–1937)

> Jazz elements of the period when it was written dominate the rhythms, melodies, and harmonies of this work. Seventh chords are the most prevalent harmonic ingredient, but ninth chords, eleventh chords, and occasionally more complicated harmonic structures occur. Gershwin was a composer of popular music primarily, but his few ventures into larger forms—this work, the *Piano Concerto in F*, *An American in Paris*, and the opera *Porgy and Bess*—achieved immediate and apparently enduring success.

By the time eleventh and thirteenth chords were accepted into the harmonic vocabulary, other methods of constructing chords were being explored. Consecutive scale tones were sounded together in *clusters*. Chord structures were derived from every third or fourth scale tone as well as from alternate scale tones. Simple chords, such as triads, were combined, and tones from different, even remote, keys were joined together. These are the harmonic materials of our time. The era was inaugurated with a bang in 1913 when Stravinsky's ballet *The Rite of Spring* was first performed in Paris. It is still a startling and exciting work after more than half a century.

IGOR STRAVINSKY: (1882–1971)	*The Rite of Spring* (1913)	29:45
	The Adoration of the Earth	
	Introduction	:00
	Dances of the Adolescents	3:00
	Game of Abduction	6:05
	Spring Rounds	7:25
	Games of the Rival Towns	10:10
	Cortege of the Sage	12:00
	Adoration of the Earth (The Sage)	12:30
	Dance of the Earth	12:50
	The Sacrifice	
	Introduction (Pagan Night)	14:00
	Mystic Circle of the Adolescents	17:35
	Glorification of the Chosen One	20:15
	Evocation of the Ancestors	21:45
	Ritual Action of the Ancestors	22:25
	Sacrificial Dance (The Chosen One)*	25:20

Every measure of *Le Sacre du Printemps,* to use its French name, contained innovations when it was written, and it breached all of the conventional boundaries with its harmonic complexity and rhythmic intricacy. The materials and procedures Stravinsky employed were ideally suited to portraying the primordial fertility ritual of spring with all its primitive compulsion. The titles of the sections give clues to the stage action, but the musical impact is not dependent upon dramatic values. The music alone is capable of evoking the pagan atmosphere and making believable the dance to death of the chosen virgin. The "Dances of the Adolescents" and the "Sacrificial Dance" are particularly appropriate for illustrating complex harmonies, but time permitting, this 20th-century masterpiece should be heard in its entirety. Sections are not always clearly delineated, so approximate elapsed times are given.

*(Record side 8 band 1)

To construct chords significantly more complex than those in *The Rite of Spring* requires a different approach to musical sonority. One such approach is explored by Penderecki in his *Threnody for the Victims of Hiroshima.* The work is for 52 string instruments, each one with an individual part. It uses *quarter tones,* that is, pitch differences only half as large as the smallest in conventional music. Sometimes every quarter-tone pitch within a specified range sounds simultaneously producing a solid mass of pitches, technically a *quarter-tone cluster.* Sounds are produced on the instruments in a variety of uncharacteristic ways, vastly expanding the string orchestra's range of tonal colors. In music like this, sonority and tone color are the most salient features. Melody and rhythm are displaced as the elements of primary interest and the focus of the listener's attention.

PENDERECKI: *Threnody for the Victims of Hiroshima* (1960) 9:00
(1933–)

Though harmonic tension and dissonance seemed for a time to have reached the saturation point with *The Rite of Spring,* the quest of composers for new sonorities never ceases, and each generation of listeners is exposed to new sound experiences.

Tonality and Mode

Tonality is that phenomenon which causes organized musical sounds to gravitate to a single focal point. This tendency exists both in melodies and in harmonic progressions. The tone which emerges as the center of the tonal system is designated the *tonic* or *keynote.* The letter name of the keynote is the *key* of the piece or passage.

There is no obvious reason for the supremacy of one tone and the subservience of others, but this orientation around a central pitch occurs spontaneously. The function of all other tones and chords is ordained by their relation to the tonic.

Tonality is an elusive quality, difficult to define but easy to demonstrate. Start singing the first stanza of *America* and stop on the word "I." Notice the sensation of being "up in the air." The impression is stronger if the harmony is added. The phrase demands completion which is accomplished by adding the tonic note and chord with the word "sing." At the end of the stanza, the tonic on "ring" is approached differently, but stopping short of it produces the same effect. A variant of this experiment is to lift the stylus from a recording before the final chord. In each case a conclusive feeling is demanded which only the tonic can supply. The interaction of tonal relationships which creates this situation is *tonality.*

Any pitch may serve as the tonic. The relation of other tones to it determines the *mode.* Between octaves of the tonic, there are eleven different pitches. Together with the tonic they comprise a *chromatic* scale of twelve tones. Commonly, music is based on scales of seven tones selected from these to form certain patterns of whole steps (major 2nds) and half steps (minor 2nds). Numbering the scale degrees up from the keynote, the most prevalent pattern has half steps between 3–4 and 7–8, whole steps elsewhere. This is the pattern associated with the syllables *do, re, mi, fa, sol, la, ti, do.* It forms a *major scale,* and music derived from it is in a *major mode* or *key*. *America, The Star Spangled Banner, Home on the Range,* and most familiar songs are in major keys.

After major, the next most common scale pattern is that of *minor*. Natural minor is a seven-tone scale with half steps between 2–3 and 5–6. *When Johnny Comes Marching Home* is a well-known song in minor. The major mode has been so predominant, elements of it customarily are incorporated in pieces which are fundamentally minor. This has led to scale resources referred to as forms of minor but which actually are hybrids combining elements of the two modes. The essential difference between major and all forms of minor lies in the 3rd degree of the scale. It is a major 3rd above the keynote in major and a minor 3rd above the keynote in minor.

Contrast the sound of the two following examples—one major, the other minor. Both pieces end with a strong return to the keynote in the melody. See if you can sing the keynote at the conclusion of the performance.

FREDERIC CHOPIN: *Preludes for Piano, op. 28* (1839)
(1810–1849)

	No. 7 in A major	:43
	No. 4 in E minor	1:52

(Record side 5 bands 5, 4)

The bulk of music written since 1600 is either major or minor. The ability to distinguish between major and minor and to discern the keynote at the end of compositions and at critical points during the course of a work is evidence of perceptive listening.

Though familiar music is preponderantly major or minor, these are not the only modes. Rich and varied scale resources of earlier periods fell into disuse when the major-minor system gained ascendency around 1600. The music of previous centuries was based on the *church modes* (or *ecclesiastical modes*), a complete system of scales that evolved over hundreds of years. The church modes are seven-tone scales like major and minor, but the half steps are in different locations. As the name suggests, early church music was derived from these modes exclusively.

GREGORIAN CHANT (codified 590–604)

Tract: *Domine non secundum*	3:10
Sequence: *Sancti spiritus assit nobis gratia*	1:10

Melodies based on the church modes, as these are, sound somewhat strange to modern ears accustomed to hearing only major and minor. The displacement of the half steps, in relation to the more familiar scale patterns, reduces the tendency of certain tones to progress in a prescribed direction and makes the contour of the melodies less predictable, less bound by conventions. These examples are included in *The History of Music in Sound* Volume II, RCA Victor LM–6015.

(Also record side 1 band 3)

Prior to 1600 Christian liturgical music was modal, but the use of the church modes was never restricted to sacred music. The modes were also used in the secular music of the period. They are still heard in folk songs, and many of the currently popular folk-rock melodies have a definite modal quality. After nearly 300 years of neglect composers rediscovered the church modes and adapted them to modern usage. Contemporary applications have little in common with Gregorian chant, but modal influences abound in 20th-century music, both popular and serious. One of the first pieces of chamber music in which modal resources were exploited deliberately was Ravel's *String Quartet.*

MAURICE RAVEL: *String Quartet in F* (1903)
(1875–1937) 1. Allegro moderato—Très doux 7:30

The composed modal melodies of this quartet are unlike the chants or folk songs with which they share scale materials. The modal influence does not extend to the harmonies, which are typical of Ravel and turn-of-the-century French music.

Toward the end of the last century composers seem to have come to the conclusion that the possibilities of musical invention within the major-minor system were approaching exhaustion. In any event the exploration of other scale resources dates from about this time. Besides reviving the church modes, composers devised and exploited new scales. One of the most distinctive of the new scales was the *whole tone scale.* In contrast to major and minor scales and the church modes, whole tone scales have no half steps and only six tones. The following composition draws its material, except for a brief passage in the middle, entirely from a whole tone scale.

CLAUDE DEBUSSY: *Preludes for Piano, book I* (1910)
(1862–1918) 2. Voiles (Sails or Veils) 2:57

The whole tone scale is ideal for creating the nebulous atmosphere of this piece.

(Record side 6 band 5)

Fascinating as the whole tone scale is, there are definite limits to its usefulness. Melodies and harmonies derived from it have a certain sameness of sound, and the very striking quality which initially attracts both composers and listeners soon leads them to tire of it. Contemporary composers have utilized many other scale formations, but the prevailing trend has been to reject the concept of selective scales.

Composers in this century have come to regard the limitations of selective scales as arbitrary. Whereas composers previously were inclined to draw their basic tonal material from preconceived scales of seven tones and to use the remaining five tones incidentally, contemporary composers are more apt to regard all twelve tones as equal in status and accessibility. The net result of this is that the previous hierarchy of tones is abolished, and the available tonal resources are expanded and freed from restraint.

Renouncing selective scales and according equal status to all twelve tones does not automatically eliminate the possibility of tonality. Tonal centers can be established which include in their orbit all eleven remaining tones, rather than the customary six that gravitate to a conventional tonic. Distinctions between major and minor disappear, and the tonality of such music is vague. However, alert listeners can detect the tonal centers in music, like the following example, which embodies the principles of this expanded tonal concept.

DMITRI SHOSTAKOVICH: *Symphony no. 1 in F, op. 10* (1925)
(1906–1975) 1. Allegretto 9:25

> The tonal centers in passages of this 20th-century symphony are almost as obvious as they are in 18th-century works, yet all twelve tones are used with equal freedom. A contemporary flavor is attained without undue complexity. Judicious balance between the old and the new have made this symphony a favorite with listeners who are a little tired of the standard repertory but not quite ready to embrace more radical new music.

Some modern music is in two or more keys at the same time. This is called *polytonality,* a device that appeals to some composers of our time, Darius Milhaud among them. Polytonality is not a technique that can be used exclusively with good effect, but it produces a delectable piquancy in brief compositions and isolated passages. The sense of tonality is never strong when two keys are used together. The perception of polytonality is usually based on the recognition of its peculiar quality rather than on the actual identification of dual tonal centers.

DARIUS MILHAUD: *Saudades do Brasil* (1921)
(1892–1974) 7. Corcovado 1:35

Milhaud spent two years in Brazil as a French diplomat. The twelve pieces of the *Saudades* are souvenirs of his visit. Each depicts some colorful district of Rio de Janeiro—this one the "hunchback" mountain which is one of its landmarks. The tonal center implied by the melody is often different from that of the accompaniment. Originally for piano, *Corcovado* can be heard transcribed for violin and piano on RCA Victor LM–1166.

Many 20th-century composers have made the final break with tradition, as far as tonality is concerned, and write music which has no key center. Music without a tonal center is said to be *atonal.* Proponents of this type of music eschew the term, but it is descriptive. Arnold Schoenberg evolved a system of "composition with twelve tones related only to one another" which assures the equal use of all twelve tones and eliminates the possibility of any tone inadvertently asserting itself as a tonic, or tonal center. A *series* of tones comprising all twelve notes in a fixed order, with none repeated, serves as the basis for a complete work. The series, subjected to specified manipulations and modifications, is repeated throughout the composition. No note is used except as it occurs in its prescribed order in the series. Actually, there is a good deal more to the philosophy and the technique of the system than this, but a detailed description is beyond the scope of a music appreciation book.[4]

Serial music, as music written according to Schoenberg's principles is commonly called, is not designed for easy listening, but it must be considered by anyone seriously interested in the music of our time. Some of the greatest creative minds of 20th-century music have regarded serial organization as the most viable compositional procedure. Every living composer is familiar with the system and, it seems safe to generalize, is influenced by it to some degree. No composer active at the present time could, or would choose, to insulate himself from such a significant development, though many do not subscribe to the method. Composers on the whole have been more intrigued by serialism and atonality than have performers and listeners. Performers find it difficult and frequently ungrateful to play. Listeners are rarely able to detect the high degree of organization implicit in the system and are perplexed by the absence of familiar tonal functions. The preceding examples illustrate various kinds of tonality. The following example contrasts with these and demonstrates the difference between music which has a tonal center, however vague, and that which has none.

---

4. For additional information see Leon Dallin, *Techniques of Twentieth Century Composition,* third edition, Dubuque: Wm. C. Brown Company Publishers, 1974.

ARNOLD SCHOENBERG: *String Quartet no. 4, op. 37* (1936)
(1874–1951) 1. Allegro molto, energico 8:10

This music is atonal. Unless you have previously heard music by Schoenberg or one of his disciples, you probably have never heard any like it before. It is not performed often, for it is extremely difficult to play. Until recently, there were few performances or recordings of music like this. You will not find singable melodies, toe-tapping rhythms, or sonorous harmonies in it. The melodic motion is disjunct, the rhythm irregular, and each part obstinately independent. Kaleidoscopic convolutions reflect the turmoil of the age which gave this music birth. In listening to it, try to put aside preconceived notions about what music should be, and accept this music on its own terms. It will not recall fond memories, and you will not go away whistling its tunes. It does provide a provocative and stimulating listening experience.

(Also record side 8 bands 2–4)

Modulation

The same melodic and harmonic devices which cause one note to emerge as a tonal center are used to shift the center from one pitch to another. This process is called *modulation.* Any change of key is a modulation.

Modulation is a constant source of variety in music and a feature of musical form. Excursions to other keys are invariably followed by a return to the original tonic in traditional compositions. One must be aware of changes in tonality, especially the departure from and return to the original key, to comprehend musical structures and procedures completely. The perception of tonality and modulation may be on the subconscious level, but static tonality produces conscious monotony.

Modulations may be made between any two keys, but most often they occur between *related keys.* Related keys are those keys which have five or more of their seven notes in common. Keys with fewer than five notes in common are *foreign* or *remote keys,* and modulations to them are *foreign* or *remote modulations.* Pairs of keys, one major and one minor, which have all seven notes in common but a different keynote are *relative keys.* The major key and the minor key with the same keynote are *parallel keys.*

Modulations are reckoned according to the relationship of the new tonic to the old. In describing key relationships the Roman numerals and the names associated with each scale degree are useful. In scale order, they are:

I—Tonic
VII—Subtonic (Leading tone)
VI—Submediant
V—Dominant
IV—Subdominant
III—Mediant
II—Supertonic
I—Tonic

Either the name or the numeral indicating the scale degree can be used in referring to modulations. For example, a modulation to the dominant key or to V would indicate that the fifth scale degree of the old key would become the new tonic. Modulations throughout a composition are related to the original tonic key established at the outset. Modulations to the dominant key are most common, followed by modulations to the subdominant (IV), supertonic (II), relative major (III), and relative minor (VI). These are closely related keys having six or all seven of their tones in common.

Modulations are illustrated in the examples of Part II in connection with the study of musical form.

Dynamics and Color

Dynamics and tone color, or timbre, cannot be ignored in a discussion of musical elements. They are not elements in the same sense as rhythm, melody, and harmony, but they are nonetheless essential components of the composer's expressive material.

Dynamics have to do with degrees of loudness and softness, prime ingredients of emotional intensity in music. Dynamic level is determined by the number and kind of instruments used and by the manner of playing. Instruments and voices are capable of wide dynamic variations, and the composer's intentions are conveyed to the players by means of signs which are a part of musical notation. There are signs for several degrees of loudness and for changes both gradual and sudden. Dynamic indications are relative, and very loud for a violin is quite different from very loud for a trombone or full orchestra. However, composers learn what to expect from each instrument and combination and score accordingly. The inbalance of tone produced by certain categories of instruments is compensated for somewhat by the numbers used. For instance, string instruments produce much less sound than brass instruments, but there are many more of them in an orchestra. In this regard it is noteworthy that doubling the number of players does not double the tone volume. Two violins playing with equal intensity are only 1.3 times louder than one.

Ten are required to double the sound of one. Securing proper dynamic levels and balancing the sound of opposing sections in larger ensembles is a strategic function of conductors.

Color in music results from the fusion of pitches and timbres. Each note on every instrument has a unique sound, even ignoring pitch differences. With various pitches and timbres mingled, the color possibilities are infinite. The art of orchestration (scoring music for orchestra) and the quest for orchestral color have been carried to new heights during the last century. This trend has been encouraged by mechanical improvements in instruments and by the astounding technical proficiency of large numbers of performers. Performances of scores which would have been deemed impossible to play before the turn of the century are commonplace today. The perfection of instruments and the artistry of players have stimulated composers to write ever more demanding scores and to tap hidden instrumental resources for new colors. Fresh orchestral colors have been produced by instruments playing in extreme registers—very high and very low. Mechanical devices have been used in and on instruments to modify their tone coloring. Unusual ways of producing tones, like strings played with the wood rather than the hair of the bow, have been used for special effects. These variegated tints added to the normal rich coloring of the orchestra provide the composer with a tempting palette.

Recent composers have taken full advantage of bounteous and relatively stable instrumental resources. They have made penetrating studies of instrumental possibilities, limitations, and peculiarities and have cultivated an idiomatic way of writing for each instrument which utilizes its capabilities to the fullest and minimizes its shortcomings. This facet of composing was largely ignored by earlier composers who were inclined to be indifferent toward instrumentation. Many of their scores do not specify the instruments to be used, an unthinkable omission in recent times. Lack of standardization in both instruments and instrumental combinations fostered the practice of writing, on occasion, parts which could be played by any of several instruments. These circumstances, coupled with the preoccupation of composers for an extended period with problems of melody, harmony, and form, delayed the full flowering of orchestral color. Ferreting out latent instrumental possibilities, skillful and colorful orchestration are hallmarks of the late 19th and 20th centuries. Certain younger composers going contrary to this trend are reverting to the older practice and producing works with variable or unspecified instrumentation.

Harmony also is a source of musical color. Some combinations of notes are rich, others stark. Some are bright, others dark. Some harmonic progressions are iridescent and some are achromatic. Words are in-

Rimsky-Korsakov

adequate to describe them, but the hues of harmony are apparent to all who listen.

The full range of dynamic levels from whispering to thundering and the full spectrum of orchestral color from infrared to ultraviolet are exploited in the following example.

Rimsky-Korsakov: *Capriccio Espagnol, op. 34* (1887)

(1844–1908)	1. Alborada	1:15
	2. Variations	4:30
	3. Alborada	1:15
	4. Scene and Gypsy Song	4:45
	5. Fandango of the Asturias	3:00

The composer's intention was to create a piece which would "glitter with dazzling orchestral color." He was satisfied with his accomplishment, as well he might have been! He took issue with critics who praised the *Capriccio* as a magnificently orchestrated piece and preferred to think of it as a brilliant composition for the orchestra, a subtle but in his mind an important distinction. The first, third, and fifth movements share thematic material. The fourth and fifth are played without interruption.

Texture

6

There are three basic kinds of musical texture, *monophonic, polyphonic,* and *homophonic.* Phonic by itself is an adjective meaning *of or pertaining to sound.* Mono- is a combining form meaning *one, single, alone.* Poly- is a combining form signifying *many, much, several.* Homo- is a combining form denoting *common, joint, like.* These terms have special connotations in music.

Monophonic Texture

Monophonic texture, or *monophony* to use the noun form, is music consisting of a single, unaccompanied melodic line. It is the most ancient of the three types. Monophonic music occupies such an insignificant position in our culture that it is difficult to realize the large span of music history devoted to its development and how large it still looms on the universal musical scene. Primitive music and that of ancient civilizations, early church and court music, and Oriental music to the present day are essentially monophonic. Most of this music was little known beyond its own time and sphere of influence until musicologists and ethnologists combined their skills with the marvels of recording to discover, collect, recreate, and disseminate music from the distant past and from the far corners of the world.

Acquaintance with old and exotic music has increased recognition of its value. Freedom and interesting detail of line in monophony compensate for its sparseness of texture. It is refreshing to discover the beauty of single lines—rediscover would be more exact. The systematic sounding together of different pitches, dating back only a little over a millennium, is a comparatively recent development.

The largest single body of monophonic music is found in the liturgy of the Catholic Church. There are nearly 3000 chant melodies in the repertory, a treasury no proper study of music can ignore. Music of the remote past should not be equated with familiar styles. The very old, like the very new, must be accepted on its own terms. Its quaint sound, unaccompanied simplicity, and unmeasured rhythm must not be taken as tokens of inferiority.

GREGORIAN CHANT (codified 590–604)
Alleluia: Vidimus stellam 1:59

The musical ritual of the Catholic Church crystallized during the pontificate of Gregory the Great (590–604), from whom the chant takes its name. The origins of some of the chants can be traced back to antiquity, while others postdate Gregory. This example is recorded on Haydn Society 9038, *Masterpieces of Music before 1750.*

(Record side 1 band 3. Notation p. 370)

Instrumental melodies are rarely unencumbered in Western music. The following examples are selected from the isolated instances in which composers have lavished their talents on a single instrumental line. In these selections the melody does not have to compete with harmony or counterpoint for attention, and listeners are free to concentrate on the details of pure melodic invention.

J. S. BACH: *Partita no. 2 in D minor for Violin, S.1004* (1722)
(1685–1750) 4. Gigue 4:00

String instruments are capable of playing double notes and chords, but this movement from the *Partita* for unaccompanied violin is an example of pure monophonic texture.

CLAUDE DEBUSSY: *Syrinx* (1912) 2:35
(1862–1918)

This work for flute is one of the very few for an unaccompanied wind instrument. Syrinx is the Greek name for panpipes, a primitive wind instrument attributed to the god Pan. It consists of a graduated series of pipes fastened together and played by blowing.

The preceding examples demonstrate that an unaccompanied melody can capture and hold a listener's attention. Though few works on modern concert programs are limited to a single melodic line, monophonic passages are common in all styles, periods, mediums, and forms. The primary function of monophonic texture is to provide variety in works which are essentially polyphonic or homophonic.

Polyphonic Texture

At an early date melodies and chanting were accompanied by stamping, clapping, and percussion instruments. The second part in such cases is lacking in pitch and the other attributes of tone, so it does not, strictly speaking, represent a combination of musical sounds. The first real departures from monophony probably resulted from minor discrepancies committed by accident or intent in the performance of a single line. The sounding together of slightly discrepant versions of the same melody produces *heterophony*. Heterophony occurred in ancient Greek music, and it persists in the music of Africa, Java, China, and particularly Japan. Neither heterophony nor percussion-accompanied melody is common in Western music, though there are isolated instances of both. These styles are prominent only in primitive and exotic music.

Another type of prepolyphony occurred early in the development of music as a result of combining male and female or boys' voices. The natural pitch of adult male voices is about an octave lower than that of preadolescent and female voices. When they sing the same melody together, they normally sing in octaves. That is, they sing identical melodic contours and notes with the same letter names, but different pitches. Two pitches in this relationship blend so perfectly that they are barely distinguishable, and the sound is more like an amplification of one pitch than a combination of two. This is the pitch relationship heard in community singing by mixed groups and also on occasion between the male and female leads in dramatic musical works.

The incidental and almost spontaneous combinations of sound such as percussion-accompanied melody, heterophony, and octave doubling which occur in ancient and primitive music did little to pave the way for subsequent development. This was delayed until pitches were combined systematically and preserved in notation. The oldest specimens with these qualifications date from the 9th century. At first the added parts duplicated the contour and rhythm of the original melody, but this stage did not last long. Soon the intervals between the parts were varied, and not long after the parts became rhythmically independent. The effect was no longer that of one line with a shadow but that of autonomous parts. These early experiments sound crude to modern ears, but the significance of this innovation cannot be overestimated. The pace of musical development quickened with this breakthrough, and it has been gaining momentum ever since.

EARLY POLYPHONY (10th and 11th centuries)

Sit Gloria Domini	:15
Alleluia: Surrexit Christus	3:00
Regi Regum Glorioso	2:00

The first example is the earliest and most primitive. It consists of a melody doubled by a parallel part a fourth lower and duplication of both parts at the octave. The second example, taken from a manuscript dated about 1100, shows marked progress. Two-part music alternates with monophonic passages. The added part no longer parallels the other voice, but frequently moves in the opposite direction. Though the two parts are rhythmically identical, the combination of different melodic contours has been accomplished. The third example employs procedures similar to those of the second except that the two parts are continuous and there are instances of momentary rhythmic independence. These examples are in *The History of Music in Sound* Volume II, RCA Victor LM–6015.

Though all early music in more than one part is classified as polyphony, the term has a special connotation implying music conceived as a combination of melodic lines rather than as a succession of chords. The texture of music consisting of two or more lines is *polyphonic* or *contrapuntal,* the terms being used interchangeably. The art of combining melodies and the study of contrapuntal music is *counterpoint.*

The simplest kind of counterpoint is created by combining a melody with itself starting at different times so that statements of the melody overlap. This is the kind of counterpoint produced when a group sings rounds like *Are You Sleeping,* also known as *Brother John* and *Frère Jacques.* Nearly everyone knows the tune. It is a four-part round, which means that the melody is sung starting at four different times. The words are aligned to show how the four parts fit together. To experience this type of contrapuntal texture firsthand, sing *Are You Sleeping* with a fourth of the class on each part. It can be repeated any number of times, since the end of the melody leads around (hence the name of the form) and back to the beginning.

When a musical idea stated in one part is immediately repeated in another, the second and any subsequent part is said to be in *imitation.* The imitation is continuous in *Are You Sleeping.* The number of beats or measures between the entrances of the parts is the *distance of imitation.* The distance of imitation between successive entrances in *Are You Sleeping* is eight beats or two measures. The difference in pitch, if any, between the starting notes is the *interval of imitation.* In rounds the imitation is at the same pitch when the parts are sung by voices of the same sex, at the interval of an octave when the entrances alternate between male and female voices.

ANONYMOUS: *Are You Sleeping*

1. Are you sleeping, are you sleeping, Brother John, Brother
2. Are you sleeping, are you

1. John? Morning bells are ringing, morning bells are ringing,
2. sleeping, Broth - er John, Broth - er John?
3. Are you sleeping, are you sleeping,

1. Ding, ding, dong, ding, ding, dong.
2. Morning bells are ringing, morning bells are ringing, Ding,
3. Broth- er John, Broth - er John? Morning
4. Are you sleeping, are you sleeping, Broth -

2. ding, dong, ding, ding, dong.
3. bells are ringing, morning bells are ringing, Ding, ding
4. er John, Broth - er John? Morning bells are

3. dong, ding, ding, dong.
4. ringing, morning bells are ringing, Ding, ding, dong, ding, ding, dong.

The old English round *Sumer Is Icumen In* is not too unlike *Are You Sleeping* in construction. It has four parts in continuous imitation at the distance of four beats, plus two accompanying parts in which two elements of a short melodic fragment alternate. A diagram of the form is given on p. 156.

ANONYMOUS: *Sumer Is Icumen In (Summer Is Coming In)* (1240) 1:38
(Record side 1 band 6)

The limitations of continuous imitation like that found in rounds are too severe for extended compositions. In most types of imitative polyphony the parts enter with the same theme or motive and then become free, or imitative passages alternate with passages in nonimitative *free counterpoint.* Sometimes the imitation consists of no more than an exchange of motives between the parts. Bach explores the full range of possibilities from fragmentary to almost continuous imitation in his *Two-Part Inventions,* of which the following are representative.

J. S. BACH: *Two-Part Inventions, S.772/786* (1720)
(1685–1750) No. 2 in C minor 1:25
No. 3 in D major 1:10
No. 7 in E minor 1:25

The two parts of *Invention 2* are in strict imitation at the interval of an octave and at the distance of two measures (eight beats) during most of the invention. The imitation is interrupted briefly in the middle and just before the end. The lower voice imitates the upper for the first half of the piece, and the upper voice imitates the lower in the last half.

In *Invention 3* the second voice enters in imitation two measures (six beats) after and an octave lower than the first voice. The imitation is dropped after two measures and not resumed, though the two parts exchange motives on several occasions. (Notation p. 371)

Invention 7 is organized around motives which pass from one part to the other carrying the burden of interest.

Attentive listening and repeated hearings are usually necessary before the individual lines of imitative counterpoint can be followed and fully appreciated. The interchange of motives between parts is less difficult to perceive. Perhaps the most common type of contrapuntal texture is that involving exchanges of material between the parts and imitation of limited duration. *Fugues* are prime examples of this type of counterpoint.

The structure of fugues is considered in greater detail in Chapter 9, but basically a fugue is a musical form in which each part enters imitatively with the same theme or *subject* and in which subsequently the subject is combined with itself and with other melodies. Melodic interest is distributed between all of the parts, and recognizing the themes wherever and whenever they appear is essential for comprehension of the musical design. The subject is announced alone at the beginning of a fugue. Hearing the subject by itself a few times facilities recognition of later entrances when it is altered and associated with other melodic lines.

J. S. BACH: *Fugue in G minor for Organ, "Little," S.578* (1700) 4:50
(1685–1750)

Bach brought the fugue to its highest perfection, and this is a classic example of the form. Counting the statements of the subject as they appear is one way to determine whether or not all of them are being detected.

(Also record side 2 band 3)[1]

Though fugue form was perfected in Bach's time, it has been adapted to changing styles through the years and is still in use. The fol-

1. See fn. p. 16.

lowing example in comparison with the previous one demonstrates that the fugue idea has diverse applications.

JAROMIR WEINBERGER: *Schwanda the Bagpiper,* opera (1927)
(1896–1967) Polka and Fugue 7:30

The opera *Schwanda* tells the tale of a jolly bagpipe player who defeats the devil himself with his magical music. The complete opera is seldom given in this country, but this excerpt is a favorite. The *Polka* is fundamentally homophonic, though countermelodies are introduced at times. It comes to a close in just over two minutes, and the violins by themselves announce the fugue subject. From this point on the fugue subject or fragments of it are passed from one section of the orchestra to another in typical fugue fashion, and the texture becomes polyphonic. Toward the end of the fugue, elements of the fugue subject and the polka theme are combined.

(Also record side 7 band 2, end)

Some polyphonic texture is entirely nonimitative, that is, it results from combining essentially independent melodies. The prelude to *Die Meistersinger* contains a stellar example of this type of polyphony. The three main themes are introduced one after another, then toward the end of the piece all three are ingeniously combined. Listeners must learn to recognize and remember the themes as they are heard separately to appreciate fully the marvelous effect when they are heard together.

RICHARD WAGNER: *Die Meistersinger (The Mastersingers),* opera (1868)
(1813–1883) Vorspiel (Prelude) 9:00

The piece and the first theme begin together with an incisive rhythmic motive followed by an ascending scale line. A new rhythmic motive and full chords in the brass and woodwind sections signal the beginning of the second theme (1:35). The first theme returns (2:20) transformed into a lyric melody. The mood changes, and the third theme, the famous "Prize Song" of the opera, enters quietly (3:35). After extensive development, all three themes are combined in the final section (6:25). The "Prize Song" theme is the principal melody. Both versions of the first theme are used in the bass, and the second theme provides the harmonic background. (Themes p. 372)

Homophonic Texture

The texture is homophonic when the melodic interest is concentrated in a single part, usually the highest, and the remaining parts serve primarily to provide an accompaniment. Supporting parts in homophonic music are designed to form a suitable rhythmic and harmonic background for the predominant melody.

The homophonic and polyphonic approaches to music, though differing in point of view, are not mutually exclusive. The difference is one of emphasis. An accompanying part in homophonic music creates a linear sequence of tones in going from one chord tone to another, but the composer strives for complete chords and smooth, unobstrusive lines rather than for engaging contours. In polyphony each part is conceived as a melody, but the melodic tones sounding together form chords. One melody is supreme in homophonic music, and all other parts cooperate to provide a setting favorable to its unfolding without competing for attention. All parts are melodies in polyphonic music, and though the center of interest may shift, one never becomes subservient to another. Except for the one melody, homophony is vertically oriented, and harmonic progression is of primary importance. Polyphony is horizontally oriented, and linear movement is of primary importance. Conversely, the lines of accompanying parts in homophony and the harmonic progressions resulting from polyphony are secondary considerations.

Ideally, the vertical and horizontal aspects of music—the chords and lines—should be in balance. Their conflicting requirements are reconciled by composers of genius with no apparent compromises. Few compositions are purely homophonic or polyphonic. One type of texture may predominate, but rarely to the exclusion of the other. The dividing line between homophonic and polyphonic texture is not always sharp, and borderline cases are probably more prevalent than clear examples of either.

The development of multipart music was melodic rather than harmonic until about 1600 when a group of poets and composers attempting to recreate Greek drama laid the foundations for both the homophonic style and opera, neither of which was implicit in their model. One aim of the group was to provide dramatic texts with musical settings that would permit the words to be clearly understood. The polyphonic style did not satisfy this requirement. Their solution was to project a single melodic line against a background of slower-moving harmonies, and the concept of homophonic music was born. Claudio Monteverdi was the most distinguished of its early practitioners.

Claudio Monteverdi: *Orfeo*, opera (1607)
(1567–1643) Tu se' morta (Thou art perished) 2:35

This is a *recitative*, a passage in declamatory style for solo voice with a simple harmonic accompaniment. The recitative style dominated the first operas and persisted between more lyric sections of operas, oratorios, and cantatas into the 19th century.

(Also record side 2 band 1, beginning)

The recitative style, in which a simple melodic line is accompanied by relatively static harmonies, is one type of homophonic texture. Another type of homophonic texture results when all of the parts, including the melody, move together in block chords. This type of homophonic texture is found in hymns, chorales, carols, patriotic songs, and the like when they are sung in parts with the rhythm and the words of the accompanying voices coinciding with those of the tune. The following example is representative of chordal homophonic texture.

ANONYMOUS: *God Rest You Merry, Gentlemen* 2:00

Congregational and community singing is generally in a chordal homophonic style. This style is preserved in the recording of this Christmas carol on Columbia MS–6499.

Pop and rock vocal groups singing in harmony also produce chordal homophonic texture, but the most prevalent type of homophonic texture consists of a single melody with a rhythmically animated accompaniment. Popular songs other than those arranged for vocal groups belong in this category, as does most art music both vocal and instrumental that is not deliberately contrapuntal in nature.

The most obvious way of motivating harmony which otherwise would be static is to repeat the chords in a rhythmic pattern. The rhythmic repetition of the chords not only adds interest and movement but, in the case of the piano, provides a means of sustaining the sound at equal intensity. The repeated notes in the *Erlkönig* accompaniment serve both purposes.

FRANZ SCHUBERT: *Erlkönig (Erl-King) op. 1* (1815) 3:54
(1797–1828)

Goethe's words and Schubert's music together make this art song one of the finest and best known in the entire literature. A translation of the poem is given on p. 212. Singers traditionally vary their vocal quality to represent the four characters whose words are heard in the song—a narrator, the father, his son, and the Erl-King (a symbol of death). The rapid repeated notes in the piano accompaniment graphically portray the frantic night ride of the father holding his dying son in his arms.

(Record side 5 band 2)

Another way to motivate harmony is to have the notes of the chords sound one at a time in succession, typically in consistent rhythm and pitch patterns. The keyboard music of the last half of the 18th century is replete with accompaniment figures fitting this stereotype. Mozart was one of the composers who used this method of motivating harmonies in a basically homophonic texture.

W. A. Mozart: *Piano Sonata no. 15 in C, K.545* (1788)

(1756–1791)	1. Allegro	3:00
	2. Andante	4:00
	3. Allegretto grazioso	1:25

Each movement of this sonata contains accompaniment figures current in Mozart's time. The patterns are varied and interrupted to avoid monotony, but the real interest is in the melody above the accompaniment.

Similar accompaniments are also possible in nonkeyboard works such as the following one for strings.

Joseph Haydn: *String Quartet in F, op. 3 no. 5* (1763)

(1732–1809)	2. Andante cantabile	5:55

This work is usually attributed to Haydn (as here) and is found in catalogs under his name, though it was actually composed by a virtually unknown contemporary named Hofstetter. An ingratiating melody in the first violin is accompanied by the other three instruments playing pizzicato (plucked) in a consistent pattern.

Harmonic progression and motivation were both highly stylized in this period leaving composers free to concentrate on melodic invention and organization, a circumstance which contributed to the tremendous fecundity of men like Mozart and Haydn without noticeably impairing the quality of their music. Men of lesser talent relying excessively upon these devices produced a quantity of undistinguished music which is no longer performed.

Another attribute of accompaniment figures, aside from those already mentioned, is their capacity to create the illusion of full chords with few notes. This combines the advantages of satisfying harmony with simplicity and clarity. There is no confusion or obscurity in the Mozart sonata, for much of the time only two notes are sounding, one melody tone and one tone of the accompaniment pattern. This fact is camouflaged by the figuration and the use of the sustaining pedal of the piano.

Composers of the next century were less inclined to settle for stereotyped patterns and harmonies. Their accompaniments generally are more elaborate and imaginative, sometimes approaching the status of secondary melodies, but still serving the same purposes as those of their predecessors. Their harmonies are more colorful, partially as a result of the fancier accompaniment patterns and partially as a product of natural evolution. Chopin was a luminary in this generation of composers.

FREDERIC CHOPIN: *Preludes for Piano, op. 28* (1839)
(1810–1849) No. 3 in G :55

> Chopin was a master in conceiving brilliant piano figurations. His music ushered in a style of piano writing which remains at the apex of piano literature. It is a rare piano program on which he is not represented. This *Prelude* is a small sample of the piano style upon which his reputation is based.

Accompaniment patterns related to those found in piano music are also found in music for other mediums, but less obviously and extensively. One reason is that most instruments, unlike the piano, are capable of sustaining tones, so it is not necessary to repeat or change pitches to maintain volume. Another reason is that repeated chords and figures submerged in the total sound of an orchestra or a large ensemble are less apparent than the same devices played on the piano. In writing for soloist, chorus, and orchestra Mendelssohn supports single melodic lines with all three types of homophonic accompaniment—sustained chords, rhythmically animated chords, and block chords moving synchronously with the melody.

FELIX MENDELSSOHN: *Elijah, op. 70,* oratorio (1846)
(1809–1847)
3. Ye people, rend your hearts :55
4. If with all your hearts 2:40
15. Cast thy burden upon the Lord 1:23

> No. 3 is a recitative with sustained chords in the orchestra accompanying a declamatory vocal line. The style is similar to the chronologically earlier recitative of Monteverdi. The homophonic texture of No. 4, an aria, consists of a melody for solo tenor plus an orchestral accompaniment of chord figures, rhythm patterns, and repeated chords. No. 15 is a chorale in which the words of the text occur synchronously in four-part chords formed by the voices. The orchestra provides bridges between phrases of the chorale and brings it to a close. The big choral numbers in *Elijah* are too contrapuntal to be appropriate examples in this context, but including one or more in the listening gives a more complete picture of the work.
>
> (Record side 5 bands 8–10. Vocal parts of no. 15 p. 373)

Composers of the present century shun everything that smacks of pattern or stereotype and consequently are not attracted to the homophonic accompaniment patterns. Finding substitutes for them magnifies the problems of composition and reduces output, but most composers now seem to feel that the added effort is not only justified, but necessary. Composers continue to write homophonic music, but their rejection of ready-made devices requires them to devote their creative energies as much to the settings as to the melodies and themes. Popular music is the one area where standardized accompaniments remain the rule rather than the exception.

The evolution of music has gone from monophony through polyphony to homophony, but the advent of a new type of texture has not meant the supplanting of the old one. Since 1600, and to some extent even before, the three types of musical texture have flourished side by side. The usual procedure is to vary the texture within a work, emphasizing first one type and then another. Extended works particularly are apt to make use of at least two types of texture, if not all three, for variety. Polyphonic and homophonic texture appear in almost equal proportion along with glimpses of monophonic texture in the finale of Mozart's *String Quartet no. 14.*

W. A. MOZART: *String Quartet no. 14 in G, K.387* (1782)
(1756–1791) 4. Molto allegro 4:00

(Also record side 3 band 4)

The Forms of Music

2

Small Homophonic Forms

7

Form in music can be defined as design or structure. It results from patterns of repetition and contrast. Form refers to the logical organization of musical elements in a sequence of time.

Musical form has points in common with architecture, language, and literature. The structure of music can be likened to the structure of an edifice. The sounds of music create patterns in time as the shapes of material create patterns in space. Phrases and sentences in language have counterparts denoted by the same terms in music. Musical ideas enter, unfold, develop, and reach climaxes in the manner of novels and plays.

In spite of certain similarities to speech and the other arts, musical organization is essentially unique. It does not convey concrete meanings, so it is free from syntactical rules. Its formations are not restricted by the pull of gravity or the necessity of bearing weight. It exists only in time. Its perception is dependent upon remembering and relating a sequence of musical events. Elusive though it may be, form is a primary concern of the composer, the performer, and the listener. Music is not fully comprehended unless its plan of organization is perceived to some degree.

The forms of music cannot be regarded as molds into which the composer pours pitches and rhythms until they are full. In a very real sense each musical idea dictates its own form, and no two are identical. However, in the evolution of music certain recurrent patterns have crystallized. Without being the same they are sufficiently uniform to yield to systematic study. Not every work is cast in a traditional form, but the traditional forms influence even the musical designs they do not determine.

The Building Blocks

Musical organization begins with a note, but a single note cannot be related to a specific work. The smallest identifiable musical unit is a *motive.* A motive may be a rhythm, a pitch pattern, a combination of these, or less often a harmonic progression. Motives are the cells which coalesce into an organic whole. The most useful motives are those easily recognized in manifold modifications and readily adapted to multiple functions. Often they serve like mortar in binding together the other elements. Motives serve to link contrasting ideas, and they may figure in accompaniments as well as in melodies. Motives are particularly useful in *sequences,* that is, repetitions at other pitch levels of rhythmic, melodic, or harmonic patterns. Some themes are constructed by expanding and extending motives sequentially. The opening motive of Beethoven's *Fifth Symphony* fulfills all of these functions and in its many guises permeates the entire first movement.

L. van Beethoven: *Symphony no. 5 in C minor, op. 67* (1808)
(1770–1827) 1. Allegro con brio 8:38

> The first four notes introduce the motive which consists initially of three short notes on the same pitch followed by a longer note a third lower. The rhythm approximates the letter "V" in Morse code used during World War II as a victory motto. The statement of the motive is followed immediately by a repetition of its rhythm and contour at a slightly lower pitch. Different versions of the motive then are strung together in sequence to form a theme. The motive is still in evidence during a transitional passage, and when a lyric melody enters, it moves to the accompaniment. The rhythm of the motive is always recognizable no matter how its shape is bent or where it appears in the texture. The motive is a primary unifying element of the *Symphony* and the germ from which this movement springs.
>
> (Record side 4 band 5. Motive p. 374)

The structural unit of music just larger than a motive is a *phrase,* borrowing a term from language. More than one phrase is generally required to complete a musical idea, so the musical idea in a single phrase is usually incomplete. The standard phrase length is four measures, but longer and shorter phrases are uncommon only in dance-inspired music. The setting of each of the following familiar lines is one phrase long. The phrases vary in length from three to six measures, as shown by the number in parentheses at the end of each line. Observe that two or three phrases of text may be set to a single phrase of music and that sometimes there are perceptible subdivisions within a musical phrase.

O say! Can you see, by the dawn's early light, (4)
O beautiful for spacious skies, for amber waves of grain, (4)
Come, Thou almighty King! (3)
My country, 'tis of thee, sweet land of liberty, of thee I sing. (6)

Each phrase ends with a *cadence,* the musical equivalent of the vocal inflections in spoken language associated with the end of phrases and sentences. The cadence effect is achieved by appropriate melodic, harmonic, and rhythmic formulas. The strength of cadences varies from a momentary pause within a musical idea to absolute finality at the end of a composition. The cadences within a musical idea are *incomplete cadences.* The cadences at the end of complete ideas and works are *complete cadences.*

Homophonic music, like language, grows by a cumulative process. In language the two parts of a compound sentence are joined to express a complete thought. Similarly, in music the incomplete ideas of two or more phrases are combined to express a complete musical thought. The resulting unit of musical form is a *sentence,* also called a *period.*[1] Sentences in music most often consist of two phrases. The first phrase in two-phrase sentences ends with an incomplete cadence, and the concluding phrase ends with a complete cadence. Interrelationships between the phrases comprising a sentence are the norm.

The most concrete way to examine typical sentence structures is to sing some familiar melodies illustrating them. Several are suggested. The phrase structure of each sentence is described and diagramed. A line under the words extends to the end of a phrase. The diagonal stroke at the end of a phrase line signifies a cadence, incomplete if the abbreviation i.c. appears below the line and complete if the abbreviation c.c. appears below the line. Phrases are identified by lower-case letters. A letter in parentheses following an identifying letter indicates a closely related phrase.

The phrases in two-phrase sentences typically have a question-answer relationship. The two phrases may begin alike and be very similar right up to the cadence points, but the cadences are different. The first phrase closes with the rising inflection of a question and an incomplete cadence. The second phrase closes with the falling inflection of an answer and a complete cadence. Stephen Foster's famous melody begins with this type of sentence.

1. Among musicians *period* is the more prevalent term, but *sentence* seems preferable for nonmusicians.

Sentence: Two phrases beginning alike

'Way down upon the Swannee River, far, far away,/

a i.c.

There's where my heart is turning ever, there's where the old folks stay./

b (a) c.c.

In the other type of two-phrase sentences the two phrases begin differently, as in the following example. The question-answer effect results from the contrasting contours of the two phrases. The ascending motion of the "a" phrase is answered by the descending motion of the "b" phrase. Unity is achieved by the repetition of a rhythmic pattern that occurs three times in each phrase. Observe that the meaning of the words and the punctuation have no bearing on the question-answer relationship of the two phrases.

Sentence: Two phrases beginning differently

Should auld acquaintance be forgot, and never brought to mind?/

a i.c.

Should auld acquaintance be forgot, and days of auld lang syne?/

b c.c.

Sentences are predominantly of the two-phrase variety with the phrases either beginning alike, like *Old Folks at Home,* or differently, like *Auld Lang Syne.* Less common are sentences of three, four, or more phrases.

In a three-phrase sentence the first two phrases end with incomplete cadences and the third with a complete cadence. The entire melody of *Silent Night* is a three-phrase sentence.

Sentence: Three phrases, all different

Silent night, holy night, all is calm, all is bright./

a i.c.

Round yon virgin mother and Child, holy Infant so tender and mild./

b i.c.

Sleep in heavenly peace, sleep in heavenly peace./

c c.c.

In sentences of three or more phrases, two of the phrases may be the same. Of the four phrases in the first sentence of *Flow Gently, Sweet Afton,* the first and third are the same except for one note. Modifications, such as this, which do not obscure the identity of a part or alter its function are indicated by adding a prime sign (′) to the identifying letter or number. The second and fourth phrases begin alike but end differently. Only the last phrase of a sentence has a complete cadence.

Sentence: Four phrases, first and third alike

Flow gently, sweet Afton, among thy green braes;/
a i.c.

Flow gently, I'll sing thee a song in thy praise;/
b i.c.

My Mary's asleep by thy murmuring stream,/
a′ i.c.

Flow gently, sweet Afton, disturb not her dream./
c (b) c.c.

The sentence structures of most music can be related to one of these four patterns illustrated from familiar songs. There are exceptions, of course, and in extended works and especially in developmental and transitional passages the divisions are apt to be vague and the phrases irregular.

Motives, phrases, and sentences—these are the building blocks of the homophonic forms.

One-Part Form

A *one-part form* differs from a sentence only in that a one-part form is complete in itself, whereas a sentence is usually part of a larger whole. All one-part forms, naturally, are sentences, and any sentence which stands by itself as a complete entity is also a one-part form. *Silent Night*, cited as an example of a three-phrase sentence, is also a one-part form. The melody of *When Johnny Comes Marching Home* is a four-phrase sentence and, likewise, a one-part form.

One-part form

When Johnny comes marching home again, hurrah, hurrah!/
a i.c.

We'll give him a hearty welcome then, hurrah, hurrah!/
b (a) i.c.

The men will cheer, the boys will shout, the ladies they will all turn out,/
c i.c.

And we'll all feel gay when Johnny comes marching home!/
d c.c.

Other familiar examples of one-part form are: *America the Beautiful, Stars of the Summer Night, Abide with Me,* and *Anchors Aweigh.* Repetitions of the melody with different words do not change the musical form.

Traditional 12-bar blues are one-part forms with three phrases. The following words from Bessie Smith's *Lost Your Head Blues* taken from the recording in the *Smithsonian Collection of Classic Jazz* are typical.

One-part form (blues)

I was with you baby, when you didn't have a dime./
a i.c.

I was with you baby, when you didn't have a dime./
b(a) i.c.

Now since you got plenty money you have throw'd your good gal down./
c c.c.

One-part forms are common in folk, patriotic, and children's songs and in spirituals and hymns. They are relatively rare in instrumental music, but not unknown. Several of Chopin's *Preludes,* for example, are one-part forms.

FREDERIC CHOPIN: *Preludes for Piano, op. 28* (1839)
(1810–1849) No. 4 in E minor 1:40
One-part form

a i.c./ b (a) c.c./

The tempo is slow, and the phrases are long in this one-part form. The two phrases, which are nearly equal in length, begin alike but end differently. The division between them is marked by the incomplete cadence and by a momentary interruption in the persistent rhythm of the accompaniment.

(Record side 5 band 4)

FREDERIC CHOPIN: *Preludes for Piano, op. 28* (1839)
(1810–1849) No. 7 in A :43
One-part form

a i.c/ b i.c./ a′ i.c./ c c.c./

In this highly unified one-part form the rhythm is the same in all of its four phrases. The first and third phrases are melodically and harmonically similar, but not identical. The melodic contours and harmonies of phrases two and four complement those of phrases one and three.

(Record side 5 band 5)

Two-Part Form: Binary

Binary is the customary designation for musical forms consisting of two distinct parts. Each part consists of a sentence or equivalent and ends with a complete cadence. The first complete cadence comes toward the middle of the form and ends the first part. The second complete cadence closes the second part and ends the work. Binary form is found in the same categories of familiar music as one-part form. The melodies of *Auld Lang Syne, Sweet and Low,* and *Aura Lee* (popularized as *Love Me Tender*) are binary. The first sentence of *Aura Lee* is the setting for the verses, and the second sentence is the setting for the refrain. In all ensuing form diagrams musical sentences and parts with sentence function are identified by capital letters.

Binary form

As the blackbird in the spring, 'neath the willow tree,/

A-a i.c.

Sat and piped, I heard him sing, singing Aura Lee./

A-b (a) c.c.

Aura Lee, Aura Lee, maid of golden hair,/

B-a i.c.

Sunshine came along with thee, and swallows in the air./

B-b c.c.

In concert music binary form is almost peculiar to the baroque period (1600–1750). It is the traditional form of the dance movements in the suites of that era. As used in the suites the form is known more specifically as *baroque binary.*

Baroque binary form is highly stylized. The tonic key is firmly established at the beginning of the first part, and then a modulation is made to a related key, ordinarily the dominant or relative major. A cadence in the new key concludes the first part. It is repeated immediately. The material of the second part is derived from and closely related to that of the first. There is no contrast of style, mood, or tempo. Frequently the only difference between the beginnings of the two parts is the change of key. The second part begins in the new key to which the first part modulated. Sometimes the second part starts as an inversion, that is, an upside-down version of the first part. After beginning in the related key the second part modulates back to the original key, sometimes passing through one or more other tonalities enroute making it somewhat longer than the first part. A complete cadence in the tonic key concludes the second part. It, too, is repeated immediately. Though repeats are invariably indicated, they are not always observed by performers. Examples of baroque binary form are legion in the suites of Bach and his contemporaries. The ones in the *French Suites* are exceptionally concise and clear.

J. S. Bach: *French Suite no. 4 in E-flat, S.815* (1722)
(1685–1750) 6. Gigue 2:32

Binary form

A Starts with a lilting figure in one voice, other two enter imitatively, ends with complete cadence in dominant key.

A Repeated. :30[2]

B Starts with single voice like A but theme inverted and in dominant key, ends with complete cadence in tonic key. 1:00[2]

B Repeated. 1:45[2]

(Record side 2 band 2. Themes p. 374)

Immediate repetitions of parts or sections do not affect the basic designations for the forms. The AB pattern of *Aura Lee* and the AA BB pattern of a typical baroque binary dance movement are both binary.

Three-Part Form: Ternary

A three-part design comprising statement-departure-return, represented by the letters ABA, is the most prevalent pattern of musical organization. It occurs in works of all sizes, small and large. When each of the three parts consists of a single idea, the form is simple *ternary.* Many familiar and popular songs are in ternary form. Ternary design is most obvious when there are no repetitions and the three parts are of equal duration, as they are in the following example.

Frederic Chopin: *Mazurka no. 24 in C, op. 33 no. 3* (1838) 1:20
(1810–1849)

Ternary form

A Sentence of four phrases, the first and third alike, ending with a complete cadence in the tonic key.

---

2. Approximate elapsed time to the beginning of the part.

B Change of key and style. Four phrases of which the third and fourth are essentially variants of the first and second respectively. Ends with a harmonically strong but rhythmically weak cadence in the new key (A-flat). :26

A Returns abruptly. First note omitted but otherwise exactly as before. :50

(Record side 5 band 6. Themes p. 374)

The function of the B section in a ternary form is to provide contrast with the A section which precedes it and to create a need for the return of A to round out and complete the design. The degree of contrast between the A and B sections varies considerably. In simple, concise examples of ternary form the thematic material of B may be derived from and very similar to that of A and the degree of contrast slight—just sufficient to establish a feeling of departure and return. In other examples of the form, especially more expansive ones, the material of B may be completely new, and the style may contrast sharply with that of A as it does in Chopin's *Nocturne no. 4.* The larger dimensions of this ternary form result from the expansion of the sections. Each of the three parts contains several phrases but only one complete idea. The high degree of contrast between the parts eliminates the necessity for decisive internal cadences.

FREDERIC CHOPIN: *Nocturne no. 4 in F, op. 15 no. 1* (1833) 4:05
(1810–1849)

Ternary form

A Slow tempo, lyric theme in major, last phrase extended to lead directly into B.

B Fast tempo, dramatic theme in minor, extension of last phrase prepares for return of A. 1:25

A′ Slow tempo, lyric theme in major as before but ending altered to arrive at a complete cadence. 2:20

(Themes p. 374)

All of the homophonic forms are routinely expanded by repetition. According to an established principle the immediate repetition of a part or group of parts does not alter the analysis of the underlying form. For example, an AB pattern and an AA BB pattern are both regarded as binary. One explanation for this is that a literal repetition is usually indicated by a sign, and the music is only written out once. Baroque binary forms with an AA BB pattern are written:

‖: A :‖‖: B :‖

The underlying structure of a piece with repeats is more apparent to one examining the music on the printed page than to one hearing it performed. Though immediate repetitions do not change the designation or the basic organizational plan, they do alter the actual sequence of musical events and complicate the aural perception of the form. However, familiarity with the conventional patterns of repetition simplifies the problem. Literal repetitions of complete parts are relatively rare in recent music, and the repeat signs prevalent in older music are not always observed in contemporary performances. These developments are perhaps a reflection of our accelerated pace of living.

In ternary forms the first part is repeated more often than not. When only the first part is repeated, the resulting pattern is AA B A. This design with each part an eight-measure sentence is standard for popular songs. It is the design of Duke Ellington's *Solitude* and also of Schumann's *Träumerei.*

ROBERT SCHUMANN: *Scenes from Childhood, op. 15* (1838)
(1810–1856) 7. Träumerei (Reverie) 2:10

Ternary form

A Two phrases beginning alike, the second ending with a complete cadence in a new key, but the rhythmic motion continues in the bass.

A Repeated. :30

B Closely related to A, two phrases with similar contours, the second higher, both cadences incomplete. 1:00

A′ First phrase the same as before, second phrase modified to remain in tonic key and to cadence conclusively. 1:30

All of the phrases in this piece begin with the same melodic contour. Emphasis is upon unity, rather than variety, which is usual in small forms.

(Themes p. 375)

In ternary forms the first sentence frequently modulates and cadences in a new key, as it does in *Träumerei.* When this occurs, the return of A is modified to remain in the tonic key, and the piece ends in the same key as it began. It is traditional to begin and end compositions in the tonic key and to explore other tonalities in between. Thus the formal principal of departure and return applies to tonality as well as to thematic material.

Any of the parts of a ternary form may be repeated individually, but the usual practice when there are two repeats is to repeat the first part by itself and to repeat the second and third parts together as a unit. The pattern then becomes AA BA BA, but the form is still regarded as simple ternary. The ternary design is apparent when the repetitions are indicated by repeat signs.

‖: A :‖: B A :‖

The returns of A may be modified or abbreviated, and sometimes B is a phrase or a group of phrases rather than a sentence. The following is an example of a ternary form with an AA BA BA pattern of repetitions in which B is a phrase.

Robert Schumann: *Scenes from Childhood, op. 15* (1838)
(1810–1856) 1. About Strange Lands and People 1:30

Ternary form

A Opening melodic motive appears three times in succession in this sentence.

A Repeated. :15

B Almost as long as A but just a phrase. :30

A First note different but otherwise as before. :45

BA Repeated together. 1:00

(Themes p. 375)

Between the end of one part of a musical form and the beginning of the next there may be a *transition.* A transition is a passage that functions as a bridge between two structural units of a form. For this reason transitions are also called *bridge passages.* A modulation (change of key) normally occurs within a transition, and transitions also serve to prepare the way for changes of tempo, mood, and style. Transitional passages are usual between the parts of the larger musical forms; less usual but not uncommon between the parts of ternary forms. The transition in the following ternary form leads from the end of the B section in a contrasting key back to the tonic key and the return of the A theme.

P. I. Tchaikovsky: *Nutcracker Suite, op. 71a* (1892)
(1840–1893) 4. Russian Dance (Trepak) 1:00

Ternary form

A Four phrases with an a-b-a-c(b) pattern.

A Repeated with somewhat fuller scoring.

B Melody moves to the bass, four phrases with the same design as A. :22

Transition based on motive common to the two parts.

A′ First three phrases essentially as before, last phrase extended several measures without a cadence until the end. :38

(Record side 6 band 2. Themes p. 375)

A *coda* is a section sometimes added to the basic design of a form to bring a composition to a more conclusive or satisfactory close. *Codetta* is a diminutive form of the term meaning "small coda" but frequently used to designate a closing section appended to a principal part within a work. Codas are not usually found in one-part or binary forms but are common in ternary and all of the larger forms. The following 20th-century work is a relatively sophisticated example of ternary form with a coda. In it the return of A is represented by a substantially modified form of its first phrase, and the two transitions plus the coda account for almost half of its duration.

PAUL HINDEMITH: *Mathis der Maler (Mathias the Painter)*[3] (1934)
(1895–1963) 2. Grablegung (Entombment) 4:08

Ternary form

A Three phrases of which the first and third are related.

Transition :45

B Oboe and then flute and oboe play two related phrases accompanied by pizzicato strings. 1:20

Transition using elements of both A and B.

A′ First phrase of A modified and extended. 2:15

Coda 2:50

(Record side 8 band 5. Themes p. 375)

March Form: Compound Binary

Just as phrases are joined in sentences and sentences are combined in binary and ternary forms, binary and ternary forms are united at the next level of musical organization. The resulting forms have specialized applications, and there is no universally accepted terminology for them. *Compound binary* is a descriptive designation for the musical form consisting of two parts, each of which is simple binary or ternary. This form

3. See Colorplate 1.

is typical of marches and rarely encountered elsewhere, so *march form* is another name for it.

The first part of a compound binary form in march style is sometimes referred to as the *march* (as it is in the following diagram) to distinguish it from the second part, which is customarily labeled and called the *trio*. There is no logical reason for calling the second part a trio, but the usual explanation is that the corresponding part in a minuet is called a trio. March trios are traditionally in the subdominant key, and the trio concludes the form. Marches, therefore, are the one consistent exception to the rule that a piece ends in the same key as it begins. The trios in marches are usually lyric in style. Their lyricism is sometimes interrupted by a contrasting middle section, after which the lyric style returns.

Marches often begin with a brief *introduction*. An introduction is a passage that precedes the main body of a form. Introductions are useful in capturing the attention of listeners, in establishing the tempo, mood, and key of the piece, and in preparing for the entrance of the first thematic idea. *Hands Across the Sea* is a march in compound binary form which begins with an introduction and adheres to the conventional march plan throughout.

JOHN PHILIP SOUSA: *Hands Across the Sea* (1899) 2:50
(1854–1932)

Compound binary form

March: Binary

Introduction, one phrase.

A Four phrases.

A Repeated.

B Four phrases. :35

B Repeated.

Trio: Ternary

A[4] Lyric melody in subdominant key, four phrases. 1:08

A Repeated.

B Begins with low and high instruments sounding alternately. 1:40

---

4. The letter "A" represents the first sentence (or passage with sentence function) in each part of a multipart-form diagram.

A′ Embellished return of A.

BA′ Repeated together, ends in subdominant key. 2:13

(Record side 6 band 3. Themes p. 376)

Composers of marches generally follow the basic plan of organization utilized by Sousa. The march proper is nearly always binary, and the trio is usually binary or ternary but is occasionally one part. Each sentence traditionally is repeated.

A plan of organization very similar to that found in marches is more or less standard for rags, which is not surprising. Marches and rags have much in common. Joplin even indicates *Tempo di marcia* (march tempo) for his *Maple Leaf Rag* and labels the second part "trio." Sousa and his famous band played a band version of this rag throughout Europe the year after it was published (coincidentally the same year as Sousa's *Hands Across the Sea*). Each strain is 16 bars long, the same as most march strains. Since all strains of a rag are similar in style, they are sometimes represented by consecutive letters and not grouped in parts. The usual pattern of themes and repetitions is then AA BB A CC DD. The similarity of this pattern to the compound binary form of marches is apparent in the following diagram of a typical rag.

Scott Joplin: *Maple Leaf Rag* (1899) 3:14
(1868–1917)

Compound binary form (Tempo di marcia)

Part I: Ternary

A Syncopated rag rhythm, tonic key.

A Repeated.

B Rhythmically similar to A and in same key. :45

B Repeated.

A As before. 1:30

Part II: Binary

A Different rhythm patterns, key changes to subdominant. 1:50

A Repeated.

B Rhythm patterns derived from I–A, modulates back to tonic key. 2:33

B Repeated.

(Record side 9 band 1)

Minuet and Trio Form: Compound Ternary

A form with an overall A B A design in which each part individually is a simple binary or ternary form is a *compound ternary* form. Compound ternary is the usual form for minuets (French, *menuet*; Italian, *menuetto*). Each part of a minuet is most often ternary. The middle part, like the second part of a march, is a trio. The trio designation apparently originated when it was the practice to write the middle part of minuets for three instruments. The name persisted long after the reason for it had disappeared. The word *minuet* is used in two ways—to identify a complete piece or movement and more specifically to refer to the parts of a minuet that precede and follow the trio. Minuet-trio-minuet is the sequence of parts in a complete minuet. The first appearance of the minuet and the trio ordinarily have a full complement of repeats, and the return of the minuet has none, producing the following pattern.

Minuet	Trio	Minuet
‖: A :‖: BA :‖	‖: A :‖: BA :‖	A B A
(AA BA BA)	(AA BA BA)	

The third movement in classic four-movement symphonies, sonatas, and quartets typically is a minuet, as in Mozart's *Symphony no. 35.*

W. A. Mozart: *Symphony no. 35 in D, K.385, "Haffner"* (1782)
(1756–1791) 3. Menuetto 3:05

Compound ternary form

Minuet: Ternary, D major.

A Two phrases—the first loud, vigorous, ascending; the second quiet, lyric, descending.

A Repeated.

B Two phrases which parallel the stylistic relationships of A. :21

A As before.

BA Repeated together. :44

Trio: Ternary, A major.

A Two phrases which begin alike. 1:06

A Repeated.

B Two phrases, the second extended. 1:29

A As before.

BA Repeated together. 1:59

Minuet: Ternary as before but without repeats. 2:29

A As before.

B As before.

A As before.

(Record side 3 band 3. Themes p. 376)

Starting with Beethoven the minuet in multimovement works sometimes was replaced by a *scherzo*. Scherzos have the same form and meter as minuets but differ in tempo, which is faster, and style, which is less graceful. Scherzo is an Italian word meaning "joke" or "play." In keeping with the name, scherzo movements may contain elements of whimsy, humor, and surprise in their bustling rhythms. The following is an extremely concise but perfectly valid example of scherzo form and style.

L. VAN BEETHOVEN: *Violin Sonata no. 5 in F, op. 24, "Spring"* (1801)
(1770–1827) 3. Scherzo: Allegro molto 1:07

Compound ternary form

Scherzo: Ternary

A Piano alone.

A′ Material repeated but violin added.

B Just a phrase, full chords in piano.

A′ First phrase only.

BA′ Two previous phrases repeated together, slightly extended.

Trio: Binary :25

A Running figure in both violin and piano.

A Repeated.

B First phrase has running figure in piano, second phrase has running figure in violin.

B Repeated.

Scherzo: Ternary :45

A As before.

A′ As before.

B As before.

A′ First phrase only but slightly extended as it was previously after the repetition of BA′ together, which is now omitted.

(Record side 4 band 4. Themes p. 377)

There are a few scherzos with two trios. The plan then becomes:

Scherzo—Trio I—Scherzo—Trio II—Scherzo

The *scherzo* in Schumann's *Symphony no. 1* has two trios, as does the *Scherzo* in his *Quintet for Piano and Strings.*

When the return of the minuet or scherzo after the trio is literal and complete except for the repeats, it is not necessary for it to be written again. This repetition is indicated by the sign *D.C.*, abbreviation for the Italian words *da capo* meaning "from the beginning." On seeing this sign performers go back to the beginning and play to the end of the minuet or scherzo proper (up to the trio), where the word *fine*, meaning "end," appears. Repeat signs are ignored when playing a da capo.

In vocal music compound ternary structures are found in the *da capo arias* of cantatas, oratorios, and operas. Da capo arias are songs for solo voice with instrumental accompaniment in which the first part returns, sometimes with improvised vocal embellishment, after a contrasting section. The return of the first part corresponds to the return of the minuet or scherzo after the trio. The repetition of Part I is indicated by the abbreviation for da capo, giving the form its name. Da capo arias were common in the music of the past. The fact that their musical design required repetitions which were not implicit in the text perhaps contributed to the failure of some works in which they were prominent to achieve a permanent place in the repertoire. *He was despised* is one of the two da capo arias Handel wrote in the *Messiah,* but they are not always performed in their entirety.

G. F. HANDEL: *Messiah, oratorio* (1741)
(1685–1759) 23. He was despised 9:35

Compound ternary form

Part I: Binary, major.

A Motives of part I introduced in orchestra, voice repeats first phrase and continues with an extended phrase which modulates and cadences in the dominant key.

B Same text and motives as A, orchestra starts in new key, voice enters after one phrase and modulates back to tonic key, repeated cadences before concluding orchestral phrase. 1:35

Part II: Binary, minor

A Contrasting style and mode, agitated rhythmic figure in accompaniment. 4:05

B Accompaniment figure continues uninterrupted as background to vocal declamation, part ends with two chords in orchestra. 4:40

Part I: Da capo, from the beginning as before. 5:20

On some recordings of this aria Part II and the da capo are omitted. It is complete as diagramed on London 1329.

(Themes p. 377)

Forms with clearly delineated parts but a thematic design that does not conform to any of the preceding binary or ternary patterns are classified as *free part forms.* In this category are patterns such as A B C A, the form of Chopin's *Mazurka no. 41 in C-sharp minor, op. 63 no. 3,* and AA BB CC A coda, the form of Schubert's *Moment Musical in F minor, op. 94 no. 3.*

Additional Examples

One-Part Form

CHOPIN: *Preludes op. 28, nos. 1, 2, 9, and 20*

Binary Form

BACH: *French Suite no. 5 in G, S.816,* all movements
HANDEL: *Concerto Grosso op. 6, no. 1 in G,* last movement
SCARLATTI: *Sonata in C, L.454*

(Record side 2 band 7)

MOZART: *Qui sdegno non s'accende* (A B, repeated)

(Record side 4 band 1)

Ternary Form

BRAHMS: *Waltzes op. 39, no. 2 in E*
RACHMANINOFF: *Prelude in C-sharp minor, op. 3, no. 2*
SCHUMANN: *Scenes from Childhood op. 15, nos. 2 and 13*

Compound Binary Form

SOUSA: *Manhattan Beach*
Fairest of the Fair

Compound Ternary Form

BEETHOVEN: *Piano Sonata no. 11 in B-flat, op. 22*

3. Menuetto

Symphony no. 3 in E-flat, op. 55, "Eroica"

3. Scherzo

HAYDN: *Symphony no. 104 in D, "London"*

3. Menuetto: Allegro

Large Homophonic Forms

8

The terms *large* and *small* are relative as applied to musical forms. A fast, terse large form may be of shorter duration than a slow, diffuse small form. A greater number of parts and a higher degree of organization distinguish the large forms from the small forms. The various *rondo forms* and *sonata form* are large homophonic forms.

Rondo Forms

In rondo forms a theme stated at the very beginning returns after each departure. In their use of a recurrent theme which alternates with contrasting material, rondo forms are similar in design to poetic forms that begin with a refrain which is repeated after each verse. The pattern produced by alternating fixed and variable elements becomes clear when the elements are represented by letters.

refrain/	verse 1/	refrain/	verse 2/	refrain/	verse 3/	refrain/etc.
A	B	A	C	A	D	A

The theme represented by the letter "A" is the *rondo theme.*

The type of rondo which most clearly illustrates the rondo principle is *old rondo form.* In old rondos each part is a single sentence with a complete close, after which the next part follows immediately. As in all rondos, the rondo theme is heard first and after each digression. The number of digressions, or contrasting themes, is not fixed. In Bach's *Gavotte en Rondeau* (gavotte in rondo form) there are four. These four plus the five appearances of the rondo theme make a total of nine parts—AA B A C A D A E A. The immediate repetition of the rondo theme after its initial statement does not constitute an additional part.

J. S. Bach: *Partita no. 3 in E for Violin, S. 1006* (1722)
(1685–1750) 3. Gavotte en Rondeau 3:05

Old rondo form

A	Rondo theme, tonic key, major.
A	Repeated.
B	Contrasting sentence in relative minor key. :27
A	As before.
C	Contrasting sentence in dominant key. :55
A	As before.
D	Contrasting sentence in supertonic key. 1:34
A	As before.
E	Contrasting sentence in mediant key. 2:15
A	As before.

This partita is number 6 when Bach's sonatas and partitas for solo violin are numbered together. A partita is a group of movements with dance characteristics. A gavotte is a dance in duple meter and a moderate tempo which first became popular in France during the 17th century.

(Record side 2 band 4. Rondo theme p. 377)

The archaic old rondo form was superseded by the classic rondo forms. The parts in classic rondos, as compared with those in old rondos, tend to be fewer in number and larger in size. Classic rondos have five or seven parts, and the individual parts frequently have a binary or a ternary design, sometimes with repeats. Transitions between parts are common, and they may be extensive. Classic rondos customarily end with a coda.

The classic rondo form with five parts, called a *five-part rondo* or a *simple rondo*, has a basic A B A C A design. Since the parts, or themes, in a rondo are generally larger than a sentence, they are represented in the form diagrams by Roman numerals, and they are sometimes known by descriptive names, as follows:

A	Theme I	Rondo theme
B	Theme II	Subordinate theme I
A	Theme I	Rondo theme
C	Theme III	Subordinate theme II
A	Theme I	Rondo theme

The second movement of Mozart's *Eine Kleine Nachtmusik* (a little night music) is a typical example of five-part rondo form.

W. A. MOZART: *Serenade in G, K.525, "Eine Kleine Nachtmusik"* (1787)
(1756–1791) 2. Romanze: Andante 6:10

Rondo form, five-part

Theme I (rondo theme), ternary.

A Sentence of two phrases.

A Repeated.

B Contrasting phrase. 1:00

A′ Reduced to a phrase.

BA′ Repeated together.

Theme II, two parts. 2:05

A Phrase which ends with a complete cadence.

A Repeated.

B Material derived from preceding phrase, dissolves without a cadence.

Transition

Theme I (rondo theme), reduced to one part. 3:10

A As before.

Theme III, two parts. 3:40

A Phrase which ends with a complete cadence like II-A, contrasting mood in minor.

A Repeated.

B Material derived from preceding phrase, dissolves without a cadence like II-B.

Transition

Theme I (rondo theme), ternary. 4:35

A As before.

B As before.

A′ As before.

Coda Three chords, then final references to rondo theme. 5:35

Repetitions indicated in the score and in the diagram of the form are not always observed in performance.

(Themes p. 378)

Compositions and movements that are labeled "rondo" by the composer usually have seven parts. *Seven-part rondo* form is also known as *rondo-sonata* form and *sonata-rondo* form, because it has features in common with sonata form, discussed next. Seven-part rondos theoretically have two more parts than five-part rondos but have the same number of themes. The two additional parts come from a return of theme II (subordinate theme I) transposed to the key of the rondo theme (the feature derived from sonata form), and an extra statement of the rondo theme. In practice the final statement of the rondo theme is usually merged with the coda. The basic plan of a seven-part rondo form is:

A	Theme I (rondo theme), tonic key.
B	Theme II (subordinate theme I), related key.
A	Theme I (rondo theme), tonic key.
C	Theme III (subordinate theme II), new key or keys. (sometimes replaced by a development section)
A	Theme I (rondo theme), tonic key.
B′	Theme II (subordinate theme I), transposed to the key of theme I, tonic.
A	This statement of theme I is usually incorporated in the coda, tonic key.

Seven-part rondo form is frequently used for the final movements of sonatas and concertos. Beethoven ends his *Piano Sonata no. 2* characteristically with a clear example of the form.

L. van Beethoven: *Piano Sonata no. 2 in A, op. 2 no. 2* (1795)
(1770–1827) 4. Rondo: Grazioso 6:35

Rondo form, seven-part

Theme I (rondo theme), ternary.

A Soaring figure begins both phrases of this sentence.

B Contrasting phrase.

A′ Reduced to a phrase.

Transition, running figures modulate to dominant key.

Theme II, one part. :47

A Extended sentence in the dominant key.

Transition, undulating figure in low register.

Theme I (rondo theme), ternary. 1:16

A Slightly embellished.

B As before.

A′ As before.

Theme III, ternary. 1:48

A Loud and vigorous, starts in parallel minor key and modulates to its relative major.

A Repeated.

B Continues style of preceding sentence.

A′ Modified and shortened version of A.

B Same material as before but now the style is soft and smooth.

A′ Partial return which dissolves into. . . .

Transition, single descending line leads to return of. . . .

Theme I (rondo theme), ternary. 3:29

A With additional embellishment.

B Embellished.

A′ Soaring figure filled in but otherwise as before.

Transition, same material as that following first statement of rondo theme, but this time it does not modulate.

Theme II, one part. 4:17

A′ Transposed to the tonic key but otherwise essentially as before.

Theme I (rondo theme) and coda merged. 4:40

This section, which is developmental in character, functions as the final statement of the rondo theme and as the coda. Ornate versions of the rondo theme at the beginning and end of this section are separated by contrasting material derived from theme III.

(Record side 4 band 2. Themes p. 378)

Sonata Form

A certain amount of confusion about the term *sonata* is inevitable, since it has different meanings in different contexts. Originally, sonata simply meant a "sound piece" which was played, as opposed to a *cantata* which was sung. This usage is no longer current, but sonata is still used to designate (a) a multimovement work for one or two instruments, and (b) a specific plan of musical organization within one continuous unit. *Sonata form* proper comes under the second heading.

Sonata form, like most musical forms, evolved over an extended period, borrowing elements from existing forms, modifying and adding to them. It emerged as a distinct form around the middle of the 18th century and was in general use by 1780. A high percentage of all larger musical compositions written since that time have fulfilled the essential conditions of sonata design. The form is ideally suited to the requirements of the classic era and readily adaptable to the changing styles of subsequent periods down to the present.

Sonata form seems to have evolved from binary form, but its broad outline is essentially ternary. The three large sections of a sonata form are concerned in turn with the presentation, the working out, and the return or summing up of its thematic material. The three sections are the *exposition,* the *development,* and the *recapitulation,* respectively.

In the exposition at least two and generally three thematic ideas are stated. The *first theme* is the *principal theme;* the *second theme* is the *subordinate theme;* and the *third theme* is the *closing theme.* The principal theme and the subordinate theme differ in character and tonality to provide the essential element of contrast. The principal theme is commonly but not invariably dramatic and masculine in nature, and the subordinate theme lyric and feminine. The closing theme may be little more than a series of cadential formulas bringing the exposition to a close, or it may be a group of thematic ideas equal in scope and importance to the first two themes. When the closing theme has distinct parts, it may be called a *closing group.* Some composers, notably Beethoven, are fond of recalling motives of the principal theme at the end of the exposition in the closing theme. The exposition traditionally is repeated before proceeding to the development.

The development section, as the name implies, is concerned with combining the themes, placing them in new keys and settings, manipulating them, and working them up to a climax.

In the recapitulation readily recognizable versions of the three themes return in their original order. The significant difference between the recapitulation and the exposition is in the keys of the second and the third themes. A transition following the first theme in the exposition modulates to the new key of the second theme, and from that point on the tonic key is avoided until the recapitulation. The beginning of the recapitulation is signaled by the obvious return of the first theme in the tonic key. The tonality is essentially tonic throughout the recapitulation, with the second and third themes transposed and the transitions adjusted as necessary.

A coda, which may amount to a second development section, customarily follows the recapitulation. First movements in sonata form frequently have an introduction. If the introduction is more than a few measures long, it normally is in a slow tempo, contrasting with the fast tempo of the body of the movement.

Beethoven's *Piano Sonata no. 8*, the *"Pathetique,"* is one of his best known works and an unmistakable masterpiece. The first movement provides a perfect introduction to sonata form.

L. VAN BEETHOVEN: *Piano Sonata no. 8 in C minor, op. 13* (1799)
(1770–1827) 1. Grave—Allegro di molto e con brio 6:00

Sonata form

Introduction

Slow tempo, somber mood.

Exposition

Principal theme (I) 1:34

Fast tempo, ascending phrase answered by descending phrase in first sentence, second sentence begins like first but ends differently.

Transition

Partially based on first phrase of principal theme.

Subordinate theme (II) 2:00

Three related sentences, the third extended to lead directly into closing theme.

Closing theme (III) 2:25

A Repeated notes in the bass and soprano with a busy figure between.

B Running figure in high register.

C Reminiscent of principal theme.

(The repeat sign in the score at this point is rarely observed in modern performances.)

Development 2:56

Section 1

Brief return to tempo and material of introduction.

Section 2

Fast tempo, principal theme developed to a climax.

Transition

Rapid single line.

Recapitulation

Principal theme (I) 4:04

One sentence exactly as in exposition, partial repetition dissolves into transition.

Transition

Based on second phrase of principal theme, only the last two measures are like the exposition.

Subordinate theme (II) 4:20

Transposed but otherwise as in the exposition.

Closing theme (III) 4:43

Transposed to the tonic key but otherwise all three parts return essentially as in the exposition.

Coda

Section 1 5:15

Tempo and material of introduction.

Section 2

Final reference to principal theme.

(Record side 4 band 3. Themes p. 379)

The design of sonata form is such that many details can be varied without destroying the identity or the logic of the plan. A theme may consist of a single idea, a group of related ideas, or be cast in the mold of a small form. The transitions may be perfunctory or as attractive and imaginative as the themes. Repeat signs are no longer written at the end of expositions, and those in older works are not always observed in modern performances. New material may be introduced in the development section, or the development section can be omitted, in which case the form is abridged and the exposition is followed immediately by the recapitulation. In the recapitulation the order and tonality of the themes may be changed. All of these variations are possible within the broad concept of sonata form. Most of them are illustrated in the Additional Examples listed at the end of the chapter.

A standardized modification of sonata form attributed to Mozart occurs regularly in the first movements of classic concertos. The special adaptation of sonata form used in concertos has a *double exposition* instead of a repeated exposition. In the first exposition the orchestra presents the thematic material all in the tonic key. After remaining silent during the first exposition, the solo instrument makes an ear-catching entrance to begin the second exposition, and thereafter dominates the musical scene. In the second exposition, which takes the place of the usual repetition, the key relationships and the order of the themes are normal for sonata form. The development and recapitulation are perfectly regular, but at the end of the recapitulation where a cadence is anticipated, the progress of the movement is interrupted to provide an opportunity for the soloist to exhibit his virtuosity. This passage for the solo instrument unaccompanied is a *cadenza*. Originally improvised spontaneously on themes of the movement, cadenzas are now composed, but the free, improvisatory style is preserved. After a brilliant cadenza a mundane coda would be anticlimatic, so the movement usually ends summarily. Mozart's *Piano Concerto no. 27* begins, like his other concertos, with a movement in modified sonata form which has a double exposition and a cadenza.

W. A. Mozart: *Piano Concerto no. 27 in B-flat, K.595* (1791)
(1756–1791) 1. Allegro 12:25

Sonata form, double exposition

Exposition I
Orchestra, tonic key.
Exposition II 2:15
Solo and orchestra, usual sonata form key relationships.
Development 5:15
Solo and orchestra, typical developmental procedures.
Recapitulation 7:10
Solo and orchestra, tonic key as usual in the form.
Cadenza 10:40
Solo, brilliant passage work using thematic elements.
Coda 12:05
Orchestra

In 20th-century examples of sonata form the order of the themes in the recapitulation frequently differs from that of the exposition. Sometimes the order of the themes is reversed, producing an A-B-C—development—C-B-A design. This form is regarded by some as a modification of sonata form, by others as a distinct *arch form* or *bow form*. Arch forms also exist with a middle theme in place of the development section and with just five parts, A-B-C-B-A.

Additional Examples

Rondo Form

F. Couperin: *Pièces de Clavecin, Fifth Ordre*
La Bandoline (old rondo—AA B A C A D A)

Bartok: *Three Rondos on Folk Tunes, no. 1* (five parts)

Beethoven: *Bagatelle in A minor, "Für Elise"* (five parts)

BEETHOVEN: *Piano Sonata no. 10 in G, op. 14, no. 2*
3. Allegro assai (five parts, long coda)

MOZART: *Violin Sonata no. 10 in B-flat, K.378*
3. Rondo Allegro (five parts)

BEETHOVEN: *Violin Concerto in D, op. 61*
3. Rondo (seven parts)

BRAHMS: *Symphony no. 4 in E minor, op. 98*
3. Allegro giocoso (seven parts with development)

SAINT-SAENS: *Introduction and Rondo Capriccioso, op. 28*
(seven parts)

Sonata Form

HAYDN: *Symphony no. 94 in G, "Surprise"*
1. Adagio cantabile—Vivace assai

MOZART: *String Quartet in G, K.387*
1. Allegro vivace

BEETHOVEN: *Symphony no. 5 in C minor, op. 67*
1. Allegro con brio

(Record side 4 band 5)

MOZART: *The Marriage of Figaro, K.492*
Overture (without development)

TCHAIKOVSKY: *Nutcracker Suite, op. 71a*
Overture Miniature (without development)

BEETHOVEN: *Violin Concerto in D, op. 61*
1. Allegro ma non troppo (double exposition)

HINDEMITH: *Mathis der Maler*
1. Engelkonzert (order of themes changed in recapitulation)

BARTOK: *String Quartet no. 5*
1. Allegro

(Arch form with the themes inverted—ascending motion becoming descending motion and vice versa—and their order reversed in the recapitulation)

Polyphonic Forms

9

Both homophonic and polyphonic forms are based on the principal of repetition, but the applications of the principal are different. In the homophonic forms repetitions of previously stated thematic elements alternate with contrasting material to establish patterns. In the polyphonic forms immediate repetition in another part (imitation) produces patterns of interlacing thematic entrances.

Polyphonic forms are conceived for a fixed number of parts, all of which participate in the unfolding of the thematic material. The number of parts dictates certain critical aspects of the organization, so the integrity of the various voices is maintained. Conflicting requirements of clarity, fullness, and freedom of movement restrict the number of parts in truly polyphonic music to a narrow range. Two-part texture tends to be sparse and harmonically incomplete. Four-part texture is more cumbersome, and following four individual melodic lines taxes the listener's ear. Three seems to be the ideal number of parts for polyphonic music, though single lines and passages in more than four parts have their place in the polyphonic forms. Rests are distributed through the parts in most polyphonic music, reducing the number of parts actually sounding together at a given instant below the total number participating. Polyphonic forms written for more than five parts are rare, but this does not preclude their being scored for orchestra and the larger ensembles. Any number of instruments can play a given part.

Canon

Continuous imitation between two or more parts produces a *canon.* Strict canonic imitation is the most rigid formal procedure in music, and even the momentary lapses allowed within the definitions of the form do not appreciably loosen the bounds. The severe limitations of canonic form make it unsuitable for extended works, but it is effective in short compositions and in brief passages of larger forms.

The part that begins a canon is called the *leader,* and those that imitate are called *followers.* The followers imitate the leader continuously at a fixed distance and interval up to a cadence point, where a momentary lapse may occur and where the leader and followers may change positions.

The following example shows the use of a canon as one part of a compound ternary form. The minuet proper (excluding the trio) is a strict and obvious two-part canon.

JOSEPH HAYDN: *String Quartet in D minor, op. 76 no. 2, "Quinten"* (1798)
(1732–1809) 3. Menuetto: Allegro ma non troppo 3:05

> Overall, this minuet is in a regular compound ternary form. Individually, the minuet proper and the trio are simple ternary forms. In addition, the minuet is a canon in two parts with exact imitation throughout. The violins play the leader in octaves, and the viola and the cello play the follower in octaves, starting a measure (three beats) later and an octave lower. The trio is purely homophonic, but the canon is resumed on the return of the minuet. Haydn's fusion of polyphonic and homophonic form is a stroke of genius.

Canons in which the end leads back to the beginning are *round canons, perpetual canons,* or *rotas.* All three names are used. Round canon or just *round* is most familiar because of its association with children's songs like *Are You Sleeping, Lovely Evening, Three Blind Mice,* and *Row, Row, Row Your Boat.* While problems of notation delayed the development of other types of polyphonic music for a time, notation presented no serious barrier to early composers of rounds. Rounds could be, and were, written as single line melodies with just an indication of the point at which the second and subsequent voices were to enter. As a result the form was highly developed at an early date. The following example is remarkable for its sophisticated handling of complex texture.

ANONYMOUS: *Sumer Is Icumen In* (*Summer Is Coming In*) (1240) 1:38

Structural Diagram

Part 1

Part 2

Part 3

Part 4

Part 1

Part 2

This is the oldest piece of secular music available in modern editions and still performed. It is an isolated example of this period and style, but its perfection attests to a considerable prior development. It consists of a four-part canon accompanied by two additional voices which continuously exchange short melodic fragments as shown in the diagram. All six parts can be repeated infinitely, and no real ending is provided. The original manuscript is reproduced in the booklet accompanying *The History of Music in Sound* Volume II, RCA Victor LM–6015.

(Record side 1 band 6)

In the absence of a composed ending, rounds and canons conclude after an indefinite number of repetitions as each voice comes to the end of the melody and drops out until none is left. Canons may be accompanied by free melodic lines or by chords. It is not a requirement that all parts participate in the imitation.

Certain manipulations of melodic lines traditional in contrapuntal music can be illustrated succinctly in canons. Interest in these manipulations is renewed because of their extensive application in 20th-century music. The theory is that melodic lines preserve their identity when played backward, upside down, in longer or shorter rhythmic values (but the same proportions), and in any combination of these. Musicians have precise names for these transformations. They are:

Retrograde, crab, or *cancrizans*—played backward, that is, from the end to the beginning.

Inversion or mirror—contrary motion or as seen in a mirror. Ascending lines become descending lines and vice versa. Skips become equivalent skips in the opposite direction.

Retrograde inversion—a combination of retrograde and inversion.

Original or *rectus*—original or unmodified form of a melody.

Augmentation—increased rhythmic values, usually doubled.
Diminution—decreased rhythmic values, usually halved.

Most of these devices figure in the canons of Bach's *Musical Offering.*

J. S. Bach: *Musical Offering, S.1079* (1747)
(1685–1750)

Perpetual canon on the royal theme	1:25
Diverse canons on the royal theme	
1. Two parts	:45
2. For two violins at the unison	:45
3. Two parts in contrary motion	:50
4. Two parts in augmentation and contrary motion	2:15
5. Two parts	2:35
Canonic fugue	2:00
Two-part canon in inversion (two versions)	2:35
Four-part canon	4:50
Perpetual canon	1:30

(The canons are listed in the order of the *Collected Edition.* The sequence is altered in some recordings.)

While one of J. S. Bach's sons, Philipp Emanuel, was employed as a musician in the court of Frederick the Great, the elder Bach was invited to the Potsdam palace to display his fabled powers of improvisation. Frederick provided a theme upon which Bach extemporized. After returning to Leipzig, he worked out and wrote down these canons and three other works which together constitute his "musical offering" to the king. The "royal theme" is present in all of the canons, sometimes as part of the canon and sometimes as a free voice. The canons have two voices in imitation and one free voice except the two-part canons, which have no free voice, and the four-part canon which has all four parts in imitation. Bach took the liberty of altering and embellishing the king's theme, so it is not always apparent. Canons involving inversion and retrograde forms of the theme are virtually impossible to detect without access to the score. Imitation of this sort serves to unify and organize musical sounds even though it functions largely on a subconscious level. Do not be disturbed if you are not consciously aware of it.

(Royal theme p. 379)

Canons are most effective when used for passages within a larger framework. Canonic imitation figures prominently in many development sections. Occasionally it is used in thematic statements. One such instance is in the Franck *Sonata for Violin and Piano.*

CESAR FRANCK: *Violin Sonata in A* (1886)
(1822–1890) 4. Allegretto poco mosso 6:05

The theme with which this movement opens is stated as an accompanied canon. In its first appearance the piano plays the leader and the accompaniment while the violin plays the follower. Each entrance of this theme is imitated canonically, with the violin and piano sometimes exchanging roles as leader and follower. The other themes of the movement are either homophonic or in free, nonimitative counterpoint.

(Record side 6 band 1)

Fugue

Fugue form occupies the same position of eminence in the baroque period (1600–1750) as sonata form does in the classic period (1750–1825). It is the form in which composers of the time cast many of their most exalted musical ideas. Fugue form embodies the principle of imitation, but in a much more imaginative and flexible manner than does canon.

The germ cell of a fugue is a pithy thematic idea called a *subject*. Fugue subjects typically contain one or more motives which are readily recognized and capable of sustained development. The subject is announced alone in one voice. It is answered immediately in another. The answer is not an exact repetition of the subject. It is on different pitches, and sometimes the shape is altered slightly, but for listening purposes the subject and answer may be considered the same and are so regarded in this discussion. Each voice of the fugue enters in turn with the subject. If it is a three-voice fugue, there will be three such entrances. If it is a four-voice fugue, there will be four. Regardless of the number, each enters in its assigned register. When all of the voices have stated the subject, the first section or main exposition is concluded.

The next section consists of a series of expositions in different keys separated by passages without the complete subject called *episodes*. Episodes normally contain fragments of the subject or of counterpoints associated with the subject.

In the final section there is a return to the tonic key and traditionally a passage with overlapping statements of the subject called a *stretto*.

A fugue is, strictly speaking, a monothematic form, but sometimes a counterpoint consistently associated with the subject achieves the status of a secondary thematic idea and is designated a *countersubject*. Following the diagram of a typical fugue while it is being played does more to explain the form than multiplying words. A structural diagram of a very regular Bach fugue is provided for this purpose.

J. S. Bach: *The Well-Tempered Clavier, vol. I, S.846/69* (1722)
(1685–1750) 16. Fugue in G minor 2:16

Structural Diagram

```
Main Exposition                          /Episode   /Relative Exposition
        SSSSSSS.....ccccc..................               SSSSSSS....ccc
SSSSSSS ccccc..........                    SSSSSSS................   SSS
                          SSSSSSS...........   ccccc..ccccc..............
                   SSSSSSS ccccc...........          SSSSSSS  ccccc ..SSSSS

___/Epis/Subdominant Exposit./Episode     /Tonic Stretto
cc   ...........SSSSSSS..ccccc.............   .....   .... .............
SSSS......ccccc.......SSSSSSS.............SSSSSSS   .....SSSSSSS.......
..     ..SSSSSSS..ccccc.......               SSSSSSS.....       SSSSSSS
SS......                      .............   SSSSSSS.....ccccc.......

Subject:  SSSSSSS           } Notation p. 379
Countersubject:   ccccc     }
Free counterpoint:   .........
```

(Record side 2 band 3)

Works other than fugues often contain fugal passages. These are called *fughettas,* meaning "little fugues." Fughettas are usually similar in structure to the main exposition of a complete fugue.

Additional Examples

Canon

Bach: *Goldberg Variations, S.988* (Every third variation is a two-part canon, most with one free voice)

Bartok: *Duos (44) for Two Violins*
22. Dance of the Fly

Bartok: *Mikrokosmos vol. I, nos. 28, 30, and 31*

Fugue

Bach: *The Well-Tempered Clavier, S.846/93,* any of the 48 fugues

Bach: *The Art of Fugue, S.1080*

Hindemith: *Ludus Tonalis* (no current recording)

Variation Forms

10

Variation is ever present in the music of virtually all periods and styles, but only a small group of forms are organized around the variation principle. Variation forms are unified by one or more constant elements such as melody, bass line, harmony, or structure. Interest is sustained by modifying the remaining elements. The type of variation is determined by the choice of fixed elements, the kinds of alteration made in the variable elements, and the manner of connecting or separating the variations.

A theme stated at the beginning of a variation form introduces the constant elements. The theme may be original with the composer or it may be borrowed from a preexistent source. *Theme and variations* is a more complete title appropriate for many sets of variations. The theme is announced in a simple, direct fashion calculated to impress its characteristics on the mind of the listener. The variations follow, ranging in number from one to more than thirty, each with a direct though sometimes obscure relationship to the theme. A set of variations may conclude with a restatement of the theme or with a final section departing from the variation principle, such as a fugue or coda.

Sectional Variations

Sectional variations begin with a theme which usually is a simple tune in one-part, binary, or ternary form sixteen to thirty-two measures in length. The parts of the theme may be repeated, and the repetitions, if any, normally are preserved in the variations. The theme comes to a full close, and there is a momentary interruption between it and the first variation and between all subsequent variations. Each variation duplicates the structure of the theme, and pauses between them divide the work into segments of equal length, though duration may vary with changes in tempo and omission or addition of repeats.

Variations in which the melody is preserved more or less intact are the easiest to hear. Changes are restricted to the setting of the theme and to the registers and instruments in which it appears. The possibilities for variation are limited, so the number of variations is small. The Haydn example, with four, is typical.

JOSEPH HAYDN: *String Quartet in C, op. 76 no. 3, "Emperor"* (1798)
(1732–1809) 2. Poco adagio, cantabile 7:06

Theme and variations

Theme—poco adagio, cantabile	
Variation I	1:23
Variation II	2:30
Variation III	3:54
Variation IV	5:15

This quartet receives its familiar name from the theme of these variations, which was the Austrian national anthem. The theme was not borrowed, however, for Haydn composed the anthem. The theme is a five-phrase sentence with an a-a-b-c-c design. The plan of the variations is simple. The first violin states the theme, and then it is assigned to a different instrument in each of the four variations, returning in the final one to the first violin. Changes in the harmony and counterpoint maintain interest through the five appearances of the theme melody. A slight extension at the end of the last variation brings the movement to a close.

(Record side 3 band 5. Theme p. 380)

A more flexible type of variation results when the melody of the theme is grouped with the variable elements. The same general plan of the previous example is followed, but the melody is embellished, altered, broken into fragments, and at times all but disappears. The structure and harmonic scheme remain as fixed elements, and the influence of the melody often is sensed even when it cannot be heard and isolated. The key center usually is constant, though changes back and forth between major and minor are common. The variation movement of Beethoven's *Piano Sonata op. 26* falls in the category just described. (Also record side 5 band 1)[1]

1. See fn. p. 16.

L. van Beethoven: *Piano Sonata no. 12 in A-flat, op. 26* (1801)
(1770–1827) 1. Andante con variazioni 7:10

Theme and variations

Theme—Andante	
Variation I—Un poco piu mosso	1:15
Variation II—Piu animato, ma non troppo	2:30
Variation III—Piu sostenuto (minor)	3:30
Variation IV—Con moto	4:30
Variation V	5:35
Coda	6:40

The theme is ternary. The melody is suggested in each of the variations, but it is never restated in its original form. The structure and cadence pattern of the theme are retained in all of the variations. Within phrases the harmonies are sometimes varied, and tempo is another variable element. In the absence of a tempo indication for a variation, the preceding tempo continues.

(Theme p. 380)

In some sectional variations only the structure and broad harmonic outline are constant. Details of harmony are changed, and allusions to the theme melody may be so vague that they go undetected by all but the initiated. The theme serves as a point of departure for almost free composition, but enough of its spirit is preserved to assure the necessary unity. Brahms excelled in writing variations of this type. For him the theme functioned as a fount of inspiration, never as a millstone on his creative imagination.

Johannes Brahms: *Variations on a Theme by Haydn, op. 56a* (1873)
(1833–1897) 17:00

Theme and variations

Theme—Andante	
Variation I—Andante con moto	2:00
Variation II—Vivace (minor)	3:15
Variation III—Con moto	4:10
Variation IV—Andante (minor)	5:50
Variation V—Poco presto	7:45
Variation VI—Vivace	8:35
Variation VII—Grazioso	9:45
Variation VIII—Poco presto (minor)	12:30
Finale—Andante	13:30

This work exists in two structurally identical versions, op. 56a for orchestra and op. 56b for two pianos. The St. Anthony Chorale melody upon which the variations are based is an old hymn of unknown origin. Brahms copied it from the second movement of a *Divertimento in B-flat* for wind instruments by Haydn.

The theme is a ternary form with repeats, giving it an AA BA′ BA′ design. The structure of the theme, including the repeats and the characteristic extension at the end, is retained in all of the variations. The bass line and the melody of the theme figure in the variations, but not in ways that inhibit their striking originality.

The finale is a set of continuous variations (discussed in the second part of this chapter) over a constantly reiterated five-measure motive freely derived from the theme melody. The motive is stated several times in the bass before migrating to the soprano. A final statement in the bass gives way to a triumphant return of the chorale melody and a brief coda, which conclude the work. It is a tribute to Brahms's ingenuity that the repeated motive never becomes obtrusive. On the contrary, it may not even be detected by melody-oriented listeners who do not know about it in advance.

(Theme p. 381)

The ultimate freedom in sectional variation form is displayed when the variations depart from the structure of the theme. In variations of this type the theme serves as a source from which the composer draws thematic material. The variations have at least a subsurface unity by virtue of their common ancestry, but they may be only "kissing cousins" with highly individual personalities. Such is the case in Rachmaninoff's *Rhapsody on a Theme of Paganini*. Though Rachmaninoff calls his work a rhapsody, it is actually a set of very free sectional variations. Since the theme used by Rachmaninoff was taken from a set of variations for solo violin by Paganini, listening to Paganini's variations provides an effective introduction to the longer and more complex Rachmaninoff composition.

NICCOLO PAGANINI: *Caprices, op. 1*
(1782–1840) 24. Theme and variations 4:27

The theme is a one-part form of 16 measures with an a-a-b (4+4+8) design. The form, key, harmonic scheme, meter, and tempo of the theme are retained in all 11 variations; the rhythm and melody are uniquely varied in each. The last variation leads directly into a brief finale which concludes the piece.

(Record side 5 band 1. Theme p. 381)

Free variations like those in Rachmaninoff's *Rhapsody* differ from the strict variations of the preceding examples in several respects. The variations do not necessarily adhere to the form of the theme in either length or design. Contrasting tempos and tonal centers are usual between variations. A derived motive may be the only element linking a variation to the theme, and secondary themes may be introduced. No two sets of free variations are alike, but all of these characteristics are illustrated in Rachmaninoff's *Rhapsody.*

SERGEI RACHMANINOFF: *Rhapsody on a Theme of Paganini, op. 43* (1934)
(1873–1943)

Introduction, theme, 24 variations, and coda 21:45

The rhapsody begins with a short introduction based on a motive from the theme. A skeletal outline of the theme, which perhaps should be regarded as the first variation, follows immediately. The theme proper comes next. Rachmaninoff repeats the last eight measures of Paganini's 16-measure theme, extending it to 24 measures with an a-a-b-b (4+4+8+8) design. Most of the variations are longer than the theme, but a few are shorter. Well-defined cadences separate some variations, some are fused together, while others are linked by cadenza-like passages. The tonic key and minor mode predominate, but other keys, including some major and very remote ones, are explored in variations 12 through 18. Rachmaninoff adds a melody from the Requiem Mass, *Dies Irae* (Day of Wrath), to the original theme in variations 7 and 10 and again in the coda.

Procedures used by Rachmaninoff in his *Rhapsody,* such as using more than one theme, fusing variations, and delaying the statement of the theme, have been used in other recent variations. Liberties such as these have released variation form from confining limitations and preserved it as a viable means of musical expression for contemporary composers and listeners.

Continuous Variations

In contrast to sectional variations, *continuous variations* flow from one into another without interruption. The requirement of continuity influences the choice of fixed elements, or perhaps the other way around, the selection of certain fixed elements is conducive to continuity. In any event, the persistent feature of continuous variations is either a bass line or a scheme of harmonic progressions rather than the melody or structure typical of sectional variations.

A *ground, ground bass,* or *basso ostinato* (literally, obstinate bass) are designations for short melodic phrases repeated over and over in the bass as a foundation for continuous variations. The possibility of transferring the phrase to a part other than the bass is not precluded, but it is exceptional. The finale of Brahms' *Variations on a Theme of Haydn* illustrates the procedures of continuous variation over a ground. Similar procedures are employed in the closing scenes of many early operas, among them the final aria in *Dido and Aeneas,* known variously as *When I Am Laid in Earth, Dido's Farewell, Lament,* and *Thy Hand, Belinda.*

HENRY PURCELL: *Dido and Aeneas,* opera (1689)
(1659–1695) Act III. Lament 4:00

After an introductory recitative a descending chromatic bass line five measures long typical of 17th- and early 18th-century grounds is heard a total of eleven times, first alone and then supporting full harmonies. It accompanies an independent melody in the voice with an AA BB design.

(Record side 2 band 1. Ground p. 381)

Passacaglia and *chaconne* are names for specific types of continuous variation forms. Their origins are shrouded in mystery, and attempts to distinguish between them have not met with success. The themes of both are traditionally in the minor mode, eight measures long, and in triple meter. The theme may be a melody introduced in the bass or a series of harmonies. Bach wrote one of each type. He called the one with a continuously repeated line initially heard in the bass a passacaglia and the one which starts with an eight-measure pattern of chords a chaconne, but this distinction is not always observed by other composers. It is of no great importance, for bass and harmony are closely related. In the period when these two forms developed, a prescribed bass line would exert a strong influence on the chord structures erected above it, and a prescribed harmonic progression would almost determine the choice of bass tones.

As with sectional variations, continuous variations may end with a section which departs from the variation process. Bach's *Passacaglia and Fugue in C minor,* as the title suggests, ends with a fugue.

J. S. BACH: *Passacaglia and Fugue in C minor, S.582* (1705) 13:45
(1685–1750)

The passacaglia begins with the theme by itself. Becoming thoroughly familiar with it is a great help in following the variations. The end of the theme leads directly back to its beginning, and there is no break in the continuity between its twenty varied appearances. The passacaglia reaches a climax, which subsides suddenly for the start of the fugue about two-thirds of the way through the work. The subject of the fugue is the bass theme of the passacaglia with the ending changed. Since the subject is already known, the countersubject enters with the first statement of the subject, unlike most fugues in which the subject is stated initially alone.

(Theme p. 381)

Additional Examples

Sectional Variations

BRAHMS: *Variations on a Theme by Paganini, op. 35*

Brahms wrote two books of *Studies for Piano*, better known by their subtitle given above, based on the same theme as Paganini's *Caprice no. 24* and Rachmaninoff's *Rhapsody on a Theme of Paganini*. Each book consists of 14 strict variations preceded by the theme and followed by a coda. Brahms, like Rachmaninoff, added a repetition of the last eight measures to the original version of the theme. (Theme p. 381)

Continuous Variations

BACH: *Partita no. 2 in D minor for Violin, S.1004*
5. Chaconne

BACH: *Mass in B minor, S.232*
16. Crucifixus (ground bass)

Multimovement Forms

11

The forms considered thus far have been closely knit entities performed, except for the brief pauses between sectional variations, without interruption. The cumulative process continues, and these separate entities are united in more expansive musical projects. The individual units retain their identity, however, for they close with final cadences and in performance are separated by periods of silence. The individual parts of these combined forms are movements. Random associations of movements are conceivable, but the orderly sequences prescribed by convention are the rule.

Complete Sonata Form

The emergence of sonata form proper together with the plan for the complete sonata marked an epoch in the history of music. These interrelated schemes have been the supreme form of musical expression from that day to this. Untold numbers of masterpieces have been spawned in the matrix of the complete sonata form. The durability of this mode of musical organization through the radically changing styles of the last 200 years attests to its adaptability and vitality.

Complete sonata form embraces far more works than those which bear its name. A trio, speaking now of the form and not the medium, is a sonata for three instruments. Likewise, a quartet is a sonata for four instruments; a symphony is a sonata for orchestra; and a concerto is a sonata for a solo instrument with orchestra. These works are variously titled according to the performing medium, but structurally they are all essentially the same.

A complete sonata, regardless of medium, consists basically of three movements with a fast-slow-fast tempo scheme. A fourth movement is often inserted between the slow and fast movements. The first movement is, with rare exceptions, a sonata form, and certain forms are associated by tradition with the other movements.

Movement	*Tempo*	*Form*
First	Fast	Sonata
Second	Slow	Compound ternary, sonata, variation, or rondo
Third (Optional)	Moderate/fast	Compound ternary
Last	Fast	Rondo or sonata

Haydn favored a four-movement plan with a minuet as the third movement. Mozart ordinarily included a minuet in symphonies and quartets but not in sonatas. Beethoven was partial to scherzos, which he included as the third of four movements, but reverted on occasion to the older minuet. Brahms was committed to the four-movement plan, but his third movements usually are without dance or scherzo connotations. There are, of course, many exceptions to the basic plans. One, which is fairly common when the first movement tends toward the slow side, is to reverse the order of the second and third movements, placing a faster rather than a slower movement after the opening movement.

A sonata, a quartet, a symphony, and a concerto will illustrate various types of complete sonata form as written for the different mediums by composers of widely separated periods.

W. A. Mozart: *Piano Sonata no. 17 in D, K.576* (1789)
(1756–1791)

1. Allegro—sonata form 4:45
2. Adagio—compound ternary form 5:25
3. Allegretto—rondo form 4:10

The pattern of tempos and forms is typical for three-movement complete sonatas, but the internal structure of the first and third movements is somewhat irregular. The first two themes of the first movement begin with the same motive, and the order of the second and third themes is reversed in the recapitulation. The third movement structure is like a seven-part rondo with the second return of the rondo theme suppressed, a modification of rondo form used by Mozart in other works. The thematic design is A B A C B′ A. The same motive is prominent in each of the three themes, producing a highly integrated movement.

Joseph Haydn: *String Quartet in D minor, op. 76 no. 2* (1798)
(1732–1809)

1. Allegro—sonata form 4:40
2. Andante o piu tosto allegretto—compound ternary form 5:00
3. Menuetto: Allegro ma non troppo—compound ternary form 3:05
4. Finale: Vivace assai—sonata form 3:45

The nickname of this quartet, "Quinten," comes from the interval of a fifth which is prominent in the themes of the first movement. The quartet as a whole follows closely the traditional plan of complete sonata forms with four movements. In the second movement the third part is elaborately embellished in the manner of a variation rather than a literal return of the first part. The menuetto was cited previously as an example of canon.

Serge Prokofiev: *Classical Symphony in D, op. 25* (1917)
(1891–1953)

1. Allegro con brio—sonata form 3:30
2. Larghetto—rondo form, five parts 3:30
3. Gavotte: Non troppo allegro—ternary 1:30
4. Finale: Molto vivace—sonata form 4:10

Those who think of a symphony as something ponderous and formidable will be surprised by the sprightly character of this one. Though adhering to classic form, as the title indicates, this work is not without its 20th-century flavor. The gavotte is substituted for the more usual minuet or scherzo, but otherwise the structural concept is very close to that of Mozart or Haydn.

(Also record side 3 bands 1–4)[1]

Bela Bartok: *Piano Concerto no. 3* (1945)
(1881–1945)

1. Allegretto—sonata form 6:10
2. Adagio religioso—compound ternary form 8:05
3. Allegro vivace—rondo form, five parts.* 7:20

The three-movement plan is usual in concertos. The first movement sonata form of this one has but a single exposition, and thus adheres more closely to the structural plan of a classic symphony than a classic concerto. The third movement follows the second immediately without any pause, which is not unusual in concertos.

*(Record side 7 band 1)

Cyclic Form

The movements of a complete sonata form have a certain underlying unity of style as a natural consequence of having been written by the

1. See fn. p. 16.

Antonin Dvorak

same composer, but the only organic unifying element consistently present between movements of classic complete sonatas is that of key. The first movement is in the tonic key, the key indicated in the title, as are the third and fourth movements. The second (slow) movement normally is in a different but closely related key. Some composers have felt the need for stronger bonds between movements, for integrating devices beyond a plan of tempos, forms, and keys. This motivation led to the use of common material in the various movements. The shared material may be only a motive which appears in more than one movement, or a common body of themes and motives may permeate all of the movements. The purpose is to achieve a higher degree of unity in multimovement compositions. Works in which the same thematic material is used in more than one movement are *cyclic*. Cyclic form is not a plan of organization but a principle that is used in conjunction with other forms. Dvorak employs the cyclic principle effectively in the complete sonata form of his *New World Symphony*, formerly known as no. 5 but listed as no. 9 in his complete works.

Antonin Dvorak: *Symphony no. 9 (5) in E minor, op. 95* (1893)
(1841–1904)

1. Adagio, Allegro molto—sonata form 9:35
2. Largo—compound ternary form 10:20
3. Scherzo: Molto vivace—rondo form, seven parts 7:20
4. Allegro con fuoco—sonata form 10:40

The structures of the individual movements are fairly regular. Common material shared by the movements is in addition to the normal complement of distinctive themes. A *motto theme,* which occurs in each of the four movements, is first heard in the opening adagio played by the low strings. Its contour and rhythm are easily recognized and remembered. The melodic line ascends by leaps in notes of unequal value to a high point, then abruptly descends to or near the starting pitch. (Motto theme p. 381)

The motto theme, faster and somewhat modified from the version in the introduction, becomes the principal theme of the first movement proper and as such figures prominently in the movement.

In the second movement the motto theme is sounded by the trumpets and trombones in an episode which functions as a transition leading to the return of the opening material of the compound ternary form and a partial restatement of the famous "Going Home" melody by the English horn.

The form of the third movement borrows features from rondo and compound ternary forms. It has an A B A C A B A design like a seven-part rondo, but the A B A at the end is written as a *da capo* like a scherzo-trio-scherzo. The motto theme makes fleeting entrances in two of the transitions and appears again in the coda, principally in the French horns.

Thematic elements from all three preceding movements are recalled in the fourth movement, both in the development section and in the coda. The themes of all four movements are combined in a sort of recapitulation of the entire symphony. In addition to the obvious recurrences of the motto theme and the general summing up at the end, similarities of rhythm and contour can be traced between several of the thematic ideas in the four movements. All of this adds up to a highly integrated multimovement work and a convincing argument for the values of cyclic form.

Suite

The *suite* as it crystallized during the baroque period was an important instrumental form consisting of a series of movements, all in the same key. Most movements bear the name of a dance from which they derive a characteristic style and rhythm. The number and order of the dances vary, but one pattern is more prevalent than any other. It consists of the four following dances in order:

Allemande—A dance of German origin with four-beat measures in a moderate tempo, running figures and short upbeats typical, style serious but not ponderous.

Courante—A quick dance frequently paired with an allemande even before both were incorporated in suites; basic three-beat rhythmic pattern sometimes obscured by shifting accents; differing French and Italian versions produce a variety of styles.

Sarabande—A dignified dance in a slow triple meter in which the second beat may be stressed, spread from Spain across Europe but may have originated in the Orient or the New World.

Gigue—A lively dance which originated in the British Isles, six (or a multiple of three) beats in measures often containing long-short rhythmic patterns.

These four dances are standard in baroque suites. Between the sarabande and the gigue one or more optional dances is usually inserted. A prelude or overture may precede the dances, and a nondance movement occasionally is included in the optional group. The form of all the dances typically is binary. The following suite contains the standard dances in their normal order and a typical selection of optional dances.

J. S. BACH: *French Suite no. 6 in E, S.817* (1723)

(1685–1750)	1. Allemande		3:00
	2. Courante		1:45
	3. Sarabande		3:45
	4. Gavotte	optional group	1:25
	5. Polonaise	optional group	1:40
	6. Bourrée	optional group	1:55
	7. Menuet	optional group	1:30
	8. Gigue		2:30

The dances of baroque suites were of international origin. The spelling of the names varied from country to country, and even within a country the spellings were not consistent. Minor discrepancies in spelling and style aside, the same dances were known and accepted throughout England and the Continent.

The obsolescence of the baroque dances brought an end to the suite as conceived by composers of that period, but the name continued as a designation for any collection of movements not classified as a symphony or a complete sonata. Suites often are drawn from stage and dramatic works. Tchaikovsky's *Nutcracker Suite,* arranged from the music of the ballet, is typical.

P. I. Tchaikovsky: *Nutcracker Suite, op. 71a* (1892)
(1840–1893)

1.	Overture Miniature	3:10
2.	Characteristic Dances	
	a. March	2:40
	b. Dance of the Sugarplum Fairy	1:45
	c. Russian Dance (Trepak)*	1:00
	d. Arabian Dance	3:50
	e. Chinese Dance	1:00
	f. Dance of the Toy Flutes	2:10
3.	Waltz of the Flowers	6:25

*(Record side 6 band 2. Themes p. 375)

The following 20th-century suite is excerpted from an opera.

Zoltan Kodaly: *Hary Janos Suite* (1926)
(1882–1967)

1.	Prelude: The Fairy Tale Begins	3:10
2.	Viennese Musical Clock	2:10
3.	Song	5:10
4.	The Battle and Defeat of Napoleon	3:45
5.	Intermezzo (Czardas)	4:25
6.	Entrance of the Emperor and his Court	2:55

Suites of this sort do not have any fixed plan. They customarily are arranged by the composer with due consideration for the requirements of balance and variety in style and tempo. Modern suites, unlike those of the baroque era, have changes of tonality between movements. Movements derived from more inclusive works, such as ballets and operas, are assured a certain underlying unity by their common source. Composers are impelled to make excerpts for concert performance and recording, because problems of presenting the original versions relegate them, whatever their merits, to the list of works infrequently performed. *Hary Janos* is a case in point. The suite is one of Kodaly's most popular works, yet the opera is rarely staged outside of Hungary. Language, casting, and staging, formidable barriers to the performance of the opera, are no problem in the suite.

Autogenous suites are also written. Like complete sonatas, they are independent multimovement works, but they are inclined to differ from the sonata type in several respects. They generally are less profound in character, depart from the prescribed forms and movements in both style and number, and sometimes they have literary or pictorial connotations. Suites, since the time of Bach, have not been sufficiently homogeneous to yield to further generalizing regarding either style or content. Milhaud's *Scaramouche* is an example of a multimovement work specifically conceived as a suite.

Darius Milhaud: *Scaramouche Suite, op. 165b* (1937)
(1882–1974)

1.	Vif	2:40
2.	Modéré	3:20
3.	Brazileira: Tempo of a Samba	2:10

Several other terms have been applied to suite-like compositions. Terms like *divertimento, partita, serenade,* and *cassation* are sometimes almost synonymous with suite, but sometimes have special implications. Divertimentos usually consist of several short movements and are written for instrumental combinations smaller than full orchestra. A partita originally was a set of variations, but in the 17th and 18th centuries the term came to be used interchangeably with suite. Serenade and cassation are names which suggest performance out-of-doors. Many works besides those with suite or one of the alternate terms in the title fall in this general category. Most multimovement instrumental compositions which are not complete sonatas can be called suites according to current usage.

Additional Examples

Complete Sonata

Beethoven: *Symphony no. 8 in F, op. 93*
Franck: *Symphony in D minor* (Cyclic)
Violin Sonata in A (Cyclic)

Suite

Milhaud: *Suite Française* (Band)
Sessions: *Black Maskers* (Suite from incidental music for the play)
Mozart: *Cassation no. 2 in B-flat, K.99*
Divertimento no. 11 in D, K.251
Serenade in G, K.525, "Eine Kleine Nachtmusik"

Free and Miscellaneous Forms

12

The homophonic, polyphonic, variation, and multimovement forms considered thus far encompass the most prevalent plans of organization in instrumental music. There remain, however, a few additional instrumental forms sufficiently common and standard to warrant attention. Terms which are more properly designations of style and medium but which are used to denote works of special types also are considered in this chapter.

Overture

The term *overture* originally was applied to the instrumental introductions to operas, oratorios, ballets, plays, and the like. Such overtures often are included on concert programs detached from the complete work. The meaning of the term has been extended to include the first movement of suite-type compositions and independent, one-movement compositions for both orchestra and band.

The earliest overtures consisted of two or three sections in contrasting tempos. The sectional concept with changes of tempo persists only in the concert (i.e., independent) overtures written for high school bands. Few of this type remain in the orchestral repertory. They were superseded by two types reflecting subsequent developments. The first embodied the structural principles of sonata form, and the second joined together in a medley tunes selected from the ensuing work.

Overtures in sonata form have the advantage of a highly developed plan of organization, especially important in concert performances. The form does not preclude the possibility of using thematic ideas from the body of the work or of foreshadowing the mood and action of the subsequent drama. The overture to Mozart's opera *The Magic Flute* incorporates these features in its sonata form and is equally effective as a prelude to the opera and as a concert piece.

W. A. MOZART: *The Magic Flute, K.620* (1791)
(1756–1791) Overture 8:00

Composers of the Mozart-Beethoven period were partial to sonata form in their overtures.

In the 19th century the other type of overture, which is simply a potpourri of melodies from an opera or similar work, emerged. A potpourri overture affords the operagoer a preview of the tunes which are to follow and gives the concertgoer an abridged version of the opera's thematic content. An overture of this type is essentially lacking in unity, because it consists of a series of unrelated melodies isolated from their dramatic context and loosely held together by transitional passages. Its melodies, culled from the best of the complete work, are the source of its strength. Medleys serve as overtures for many French and Italian operas and for most Broadway musicals. The overture to *My Fair Lady* is representative of the type.

FREDERICK LOEWE: *My Fair Lady* (1956)
(1904–) Overture 3:10

> This overture is made up from the melodies of three songs plus a motive from a fourth. A brief introduction captures the listener's attention before the theme of *You Did It* is heard. *On the Street Where You Live,* and *I Could Have Danced All Night* follow, with only a perfunctory transition between them. A motive from *Show Me* serves as a coda to the overture and leads directly into the opening song, *Why Can't The English,* sung by Professor Henry Higgins.

The rock opera *Jesus Christ Superstar* begins with a more recent and less typical potpourri overture.

ANDREW LLOYD WEBBER: *Jesus Christ Superstar* (1970)
(1948–) Overture 3:59

> This overture is virtually an instrumental condensation of three scenes near the end of the opera—*Trial before Pilate, Superstar,* and *The Crucifixion.* It is more a series of motives and fragments than a succession of melodies, but it introduces thematic elements which are prominent in the body of the work and which contribute significantly to the opera's overall unity.

Concert overtures for orchestra generally follow the plan of sonata form. They provide composers with a substantial vehicle less extensive than the symphony, and on concert programs they serve a very practical purpose. Interruptions between movements of major works while latecomers are being seated can be avoided by opening the program with a shorter number. Overtures are ideal in this capacity. They become, in a sense, overtures to the concert. It is customary to provide concert overtures with names, often with pictorial or literary implications as in Mendelssohn's *Fingal's Cave Overture*.

FELIX MENDELSSOHN: *Fingal's Cave Overture, op. 26* (1832) 9:15
(1809–1847)

Mendelssohn conceived the opening of this overture while visiting Fingal's Cave, the largest cave on Staffa, a small uninhabited island of the Hebrides archipelago off the coast of Scotland. The overture is also known as *Hebrides Overture*. Its sonata form did not inhibit the composer's romantic tone painting vividly conveying his impression of the surging sea, the barren coastline with its precipitous basaltic cliffs, and the yawning mouth of the mammoth cave.

Ritornello Form

Ritornello is a form peculiar to the baroque era when texture and tonality were paramount considerations in musical organization. A ritornello form ordinarily has a solo voice, instrument, or combination of instruments that are assigned certain responsibilities in the musical design, the other responsibilities being assigned to the accompanying group. A ritornello form starts with an incisive *ritornello theme* played by the whole ensemble. The solo, voice or instrument(s), enters at the close of the ritornello theme and participates in a passage which ultimately modulates to a new key. The ritornello theme, or a fragment of it, is then stated in the new key. Modulatory passages, called *episodes*, alternate with statements of the ritornello theme in various keys until the last episode modulates back to the tonic key, and a final (usually complete) statement of the ritornello theme in the tonic key completes the form. The number of episodes and keys is flexible, and the basic plan is subjected to many modifications. The last movement of Vivaldi's *Violin Concerto in A minor* is one of the clearer examples of ritornello form. (Also record side 2 band 6)[1]

1. See fn. p. 16.

Antonio Vivaldi: *Violin Concerto in A minor, op. 3 no. 6* (1712)
(1678–1741) 3. Presto 2:40

Ritornello form

Ritornello theme
Tonic key (A minor), orchestra.

Episode
Solo prominent, starts with embellishment of motive from ritornello theme, modulates to dominant key. :30

Ritornello theme
Starts in dominant key (E minor), orchestra with solo interspersed. :55

Episode
Solo prominent, modulates to relative major key. 1:15

Ritornello theme
Fragment in relative major key (C) followed by same fragment in dominant key (E minor), orchestra. 1:40

Episode
Solo prominent, modulates back to tonic key. 2:00

Ritornello theme
Tonic key (A minor), solo and orchestra. 2:05

Coda
Solo and orchestra. 2:30

This concerto, one of twelve known collectively as *L'Estro Armonico* (The Harmonic Whim), is scored for one solo violin, string orchestra, and cembalo (harpsichord). When the solo violinist is not playing an independent part, he joins in with the violins of the orchestra. Though written for one solo instrument, solo and tutti passages alternate in this movement as in a concerto grosso (see next).

(Ritornello theme p. 382)

Concerto Grosso

The distinguishing characteristic of the *concerto grosso* is the medium. A concerto grosso is written for a small group of solo instruments—usually two violins, cello, and a keyboard instrument—and string orchestra. The solo group may be differently constituted, and wind instruments are occasionally included in both the solo group and the orchestra. Contrasting the full sonority of the orchestra with the lighter sound of the solo group is the essential feature of the form.

A concerto grosso normally has at least three movements, usually more. The individual movements may be simple part forms, ritornello form, or fugal. The concerto grosso flourished from the end of the 17th century to the middle of the 18th century, and it has been revived in the

20th century. Corelli was one of its leading exponents, perhaps its originator.

Arcangelo Corelli: *Concerto Grosso, op. 6 no. 8 "Christmas"*

(1653–1713)	1.	Vivace—Grave	1:30
	2.	Allegro	2:00
	3.	Adagio—Allegro—Adagio	3:50
	4.	Vivace	1:10
	5.	Allegro	2:45
	6.	Pastorale: Largo	3:45

This concerto grosso bearing the inscription, "Composed for the night of the Nativity," was published posthumously in 1714. The date of composition is not known. It is for the standard solo group (two violins, cello, and a keyboard instrument) and string orchestra. The contrast between the solo group and the larger body of strings is exploited with special effect in the first and last *allegro* sections and in the *vivace* following the *adagio.*

Prelude

Composers seem to have ignored the literal meaning of the term as often as they have observed it in naming compositions *prelude.* Some have used it literally for the first of two pieces in *preludes and fugues* and for the first movement of suites, while others have written collections of piano pieces all of which are called preludes. The most famous of the former category are the 48 Preludes and Fugues of Bach's *Well-Tempered Clavier.* Notable collections in the latter have been written by Chopin, Shostakovich, Debussy, and Gershwin.

Introductory preludes are apt to be based on a single motive or figure and often make extensive use of scale and arpeggio figures. Bach's *C Major Prelude,* the first of the 48 and probably the best known, utilizes one pattern and a constant rhythm throughout.

J. S. Bach: *The Well-Tempered Clavier, vol. I, S.846* (1722)

(1685–1750)	1.	Prelude in C	2:10

Not much can be said about independent preludes except that they are brief character pieces. They may be in any of the smaller forms, and some are descriptive. The following are representative.

Claude Debussy: *Preludes for Piano, book I* (1910)

(1862–1918)	2.	Voiles (Sails or Veils)	2:57
		(Record side 6 band 5)	

George Gershwin: *Preludes for Piano* (1926)
(1898–1937) No. 1 in B-flat 1:25
(Also record side 5 bands 4–5)

Prelude is also used instead of overture to designate the instrumental introduction to an opera, especially when the form is other than sonata or potpourri. Wagner used the term, or at least its German equivalent (*Vorspiel*), for instrumental introductions that lead directly into the first and sometimes subsequent acts of his music dramas. Special endings are provided for concert performances.

Richard Wagner: *Lohengrin* (1850)
(1813–1883) Act I. Prelude 7:40
Act III. Prelude 2:40

The *chorale prelude* is a special type of composition for organ which developed as an introduction to the singing of the chorale by the congregation in Protestant churches. The form, originally intended for a specific function, has since been used detached from religious services. A chorale prelude is basically an elaboration of the chorale melody, a kind of variation before the theme. In concert performances organists sometimes play the chorale before the prelude, reversing the normal order and placing the prelude in a curious position. This arrangement has the advantage of announcing the theme, which otherwise might be unfamiliar, before the variation.

Several methods of elaboration are employed in chorale preludes. Some are merely enriched settings of the chorale melody, which may be in any voice, and which usually moves slowly against a more animated background. In others the melody itself is embellished. A third procedure is to derive fugue subjects from the chorale, usually one from each phrase, and to use them in a succession of fughettas. Overlapping of methods is not unusual.

J. S. Bach: *Schübler Prelude no. 1, S.645* (1746)
(1685–1750) Wachet auf, ruft uns die Stimme (Sleepers Awake) 4:37

This chorale prelude, the first of a group of six published by Schübler in 1746, is based on a chorale melody by Philipp Nicolai (1556–1608). In this prelude an independent, flowing melody is announced against which the chorale tune is projected a phrase at a time.

(Record side 2 band 5. Chorale melody p. 382)

Though it is unique rather than one of a type, no discussion of preludes is complete without mentioning Debussy's incomparable *Prelude to the Afternoon of a Faun*. Being an independent descriptive work for orchestra, it neither fits the literal meaning of the word nor bears any direct resemblance to traditional prelude types, but it illustrates the latitude with which the term has been used by composers.

CLAUDE DEBUSSY: *Prelude to the Afternoon of a Faun* (1894) 9:00
(1862–1918)

This work was inspired by the poem of the impressionist poet, Stephane Mallarmé. Its content may be summarized. "A faun is lying on the borderland of waking and sleeping in a grove. The atmosphere is palpitating with the golden midday heat. He has seen some slender-limbed, light-footed nymphs flit by; he would perpetuate the lovely vision. But he asks himself, am I in love with a dream? Fully awake, he begins to reflect and analyze, to dissect his sensations and emotions. His thoughts become exaggerated, distorted; his senses predominate. Delicate imagery takes shape in his mind. Had he seen a flight of swans? The current of his ideas becomes more realistic, and he imagines himself under the shadow of Etna with Venus in his arms. While anticipating punishment for such desecration, sleep visits his eyelids once more; he bids adieu to facts and reality and in the shades of oblivion goes in quest of the shadowy, vanished dream."

Rhapsody and Fantasia

Rhapsody and *fantasia* are terms generally applied to freely and often loosely constructed works which follow no prescribed plan of organization. Often they are improvisatory in style, and composers writing them indulge in flights of fancy without the usual regard for conventions of form and style. These procedures are illustrated in the following examples.

FRANZ LISZT: *Hungarian Rhapsody no. 2 in C-sharp minor* (1851) 9:20
(1811–1886)

Liszt's *Hungarian Rhapsodies*, which served to popularize the form, incorporate Hungarian and gypsy elements in several vividly contrasted, tenuously connected sections. Of the nineteen he composed for piano, the second is most famous. It is included as the fourth of the six Liszt arranged for orchestra.

Ralph Vaughan Williams: *Fantasia on a Theme by Tallis* (1910) 15:45
(1872–1958)

This fantasia is based on a theme of the early English composer, Thomas Tallis (1505–1585), but the theme serves only as a point of departure. It is freely molded and expanded without obeisance to preconceived notions of structure, unlike the composer's similarly titled and better known *Fantasia on Greensleeves,* which has a broad ternary design.

There are, of course, many other terms, such as *toccata, impromptu, pastorale, song without words, ballade, nocturne,* dance-inspired names, and a host of others too numerous to mention, which are used as designations for musical works. Toccatas are brilliant, idiomatic works for keyboard instruments and, by extension, for other mediums as well. The other appellations are used for brief character pieces reflecting the mood or style indicated by the title but otherwise without special distinctions.

In addition there are compositions, especially from the romantic and contemporary periods, which do not follow any prescribed plan of organization. This is true in a sense of rhapsodies and fantasias, but works in these categories have enough in common to create a type if not a pattern. Unique design is relatively rare in conventional music, but not unknown or undesirable. Setting a text or depicting a story may provide the impulse for an unusual sequence of musical ideas. Composers in this century have revolted against the conventions of form as well as those of harmony, tonality, and line. Their new musical language has demanded a new syntax. Musical structures are now more than ever before a product of their content, and free forms—those with no standard organizational plan—are the rule rather than the exception.

Free or unique form is not to be confused with lack of form. On the contrary, the most skillfully integrated musical expression may defy classification. Works in which ties with traditional patterns are absent or stretched beyond recognition are grouped together as free forms. Their eccentric nature renders impossible generalization and illustration.

A special kind of free form results when the sequence of events and the precise nature of the events in a musical work are not predetermined by the composer. In such cases the compositional decisions not made by the composer are made by the performers or left to chance and presumably differ in each performance. Leaving some elements of a composition indeterminate in notation and variable in performance has emerged as a major trend in avant-garde music. Works of this genre in which responsibility for the ordering of musical events is delegated to the performers and/or dictated by chance tend to be unique in concept and to have in common only their indeterminacy. Representative indeterminate compositions and procedures are described in Chapter 23.

Additional Examples

Overture

ROSSINI: *William Tell Overture* (opera)
RODGERS: *The King and I Overture* (musical show)
BEETHOVEN: *Egmont Overture, op. 84* (drama)
BARBER: *Overture to the School for Scandal* (drama)
BRAHMS: *Academic Festival Overture, op. 80* (concert)
Tragic Overture, op. 81 (concert)
BERLIOZ: *The Corsair, Overture for Orchestra, op. 21* (concert overture inspired by Byron's narrative poem)

Ritornello Form

HANDEL: *Messiah*
9. O thou that tellest good tidings to Zion
(Record side 2 band 6)

Concerto Grosso

VIVALDI: *L'Estro Armonico, op. 3 no. 11 in D minor*

Prelude

WAGNER: *Prelude to Tristan and Isolde* (opera)
BACH: *Orgelbüchlein Chorale Prelude no. 10, S.608*
In Dulci Jubilo (In Sweet Jubilation)

Rhapsody and Fantasia

ENESCO: *Roumanian Rhapsody no. 1, op. 11*
BRUCH: *Scottish Fantasy for Violin and Orchestra, op. 46*

Program Music

13

Program music is a general classification for music which depicts or is inspired by extramusical ideas, in contradistinction to *absolute music* which is pure music, free of any such influences. Though all music with a text or used in dramatic productions is programmatic in a sense, the designation is commonly used only for instrumental works with literary or pictorial connotations or which imitate the sounds of nature.

The influence of the program on the music ranges from the merest suggestion of a mood to the graphic depiction of specific incidents and scenic details. The crudest examples of program music attempt to generate interest by the realistic portrayal of natural sounds, events, and things. Such exercises may prove that a composer is clever or ingenious, but they rarely transcend the level of short-lived novelties. In contrast with these are the works which pay homage to the programmatic concept with descriptive titles or suggestions of a story but which have their foundations firmly anchored in purely musical values. Form would seem to be the aspect of music most seriously undermined by the requirements of a predetermined program, but this is not necessarily so. Many pieces of program music are in perfectly regular, conventional forms.

The sounds of music are not well suited to conveying concrete visual or dramatic impressions. Not a single idea can be expressed effectively by means of musical sounds alone. The perception of the program underlying a piece of music is dependent in large measure, if not entirely, upon providing the listener with sufficient clues in advance. When descriptive titles are inadequate for the purpose, composers resort to verbal descriptions of what the music is about. Pertinent sections or résumés of literary works are sometimes quoted in scores and reprinted in program notes and on record jackets as an aid to comprehending program music.

The validity of the fundamental precepts of program music is open to question. It is argued that music is incapable of expressing ideas, or at least that it is a poor substitute for words. Proponents of absolute music feel that attaching a program to music robs it of the abstraction which makes it unique among the arts. For this philosophy's adherents music ideally is pure sound stimulating the senses and triggering the emotions directly, and it is most effective when extramusical associations do not intrude.

On the other hand, there is no denying the existence of programmatic musical masterpieces or the popularity of works which tell a story. For many listeners the program serves as a bridge to the realm of music. Its mysteries seem somehow less formidable when a link with tangible reality is provided. There can be no objection to the composer's sharing the source of his inspiration with the listener. However, the practice of inventing stories to go with music when none is intended by the composer is undesirable, even as sugarcoating for music presented to the very young. False values thus established, eventually if not immediately, defeat the avowed purpose of making abstract music more palatable.

The most defensible position with reference to program music is that a program neither assures nor denies the creation and appreciation of admirable music. Descriptive music is not per se either good or bad. A program is no substitute for solid musical value, but the two may exist side by side, as they do in all the best examples of program music.

An undeniable advantage of program music is that its fanciful titles are more easily remembered, even by musicians, than the numbers and keys used to identify absolute music. One wonders if it is coincidental that of Beethoven's 32 piano sonatas, all of the most famous are included in the half-dozen or so associated with names.

The beginnings of tone painting can be traced back to 14th-century vocal music, but in these early examples the music merely illustrates words or ideas occurring more or less simultaneously in the text. One of the first examples of instrumental program music is a fantasia by John Munday (d.1630) in the *Fitzwilliam Virginal Book*. It depicts thunder, lightning, and fair weather. Kuhnau's six *Biblical Sonatas* (1700) are somewhat later and more sophisticated examples of program music for a keyboard instrument. The meaning of each movement is described explicitly in the score. Kuhnau must have anticipated opposition to his ideas, for he explained and defended his approach in a preface to the sonatas. Couperin carried the programmatic concept a step further and correlated his musical ideas with both human attributes and colors.

François Couperin: *Les Folies Françoises* (1722) 10:20
(1668–1733) (*Follies of the French*)

1.	Virginity—invisible	
2.	Modesty—red	:40
3.	Ardor—scarlet	1:20
4.	Hope—green	2:10
5.	Loyalty—blue	2:55
6.	Perseverance—flaxen gray	4:10
7.	Languor—violet	4:50
8.	Coquetry—various colors	6:05
9.	Aged gallants—purple	6:35
10.	Benevolent cuckoos—yellow	7:30
11.	Jealousy—dark gray	8:20
12.	Frenzy or despair—black	9:35

Title and color designations notwithstanding, this is a series of variations on a harmonic-bass theme. Virginity is the theme, and each following attribute is a variation. The similarity of the variations to each other and to the theme is especially apparent in the cadences which separate them. The variation form and the program are not only compatible, but complementary. (Recording: Serenus 12054)

Program music occupied an insignificant place in the music of the classic era, but with the rise of romanticism in the 19th century it assumed a position of importance and for a time challenged the supremacy of absolute music. Music of every dimension from miniatures to immensities and for every medium from one instrument to full orchestra would be embraced by a catalog of romantic program music. The suggested listening barely hints at its magnitude and scope. Mussorgsky's *Pictures at an Exhibition* is a piece of 19th-century program music in the tradition of Kuhnau and Couperin, but with some added touches.

Modest Mussorgsky: *Pictures at an Exhibition* (1874) 29:30
(1839–1881)

Promenade (theme p. 382)

Depicts the viewer (Mussorgsky) as he moves between pictures in the art gallery; theme provides a connecting and unifying element between sections, and appears in the finale.

The Gnome 1:30

A misshapen, comical figure supposedly fashioned as a Christmas tree ornament.

Promenade 4:00

The Old Castle 4:50

A troubadour sings his lay before a medieval castle.

Promenade 8:30
Tuileries 9:00
The famous gardens with children and their nurses.
Bydlo 10:10
A two-wheeled ox-drawn cart lumbering across the fields.
Promenade 12:50
Ballet of the Unhatched Chicks 13:25
Dancers costumed as chicks emerging from their shells.
Samuel Goldberg and Schmyle 14:45
A dialogue between a rich Jew and a poor one.
The Market Place at Limoges 17:00
Women wrangling furiously.
The Catacombs 18:20
The artist exploring the catacombs of Paris by lantern light.
Baba-Yaga 21:55
A grotesque clock representing the house of Baba-Yaga, a witch character of Russian folklore.
The Great Gate of Kiev 25:20
Hartmann's design for a triumphal arch through which passes a pageant of Russian history.

A posthumous exhibition of paintings by Mussorgsky's friend, Victor Hartmann, included the ten canvasses which inspired this composition. It was composed for piano but is better known in transcriptions for orchestra. The recurrent promenade theme serves as an overall unifying element. The other parts have independent themes and their own internal structures.

The sounds of nature are still heard—sometimes subtly, sometimes humorously—in 19th-century program music. Animal and bird sounds are imitated by instruments in *The Carnival of the Animals.* These are served up with parodies of borrowed melodies and engaging original tunes to make musical fare which is certain to entertain children and amuse adults. Ironically, Saint-Saens regarded this, his most popular work, as such a trifle that he did not allow it to be published or publicly performed during his lifetime.

C. SAINT-SAENS: *The Carnival of the Animals* (1886) 21:00
(1835–1921)

1. Introduction and Royal March of the Lion
2. Hens and Cocks 1:55
3. Fleet-footed Animals (Hemiones) 2:40
4. Tortoises 3:20
5. The Elephant 5:00
6. Kangaroos 6:30
7. Aquarium 7:20
8. Personages with Long Ears 9:40

9.	Cuckoo in the Woods	10:15
10.	Aviary	12:30
11.	Pianists	13:45
12.	Fossils	14:55
13.	The Swan	16:10
14.	Finale	19:00

Borrowed melodies are heard in Sections 4, 5, 11, and 12. "Tortoises" begins with the cancan melody from Offenbach's *Orpheus in Hades* and ends with a few measures from Act I of the same opera. "The Elephant" has a parody of the "Dance of the Sylphs" from *The Damnation of Faust* by Berlioz and a hint of the *Midsummer Night's Dream* "Scherzo" by Mendelssohn. Exercises à la Czerny are practiced in "Pianists." The themes of "Fossils" are from Saint-Saens' *Danse Macabre* and Rossini's *Barber of Seville*, with added bits from the French folk songs *J'ai du bon Tabac, Ah! Vous dirai-je Maman,* and *Partant pour la Syrie*. Material from previous sections is recalled in the finale.

The *symphonic poem* or *tone poem* is an important type of 19th-century program music. A symphonic or tone poem is a large-scale, single-movement, programmatic work for orchestra. The concept is attributed to Franz Liszt (1811–1886), who composed twelve works in the form (see p. 275). His innovation was enthusiastically received and widely imitated. The symphonic poem ranks as the most characteristic expression of the romantic impulse in instrumental music.

Goethe's ballad *The Sorcerer's Apprentice* is such a natural subject for a symphonic poem that someone was bound to use it. Dukas did, and it is difficult to decide whether the music or the story contributes most to the success of the piece, not that it matters. The details of the story are graphically portrayed without sacrificing musical values in this inimitable tone painting.

PAUL DUKAS: *The Sorcerer's Apprentice* (1897) 8:45
(1865–1935)

This work tells in tones the story of an apprentice sorcerer who, in his master's absence, repeats a magic formula he has overheard which enables him to bring a broomstick to life. He commands it to carry water from the well, and it obeys perfectly until the task is completed. Then the apprentice discovers that he does not know the formula to stop it. The broomstick carries bucket after bucket of water until the room is overflowing. In desperation the apprentice chops it in two, and to his dismay both halves carry water faster than ever. At last the sorcerer returns, pronounces the magic words, and restores order.

Multimovement counterparts of the symphonic poem are the *program symphony* and the *program suite.* Because of the less rigid application of structural principles in program music generally, distinctions between program symphonies and suites are not so well defined as between absolute symphonies and suites. Evidence of the closer relationship between program symphonies and suites is manifest by the addition of movements beyond the normal four in some program symphonies. Berlioz's *Symphonie Fantastique,* with five movements, is deservedly one of the most celebrated.

HECTOR BERLIOZ: *Symphonie Fantastique, op. 14* (1831)
(1803–1869)

1.	Dreams and Passions: Largo—Allegro agitato e appasionata assai	12:50
2.	A Ball (Waltz): Allegro non troppo	5:40
3.	Scenes in the Country: Adagio	15:30
4.	March to the Scaffold: Allegretto non troppo	5:00
5.	A Witches' Sabbath: Larghetto—Allegro	9:10

Berlioz himself outlined the story of the symphony in a preface to the work:

> A young, morbid, ardent musician in a state of amorous despair poisons himself with opium. The dose, insufficient to kill him, plunges him into a delirious sleep during which his sensations take the form of musical ideas in his sick brain. His beloved becomes a melody, an *Idée Fixe* (fixed idea) which he hears everywhere. (*Idée Fixe* p. 383)
>
> Dreams and Passions. He at first recalls the vague melancholy and joy which alternated without apparent reason before he met his beloved; then the volcanic passion with which she inspired him, his jealous fury, his return to tenderness and religious consolation.
>
> A Ball. He finds his beloved waltzing in the tumult of a brilliant fete.
>
> Scenes in the Country. On a summer evening in the country he listens to two shepherds playing a pastoral duet to summon their flocks. The rustic scene, the gentle rustling of the trees in the breeze, hopeful prospects he has recently entertained, all combine to produce an unaccustomed calm but with a bitter tinge. The beloved returns again . . . his heart throbs . . . he is disturbed by forebodings that she might deceive him . . . one of the shepherds resumes his naive melody . . . the other no longer answers . . . the sun sets . . . in the distance thunder rumbles . . . solitude . . . silence . . .

> March to the Scaffold. He dreams he has killed his beloved, that he has been condemned to death and is being led to the scaffold. The procession advances to the sound of a march now sombre, now wild, now brilliant, now solemn. Loud outbursts are followed without pause by the plodding sounds of marching feet. The *Idée Fixe* appears for a moment like a last thought of love cut short by the fatal blow of the guillotine.
>
> Witches' Sabbath. He finds himself at a witches' revel in the midst of a horrible group of spectres who have come to attend his funeral. Strange noises are heard—groans, bursts of laughter, distant shrieks to which other shrieks seem to reply. The melody of the beloved appears once more but transformed from its character of nobility and gentleness to a common, grotesque dance tune. Howls of joy accompany her arrival and participation in the diabolic orgy . . . funeral bells . . . parody on the *Dies Irae* . . . witches' dance . . . witches' dance and the *Dies Irae* together.

Berlioz departs from the traditional sequence of movements in this symphony, but his procedures are not unrelated to convention. He substitutes a waltz and a march for a minuet or scherzo, but this is a logical extension of the basic concept. A minuet or corresponding movement usually follows the slow movement, but sometimes preceeds it. Berlioz places the one before and the other after. This provides an ideal balance with the slow movement, longest of the five, flanked on each side by a shorter movement in a relatively moderate tempo. The first and last movements correspond both in tempo and duration. In spite of the program, Berlioz abandons typical structural patterns only in the last movement. The first movement is a sonata form. The second, third, and fourth movements have compound ternary designs. The final movement has a free sectional structure of four large parts.

The appearance of the *Idée Fixe* in each movement provides a cyclic element. It is announced after the slow introduction of the first movement by the violins and flutes in the prevailing fast tempo of the movement. It is the principal theme of the sonata form. In the second movement this theme appears, rhythmically transformed, in the middle section of the waltz played first by flute and oboe and then by flute and clarinet. The *Idée Fixe* in a different rhythmic transformation serves as an answering phrase in flute and oboe in the middle section of the third movement and enters briefly at the end. The hero's memory of his beloved is recalled by her theme just before the end of the fourth movement. The *Idée Fixe* completely transformed into a derisive and sarcastic dance tune by grace notes and trills immediately follows the opening Larghetto section in the final movement. Thus the *Idée Fixe* provides a cyclic as well as a programmatic element.

With the decline of romanticism the appeal of program music waned for composers but not for listeners. Many of the staple items in the current repertoire and some of the most widely accepted and appreciated compositions of all time were products of program music's heyday during the last century.

Additional Examples

Program Music

BEETHOVEN: *Symphony no. 6 in F, op. 68, "Pastoral"*

DEBUSSY: *Preludes for Piano, book I*
2. Voiles (Sails or Veils)
(Record side 6 band 5)

ELLINGTON: *Harlem Air Shaft*
(In the *Smithsonian Collection of Classic Jazz*)

HINDEMITH: *Mathis der Maler (Matthias the Painter)*
2. Grablegung (Entombment)
(Record side 8 band 5)

HONEGGER: *Pacific 231*
(Available on disc recordings and also as the sound track of a Young America Film showing the locomotive from which the work takes its name and giving a visual interpretation of the music.)

IVES: *Three Places in New England*
2. Putnam's Camp, Redding, Connecticut
(Record side 6 band 6)

RIMSKY-KORSAKOV: *Scheherazade, op. 35, Symphonic Suite after the Thousand and One Nights*

SMETANA: *Ma Vlast (My Fatherland)*
2. The Moldau

STRAUSS: *Till Eulenspiegel's Merry Pranks, op. 28* (see p. 280)

Dramatic Music

14

Dramatic music is the general classification for music associated with stage presentations and their more recent counterparts, motion pictures and television. Dramatic music is the type least successfully captured in recordings. The visual aspect of a dramatic presentation vies with the aural in actual performance, and a serious void is created by its absence. The full impact of a live production can never be matched by the pale image of the sound alone. The appreciation of dramatic music is immensely stimulated by the experience of seeing and hearing an actual performance. The appeal of the theater is age-old and universal. The combined attraction of beauty in sound, line, color, and motion is irresistible. Of these elements, which are real and abundant on the stage, all but the sound must be supplied by the imagination in recorded performances.

Opera

Broadly defined, *opera* is sung drama, with all the adjuncts of staging, accompanied by orchestra. An opera is a play set to music. Many are based on successful plays. The definition of opera attributed to Saint-Evremonde as "a bizarre affair of poetry and music in which the poet and the musician, each equally obstructed by the other, give themselves no end of trouble to produce a wretched result" probably would find some support even today. Actually, a musical setting endows a drama with special qualities and imposes on it certain limitations. The amalgamation of music and drama is not accomplished without compromises. The success of the union depends somewhat upon the skill of the practitioners and somewhat upon the point of view. If an undue portion of the American public reacts negatively to opera, misunderstanding of what opera is must share the blame with the poor rapport between typical opera and current taste. A survey of the operatic scene should allay misconceptions about its aims and purposes. Recent endeavors both in the creation and production of opera have progressed toward bringing it in line with the requirements of present-day entertainment.

Enjoyment is contingent upon accepting opera as a highly artificial art form. It is not natural to burst into song under the impact of emotional stress or to hit a high C with one's dying breath, but these are conventions the operagoer must be prepared to accept. Opera is remote from reality, but realism in any art is only relative. Though opera is one of the least realistic, this is not a debilitating admission. Frames around landscape paintings and rhymes in play dialogue are equally artificial but widely accepted conventions.

The particular conventions of opera have a long history. The association of music with drama dates back to the ancient Greeks. Their musical achievements were not handed down, but in attempting to revive Greek tragedy, a group of Florentine noblemen known as the *Camerata* laid the foundations of modern opera just before 1600. This group, conforming to their concept of Greek drama, evolved a musical style which consisted of vocal declamation with careful attention to the natural rhythm, accent, and inflection of the text. This vocal declamation, a sort of intensified speech, was carried out over a simple, instrumental harmonic background. The concept was revolutionary in its time, and though its influence on the course of music was immense, the limitations of melodies inseparably bound to natural speech were apparent as soon as the novelty wore off. The advantages of this style were that the text could be understood and that the action progressed almost as fast as in spoken drama. Subsequent attempts to enhance the musical value with more appealing melodies and more expressive harmonies invariably sacrificed these virtues.

From the beginning of opera, scenes occasionally closed with metric songs and choruses and with dancing. These features became increasingly prominent as opera developed. Soon there were distinct sections. *Recitatives* (see p. 246) in declamatory style were followed by lyric and metric *arias*. Meanwhile the size and importance of the orchestra were expanded to provide overtures and interludes in addition to accompaniments. The relative emphasis on the various aspects of opera differed widely with the region and the period.

Arias, ballets, choruses, and instrumental interludes contributed musical interest to the spectacle at the expense of the drama. The plot, often reduced to the barest thread, was stationary during these episodes and progressed only in the recitatives. The portions between recitatives, uninhibited by dramatic requirements, developed into closed forms structurally complete in and of themselves. This facilitated not only detaching the numbers from the opera but also exchanging them between operas. In the absence of copyright restrictions, unauthorized borrowing of whole sections was a flagrant practice which reached its ridiculous conclusion in the *pasticcio* (Italian for pie or pastry). These entertainments consisted simply of an uninterrupted succession of favorite operatic selections without regard for the source or sequence.

The demand by singers and audiences alike for vocal display vehicles also detracted from the dramatic possibilities of opera. Star singers demanded roles exploiting their capacity for vocal pyrotechnics and stopped the show to acknowledge applause after each brilliant number. A succession of reformers raised their voices and pens against the forces inimical to the dramatic element in opera, but abuses persist in varying degrees throughout most of the operatic literature. In spite of certain inherent limitations, genuine masterpieces were conceived within the framework of the *numbers opera,* that is, an opera consisting of a series of numbers—recitatives, arias, ensembles, choruses, ballets, and instrumental interludes. As a composer of numbers operas Mozart has no peer, and *The Marriage of Figaro* is an attractive introduction to the type, especially if it can be heard in the new English translation.

Richard Wagner (1813–1883) revolted against traditional opera and fused music and drama in a new relationship which he called *music drama.* The Wagnerian concept of music drama as a transcendental art form required the subjugation of the constituent arts and some negation of their special properties. He composed the music to his own librettos and regarded them as complementary equals in the finished product. There are no divisions or interruptions within scenes of his music dramas. Melodies are continuous and, in a conventional sense, formless. The orchestra participates, almost competes, in the drama, underlining not only the vocal melodies but the emotions and actions as well. Musical motives, called *leitmotivs* in music drama, are associated with particular characters, objects, emotions, or ideas. Leitmotivs, varied and transformed in response to changing dramatic situations on stage, often explain and reinforce the mood and action of the drama in addition to serving as unifying elements. The leitmotiv concept was one of Wagner's outstanding contributions to music, and he was an innovator in the realms of harmony and orchestration as well. Wagner's ideas are most fully realized in the four monumental music dramas comprising *The Ring of the Nibelung,* but as an initiation to his dramatic music *Die Meistersinger von Nürnberg* is recommended.

Richard Wagner

In Wagner's music dramas there are no interruptions between numbers or musically sterile recitatives as there were in earlier operas, but his approach left many of the problems of opera as an art form unsolved for those not completely sold on the idea of music drama as the successor to traditional opera. For many opera buffs the separate numbers in which musical interest is concentrated are the reason for an opera's existence, and music dramas do not have them. The plot of Wagner's music dramas unfolds continuously, but at a snail's pace, and his preoccupation with mythical subjects, which he regarded as the proper province of music drama, is out of vogue. Though Wagner's music dramas are performed regularly in the major opera houses of the world, no other composer has wholeheartedly adopted his philosophy, and no other work conceived along similar lines has achieved notable success. Richard Strauss (1864–1949) perpetuated and developed a style and technique inherited from Wagner but without subscribing to all tenets of Wagner's artistic credo.

During the time Wagner was formulating the principles of music drama, Giuseppe Verdi (1813–1901) was composing more conventional operas with melodramatic plots and separate numbers but at the same time striving for unity between the music and drama, elimination of extraneous elements, vivid characterization, and effective dramatization. His success in achieving these aims and his apparently inexhaustible supply of captivating melodies have established his operas as interna-

GIUSEPPE VERDI

tional favorites. Of the nineteen that can be heard on recordings, *Aida* and *Rigoletto* are perhaps the best known, with *La Traviata* and *Il Trovatore* not far behind.

Verdi's successor and the composer in whose operas many find the ideal fusion of music and drama is Giacomo Puccini (1858–1924). His operas, in relation to those of Verdi, are characterized by greater continuity and more emphasis upon the realistic treatment of contemporary subjects. *Madame Butterfly, La Bohème,* and *Tosca* are representative of his stellar achievements as a composer of operas.

Georges Bizet (1838–1875) by virtue of one fantastically successful work, *Carmen,* must also be listed with the opera composers of first rank. Ruggero Leoncavallo (1858–1919) and Pietro Mascagni (1863–1945) likewise achieved fame on the basis of one operatic work, *Pagliacci* and *Cavalleria Rusticana* respectively. Omitting a host of less distinguished opera composers, this brings us to the present century.

Since opera combines the most attractive elements of stage entertainment—music, drama, and dancing—why is it not the most appealing form of art? An important reason is that each of the arts sacrifices something when combined with the others. Music tied to a text and the human voice lacks the freedom of absolute instrumental music, and an orchestra supporting singers from the pit lacks the power and eloquence of an unencumbered symphony. The slow pace of singing as compared to

Giacomo Puccini

speaking causes the drama to suffer as does the difficulty of understanding words in song. Dancing in opera adds color and variety but does so at the expense of the drama except when carefully integrated. Anyone expecting to find in full measure all the attributes of a concert, a play, and a ballet in an opera is certain to be disappointed. Opera, to be properly enjoyed, must be accepted as a distinct medium separate and apart from its components.

Accepting opera on its own terms still leaves several unsolved problems. Opera is expensive to produce, and opera companies must be subsidized or charge exorbitant prices for admission. Government subsidy is the usual solution in Europe. The absence of official public support restricts full-fledged professional opera in the United States to a few metropolitan areas and severely limits the number of people who have regular access to live opera. This lends a certain snob appeal but in the long run augurs against true popularity.

The biggest barrier to the widespread popularity of opera, however, is language. This country, more than most, is monolingual, yet the custom of singing opera in other languages is general. Only a dedicated music lover finds satisfaction in an opera without understanding its language, and a school-book knowledge is insufficient for comprehension of a text sung in a foreign tongue.

The present status and outlook for opera in this country is by no means as dismal as a survey of its problems suggests. Securing for opera its rightful place in the hierarchy of the arts is a formidable but not an

Georges Bizet

insurmountable task. The omens are favorable for a brighter future for opera in America.

In the first place there is a growing tendency to perform opera in English. Excellent translations of several standard works issued recently reflect this trend. Translation is perhaps a makeshift, but it cannot fail to attract new devotees. Opera in English is suitable fare for radio and television, and the sparse but laudable offerings of opera on television have attracted favorable attention. Television also solves the problem of cost, at least for the individual viewer.

The most significant new development in the field of opera, however, is the surge of interest by college and university music departments. There are now more than 900 groups, amateur and professional, performing opera in the United States. Areas which never could support a professional company now are offered high calibre collegiate performances while increasing numbers of talented students are gaining invaluable training and experience. Grass roots opera played before relatively unsophisticated audiences by young performers has special requirements. In response to this demand a virtually new concept of opera is emerging.

Operas are being composed to English texts with plots designed to appeal to contemporary audiences. Extraneous elements are eliminated and the dimensions scaled down to practical limits. Composers are writing chamber operas requiring few principals, small choruses or none, small orchestras, and a modest staging budget. Far from suffering from these limitations, operas in this new style are thriving. Making opera a believable and exciting dramatic experience is part of the movement, and in this too it is achieving striking success. With these developments a more general acceptance of opera as a form of entertainment seems assured.

A pioneer librettist-composer in this field who has several successful operas to his credit is the Italian-born, American-trained Gian-Carlo Menotti. He has combined his dramatic and melodic gifts with a real flair for the theater to produce a series of flourishing operas. His works have been produced by the Metropolitan Opera Company and innumerable college opera workshops, broadcast on radio and television, and filmed. Perhaps his most spectacular success and the opera probably seen by more people than any other in a comparable span of time is his *Amahl and the Night Visitors.* The NBC telecasts of *Amahl* were annual Christmas events for many years following its first performance in 1951. It certainly is one of the most appealing operas of the new type.

GIAN-CARLO MENOTTI: *Amahl and the Night Visitors* (1951) 45:45
(1911–)

The full worth of this small masterpiece is perceived only when it can be seen as well as heard. Menotti displays rare skill in creating a setting, developing a plot, delineating character, working up emotional intensity, and bringing off a stunning climax. The music and text contribute in equal measure to the unfolding of this simple yet powerful drama.

The opera is extremely concise, but it has all the ingredients of traditional opera including chorus and dancing. For performance it requires only a modest number of principals, a small chorus and orchestra, a few dancers, and one stage setting. The scene is the interior of a humble dwelling on the road to Jerusalem on the night of the Nativity. Amahl, a crippled shepherd boy, and his widowed mother are visited by the Three Kings. The memorable events of that night in the lives of Amahl and his mother provide the material of the story. The English text and the fine diction of the singers on the recording render further comment unnecessary.

Broadway *musical shows* represent America's best claim to an indigenous tradition of drama with music. Except for the use of spoken dialogue in place of recitative, they preserve the pattern originated centuries ago in Italian opera. While continuing a venerable form, their style and content are strictly current-popular and change with the season. Irving Berlin, George Gershwin, Jerome Kern, Cole Porter, Richard Rodgers, Meredith Willson, and Frederick Loewe are illustrious names in the annals of the Broadway stage. The impressive list of smash hits they composed over the years prove that musical drama can be tremendously popular and financially rewarding. That which prospers in this country thrives, so the Broadway musical tradition can look forward to a glorious future. There will be no shortage of composers and librettists searching for the magic formula to produce a hit. Whether any of the hits will have enough substance and value to survive as works of art is another question. Gershwin's folk opera *Porgy and Bess* is one descendant of the Broadway tradition which as yet shows no sign of succumbing to the fate of most musicals. Perhaps it will escape the early oblivion

George Gershwin

which seems inevitably to be the price of immediate popularity. Leonard Bernstein's *West Side Story* is another work that may presage a more significant future for American music theater. Until the styles become more stabilized, one hesitates to suggest a specific example for listening.

An original cast recording of any show now on Broadway will illustrate the latest trends in musical shows.

Light operas and *operettas* are in a style somewhere between that of grand operas (or music dramas) and that of musical shows and comedies. Light operas and operettas usually have spoken dialogue and music in a light but not a popular vein. They are staple fare in amateur and outdoor summer productions.

The rock opera *Jesus Christ Superstar* (1970) and the New York musical hit *Godspell* (1971), both subsequently made into motion pictures, may be harbingers of a new type of dramatic music.

Ballet

A performance by a troupe of dancers in costume to the accompaniment of music is a *ballet*. Ballet exists in four more or less distinct types: *classic ballet, modern ballet, modern dance,* and *incidental ballet* connected with other types of entertainment, especially opera and recently, motion pictures.

Classic ballet often is adapted to existing absolute music. It is done in attire without special significance but which by color or design may contribute indirectly to the general mood of the dance. The stage customarily is bare except for a plain backdrop. The highly stylized steps, gestures, and movements of the ballet are executed with absolute precision. Episodes featuring individual dancers and small groups alternate with those involving the entire company. The motions are graceful and restrained. Evidence of effort is carefully concealed. The ballerinas wear special slippers which permit them to dance on the very tips of their toes, and steps executed thus are a characteristic feature of ballet. Classic ballet is abstract. It tells no story and conveys no message. Aesthetic satisfaction derives from the beauty of line and movement of the individuals, from fluid patterns and designs created by the movement and disposition of groups, and from the music. The music itself has no special properties. The choreographer who conceives the dance selects a composition and adapts appropriate movements to it.

The most obvious difference between classic and modern ballet is that modern ballet dramatizes a story in pantomime. Costumes are used to delineate characters, but they are often more fanciful and suggestive than realistic. Ballerinas wear the same shoes as for classic ballet, and all the classic steps are employed, plus any others required by the story. Because of the limitations of pantomime, plots are relatively uncomplicated. Even so, audiences usually are provided an outline of the story in the program. The stage is kept relatively unobstructed, but scenery, stage properties, and lighting contribute to the total effect. Colorful stories suggestive of varied actions and providing for solo, small group, and full company scenes are most likely to be used. Music for modern ballets ideally is specifically composed for a given story with the composer and choreographer working in close collaboration. Several of the most celebrated works of the 20th century were created in this way on commissions from Sergei Diaghilev (1872–1929), impresario of the renowned Russian Ballet. Among them is *The Firebird* with music by Igor Stravinsky and choreography by Michel Fokine. This is the work which first brought Stravinsky international acclaim. It was followed by a series of ballets in the same genre which solidly established his reputation as the leading composer of his time.

IGOR STRAVINSKY: *The Firebird* (1910) 21:00
(1882–1971)

- Introduction and Dance of the Firebird
- Dance of the Princesses
- Dance of Kastchei
- Berceuse
- Finale

In the ballet, based on Russian legend, young Prince Ivan wanders at night through the enchanted forest and captures the radiant Firebird. In return for her release the Firebird rewards him with one of her feathers. The darkness dissipates and twelve beautiful princesses are seen playing with the golden fruit of a silver tree in front of an imposing castle. The princesses warn Ivan that the castle is the abode of the infernal monster, Kastchei, who casts spells over intruders in his domain. Ivan is saved from destruction by the magic feather. The Firebird lulls the demon to sleep and reveals to the Prince the source of the monster's evil power, an egg hidden in the trunk of the silver tree. Ivan smashes the egg, vanquishing the monster and freeing his captives. The most beautiful of the princesses becomes his bride.

There are three different concert versions of this ballet music. The most familiar consists of the sections listed above as rescored by the composer in 1919.

(Also record side 8 band 1)[1]

Music from preexisting scores is sometimes used for modern ballets. This is feasible especially when the music itself suggests a story. Ballets using the music of Debussy's *Prelude to the Afternoon of a Faun* and Rimsky-Korsakov's *Scheherazade* are in this category. There are instances, too, in which music from various sources is arranged and adapted to accompany the intended story and action.

The distinctions between modern ballet and modern dance are by

1. See fn. p. 16.

no means clearly defined. In general, modern dance has in common with modern ballet a pantomimed story, specially composed and arranged music, stage effects, and costumes. Differences lie in the types of movements and gestures used by the dancers. Modern dance places more emphasis on realism and less on stylized motions. Ballet dancers are thoroughly schooled in the traditions of classic ballet, whereas modern dancers stress individual expression through bodily movement. The subject matter of modern dance tends to be more earthy and the action more violent, but tender and sentimental moods are not excluded. Ballet slippers are an artifice usually discarded by modern dancers, and bare feet are common. Precision of group movement is less in evidence in modern dance, as rigid order yields to spontaneity. Martha Graham is a leading exponent of modern dance. Her *Appalachian Spring* with music by Aaron Copland is a magnificent example both musically and choreographically. Modern dance is not, of course, a separate art but an aspect of ballet, and no distinction between types can be detected in the music.

AARON COPLAND: *Appalachian Spring* (1944) 20:00
(1900–)

Appalachian Spring was commissioned by the Elizabeth Sprague Coolidge Foundation for Martha Graham. It received the 1945 Pulitzer Prize for music and the Music Critics Circle award for the outstanding theatrical work of the 1944–45 season. Originally scored for a chamber ensemble of thirteen instruments, the music was subsequently arranged by the composer for full orchestra. This version, heard in concerts and on recordings, contains the essence of the ballet music but omits sections in which the interest is primarily choreographic. The music has no formal divisions and is played without pause. The action of the ballet is summarized in the Boosey & Hawkes score of the music as follows:

> A pioneer celebration in spring around a newly-built farmhouse in the Pennsylvania hills in the early part of the last century. The bride-to-be and the young farmer-husband enact the emotions, joyful and apprehensive, their new domestic partnership invites. An older neighbor suggests now and then the rocky confidence of experience. A revivalist and his followers remind the new householders of the strange and terrible aspects of human fate. At the end the couple is left quiet and strong in their new house.

(Also record side 6 band 7)

Until recently ballet was rarely seen in the provinces, but this is changing. Now dance troupes are regularly included on civic and community concert series, albeit often small companies with piano accompaniment in place of orchestra. Even under these less-than-perfect circumstances, packed houses attest to the popularity of these events and portend a growing market for ballet. Motion pictures and television, too, have discovered the magic of music and the dance. Music and dance production numbers are thoroughly exploited in Hollywood extravaganzas. More significant was the spectacular success several years ago of *The Red Shoes*, a British motion picture with a ballet milieu and a cast of renowned dancers in which complete scenes from several ballets were shown. Television, besides showing motion pictures containing ballet scenes, occasionally programs live broadcasts of ballet. Through these mediums, ballet undoubtedly is reaching and pleasing a wider audience than ever before. The producers and sponsors of these shows are to be applauded for providing brief respites from the tedium of game shows, soap operas, and westerns and for their contribution to the progress of art.

Dancing incorporated in other forms of entertainment such as operas and motion pictures is not a distinct type. Most often it is of the modern dance variety loosely connected to the main action by some specious pretext. Only rarely does it become an integral part of the story line and advance the plot, though it is most effective in this role. Obviously not all dancing in motion pictures bears a resemblance to ballet. Tap, acrobatic, ballroom, soft shoe, and the like occupy a secure if lowly niche in the realm of the dance similar to that of pop tunes in the realm of music.

Incidental Music

Incidental music is a classification for music which is subservient to drama. Though sometimes extended to include music played before and between acts, its particular function is to heighten the effect of the drama during the course of the action.

The use of incidental music can be traced throughout the history of drama. It figured prominently in Greek drama, in the Mystery and Miracle plays of the Middle Ages, and in the Elizabethan theater. If practical limitations restrict its use currently on the legitimate stage, its expanded role in motion pictures and television more than compensates. Sound motion pictures and tape recording have revolutionized concepts of incidental music and have added a fascinating new tangent to the art of music. Most dramatic television shows are filmed or video taped, so their processes are identical with those of the movies. The functions of incidental music are the same regardless of medium.

A paramount function of incidental music is to intensify the emotional impact of important scenes. Whether the emotion conveyed is one of joy or sorrow, elation or dejection, appropriate music has an uncanny power to evoke greater audience response. Used in this manner, incidental music supplements and augments the effect of words and actions. It underlines turning points and heightens climaxes in the story line.

Closely related to this is music with psychological significance. Music in this category is used to suggest subconscious thoughts and emotions and the presence of the unseen. Also included is music employed to create moods, to develop suspense, and to foreshadow impending action.

Music has utilitarian functions, too. It serves to indicate the passage of time. It fills voids created by the suspension of dialogue and sound effects. It smooths transitions between contrasting scenes. It aids in establishing the locale by exploiting indigenous musical devices, for example, native drums for Africa, Spanish rhythms for the Iberian peninsula, and oriental scales for the Far East. In these capacities incidental music helps to maintain the pace and continuity of the drama and to place it in the proper time and setting.

Actions sometimes are portrayed musically in an exaggerated and ludicrous manner for humorous effect. In this case the music has no psychological implications but simply mimics in an obvious fashion the visual elements. This procedure, called "Mickey Mousing" the action, is the stock approach to scoring cartoons and certain types of comic situations.

Incidental music occasionally is introduced realistically, that is, showing the musicians playing, and stories sometimes require a character to sing or to play an instrument on camera. Music in such cases may be an essential part of the plot, a diversion from the main argument, or a contrived device to display special talents of a star. Incidental music of this type is of necessity confined to situations where it is not inconsistent with the requirements of the story.

And finally, *title music* occupies the two spots where film music is most likely to command the listeners' attention, during the credits at the beginning of a picture and during the notice of completion at the end. *Opening title* music provides background for the studio trademark, the title of the picture, the list of characters and actors, credit lines, and notices. It is interesting to observe the location of the musical climax in this section, whether it coincides with the name of the star, the producer, the director, or perhaps with that of the composer himself! Besides providing background for the preliminaries, the opening title music establishes the tenor of the drama or the mood of the opening scene. *End title* music rarely is more than a cadence swelling up under the fadeout of the last scene and reinforcing the sense of finality at the end. It would be revolutionary for a film score to end quietly.

Recording the sound track of a motion picture is an intricate and demanding process. The casual viewer rarely is aware of the care and effort devoted to it. The composer's work really begins after the final editing of the film is completed. A product sometimes costing in the millions awaits his crowning touch before it can be marketed. This puts considerable pressure on the composer to work fast and jeopardizes the artistic quality of the music. The first step is to decide where music is to be used. This is done by production executives in collaboration with the music staff. The amount of music averages about half the total running time of the picture, but it may be much more or less. The location and extent of the music is largely a matter of personal taste, but in general it appears wherever it can provide one of the functions outlined above.

The film composer is furnished a *cue sheet* giving a synopsis of the action and the dialogue with timing to a fraction of a second for scenes involving music. From this he knows whether the music is to be under voices, with sound effects, or *in the clear.* He has unlimited access to the film and views repeatedly on a Moviola machine the scenes he is to underscore. Though he may have done some preliminary sketching of thematic ideas, only now is he ready to start composing music for specific scenes.

Music cues vary in duration from a few seconds to a few minutes. Composing within rigid time limits poses a problem, but those with experience working in the medium do not find this restriction burdensome. The episodes are brief, and the predetermined mood and function of the music stimulates the composer's imagination. Music's mission in relation to drama is achieved more readily than innate artistic merit, and it is not subjected to the same scrutiny as concert music. On the whole, dramatic music is written faster and less laboriously than nondramatic music.

Film music is turned out on a sort of assembly line by a small group of specialists. The composer's draft is handed to an orchestrator who arranges it for orchestra. A copyist then prepares parts for the individual players. Before the ink is dry on the last page, a recording time is set.

The orchestra is assembled on a sound stage equipped with the most advanced recording facilities. The conductor, usually the composer or the music director of the studio, faces a screen on which the picture is projected during the recording. The picture is started a bit before the music entrance, and preparatory signals are flashed on the screen. The conductor starts on cue and synchronizes the music with the action. He is assisted by a battery of timing devices including, when necessary, a *clicktrack* which produces clicks in an earphone at a preset rate. A run-through just before recording is the only rehearsal, so superb players are essential. Each scene is recorded as many times as necessary to achieve a "perfect take." Then the sound technicians take over.

Each facet of the sound—music, dialogue, sound effects, and background noise—is recorded on a separate sound track. These are synchronized with the picture and combined on a master sound track with strict attention to balancing the dynamic levels of the various components. The recording up to this point is done on magnetic tape. The completed master sound track is transferred to film where it appears as a narrow line of variable area and/or density running along the side of the picture.

This line is scanned by a light focused on a photoelectric cell in the projector which reproduces it as sound in the theatre sound system.

The procedures are different when singing, playing, or dancing is shown on the screen. Music for these scenes is prerecorded. The recording then is played back while the action is being filmed, and the action is synchronized with the music. Performances of professional musicians are *dubbed in* when the musical ability of the actors is inadequate. The dubbing technique is used most frequently when a movie star is shown singing a song. Though the *lip sync* (synchronization of the lips with the music) may be flawless, odds are that the voice heard on the film is that of a professional singer. Even so, the song's association with a big star, whose photograph may be on the cover of a recording, greatly enhances its chance of becoming a top forty hit.

Except in musicals, incidental music is a subsidiary of the drama. How conscious should the audience be of its presence? Ideally, the viewer should not be aware of the music as such, but should miss it if it were stopped. Incidental music which intrudes or detracts from the drama is objectionable. The task of film composers is rather menial, but in comparison with composers of symphonies and string quartets their remuneration, if not their satisfaction, is greater. They are accused of writing in imitative and derivative styles, but their contribution to the success of the total production is significant.

Cinema composers, following the lead of ballet and opera composers, have arranged excerpts from film scores for concert performance and have released recordings taken from original sound tracks. On recordings from movie sound tracks, like the following, the musical excerpts are usually identified by the scenes they accompany in the film.

JOHN CACAVAS: *Airport 1975*		33:45
(1930–)	Main Title, "Airport 1975"	2:50
	Destination Elko	1:40
	How Insensitive	2:17
	Interludium	1:55
	Airborne; Three Moods	3:00
	(a) Realization	
	(b) A Man and a Woman	
	(c) Scott's Rendezvous	
	Inflight Collision	3:45
	Theme, "Airport 1975"	2:20
	Montage	3:48
	Alexander's Death	2:15
	Murdock Makes It!	1:40
	Suspense, Approach and Landing	5:05
	Finale, End Title	3:10

> Though the album is strictly instrumental, the names of the stars in the film are listed on the record jacket in type twice as large as that used for the name of the composer/conductor. Like most composers of background music, John Cacavas is not well known outside of music circles despite the fact that he previously did the scoring for the popular *Kojak* television series.

Sound track music isolated from the film it was intended to accompany may be attractive, but incidental music is best appreciated in context as a part of the total dramatic experience. The next time you see a motion picture or watch a drama on television, concentrate on the music. If you are among the many who have always taken it for granted, its scope and importance probably will come as a revelation.

Additional Examples

Opera

Gershwin: *Porgy and Bess*
Menotti: *The Telephone*
Weill: *Three Penny Opera*
Britten: *Peter Grimes*
Ward: *The Crucible*

Musical Show

Loewe: *My Fair Lady*
Rodgers: *South Pacific*
Bock: *Fiddler on the Roof*

Operetta

Lehar: *The Merry Widow*
Romberg: *The Desert Song*
Strauss: *Die Fledermaus (The Bat)*

Ballet

Falla: *El Amor Brujo (Love, the Sorcerer)*
Ritual Fire Dance (record side 6 band 7)

Stravinsky: *The Rite of Spring*
Sacrificial Dance (record side 8 band 1)
Bernstein: *Fancy Free*
Khachaturian: *Gayne*

Incidental Music

MENDELSSOHN: *A Midsummer Night's Dream* (incidental music for Shakespeare's play)

HAMLISCH: *The Way We Were* and *The Sting* (sound tracks which won 1974 Motion Picture Academy Oscars)

PROKOFIEV: *Lieutenant Kije Suite, op. 60* (from the film score)

Song Forms

15

The forms used for instrumental music are also used in music for voices, and the small forms, even in instrumental music, are sometimes called song forms. The song form classification as used in this book, however, encompasses only the three plans of musical organization peculiar to music with words and found in song literature.

Strophic Form

When each stanza, or strophe, of a poem is set to the same music, the form of the resulting song is *strophic*. Strophic form is common in folk and familiar songs, children's songs, patriotic songs, hymns, and chorales, as well as in art songs. In art music this type of setting is appropriate only for simple, lyric poems with a limited number of uniform stanzas. From a musical point of view strophic form has several limitations, consisting as it does of an uninterrupted series of literal repetitions. There is no provision in the form for departure, return, variation, or development. The emotional range of the music, and consequently of the text, cannot be great. Musical interests must be concentrated in a single, cogent statement which fits all of the stanzas of the poem. Within the relatively narrow confines of strophic form many gems of the song literature, both traditional and art, have been conceived. One such gem, *Who Is Sylvia,* is a perfect example of the form, with identical music for each of its three verses.

Franz Schubert: *Who Is Sylvia, op. 106 no. 4* (1826) 2:42
(1797–1828)

Strophic form

A Who is Silvia, what is she,
That all our swains commend her?
Holy, fair, and wise is she;
The heavens such grace did lend her,
That she might admired be.

A Is she kind as she is fair?
For beauty lives with kindness.
Love doth to her eyes repair
To help him of his blindness,
And, being helped, inhabits there.

A Then to Silvia let us sing,
That Silvia is excelling;
She excels each mortal thing
Upon the dull earth dwelling;
To her let us garlands bring.

—William Shakespeare: Two Gentlemen of Verona

In the song the last line of each stanza is repeated. Schubert's spelling of the name does not agree with Shakespeare's.

(Record side 5 band 3. Melody p. 370)

Through-Composed Form

The procedures in a *through-composed form* are just the reverse of those in a strophic form. For each part of the text a distinctive musical setting is created which is uniquely suited to the rhythm and sentiment of the words. Unifying elements may appear more than once, but there is no systematic repetition of sections. The sequence of musical ideas is dictated by the logic of the words rather than by the requirements of abstract musical design. This type of setting is appropriate for dramatic and narrative poems and those expressing a wide range of emotions. It is the only feasible way of setting blank verse and poems in which the rhythms are inconsistent or the stanzas irregular.

The fact that a through-composed song is organized around the text does not mean that unifying elements are lacking in the music. Tonality, style, and tempo give a sense of direction and purpose to musical events, even in the absence of a preconceived structural design. Melodic, motivic, rhythmic, and harmonic elements may be repeated, modified and adapted in the process of illuminating the text. Literal repetitions inspired by textural rather than musical considerations do not violate the concepts of through-composition.

Goethe's *Erlkönig* is a poem that demands a through-composed setting, and Schubert masterfully delineates every feature of the dramatic text in his music. The musical style changes with each shift from narration to dialogue and for each character—the father, the son, and the Erl-King, a symbol of death. The first stanza is preceded by an introduction in which the piano establishes the mood and states the leading motive four times. This motive is heard throughout the song, but always in the accompaniment, never in the voice part. The complete fusion of poetic and musical ideas produces a spectacular example of through-composed form.

FRANZ SCHUBERT: *Erlkönig (Erl-King), op. 1* (1815) 3:54
(1797–1828)

Through-composed form

Introduction

A Who rides there so late through night so wild?
A loving father with his young child;
He clasped his boy close with his fond arm,
And closer, closer to keep him warm.

B "Dear son, what makes thy sweet face grow so white?"
"See, father, 'tis the Erl-King in sight!
The Erl-King stands there with crown and shroud!"
"Dear son, it is some misty cloud."

C "Thou dearest boy, wilt come with me?
And many games I'll play with thee;
Where varied blossoms grow on the wold,
And my mother hath many a robe of gold."

D "Dear father, my father, say did'st thou not hear,
The Erl-King whisper so low in mine ear?"
"Be tranquil, then be tranquil, my child,
Among withered leaves the wind bloweth wild."

E "Wilt come, proud boy, wilt thou come with me?
Where my beauteous daughter doth wait for thee;
With my daughter thou wilt join in the dance every night,
She'll lull thee with sweet songs to give thee delight,
And lull thee with sweet songs to give thee delight."

D′ "Dear father, my father, and can'st thou not trace
The Erl-King's daughter in yon dark place?"
"Dear son, dear son, the form you there see
Is only the hollow gray willow tree."

F(D) "I love thee well, with me thou shalt ride on my course,
And if thou art unwilling, I'll seize thee by force!"
"Oh father, my father, thy child closer clasp,
Erl-King hath seized me with icy grasp!"

G The father shuddered, his pace grew more wild,
He held to his bosom his poor swooning child,
He reached that house with toil and dread,
But in his arms, lo, his child lay dead!

—J. W. von Goethe
(Translation by Theodore Baker)

(Record side 5 band 2)

Song Cycle

A *song cycle* is a group of songs related by text, thought, medium, or style which collectively constitutes a musical entity. Songs joined together in a unified group expand the scope and dimensions of the art song concept. The texts for a song cycle are usually the work of one poet, but they may be selected by the composer from random sources. The number of songs in a cycle varies considerably. There are three in Hugo Wolf's *Michelangelo Songs* and twenty-four in Franz Schubert's *Winterreise* (Winter Journey). In other respects song cycles are similarly lacking in uniformity, so to attempt to generalize about them is futile.

The number of existing song cycles is not large as compared with, for instance, the number of symphonies. Each one tends to be a law unto itself and unlike any other. If any cycle can be regarded as typical, it is Schumann's *Frauenliebe und Leben* (Woman's Love and Life). Its eight songs collectively constitute a model song cycle and individually illustrate three distinct approaches to setting a text. Two songs are essentially strophic; one is through-composed; and the other five are in forms associated with instrumental music.

ROBERT SCHUMANN: *Frauenliebe und Leben, op. 42* (1840) 20:15
(1810–1856)

1. Ever since I saw him
2. He of all mankind 2:30
3. I can't believe it 5:30
4. O ring upon my finger 7:30
5. Help me dear sisters 9:45
6. Dearest man 11:30
7. Here at my breast 15:35
8. Now hast thou hurt me first 16:50

Song Cycle

1. Strophic, tonic key (B-flat)

A Ever since I saw him,
I seem blind to be,
For whate'er I look at,
Only him I see;
Stays his face before me
As in waking dream,
In the deepest darkness
Brighter, brighter doth it gleam.

A All the world without him's
Colorless and bare,
For my sisters' pastimes
No more can I care,
To my little chamber
I would weeping flee;
Ever since I saw him,
I seem blind to be.

2. Rondo, five-part, subdominant key (E-flat)

A He, of all mankind the noblest,
And so gentle, and so kind!
Lips of frankness, eyes of crystal,
Steadfast courage, flashing mind.

A As, in those blue heights above us,
Bright and noble is yon star,
So is he, in my own heaven,
Bright and noble, high and far.

B Forward, forward on thy highway;
Let me but thy glory see,
In all humbleness but see it,
Blessed in my sadness be.

A Do not hear my silent prayer,
Thy high fortunes follow free;
Heed not me, a lowly maiden,
Lofty star of majesty!

C None but worthiest of women
May deserve thy happy choice;
I will bless high heaven always,
Thousand times rejoice!

C′ I will joy then in my weeping,
Blessed, blessed will I sit;
And if my poor heart be breaking—
Break, my heart! What matters it?

A′ He, of all mankind the noblest,
And so gentle, and so kind!
Lips of frankness, eyes of crystal,
Steadfast courage, flashing mind.
And so gentle, and so kind!

3. Free part form, supertonic key (C minor)

A I can't believe it, conceive it,
'Tis all a dream and a lie,
For how could he over others
Poor me have set happy and high?

B Methought his voice was speaking:
"Forever I love thee!"
Methought—I must have been dreaming,
It never, never can be!

C So dreaming, fain would I die now,
Here cradled upon his breast;
How welcome were death, by rapture
Of tears everlasting caressed!

A I can't believe it, conceive it,
'Tis all a dream and a lie,
For how could he over others
Poor me have set happy and high?

Coda I can't believe it, conceive it,
'Tis all a dream and a lie!

4. Rondo, five-part, subdominant key (E-flat)

A O ring upon my finger,
My little ring of gold,
Dear jewel, devoutly I kiss thee,
Devoutly I kiss thee,
To my heart I hold.

B I had awaked from dreaming
My childhood's dream of peace and grace;
I found me lost and forsaken
In boundless untenanted space.

A O ring upon my finger,
'Twas taught to me first by thee,
From thee the revelation
How precious a jewel our life can be.

C I'll live for him, I will serve him,
Belonging to him whole,
Will give him myself, and discover transfigured
Discover transfigured in him, my soul.

A′ O ring upon my finger,
My little ring of gold,
Dear jewel, devoutly I kiss thee,
Devoutly I kiss thee,
To my heart I hold.

5. Rondo, five-part, all parts begin alike, tonic key (B-flat)

A Help me, dear sisters,
Help to adorn me,
Me, the fortunate, tend me now;
Busy your fingers,
Daintily wreathing
Myrtle flowers about my brow.

B(A) When, with a tranquil
Heart and a happy,
Safe in the arms of my love I lay,
Often he whispered
All his impatience,
All his longing to hasten the day.

A Help me, dear sisters,
Help me to banish
Foolish fears that my heart oppress,
That with unclouded
Eyes I may greet him,
Him, the fountain of happiness.

C(A) When, my beloved,
Thou art before me,
When thou, my sun, dost on me shine,
Let me devoutly,
Let me all humbly,
Let me bow down to thee, lover mine.

A′ Strew for him, sisters,
Strew for him flowers,
Bring for him beautiful rosebuds too.
And to you, sisters,
Love and leave-taking;
Sadly, gladly I part from you.

6. Ternary, major submediant key (G)

A Dearest man, thou eyest
Me with wonder deep;
Dost not guess the reason
Why today I weep?
See the liquid pearl-drops,
Gems I seldom wear,

Tremble bright and happy
On my eyelid there!

A Why my bosom flutters,
Why my heart is proud,
Would my lips were able
To confess aloud;
Come and hide thy face here
On my trembling breast—
In thine ear I'll whisper
How our love is blest.

B Now thou knowest the reason
Of the tears that ran,
Though thou canst not see them,
My beloved, beloved man!
Stay upon my heart here,
Feel it beat and thrill,
So that close and closer
I may clasp thee still!
Close and closer!

A Look, beside my bed here
Will the cradle bide
Where the pretty picture
Of my dream I'll hide;
Soon will come the morning,
Waked the dream will be;
There will lie thine image
Laughing up at me!

Coda Thine image!

7. Strophic, modified, parts begin alike, end differently, major mediant key (D)

A Here at my breast, my beautiful boy,
Thou art my treasure, thou art my joy.
O love it is gladness, and gladness is love;
So have I said, and so it will prove.

A′ I deemed my fortune all too high,
But still more happy now am I;
Only the heart, only the breast
That baby lips have sweetly pressed.

A″ Only a mother knows full well
What love and happiness may spell.
Pity on man I must bestow,
Who mother's joy can never know.

A‴ My darling, darling angel, thou,
Thou lookest at me and smilest now!

Here at my breast, my beautiful boy,
Thou art my treasure, thou art my joy!

8. Through-composed, mediant key (D minor)

A Now hast thou hurt me first since love began,
And wounded deep!
Thou sleepest, O cruel, most unpitiful man,
Death's endless sleep.

B The world is empty now for me, a wife
Left all alone—alone;
For I have loved and I have lived, but life
I now have none.

C I shrink away into my heart's recess,
The veil doth fall;
I there find thee and my lost happiness
My world and all!

Coda The piano part of the first song, complete but without the voice part or the repetition, returns as a coda to the complete cycle; tonic key (B-flat).

—Adelbert von Chamisso
(Translation by Robert Randolph Garran)

Additional Examples

Strophic Form

SCHUBERT: *Heiden-Röslein (Hedge Roses)*
Die Schöne Müllerin (The Maid of the Mill)
1. Das Wandern (Wandering)

Through-Composed Form

SCHUBERT: *Der Tod und das Mädchen (Death and the Maiden)*
Morgenständchen (Hark, Hark! the Lark)
R. STRAUSS: *Cäcilie (Cecilia), op. 27 no. 2*

Song Cycle

BEETHOVEN: *An die Ferne Geliebte (To the Distant Beloved), op. 98*
BRAHMS: *Ernste Gesänge (Serious Songs), op. 121*
DEBUSSY: *Chansons de Bilitis (Songs of Bilitis)*
BRITTEN: *Serenade for Tenor, Horn, and Strings, op. 31*

Choral Forms and Religious Music

16

Choral music is linked inseparably with religion. The arts have occupied a central position in sacred ceremonies from their beginnings down to the present. Music, painting, architecture, poetry, prose, drama, and the dance all have drawn nurture and sustenance from the font of religion. In turn the arts have given expression to the faith and aspirations of mankind through the ages. Art and religion are almost synonymous in primitive societies. The striving for beauty independent from service to divinity and the cultivation of art for art's sake are characteristics of advanced civilizations. Varying concepts of deity in different places and times have led to the development of appropriate modes of worship with attendant arts. Those displayed only within the confines of a holy edifice are of interest primarily to communicants of a particular faith. Between the sacred and the profane lies a body of art, religiously inspired but universal in appeal, which reaches beyond the place of worship and into the museums and concert halls of the world. What is true of the arts and music in general is especially apropos in regard to choral music. The choral repertory is preponderantly of religious derivation.

Mass and Requiem

The *Mass* is a solemn rite of the Roman Catholic Church commemorating the sacrifice of Christ. The complete ritual has a complex structure of many sections only part of which are sung. Some portions of the text change with the day and the season, while others are constant. Composed Masses provide settings for five unchanging texts, the *Kyrie,*

Gloria, Credo, Sanctus/Benedictus, and *Agnus Dei.* The Mass (Latin *missa*) derives its name from an ancient phrase *Ite, missa est* (Go, the Mass is ended). This phrase, sung or intoned by the priest or deacon at the conclusion of the service, dismisses the congregation.

The text of the Mass is drawn from several sources. The Kyrie, a supplication for mercy, is part of an old Greek litany. Originally the Kyrie was in Greek and the remainder of the Mass in Latin, but the vernacular was authorized by Vatican Council II (1962–65). The Gloria, a series of acclamations, is from Luke 2:14 and Eastern liturgies. The Credo is the profession of faith formulated by the First Council of Nicaea in A.D. 325. The Sanctus/Benedictus text is derived from Isaiah 6:3 and Mark 11:9–10. In the Agnus Dei petitions are addressed to Jesus as He is characterized in John 1:29. These texts, which have inspired some of the most eloquent pages in the annals of music, are given in the traditional languages and in English. The Kyrie, Gloria, Credo, and Sanctus/Benedictus translations are based on the English version by the International Consultation on English Texts, but with adjustments as necessary to parallel the original Latin. The translation of the Agnus Dei is a more literal alternate version prepared by the International Commission on English in the Liturgy.

Text of the Mass

KYRIE

Kyrie eleison.	Lord, have mercy.
Christe eleison.	Christ, have mercy.
Kyrie eleison.	Lord, have mercy.

GLORIA IN EXCELSIS DEO,	Glory to God in the highest,
et in terra pax hominibus	and on earth peace to men of
bonae voluntatis.	good will.
Laudamus te, benedicimus te,	We praise you, we bless you,
adoramus te, glorificamus te.	we worship you, we glorify you.
Gratias agimus tibi propter	We give you thanks for your
magnam gloriam tuam.	great glory.
Domine Deus, rex coelestis	Lord God, heavenly King,
Deus pater omnipotens.	God the Father almighty.
Domine Fili unigenite Jesu Christe,	Lord Jesus Christ, the only-begotten Son,
Domine Deus, agnus Dei,	Lord God, Lamb of God,
Filius Patris,	Son of the Father,
qui tollis peccata mundi:	you take away the sin of the world:
miserere nobis;	have mercy on us;
qui tollis peccata mundi:	you take away the sin of the world:
suscipe deprecationem nostram;	receive our prayer;
qui sedes ad dexteram Patris:	you are seated at the right hand of
miserere nobis.	the Father: have mercy on us.
Quoniam tu solus sanctus,	For you alone are the Holy One,
tu solus Dominus,	you alone are the Lord,

tu solus altissimus,	you alone are the Most High,
Jesu Christe,	Jesus Christ,
cum sancto spiritu,	with the Holy Spirit,
in gloria Dei Patris. Amen.	in the glory of God the Father. Amen.
CREDO IN UNUM DEUM,	We believe in one God,
Patrem omnipotentem,	the Father, the Almighty,
factorem coeli et terrae,	maker of heaven and earth,
visibilium omnium et invisibilium.	of all that is, seen and unseen.
Et in unum Dominum, Jesum Christum,	We believe in one Lord, Jesus Christ,
Filium Dei unigenitum,	the only Son of God,
et ex patre natum ante omnia saecula.	eternally begotten of the Father,
Deum de Deo, lumen de lumine,	God from God, Light from Light,
Deum verum de Deo vero.	true God from true God,
Genitum, non factum,	begotten, not made,
consubstantialem Patri,	of one Being with the Father.
Per quem omnia facta sunt.	Through him all things were made.
Qui propter nos homines et propter nostram salutem descendit de coelis:	For us men and for our salvation he came down from heaven:
et incarnatus est de Spiritu Sancto ex Maria virgine, et homo factus est.	by the power of the Holy Spirit he became incarnate from the Virgin Mary, and was made man.
Crucifixum etiam pro nobis, sub Pontio Pilato passus, et sepultus est.	For our sake he was crucified under Pontius Pilate; he suffered death and was buried.
Et resurrexit tertia die secundum scripturas;	On the third day he rose again in accordance with the Scriptures;
et ascendit in coelum sedet ad dexteram Patris.	he ascended into Heaven and is seated at the right hand of the Father.
Et iterum venturus est cum gloria judicare vivos et mortuos,	He will come again in glory to judge the living and the dead,
cujus regni non erit finis.	and his kingdom will have no end.
Et in Spiritum Sanctum,	We believe in the Holy Spirit,
Dominum et vivificantem,	the Lord, the giver of life,
qui ex Patre Filioque procedit.	who proceeds from the Father and the Son.
Qui cum Patre et Filio simul adoratur et conglorificatur.	With the Father and the Son he is worshiped and glorified.
Qui locutus est per Prophetas.	He has spoken through the Prophets.
Et unam sanctam catholicam et apostolicam ecclesiam.	We believe in one holy catholic and apostolic Church.
Confiteor unum baptisma in remissionem peccatorum.	We acknowledge one baptism for the forgiveness of sins.
Et expecto resurrectionem mortuorum, et vitam venturi seculi. Amen	We look for the resurrection of the dead, and the life of the world to come. Amen.
SANCTUS/BENEDICTUS	
Sanctus, sanctus, sanctus Dominus,	Holy, holy, holy Lord,
Deus Sabaoth,	God of power and might,

pleni sunt coeli et terra gloria tua. Hosanna in excelsis.	heaven and earth are full of your glory. Hosanna in the highest.
Benedictus qui venit in nomine Domini. Hosanna in excelsis.	Blessed is he who comes in the name of the Lord. Hosanna in the highest.
AGNUS DEI	
Agnus Dei, qui tollis peccata mundi: miserere nobis.	Lamb of God, you take away the sins of the world: have mercy on us.
Agnus Dei, qui tollis peccata mundi: miserere nobis.	Lamb of God, you take away the sins of the world: have mercy on us.
Agnus Dei, qui tollis peccata mundi: dona nobis pacem.	Lamb of God, you take away the sins of the world: grant us peace.

Palestrina's *Pope Marcellus Mass* is often cited as a model liturgical Mass. The words are projected with exceptional clarity by unaccompanied voices, and the refined contrapuntal lines and ethereal harmonies perfectly reflect Palestrina's reverence for the sacred text. The five sections of the Mass text are usually subdivided when they are set to music. In the *Pope Marcellus Mass* the Sanctus and Benedictus are treated as separate parts, and the Agnus Dei is divided into Agnus Dei I and Agnus Dei II.

G. P. da Palestrina: *Pope Marcellus Mass* (1555) 26:20
(1525–1594)

Kyrie*
Gloria in excelsis Deo
Credo in unum Deum
Sanctus
Benedictus
Agnus Dei I
Agnus Dei II

Palestrina is regarded as the greatest 16th-century composer of church music, and the *Pope Marcellus Mass* is one of his most famous works. It presumably was composed during or immediately following the brief pontificate in 1555 of Marcellus II for whom it is named. The first known performance was in the Sistine Chapel ten years later. It was published in 1567.

*(Record side 1 band 9)

Many composers have used the text of the Mass for works not intended for liturgical use. Concert Masses range all the way from the monumental *B minor Mass* of Bach and the *Missa Solemnis* of Beethoven to *The Jazz Mass* of Joe Masters (Columbia CS9398). Where liturgical Masses originally were for unaccompanied voices, concert Masses usually are for chorus, soloists, and orchestra. In the more expansive examples the Mass texts, especially the lengthy ones of the Gloria and Credo, are sectioned, with phrases and sentences being treated musically as distinct parts. Masses of this type require resources not ordinarily available for religious services, but they illustrate another facet of music inspired by the rituals of religion.

A *Requiem* is a *Mass for the Dead.* It differs from the usual Mass in that the joyous Gloria and the Credo are omitted, and the sections peculiar to the Requiem are inserted. The Introit *Requiem aeternam* (Rest eternal) from which the service takes its name precedes the Kyrie. A long Latin hymn, *Dies irae* (Day of wrath), and the Offertory *Domine Jesu Christe* (Lord Jesus Christ) follow the Kyrie. The Requiem concludes with the Communion *Lux aeterna* (Light eternal).

Mozart's last work, left unfinished at his death, was his *Requiem in D minor.* It is scored for a quartet of solo voices (of which the soprano is most prominent), chorus, and orchestra. The five large sections of the text are subdivided and set as 12 distinct parts. The setting of the Kyrie does not conform to liturgical usage. The phrases *Kyrie eleison* and *Christe eleison* are sung simultaneously as the two subjects of a double fugue. This *Requiem* is a superlative example of religious music not intended primarily for liturgical use.

W. A. MOZART:	*Requiem in D minor, K.626* (1791)	53:38
(1756–1791)	Requiem and Kyrie	
	Dies irae	8:13
	Tuba mirum	10:08
	Rex tremendae	13:53
	Recordare	16:35
	Confutatis	22:30
	Lacrimosa	25:20
	Domine Jesu Christe	28:25
	Hostias	32:32
	Sanctus	37:07
	Benedictus	38:57
	Agnus Dei and Lux aeterna	44:50

An anonymous stranger under conditions of absolute secrecy commissioned Mozart to compose a Requiem just five months before his death. Mozart became obsessed with the idea that the stranger was an emissary of death and that the Requiem was his own. He was obliged to interrupt his labor on this work, and it was incomplete when he died. The night of his death he gave the score to his friend and pupil, Franz Xaver Süssmayr, who finished it and delivered it to the mysterious stranger. It turned out that he was acting as agent for a nobleman, Count Franz von Walsegg, who wished to pass off the Requiem as his own composition. The Count actually was listed as the composer at the first performance.

Brahms's *German Requiem* is a noteworthy exception to the usual plan. Its text was selected by the composer from the German Bible without reference to the traditional content of the Roman Rite. It is in every respect a unique work.

Motet and Madrigal

The meaning of the term *motet* has varied considerably during the 700 years that it has been in use, and no single definition covers all of its ramifications. Motets are most often unaccompanied choral compositions with sacred Latin texts and polyphonic texture, but there are many exceptions. Motets were an important adjunct of the Catholic service during the Middle Ages and the Renaissance. Such motets, of which the following by Des Prez and Palestrina are representative, have great historical significance.

JOSQUIN DES PREZ: *Ave Maria* 3:50
(1450–1521)

Des Prez composed at least two *Ave Marias*. They have in common only the words of the initial phrase—*Ave Maria, gratia plena, Dominus tecum* (Hail Mary, full of grace, the Lord is with you). Both are equally valid examples of the motet as described in the preceding paragraph.

(Record side 1 band 8)

G. P. DA PALESTRINA: *Super flumina Babylonis* (1585) 3:15
(1525–1594)

Both in treatment and text (Latin from the Vulgate, Psalm 136 verses 1 and 2) this is a typical motet. The words in the King James translation (Psalm 137) are: "By the rivers of Babylon, there we sat down, yea we wept, when we remembered Zion. We hanged our harps upon the willows in the midst thereof." This motet is included in several collections of 16th-century and Palestrina motets.

Madrigals are the secular counterpart of motets. Though the term was used for a 14th-century poetic form and its musical settings, it now implies unless otherwise qualified a type of vocal music that flourished in the 16th and 17th centuries, primarily in Italy and England. The texts for these madrigals are mostly contemplative and idyllic poems, in the vernacular, with amorous or pastoral subjects. The settings are for unaccompanied voices in four to six parts. The texture is less consistently polyphonic than in motets.

The high order of concurrent Italian and English poetry available as texts gave impetus to the madrigal movement. The words inspired the music, and it reflects directly the moods and thoughts of the text, sometimes portraying a particularly piquant word or phrase realistically.

Madrigals were intended principally as a source of entertainment for those participating in the performance. The ability to sing a madrigal part at sight was a social grace expected of every gentleman and lady. The singing of madrigals was one of the most prevalent forms of entertainment at intimate social gatherings of the period. The vocal skills of a vast public must have been unusually well developed, for the intricate music customarily was performed with the singers seated around a table reading from part books with no conductor and with only one on a part.

The madrigal originated in Italy, and Orlandus Lassus (also known as Roland de Lassus and Orlando di Lasso) is generally grouped with the Italian madrigalists, though he was born in the Netherlands and died in Munich. His formative years were spent in Italy, and his first printed work contained 22 madrigals to poems of Petrarch. His *Echo Song,* with its double chorus and homophonic texture, is not exactly a typical madrigal, but it illustrates the typical affinity between the text and the music in a most engaging manner.

ORLANDUS LASSUS: *O là, O che bon'eccho (Echo Song)* (1580) 1:05
(1532–1594)

A series of questions and invectives are echoed, rather than answered, by an antiphonal chorus. This novel piece is one of the most celebrated of the Italian madrigals. It is recorded in several madrigal collections, Dover 7269 among them.

(Also record side 1 band 10)[1]

Influence of the Italian madrigal was evident in England during the last half of the 16th century. Lassus may have visited there briefly in 1554 or 1555. A collection of Italian madrigals provided with English texts, *Musica Transalpina,* was published in 1588 and widely disseminated. It firmly established the Italian madrigal style in England. The time was ripe for the new form. English poets and composers were of a high order. They adapted the Italian madrigal style to the English language and tastes and produced a large number of indigenous madrigals that are still sung and enjoyed. An innovation of the English madrigal school was the use of the nonsense syllables "fa la la" in the texts. Thomas Morley was a first-generation English madrigalist.

1. See fn. p. 16.

Thomas Morley: *My bonny lass she smileth* (1595) 1:45
(1557–1602)

Written just seven years after the publication of *Musica Transalpina*, this example illustrates all of the characteristic features of the English madrigal style, including "fa la las" between phrases of the text.

(Record side 1 band 11)

Thomas Weelkes, one of the greatest madrigal composers, published the set of five-part madrigals, from which the following was taken, when he was only 25 years old.

Thomas Weekles: *O care, thou wilt despatch me* (1600) 2:05
(1575–1623)

This madrigal is slower in tempo and more contemplative in style than most. It has the "fa la la" syllables but not in the quick rhythms with which they are usually associated. It is included in *The History of Music in Sound, Volume IV*, RCA Victor album LM–6029.

Cantata

No precise and all-inclusive definition for *cantata* is possible, but in general cantatas are works consisting of several distinct sections for one or more voices with instrumental accompaniment. The sections often contrast in style and medium, with recitatives, arias, duets, choruses, and instrumental episodes common ingredients. The texts of the various sections are related parts of a single narrative which may be sacred or secular in subject matter, lyric or dramatic in style.

Bach's cantatas (almost 200 extant out of a much larger production) represent the largest body of relatively consistent works in the form. A typical Bach cantata opens with a polyphonic chorus followed by a series of recitatives and arias and closes with a harmonized chorale. The chorale with which a canata closes often provides a basic source of material, both textual and musical, for the entire cantata. One practice is to use each stanza of the chorale text or a paraphrase of it as the basis for one section of the cantata. The chorale melody, too, may figure in the various sections. Embellished versions of the chorale tune sometimes are used, and at other times phrases of the chorale melody in long notes are given a florid contrapuntal setting. These procedures are illustrated in Bach's Cantata no. 1, *Wie schön leuchtet der Morgenstern* (How brightly shines the morning star).

J. S. Bach: *Wie schön leuchtet der Morgenstern* (1736) 24:50
(1685–1750)
1. Chorale fantasia (chorus and orchestra)
2. Recitative (tenor with continuo)
3. Aria (soprano with oboe da caccia and continuo)
4. Recitative (bass with continuo)
5. Aria (tenor with 2 solo violins, strings and continuo)
6. Chorale (chorus and orchestra)

This cantata is based on a hymn tune by Philipp Nicolai (1556–1608) and a six-stanza text from which it takes its name. The six sections of the cantata correspond with the six stanzas of the hymn. The chorale fantasia begins with an instrumental introduction, after which the chorus sopranos sing the words of the first stanza and the hymn tune doubled by the horns with an elaborate contrapuntal setting provided by the other voices and instruments. The words of the tenor recitative are a paraphrase of the second stanza of the hymn. The soprano aria is in effect a duet between the voice and the oboe da caccia, an obsolete instrument resembling an English horn (which is often substituted in modern performances). In the tenor aria two solo violins form a trio with the solo voice. The cantata concludes with a straightforward chorale-style harmonization of the hymn tune. The instruments double the voices in the chorale except for a brilliant countermelody in the horn.

The numbers used to identify Bach cantatas are derived from their order in the collected edition of his works and have no chronological significance. This cantata, though numbered 1, is a product of his maturity. It was written for the Feast of Annunciation, March 25, and reflects the joyous mood appropriate to the occasion.

(Chorale melody p. 383)

Oratorio

Oratorios in general are dramatic compositions of large dimensions for soloists, chorus, and orchestra based on religious but nonscriptural texts. They are distinguished from operas by the absence of scenery, costumes, and action as well as by subject matter and from sacred cantatas by their size. The chorus is prominent, more so than is customary in either operas or cantatas. An overture or opening orchestral introduction is usual. Recitatives by the soloists carry the burden of the narrative. One of the soloists sometimes is a narrator who explains the action, introduces the characters, and provides continuity between the various numbers, all in recitative. Arias generally follow the recitatives. Choral numbers usually are comments on or reactions to the immediately preceding passage, frequently with the chorus representing a crowd in the dramatic situation.

Not all oratorios conform to this plan. Some have secular subjects, and some are done in costume. These must be regarded as departures from the norm, which is represented perfectly in the most famous of all oratorios, Handel's *Messiah.*

G. F. HANDEL: *Messiah* (1741) 2:25:00
(1685–1759)

Part I

1. Overture
2. Recitative (Tenor): Comfort ye
3. Air (Tenor): Every valley shall be exalted
4. Chorus: And the glory of the Lord
5. Recitative (Bass): Thus saith the Lord of hosts
6. Air (Bass): But who may abide the day of His coming
7. Chorus: And He shall purify the sons of Levi
8. Recitative (Alto): Behold, a virgin shall conceive
9. Air (Alto and chorus): O thou that tellest good tidings to Zion*
10. Recitative (Bass): For, behold, darkness shall cover the earth
11. Air (Bass): The people that walked in darkness
12. Chorus: For unto us a Child is born
13. Pastoral Symphony (Orchestra)
14. Recitative (Soprano): There were shepherds abiding in the field
15. Recitative (Soprano): And the angel said unto them, "Fear not"
16. Recitative (Soprano): And suddenly there was with the angel
17. Chorus: Glory to God in the highest
18. Air (Soprano): Rejoice greatly O daughter of Zion
19. Recitative (Alto): Then shall the eyes of the blind be opened
20. Air (Alto): He shall feed His flock
    Air (Soprano): Come unto Him
21. Chorus: His yoke is easy and His burden light

Part II

22. Chorus: Behold the Lamb of God
23. Air (Alto): He was despised and rejected of men
24. Chorus: Surely He hath borne our griefs
25. Chorus: And with His stripes we are healed
26. Chorus: All we like sheep have gone astray
27. Recitative: (Tenor) All they that see Him, laugh Him to scorn
28. Chorus: He trusted in God

29. Recitative (Tenor): Thy rebuke hath broken His heart
30. Air (Tenor): Behold, and see if there be any sorrow
31. Recitative (Tenor): He was cut off out of the land of the living
32. Air (Tenor): But Thou didst not leave His soul in hell
33. Chorus: Lift up your heads
34. Recitative (Tenor): Unto which of the angels said He
35. Chorus: Let all the angels of God worship Him
36. Air (Bass): Thou art gone up on high
37. Chorus: The Lord gave the word
38. Air (Soprano): How beautiful are the feet of them that preach
39. Chorus: Their sound is gone out into all lands
40. Air (Bass): Why do the nations so furiously rage together
41. Chorus: Let us break their bonds asunder
42. Recitative (Tenor): He that dwelleth in heaven
43. Air (Tenor): Thou shalt break them with a rod of iron
44. Chorus: Hallelujah

Part III

45. Air (Soprano): I know that my Redeemer liveth
46. Chorus: Since by man came death
47. Recitative (Bass): Behold, I tell you a mystery
48. Air (Bass): The trumpet shall sound
49. Recitative (Alto): Then shall be brought to pass the saying that is written
50. Duet (Alto and tenor): O death, where is thy sting
51. Chorus: But thanks be to God
52. Air (Soprano): If God be for us
53. Chorus: Worthy is the Lamb

Amen

Messiah ranks as one of the great artistic creations of all time. It was received enthusiastically at its first performance, and its appeal has continued undiminished through the years. It is practically never given in its entirety. Numbers 34, 35, 36, 49, 50, 51, and 52 are customarily omitted, and they are not included in the timing. More severe cuts are often made, and it is not unusual for the order of the numbers to be rearranged.

*(Record side 2 band 6)

Several passages of scripture and liturgy have been used repeatedly in choral compositions. Among them are: the Gospels of Matthew, Mark, Luke, and John which provide the texts for *Passion Music;* the *Te Deum,* a hymn of praise and thanksgiving in the Catholic liturgy which is freely set, often commemorating joyous occasions; the *Magnificat,* canticle of the Virgin in both the Catholic and Anglican rites; and the *Stabat Mater,* a 13th-century poem sung at the Feast of the Seven Dolors. The

Jewish *Sacred Service* is represented in one superlative example by Ernest Bloch (1880–1959). Specific works in these categories and some more recent and less traditional examples of the types of choral music discussed in the chapter are included in the list of additional examples,

Additional Examples

Mass and Requiem

BRUCKNER: *Mass no. 3 in F minor, "Great"*
STRAVINSKY: *Mass*
BERNSTEIN: *Mass, A Theatre Piece for Singers, Players, and Dancers*
FAURÉ: *Requiem, op. 48*

Motet

BACH: *Motet no. 5, Komm, Jesu, komm, S.229*
BYRD: *Ego sum panis vivus*

Madrigal

GESUALDO: *Tu m'uccidi, o crudele*
BYRD: *I thought that love had been a boy*

Cantata

BARTOK: *Cantata Profana*
PROKOFIEV: *Alexander Nevsky, op. 78* (cantata arranged from the film score)

Oratorio

MENDELSSOHN: *Elijah, op. 70*
WALTON: *Belshazzar's Feast*

Passion

SCHUTZ: *St. John Passion*
BACH: *St. Matthew Passion, S.244*
PENDERECKI: *Passion According to St. Luke*

Te Deum

KODALY: *Te Deum*

Magnificat

BACH: *Magnificat in D, S.243*
HOVHANESS: *Magnificat, op. 157*

Stabat Mater

PERGOLESI: *Stabat Mater*

Sacred Service (Jewish)

BLOCH: *Sacred Service, "Avodath Hakodesh"*

The Periods and Styles of Music

3

Chronology*

2000 B.C.	Earliest notation	
1800 B.C.	First surviving song	
700 B.C.	Terpander	
138 B.C.	First Delphic Hymn	
100 A.D.	Skolion of Seikilos	
130	Mesomedes: Hymn to the Sun	
540	Pope Gregory I	604
850	Beginnings of polyphony	
1100	Troubadours and trouvères	
1200	Minnesingers	
1240	Sumer Is Icumen In	
1300	Machaut	1377
1450	Des Prez	1521
1501	First music printing	
1505	Tallis	1585
1525	Palestrina	1594
1532	Lassus	1594
1543	Byrd	1623
1546	Caccini	1618
1557	Morley	1602
1560	Gesualdo	1613
1575	Weelkes	1623

(Record side 1 bands 1–11)

* Composers and milestones of music mentioned in the text. Some of the dates are approximate.

Music Before 1600

17

The origins of music are shrouded in mystery. Its beginnings can only be inferred from indirect evidence supplied by studies in anthropology and archaeology. By the dawn of history music was firmly established as an adjunct of rituals, ceremonies, and festivals. The singing and dancing of the celebrants was accompanied by a variety of percussion, wind, and string instruments.

Music was highly developed and widely practiced in the ancient civilizations of Egypt, Sumer, Babylonia, Assyria, Arabia, India, China, and throughout the Orient. Jewish musical traditions date back to 2000 B.C. Influences of pre-Christian Hebrew chants have survived in the synagogues of isolated Jewish tribes and in Christian chants, though none of the actual music has been preserved.

The earliest known musical notation is on a 4,000-year-old clay tablet in the University of Pennsylvania museum. The tablet was one of thousands excavated by a museum archaeological expedition to Mesopotamia around the turn of the century. Its significance was undetected until Dr. M. Duchesne-Guillemin visited the museum in 1967. She identified the inscription as a Sumerian scale. The notation was etched on the clay tablet using the same wedge-shaped cuneiform script employed by the Sumerians in their writing. Their culture was very advanced, and they used music extensively in their festivals, pageants, and religious rites. The death pits of Ur have yielded the remains of court musicians buried with their lyres and harps which were richly ornamented with gold, silver, shell, lapis lazuli, and red stone.

In the early 1950s French archeologists excavating on the coast of

Syria, where an ancient culture thrived from 2000 to 600 B.C., unearthed the pieces of a clay tablet from circa 1800 B.C. etched with the same type of wedge-shaped cuneiform symbols used for the Sumerian scale. The ten lines of writing on the tablet have been partially deciphered by Dr. Anne Kilmer of the University of California at Berkeley. The first four lines give the music and words, in the Hurrian language, of a sacred love hymn. The remaining six lines describe how the music is to be played and sung. The first modern performance was given in 1974 by Dr. Richard Crocker, also of the University of California, singing and playing a replica of the 11-string lyre used by ancient Hurrian musicians. The sound of the music apparently is less strange than would be expected due to the fact that it is based on a seven-tone scale familiar to modern Western ears. The three-minute piece has been characterized as being rhythmic and divided into short, rather colorless phrases. Such observations relate to current standards and assume that the transcription of the ancient notation is accurate and the performance authentic, which are matters for speculation by experts and questions that apply to all re-creations of music from the distant past.

Until the recent discovery of the Sumerian scale and the Hurrian song, the only music notation preserved from antiquity consisted of a few remnants of Greek music. In Greek culture music occupied an exalted position. Music was included in the quadrivium of liberal arts, along with arithmetic, geometry, and astronomy. Greek philosophers wrote in detail about music theory and the place of music in society. During the 7th century B.C., Terpander established the first music school in Greece. He is regarded as the father of Greek lyric poetry and is credited with being the first to set poetry to music, but this honor would now seem to belong to the unknown composer of the Hurrian song. The poems of Sappho were sung, and music figured prominently in Greek drama. The quantity of Greek music must have been great, but only one brief song and some 20 fragments survived the collapse of the Hellenic world. The following examples have been transcribed into modern notation and recorded.

ANONYMOUS: *First Delphic Hymn* (138 B.C.) 3:30

Though incomplete, this is the longest extant example of Greek music. Some reconstruction of the melody is necessary, and transcribed versions are not in complete agreement. A translation of the text and the melody in modern notation are included with the recording in *The History of Music in Sound,* Volume I, RCA Victor LM–6057.

ANONYMOUS: *Skolion of Seikilos* (before A.D. 100) :22

This epitaph engraved on the tombstone of Seikilos's wife at Tralles in Asia Minor is the earliest piece of Greek music preserved intact. Its message is still timely: "As long as you live, be cheerful; let nothing grieve you. For life is short, and time claims its tribute." This example follows the *First Delphic Hymn* in *The History of Music in Sound* album, and it is included with a different translation in *2000 Years of Music,* Folkways 3700.

(Record side 1 band 2)

MESOMEDES: *Hymn to the Sun* (A.D. 130) 2:02

This hymn is ascribed to Mesomedes of Crete, a musican attached to Hadrian's court. It is recorded in *2000 Years of Music,* Folkways 3700.

(Record side 1 band 1)

Little is known about Roman music beyond the fact that it was influenced by the theories and practices of the Greeks. The separation of music from poetry and drama and the development of brass instruments are attributed to the Romans. Slaves played music in the homes of the rich citizens and in theaters. The *hydraulis,* an organ of Greek origin, was popular at outdoor entertainments such as the exhibitions by gladiators.

Music in the early Christian era was concerned principally with the development of the sacred monody of the Catholic liturgy. Between roughly A.D. 200 and 1300 a supreme body of unaccompanied vocal music was collected under the patronage of the Church. It is known variously as *plainsong, plainchant, Gregorian chant,* or by its Latin name *cantus planus.* The codification of the chant was accomplished during the pontificate of Gregory I (590–604), and it is most often known by his name. The Benedictine monks of Solesmes (a village near Le Mans, France) have dedicated themselves to restoring and performing authentic versions of Gregorian chant. Several London recordings are devoted to their performances, any one of which will serve to supplement the following example.

GREGORIAN CHANT (codified 590–604)
Alleluia: Vidimus stellam 1:59

The *Alleluia* belongs to that group of chants in the Mass which changes according to the season or occasion. Solo voice and chorus alternate in the *Masterpieces of Music before 1750* recording, Haydn Society 79038

(Record side 1 band 3. Notation p. 370)

By the 9th century a second part was sometimes added to a Gregorian melody in a type of polyphonic music called *organum.* In its most archaic form the added part moved parallel with the original at the interval of a fourth or fifth throughout, with both parts often doubled at the octave. The following example of *parallel organum* illustrates the next step in which the strict parallelism is maintained during the middle of the phrase but not at the beginning or end. In *free organum* there is some rhythmic independence and greater variety in the intervals between the voices. *Melismatic organum* is characterized by a free-flowing line added to a chant melody in long sustained notes, as illustrated in the suggested listening.

ORGANUM

Parallel: *Sequence, Rex caeli, Domine* (9th century)	:30
Free: *Trope, Agnus Dei* (12th century)	:55
Melismatic: *Benedicamus Domino* (12th century)	:45

These three examples occur in succession on Haydn Society recording 79038.

During the centuries when the early development of polyphonic music was taking place, both sacred and secular music continued to be preponderantly monophonic. Secular monophonic songs were being disseminated by traveling minstrels and students in minor church orders who roamed Europe. At first the language was Latin as in the music of the church, but by the 12th century poet-musicians were writing aristocratic poetry in the dialect of southern France and setting it to music. These poet-musicians were the *troubadours*. Raimbaut de Vaqueiras was one of the 400 known troubadours who left a legacy of some 2500 poems and 250 melodies. His *Kalenda Maya* was set to a dance tune played on a vielle, an important string instrument of the 12th and 13th centuries.

RAIMBAUT DE VAQUEIRAS: *Kalenda Maya* (1195) :45
(Died 1207)

A recording of this troubadour song is included in *2000 Years of Music,* Folkways 3700.

(Record side 1 band 4)

The *trouvères* wrote and sang songs similar to those of the troubadours but using the dialect of northern France. Hundreds of melodies and thousands of poems have been preserved in trouvère manuscripts, some of which are now available in facsimile editions. Richard the Lion-hearted (1157–1199) was the most illustrious of the trouvères, but Adam de la Halle (1240–1287) was the author of the most extensive work, *Le Jeu de Robin et Marion* (The Play of Robin and Marion). This pastoral drama is recorded (Telefunken S–9504), and Darius Milhaud has made a delightful adaptation of it for contemporary stage presentation.

The practices of the troubadours and trouvères, and even some of their melodies, were taken up about a hundred years later in Germany by the *minnesingers.* The Germans were less influenced by popular dance music than the French, and the style and subject matter of their songs were sometimes of a religious nature. Walter von der Vogelweide's *Palästinalied* (Palestine Song) commemorates the Crusade of 1228.

WALTER VON DER VOGELWEIDE: *Palästinalied* (1228) :54
(1170–1230)

> The text of this song says, in essence: "Only now, since I have come to the place where God walked as man, do I live a true man's life." A translation is given in the *2000 Years of Music* album, Folkways 3700.
>
> (Record side 1 band 5)

The English produced some monophonic songs during this period, but an insignificant number in comparison with the French and Germans. By this time the English were already writing multipart music like the monumental *Sumer Is Icumen In* (see p. 156).

GUILLAUME DE MACHAUT (1300–1377) was a cleric, courtier, poet, and the greatest musician of his age. He composed in a wide range of forms and styles—monophonic, polyphonic, secular, and sacred. He secured a unique place in the history of music by being the first individual to write a complete polyphonic setting of the Ordinary of the Mass. The assumption that this Mass was performed in 1364 at the coronation of Charles V of France, whom he served, is not well founded. The entire Mass, sometimes identified as the *Mass of Notre Dame,* is recorded, and excerpts are included in various anthologies. The technical devices characteristic of Machaut's style are evident in the *Agnus Dei.* It is *isorythmic,* that is, it has rhythm patterns which are repeated with different pitches, a common 14th-century practice. The harmonies sound crude to modern ears, because the principles of chord structure and progression we have come to accept were not yet formulated.

GUILLAUME DE MACHAUT: *Mass of Notre Dame* (before 1364)
(1300–1377) Agnus Dei 3:19

> The first and third sections of the *Agnus Dei* have identical music. The next to the lowest of the four parts is a Gregorian melody for which Machaut has provided a polyphonic setting.
>
> (Record side 1 band 7)

In the century following Machaut the procedures of polyphonic music were refined and perfected at an accelerated rate facilitated by improvements in the system of rhythmic notation. Music history books list an array of distinguished names and achievements for this period, but the first composer whose music is apt to appeal immediately to 20th-century listeners is Josquin Des Prez (spelled a variety of ways and alphabetized under J, D, and P).

Des Prez (1450–1521) was born in Belgium but studied in Paris and spent 30 years as a musician in the chapels of Italy before returning to his homeland where he was provost of a cathedral until his death. He met many of the notables of his day in his extensive travels. His music was sung everywhere, and his influence was enormous. Some of his compositions still display the intricate contrapuntal manipulations typical of his predecessors, but the style for which he is remembered places greater emphasis on harmonic considerations. For the first time chord structures and progressions are consistently governed by principles that later became standard. The horizontal and vertical aspects of his music give the impression of being in perfect balance and under complete control. The *Ave Maria* cited on page 224 is typical of the style found in the sacred and serious compositions of Des Prez. The style of the frivolous *El Grillo* is too homophonic to be typical, but it demonstrates clearly his mastery of harmony.

Josquin Des Prez: *El Grillo (The Cricket)* (1505) 1:20
(1450–1521)

Des Prez is represented in Volume III of *The History of Music in Sound* by this and three other examples.

(Also record side 1 band 8)[1]

The printing of music was first accomplished during Des Prez's lifetime. A liturgical book containing monophonic music was printed in 1476, just 21 years after Gutenberg's Bible. The first printing of polyphonic music was done by Ottaviano dei Petrucci of Venice in 1501. The publication was a collection of multipart songs, supposedly 100 but actually only 99. Des Prez was amply represented by eight. Subsequent publications by Petrucci contained many works by Des Prez, including *El Grillo*. The printing of their music enhanced the reputations of composers and diffused their musical styles throughout Europe.

Prior developments culminated in the 16th century with a period known as "the golden age of vocal polyphony" which matched the

1. See fn. p. 16.

splendor of Renaissance painting and literature. The art of creating beautiful, euphonious texture by interweaving graceful, fluid, melodic lines was developed to the ultimate degree. Sacred music fostered by the Church and secular music fostered by the courts vied for the first time on nearly equal terms. The two composers who contributed the most to vocal polyphony's golden age were Giovanni Pierluigi da Palestrina and Orlandus Lassus.

PALESTRINA (1525–1594) for almost 400 years has been universally regarded as the greatest composer of Catholic church music. He was a choirboy from the age of seven until his voice changed. After a period of study he became an organist and choirmaster. In 1551 he was appointed maestro of the Cappella Giulia, the post he held at his death, but between 1555 and 1571 he held appointments in other churches and was for a time music director of a seminary. He and Annibale Zoilo under a decree issued in 1576 by Pope Gregory XIII prepared a revised version of the Gradual, the variable parts of the Mass sung by the choir. Though Palestrina's creative and professional life was inseparably bound with the Church, he was no ascetic. Emperor Maximilian and the court of Mantua sought his services but would not meet his terms. He was married twice, had two sons, and during the last years of his life ran a successful fur business in addition to holding a church post. He was a prolific composer. His complete works fill 33 volumes. His compositions, particularly the *Pope Marcellus Mass* (see p. 64, p. 97, and p. 222), have been cited repeatedly as models of the purest religious style. In 1903, more than 300 years after his death, Pope Pius X singled out his works for special commendation in the *Motu Proprio* on sacred music. The motet *Hodie Christus natus est,* with its triadic harmonies and free-flowing lines, is another magnificant example of Palestrina's music and 16th-century vocal polyphony.

G. P. DA PALESTRINA: *Hodie Christus natus est (Today Christ is born)* 2:50
(1525–1594)

(Also record side 1 band 9)

ORLANDUS LASSUS (1532–1594) was a most versatile composer. He wrote in the reserved style of the church and in the popular idiom of the day with equal fluency, and he set Italian, French, German, and Latin texts with equal skill. He was born in the Netherlands and, like Palestrina, started in music as a choirboy. By the time he was 12 he was in the service of the viceroy of Sicily. He held posts briefly in Milan, Laterano, and Naples and perhaps visited England and France before settling in Antwerp in 1555, the year his first compositions were published in Venice. The following year he accepted a court appointment in Munich where he remained, except for occasional journeys, until his death. He wrote in all the styles and forms of his day, and his output totals an incredible 2000 compositions. Emperor Maximilian made him a hereditary nobleman, but he may have been even more proud of the title conferred by fellow musicians, "Prince of Music." Two madrigals, *Matona mia cara* written when he was only 18 years old and *Il grave de l'eta* composed 37 years later, give some idea of the range of his style in this one type of composition.

ORLANDUS LASSUS: *Matona mia cara (Matona my dear)* (1550) 2:45
(1532–1594)

> This delightful little piece is still a favorite with madrigal singers and a cappella choirs. Its text is humorous, and slightly suggestive.
>
> (Record side 1 band 10)

ORLANDUS LASSUS: *Il grave de l'eta (The burden of age)* (1587) 2:40
(1532–1594)

> Lassus dedicated his last volume of madrigals to the physician who attended him during his declining years. The words by Gabriele Fiamma contain the phrases, "In the war of daily living I weaken. In vain do I search for peace or armistice."

When Palestrina and Lassus died, the golden age of vocal polyphony and the Renaissance were drawing to a close. Music was on the threshold of a new era, one that would have to suffer through its growing pains before it could rival the splendor of the past.

References

Brown, Howard Mayer. *Music in the Renaissance.* Englewood Cliffs: Prentice-Hall, 1976.

Bukofzer, Manfred F. *Studies in Medieval and Renaissance Music.* New York: W. W. Norton, 1964.

Reese, Gustave. *Music in the Renaissance.* Rev. ed. New York: W. W. Norton, 1959.

Sachs, Curt. *The Rise of Music in the Ancient World.* New York: W. W. Norton, 1943.

Seay, Albert. *Music in the Medieval World.* 2d ed. Englewood Cliffs: Prentice-Hall, 1975.

G. P. da Palestrina

Photo courtesy of Brown Brothers

Orlandus Lassus

Photo courtesy of Brown Brothers

Chronology

1546	Caccini	1618
1551	Gabrieli	1612
?	Munday	1630
1567	Monteverdi	1643
1582	Allegri	1652
1585	Schütz	1672
1588	Musica Transalpina	
1590	Florentine camerata	
1597	First opera	
1600	First use of figured bass	
1602	Nouve Musiche	
1653	Corelli	1713
1659	Purcell	1695
1660	Kuhnau	1722
1668	F. Couperin	1733
1678	Vivaldi	1741
1681	Teleman	1767
1683	Rameau	1764
1685	J. S. Bach	1750
1685	D. Scarlatti	1757
1685	Handel	1759
1710	Pergolesi	1736

(Record side 2 bands 1–7)

The Baroque Period (1600-1750)

18

The baroque was a period of bustling activity in science, politics, and the arts. Baroque music trailed a similar movement in painting and architecture by half a century. In keeping with the spirit of the times, it is characterized by luxuriant elaboration, grandiose concepts, and spectacular designs. Theatricalism, heretofore limited to an occasional picturesque passage, became a significant trend. The period saw decisive changes in the materials, styles, forms, and mediums of music and the birth of the first great universal musical geniuses.

During the baroque era Protestant church music was established on a par with that of the Catholic church. New forms appropriate to the Protestant services evolved. The production of secular music, encouraged by the nobility and upper classes, exceeded that of sacred music. Emphasis on secular music coupled with mechanical and technical improvements in instruments stimulated the writing and performance of instrumental music. For the first time the supremacy of vocal music was challenged by instrumental music. Concurrently an independent instrumental style began to emerge. In this period melodies and harmonies were based almost exclusively on major and minor scales, which supplanted the earlier church modes. Major/minor tonality became a prime factor in musical organization. Loud and soft passages were deliberately juxtaposed, creating patterns of terraced dynamics. Rhythms became more obviously metric, and on occasion incessant streams of equal quick notes produced a sort of perpetual motion. It was, indeed, a time of change and innovation.

That the participants were aware of the revolutionary aspects of their musical activities is apparent from the title of a song collection by Giulio Caccini (1546–1618), *Nouve Musiche* (New Music), subsequently applied to the whole period and style. A revolt against the mannered polyphony of the previous age generated the impulse which led to the new music. Three basic innovations stemmed directly or indirectly from this revolt: *recitative, figured bass,* and *homophonic texture.*

Recitative was the direct outgrowth of the emphasis placed on the text of vocal music by baroque composers. To quote Claudio Monteverdi (1567–1643), "The text should be the master of the music, not the servant." This was not possible in the 16th-century polyphonic style, because the imitative entrances and overlapping phrases made the words and syllables of the text occur at different times in the various parts. With each of four or more voices singing different syllables at the same time, comprehension of the text was impossible. The baroque solution to this problem was recitative, a sort of inflected declamation by a solo voice. This style of singing was used almost exclusively in the first operas and throughout the period in operas, oratorios, and cantatas whenever the text was of primary importance.

The recitative style was ideal for enunciating a text, but it was musically uninteresting. However, the declamatory vocal line had only to be made more lyric and continuous to produce the solo song and aria, developments which were not long in the making. Musical values were thus enhanced without reducing the text to the status of "servant." The first objective of the new music was accomplished.

This new style was conducive to a kind of musical shorthand. The accompaniment for the voice part involved no carefully prescribed lines, only a simple harmonic background played by instruments. This could be notated by writing just the bass line with numbers below it to indicate the other chord components. This type of notation is called *figured bass* or *thorough bass.* Except for the bass line, it does not indicate the specific notes to be played but does provide a basis for improvisation. The realization, that is the performance, of the figured bass part was done on a keyboard instrument, ordinarily with the bass line reinforced by one or more melody instruments. The complete realization, which customarily proceeded without interruption throughout a composition, was called *basso continuo* (continuous bass) or just *continuo.* It served both as foundation for the musical edifice and as mortar in the musical texture. Its importance can be deduced from the fact that performances were directed by the player at the harpsichord or organ, who often was the composer, while at the same time realizing the figured bass part. The practice of writing out the melody and the bass, leaving the inner parts to the discretion of the performer, had the effect of polarizing interest in the outer voices. Because the use of figured bass was general in both vocal and instrumental music, the entire period sometimes is known as the *thorough bass period.*

The vertical concept of chords built over bass tones implicit in the figured bass system is diametrically opposed to the horizontal-linear concept of polyphony. Music conceived as a single, predominant melody supported by vertically ordered harmony is homophonic. Homophonic texture is the third basic innovation of the baroque period. The homophonic style did not supersede the polyphonic style. The two flourished side by side. Elements and passages were intermixed. A recitative and aria in the new style might be followed immediately by a fugue in the old. Elaborate polyphonic texture, both instrumental and vocal, often was provided with a figured bass part. After the beginning of the baroque the relative emphasis between homophonic and polyphonic texture varied, but neither disappeared. By 1750 the homophonic style was gaining ascendency, but the baroque era closed with the death of Bach, the greatest contrapuntalist of all time.

Inventiveness in the matter of musical form was also a baroque characteristic. The 17th century probably contributed more than any comparable period to the introduction and crystallization of enduring modes of musical expression. Continuous variation, sectional variation, suite, sonata, rondo, concerto, opera, oratorio, overture, chorale, chorale prelude, and fugue all were either conceived or perfected during the baroque period. While it is true that modern examples of these forms are rather different from those of the baroque, the foundations of musical organization were well defined before the period ended. Conventional plans of musical organization not anticipated before 1750 are few in number.

Opera was the first great achievement of the baroque. Several of the most characteristic features of the period were incorporated in this one composite form. It was well suited to the exploitation of spectacular theatrical effects. Recitatives and arias were conspicuous elements. Figured bass was used consistently. Rather early the accompanying ensembles of opera were expanded to include large numbers of diverse instruments, paving the way for future development of orchestras. Instrumental *sinfonias* before and between operatic scenes and dramatic accompaniments utilized distinctive instrumental effects and contributed to the development of an independent instrumental style. The da capo aria, in which the opening section is repeated at the end, became a standard pattern. Operatic finales were often continuous variations over a ground bass (constantly repeated melodic pattern in the bass.) All in all, baroque opera represented a remarkable artistic achievement which strongly influenced subsequent music, nondramatic and instrumental as well as operatic.

Claudio Monteverdi (1567–1643) was easily the most significant of the early opera composers. Before 1600 he was well established in the court of Mantua as a viol player, singer, and composer in the old style. At middle age he turned from aristocratic chamber music to the stage and a wholehearted endorsement of the then revolutionary style of the rising baroque. He composed several operas between his first, *Orfeo* (1607) and his last, *The Coronation of Poppea* (1642). From 1613 until his death he was director of music at St. Mark's Cathedral in Venice, writing much church music. His genius knew no bounds. He was equally adept at writing court, church, and dramatic music, but it is in the field of opera that the striking originality of his genius is most apparent. Though one of the great innovators of music, Monteverdi was astute enough to temper the revolutionary practices of the Florentine Camerata (see page 193) in writing opera with more conventional means. He adopted the new recitative style for the most part in *Orfeo*, but he breathed the breath of melody into his declamation and was not disdainful of polyphony when it served his purpose.

Claudio Monteverdi: *Orfeo* (1607)
(1567–1643) Overture and Prologue 10:00

> *Orfeo* requires a large and varied orchestra with assorted wind, string, and keyboard instruments. The orchestra contributes to the drama in the accompaniments and supplies many instrumental interludes. The harmonic materials are unusually rich for the period and style. It is a tribute to Monteverdi's creative gifts that so mature an opera could be brought to fruition within a decade after the birth of the form. *Orfeo's* first performance under the auspices of the Duke of Mantua was received enthusiastically. Unlike the first opera which was lost and the other early operas which remained in manuscript, the score of *Orfeo* was published in 1609 and reissued in 1615, spreading the practices of the early baroque.

Antonio Vivaldi (1678–1741) was another Venetian famous during his lifetime as a composer of operas but now remembered primarily for his concertos, of which about 450 are extant. He began an intensive study of music with his father, who was a leading violinist at St. Mark's Cathedral, and he also prepared for the priesthood. A redhead, he was known throughout his life as *il Prete Rosso* (the Red Priest), though he served actively as a priest for only a year. Thereafter he devoted himself to music exclusively, and until the last year of his life he held a permanent appointment at the Musical Seminary of the Pietà, where orphaned and illegitimate girls were sheltered and trained in music. He played and taught violin, conducted, and served as chief administrator at the school, all the while composing profusely. Many of his works were written for special concerts and festivals at the Pietà and were first performed by the girls under his direction, but he fulfilled other commissions, enjoyed prolonged leaves, and traveled extensively. Attracted by presumably more favorable musical opportunities in the court of Charles VI, Vivaldi moved from Venice to Vienna in 1740. His genius was unrecognized there, and he died in destitute circumstances the next year.

Vivaldi wrote concertos for single and multiple solo instruments, that is, for solo concerto and concerto grosso instrumentation (see p. 178), with the former outnumbering the latter about two to one. The fast movements are characterized by vibrant rhythms in well-defined meters; the slow movements by singing Italianate lyricism. Drawing on his experience as a violinist and conductor, he wrote equally idiomatic and colorful parts for the solo and accompanying instruments. Typical baroque terracing of dynamic levels is achieved in two ways—by contrasting the full tutti with the solo instrument or group and by marking abrupt dynamic changes in the score. The concertos more often than not are in three movements and have a fast-slow-fast tempo scheme. The formal structures and key patterns are clear and straightforward. Ritornello form (see p. 177) predominates in the fast movements, though some are fugal. The slow movements are jewelled intermezzos. Vivaldi's opus 3 is a collection of 12 concertos, including both solo concerto and concerto grosso types. *The Concerto no. 6 in A minor* is representative of the solo variety.

ANTONIO VIVALDI: *Violin Concerto in A minor, op. 3 no. 6* (1712)

(1678–1741)		
	1. Allegro	3:30
	2. Largo	2:15
	3. Presto*	2:40

The 12 concertos of Vivaldi's opus 3 are known collectively as *L'Estro Armonico* (the harmonic whim). The first and third movements of this concerto are in ritornello form. The second movement is a small binary form without repeats. The three movements and fast-slow-fast tempo scheme of this work anticipate the overall plan of classic concertos, but the form and style of the individual movements are pure baroque.

*(Ritornello theme p. 382)

Vivaldi was paid the supreme compliment when a number of the concertos he had composed for solo string instruments, including six from his opus 3, were transcribed for keyboard instruments by the great J. S. Bach. Bach admired the freshness and vitality of the Italian baroque style, and he was obviously influenced by the intimate knowledge of it he

Antonio Vivaldi

acquired in the process of transcribing the Vivaldi concertos. Baroque stylistic innovations were conceived and nurtured in Italy, but in music they reached their ultimate maturity and fulfillment in the hands of two composers of German birth, Bach and Handel.

Johann Sebastian Bach (1685–1750) was the most imposing member of a prodigious dynasty of musicians who established the name Bach as a synonym for musician. He was exposed to music at an early age, and his training while unsystematic was typical for the times. His first significant position was as court organist and chamber musician at Weimer (1708–1717) during which time he wrote extensively for organ. In 1717 he was appointed director of chamber music by Prince Leopold of Anhalt at Cöthen, a position he held until 1723. This period was especially rich in the production of chamber and orchestral music. From 1723 on he lived in Leipzig as organist and music director (cantor) of the St. Thomas Church and School and eventually also as director of music in the university. These duties did not require him to relinquish the title of chamber music director in the service of Leopold. He enjoyed further honorary appointments from the Duke of Weissenfels and the King of Poland, Elector of Saxony. His most significant church music was written during his tenure at Leipzig.

A cursory review of Bach's appointments and areas of activity gives little clue to the tremendous magnitude and scope of his genius. Bach's complete works, which due to many losses are by no means complete, fill 47 massive volumes. Practically every form, medium, and style of his time with the exception of opera and ballet is represented with incomparable masterpieces. He was a consummate master of contrapuntal technique and achieved an ideal balance between the horizontal and

JOHANN SEBASTIAN BACH

vertical aspects of musical texture. Coming as he did at the end of an epoch when music was on the verge of another metamorphosis, his music was not appreciated by his immediate successors or even by his own sons, distinguished musicians who continued the family tradition. Felix Mendelssohn (1809–1847) is credited with starting the Bach revival which each succeeding year heaps new tribute on his already lustrous reputation. In a poll conducted by Paul R. Farnsworth, Professor of Psychology at Stanford University, the members of the American Musicological Society ranked J. S. Bach as the most eminent composer of all time.

There is no single work which summarizes Bach's creative activity. His range was too broad and his approach too varied to be reduced to generalities and isolated monuments. This volume, as any concerned with the history or literature of music must be, is replete with references to Bach and his music. One final example must suffice for here and now, though volumes and courses devoted to a single phase of Bach's creative life leave much unsaid. The *Brandenburg Concerto no. 3* is one of six for various instrumental combinations commissioned by and dedicated to Christian Ludwig, Margraf of Brandenburg.

J. S. BACH: *Brandenburg Concerto no. 3 in G, S.1048* (1721)

(1685–1750)	1. Allegro moderato	7:00
	2. Adagio	:10
	3. Allegro	6:10

This concerto, like the others in the group, is of the concerto grosso type but somewhat atypical. It has three parts each for violins, violas, and cellos, plus string bass and continuo. There is no solo group as such, but the scoring contrasts the massive sound of the entire ensemble with the lighter sound of small sections. The first movement is a ritornello form. The Adagio consists of just two chords, which may have been intended as a point of departure for the harpsichord (continuo) player to improvise a slow movement. An elaborate binary form concludes the work, a magnificent example of baroque instrumental polyphony and a prime example of Bach's incomparable contrapuntal technique.

George Frideric Handel (1685–1759) was born in Halle, Saxony in close proximity to Bach in both time and place. If the two men had been regarded as competitors, Bach surely would emerge the victor, but their paths never crossed. Bach made a trip to Halle hoping to meet Handel, but Handel had already left for England. Artistically, too, these giants of the late baroque pursued divergent courses. Their temperaments ordained it. Bach was essentially a provincial burgher who never traveled far from his birthplace, a devoted family man who produced 20 children in two happy marriages, a man whose personal tranquillity was ruffled by bickering with local church, town, and school authorities. Handel, by contrast, was a true cosmopolitan who traveled widely and lived and worked in Germany, Italy, and England. He was a gregarious extrovert who fraternized with artists and persons of rank. His difficulties were with his patrons, the divas who sang his music, and with other composers who vied with him for royal favor. As would be expected, Bach's music is predominantly introspective and contemplative; Handel's is mostly dramatic and theatrical.

Overcoming strenuous parental objections, Handel obtained a broad and thorough musical training including studies in counterpoint, canon and fugue, and lessons on the harpsichord, organ, violin, and oboe. He became in turn a church organist and a violinist in an opera orchestra. While in the latter position he composed his first operas. Before he turned permanently to other forms, he wrote 46 operas in the Italian language and style in addition to four early ones in German. After 1712 Handel lived permanently in England which placed him in the curious position of being a German composer writing Italian operas for the English. His fortunes fluctuated drastically with the taste and favor of the times. The complete disenchantment of the English with the artificialities of Italian opera brought Handel to bankruptcy. Though a crushing blow at the time, it was a blessing in disguise. With the failure of his operatic ventures, Handel turned to the form which was to assure his immortality —oratorio.

As a young composer in Italy he had essayed the form. In the full maturity of his fifties he returned to it, and though the form was no longer new, his treatment of it was unprecedented. The epic proportions of his scores, the sheer mass of his performing groups, the vigor of his music, and the eloquence of his Biblical heroes combined to overwhelm audiences. The success of his oratorios surpassed by far that of his operas, reestablished his reputation, and recouped his financial position. The greater part of his creative career was devoted to operas, but the vagaries of time and taste consigned them for nearly 250 years to the limbo of forgotten music. Amazingly, a few of them are again being staged, and they are receiving enthusiastic receptions by operagoers. Handel's place in the history of music would be secure if he had written nothing but the English oratorios, but in addition to these and the operas he composed an enormous quantity of chamber music and a large number of concertos which further exalt his position. His productivity surpasses even that of Bach. The collected edition of his works with index runs to 110 large volumes.

George Frideric Handel

Handel's masterpiece unquestionably is his *Messiah* (see p. 228). Excluding *Messiah,* one of Handel's most familiar and most performed works, and certainly one of the most ingratiating, is his *Water Music*.

G. F. HANDEL: *Water Music* (1717)
(1685–1759)

1.	Allegro	2:25
2.	Air	4:25
3.	Bourrée	:45
4.	Horn pipe	:50
5.	Andante	2:40
6.	Allegro deciso	2:45

A fanciful tale persists about the origin of the *Water Music* to the effect that Handel composed it in an attempt to regain the good graces of the King. Handel was granted a limited leave by his employer, the Elector of Hanover, for the purpose of visiting England, so the story goes. Handel overstayed his leave (as a matter of fact stayed in England permanently) and was still in England when his former employer mounted the throne of England in 1714 as George I, placing Handel in an extremely embarrassing position. The truth seems to be that Handel composed some 20 odd pieces of "water music" over a period of years for various entertainments held on barges floating down the Thames. Several suites have been made from this music, the best known of which consists of the six movements listed arranged for modern orchestra by Sir Hamilton Harty.

The similarities and the differences between the styles of Bach and Handel are apparent when the *Brandenburg Concertos* and cantatas of the former are compared with the *Water Music* and oratorios of the latter. These were the styles of instrumental and vocal music at the end of the baroque period.

References

Arnold, Denis. *Monteverdi.* New York: Octagon Books, 1963.

Borroff, Edith. *The Music of the Baroque.* Dubuque: Wm. C. Brown Company Publishers, 1970.

Deutsch, Otto Erich. *Handel: A Documentary Biography.* 1954. Reprint. New York: Da Capo Press, 1974.

Geiringer, Karl and Irene. *Johann Sebastian Bach: The Culmination of an Era.* New York: Oxford University Press, 1966.

Palisca, Claude V. *Baroque Music.* Englewood Cliffs: Prentice-Hall, 1970.

Pincherle, Mark. *Vivaldi: Genius of the Baroque.* New York: W. W. Norton, 1962.

Prunières, Henry. *Monteverdi: His Life and Work.* 1926. Reprint. New York: Dover Publications, 1975.

Claudio Monteverdi

Photo courtesy of The Bettmann Archive

Chronology

1683	Rameau	1764
1719	L. Mozart	1787
1732	Haydn	1809
1735	J. C. Bach	1782
1756	W. A. Mozart	1791
1770	Beethoven	1827
1782	Paganini	1840
1786	Weber	1826
1792	Rossini	1868
1797	Schubert	1828

(Records side 3 band 1 to side 5 band 3)

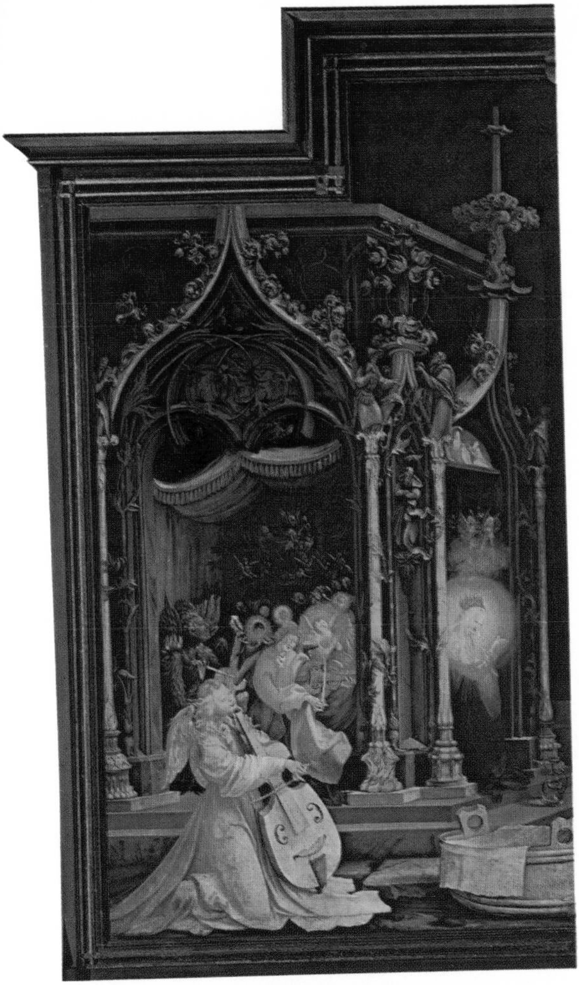

Angelic Concert

Temptation of St. Anthony

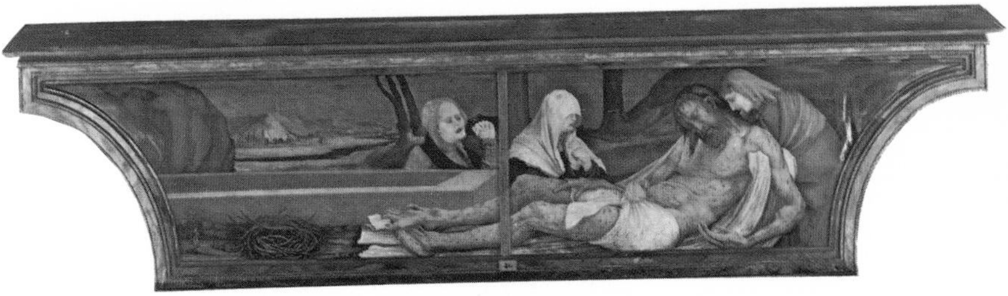

Entombment

Colorplate 1. MATHIS GRÜNEWALD: Isenheim Altarpiece (1515)

Incidents in the life of the painter Mathis Gothart Nithart, known as Grünewald, are dramatized in Paul Hindemith's opera *Mathis der Maler.* The three movements of the symphony (see p. 306) derived from the opera depict the scenes from the Isenheim altarpiece illustrated.

Courtesy of Art Reference Bureau

Colorplate 2. REMBRANDT VAN RIJN: The Night Watch (1642)

Comparison of Rembrandt's *Night Watch,* also known as *Sortie of Captain Banning Cocq's Company,* with the scenes from Grünewald's altarpiece reveals revolutionary changes in style and technique similar to those that occurred in music during the same period.

Courtesy of Rijksmuseum, Amsterdam

The Viennese Classic Period (1750-1825)

19

Three great names dominate the music of the Viennese classic period: Haydn, Mozart, and Beethoven. Their art did not spring full-blown from the ashes of the waning baroque. Portents of the new style were stirring at least a quarter of a century earlier. Even then, in a transitory period generally designated as *rococo,* the majesty and pomposity of the baroque were being replaced on occasion by aristocratic elegance. Specifically in music the advent of rococo is signaled by the gallant style or, in French, *le style galant* of which Jean Philippe Rameau (1683–1764) was a leading exponent (see p. 98). At about the same time a different reaction to austere polyphony was leading to musical expressions of moving simplicity and direct appeal to the common man. The best elements of these movements took root in another of the periodic returns to classic ideals.

Classicism is defined as conformity to classic principles of lucidity, simplicity, dignity, symmetry, restraint, refinement, and objectivity. In music these objectives were achieved by: (1) clarification of formal structures with emphasis on sectional homophonic forms, sonata form preeminent, (2) preference for compact, vocally inspired melodies possessing the quality of direct simplicity typical of folk songs, (3) elevation of homophonic texture to a position of dominance with extensive use of patterned harmonic motivation in broken-chord accompaniment figures, (4) employing imitative counterpoint essentially as a developmental device, abandoning contrapuntal forms, (5) giving harmonic clarity and simplicity precedence over complexity and ingenuity, and (6) consistently casting ideas in well-defined, regular phrases of four and eight measures.

Not all contributions of the Viennese classic period were directly inspired by classic ideals. Greater standardization of mediums also was accomplished during this time. The prior practice of scoring for available players in a particular court or church gave way to artistic conviction regarding suitable instrumental combinations. Toward the middle of the 18th century fairly uniform orchestras consisting of first and second violins, violas, cellos, basses, flutes, oboes, bassoons, trumpets, horns, and timpani began to take shape. By the end of the century orchestras with these constituents plus clarinets provided composers with a perfected and widely available medium of musical expression. The art of orchestration became an essential adjunct of composition. Basso continuo was discarded, and all of the parts in a composition were written out completely. At the same time the string quartet of two violins, viola, and cello was established as the predominant chamber music medium.

Dynamic shading became an essential feature of musical expression during this time. The terraced dynamics of the baroque typified by the alternating loud and soft passages of the concerto grosso were augmented by gradual changes from soft to loud *(crescendo)* and loud to soft *(decrescendo)*, by sudden outbursts, and by moments of silence. These features were first cultivated by a series of composers attached to the court in Mannheim who wrote in the gallant style. In many ways—general style, choice and use of mediums, exploitation of dynamic effects, and employment of novel instrumental procedures—the Mannheimers were direct forerunners of the Viennese classic masters.

The names (Franz) Joseph Haydn (1732–1809) and Wolfgang Amadeus Mozart (1756–1791) are frequently uttered in the same breath and with the same degree of reverence. The tragic brevity of Mozart's life is illuminated by the fact that Haydn, born 24 years earlier, survived him 18 years. Influence between them was strong and mutual. Young Mozart learned much from Haydn's music, and the older Haydn learned much from Mozart. Each acknowledged his indebtedness to the other, Mozart by dedicating six string quartets to Haydn. Their personal fortunes were very different. Haydn, starting in more humble circumstances, came along early enough to benefit from the vanishing custom of a court appointment. Mozart, though intermittently attached to a church or court, never enjoyed the security of a suitable permanent appointment. Neither did he profit much from publication or performances of his works, avenues of remuneration newly opened to composers.

Haydn's parents were amateur musicians in menial circumstances. There was music in the home, and at an early age his aptitude drew attention. From the age of 5 he had elementary instruction and soon was furthering his musical training while singing as a boy soprano in a church choir. When a teacher was negligent in his duty to provide instruction in theory and composition, Haydn purchased textbooks and pursued the

(Franz) Joseph Haydn

study on his own initiative. He was dismissed from the choir when his voice changed. For the next ten years he eked out a meager subsistence playing accompaniments and giving music lessons, all the while working assiduously to perfect his own playing and composing. He was already in his late twenties when he obtained his first appointment. A short time later he joined the entourage of the Hungarian Esterhazy Princes. His status was essentially that of a servant, but the position provided security and not only the incentive but the necessity for composing. His initial success was not sensational, but he never ceased growing as a composer. Gradually his fame spread throughout Europe. By the time his last patron, Prince Nikolaus, died and his orchestra was dissolved in 1790, Haydn had a pension from the estate and an international reputation. That same year he accepted an urgent invitation from the impresario Johann Salomon to perform in London. He remained there until 1792 and returned in 1794–95, scoring spectacular successes both times. The age of the public concert featuring celebrities to attract paying audiences had arrived, but Mozart had not lived to see it. Haydn returned to Vienna where he lived in affluence the rest of his days. Recognized as the grand master of chamber and symphonic music, he turned after hearing the Handel festivals in England to the composition of choral music, producing six great masses and two oratorios. Though lesser known, the operas he composed while in the employ of the Esterhazys round out a career that embraced every sphere of musical activity and spanned an entire epoch. The *Surprise Symphony* is one of the 12 symphonies Haydn composed for the Salomon concerts in London.

JOSEPH HADYN:	*Symphony no. 94 in G, "Surprise"* (1792)	
(1732–1809)	1. Adagio cantabile—Vivace assai	7:30
	2. Andante	5:40
	3. Menuetto: Allegro molto	4:50
	4. Allegro di molto	3:45

As was customary with Haydn, the otherwise brisk first movement in sonata form begins with a slow introduction. The second movement, a set of variations, contains the "surprise"—a sudden loud chord in a soft passage—about which Haydn is reputed to have said, "That will make the ladies jump." Wit and good humor are characteristics of his music. The menuetto is more rustic than courtly. Few conductors play it as fast as Haydn's marking would indicate. Literal interpretation of this tempo marking would result in a pace and mood approaching that of a scherzo. The fourth movement, in rondo form, displays the verve and sparkle expected of a Haydn finale.

W. A. Mozart certainly ranks as the most precocious musical prodigy of all time. His father, Leopold (1719–1787), was a violinist, author of a method for violin, and a recognized composer. He started the musical training of his son at the age of four in response to eager and intelligent interest. By the time he was six, young Wolfgang had composed little minuets and had appeared in his first public concert playing the harpsichord. When he was seven he made the first of his many foreign journeys, this one to Paris. His appearances now included giving exhibitions of improvisation in addition to playing concertos on the harpsichord and the violin. His first published compositions, four sonatas for harpsichord with violin ad libitum, were issued in Paris in 1764 when he was eight. That same year the Mozarts were cordially received in England where Wolfgang's first symphonies were written and repeatedly performed. He astounded the King with his ability to read at sight the music of contemporary composers such as Johann Christian Bach (1735–1782), son of J. S. Bach, who was then a leading musican in London. Mozart visited the music capitals of Europe in rapid succession, met most of the prominent musicians of the day, absorbed the latest styles and techniques like a sponge, turned out an uninterrupted torrent of compositions, and dazzled audiences with his performing feats. During a brief respite in Salzburg Mozart devoted himself to serious study and to the composition of his first oratorio. In 1768 he was on the road again, visting Vienna where he wrote his first opera and conducted a performance of his *Solemn Mass* before a large audience. After brief service to the Archbishop of Salzburg, he took leave to visit Italy. The Italian tour was undertaken primarily for the purpose of broadening his musical experience, but it turned out to be an unbroken succession of triumphs. His concerts were jammed, his compositions praised, his genius applauded, and honors were bestowed on him. In Rome Mozart wrote from memory the entire score of the nine-part *Miserere* by Gregorio Allegri (1582–1652) after hearing it only twice. At the age of 15 his meteoric career was at its zenith.

Wolfgang Amadeus Mozart

The next year the Archbishop of Salzburg, his friendly protector, died. The Archbishop's successor was unsympathetic to the young composer and subjected him to totally unwarranted indignities. Mozart obtained a leave of absence to seek another appointment. His efforts were unsuccessful, and he returned to his unhappy position at Salzburg. The situation became unbearable, and in 1781 he resigned and settled permanently in Vienna. The wife whom he married shortly after arriving in Vienna was as improvident as he. The scanty returns from the unending stream of masterpieces that flowed from his pen and a pitifully inadequate stipend tardily granted by the emperor were squandered. Production of some of the greatest music in the entire literature, operas and symphonies which have been played untold thousands of times on programs all over the Western world from that day to this, never succeeded in raising their creator above the level of pecuniary anxiety. At thirty-five he was buried in a pauper's grave without an inkling of the untold fortunes that would be made and spent on his efforts. His genius knew no limits. He is the one composer whose operas, symphonies, chamber music, and solo works are of equal monumental significance. His concertos for violin and for piano served to crystalize the form. Typical examples of his work could be as easily selected from one category as another, but the *Symphony no. 40* epitomizes his mature style.

W. A. Mozart: *Symphony no. 40 in G minor, K.550* (1788)
(1756–1791)

1.	Allegro molto	7:15
2.	Andante	7:50
3.	Menuetto	4:20
4.	Allegro assai	4:45

This is the second of three equally great symphonies composed between June 26 and August 10, 1788. That three such masterpieces could have been conceived within a period of six weeks seems almost incredible. Even more amazing is the fact that each has a distinct and separate personality. They stand as incontrovertible evidence of the depth and strength of Mozart's genius and mark a high point in the Viennese classic period.

(Also record side 3 bands 1–4)[1]

Ludwig van Beethoven (1770–1827), towering giant of music and third in the triumvirate of Viennese classic composers, probably is regarded as *the* greatest composer of all time by the majority of people, both musicians and nonmusicians. This is partially because of the transcendental power of his musical achievement, the unquestioned authenticity of his genius, and partially because he exemplifies as no other composer before him or since the qualities commonly associated with the creative artist.

Beethoven, son and grandson of Flemish musicians of modest abilities who had settled in Bonn on the Rhine, began his musical training at an early age under the strict and stern tutelage of his father, who had pretensions of producing another wonderchild of the Mozartean cast. He displayed remarkable talent but nothing to rival the phenomenal abilities of Mozart. In his early teens he was assistant organist in the

1. See fn. p. 16.

church, harpsichordist in the court orchestra, and violist in the theatre orchestra. He attended the public schools in Bonn and continued his studies with the local musicians. He met and elicited praise from Mozart during a short visit to Vienna in 1787. Haydn, on his way back to Vienna in 1792 after his first engagement in England, stopped over in Bonn and warmly praised a cantata by Beethoven. With this encouragement and a letter from the Elector, he left his provincial birthplace and moved to Vienna, capital of the musical world. Beethoven studied with Haydn for a time, but, being dissatisfied with him as a teacher, switched to others. At this stage of development, Beethoven evidently was not a tractable student, and the teachers were not impressed with his scholarship. He was, however, welcomed in the palaces of music-loving aristocrats of Vienna and fraternized as an equal with the social elite of the city. His genius and nobility of character were appreciated and his uncouth appearance and occasional ill manners were tolerated if not forgiven.

Beyond his youth Beethoven never held any of the positions which till then had supported composers and had elicited from them routine quotas of music for immediate consumption. His income was from sales of his works and allowances granted him by the wealthy without exacting tribute. This left him free to compose what, when, and how he pleased and if need be to wait for inspiration, an option he often elected if one were to judge by comparing his output with that of Mozart or Haydn.

But there is more to it than that. His whole manner of working was different. Whereas with Mozart whole symphonies seem to have been conceived in a flash and dashed off at blinding speed, Beethoven started with germ motives in the rough which he inscribed in a series of sketchbooks. Motives and themes often were transformed, polished, perfected and left to season before they found their way into finished works. His monuments were hewn from granite, not molded in clay. Each work is a distinct and separate entity which by compelling inner logic forges its own peculiar shape. Beethoven for the most part takes cognizance of conventional forms but strives for a higher degree of integration than his predecessors. Beethoven's form is progressive. There is little literal repetition beyond that accomplished by signs in the traditional places. Otherwise each return of a theme is projected against a different background or exposed to new and more penetrating illumination. Transitions are not perfunctory passages which merely accomplish a change of key or mood. They are occasions for additional development of thematic ideas, opportunities for unexpected modulations and harmonic experimentation. Creative imagination is ever at work in Beethoven's music. Nothing is superfluous. The musical drama unfolds in every measure. He wrote few potboilers. One has the feeling that every time he took his pen in hand it was in a deliberate attempt to create a masterpiece. With a goal so high, his percentage of successes is astounding.

All of his nine numbered symphonies remain in the repertory, as do his two independent overtures and various overtures for his one opera, *Fidelio* (*Leonore*). Opera was admittedly not his forte, but his single attempt in the form is still staged in spite of an absurd libretto. All of his piano music has been recorded and much of it, which includes five concertos and thirty-two sonatas, is programmed regularly. All violinists and cellists play his sonatas for these instruments. His one violin concerto is an enduring favorite. His sixteen string quartets are paragons of the form. Considering the quality, it is a respectable list. It is strongly slanted, as was his talent, toward instrumental music. In this realm he has never been equalled. His nine symphonies have been a decisive force in shaping all subsequent development of the form. No composer since Beethoven has been able or would want to escape his pervading influence. After Beethoven had composed all of his symphonies except the last, the *Eroica* was still his favorite.

L. van Beethoven: *Symphony no. 3 in E-flat, op. 55 "Eroica"* (1804)
(1770–1827)

1.	Allegro con brio	15:15
2.	Marcia funebre: Adagio assai	15:45
3.	Scherzo: Allegro vivace	5:55
4.	Finale: Allegro molto	11:45

In more ways than the inscription on the score, this is a "heroic" symphony. It is heroic in proportions, content, and realization. Paul Henry Lang ranks it as ". . . one of the incomprehensible deeds in arts and letters, the greatest single step made by an individual composer in the history of the symphony and in the history of music in general." One has only to compare it with Mozart's *Symphony no. 40* or Haydn's *Symphony no. 94* previously cited to grasp the magnitude of Beethoven's accomplishment and to perceive the transformation of the form within a span of 16 years. This symphony is intensely dramatic, personal, powerful, monumental; terms that would scarcely be applied in the same context to any prior symphony. The music bursts the classic restraints and overflows the traditional forms. Portents of rising romanticism are evident everywhere, even in the somewhat programmatic inspiration for the work. The symphony originally was dedicated to Napoleon Bonaparte, but Beethoven tore up the title page when Napoleon proclaimed himself Emperor, betraying the ideals of equality and liberty that Beethoven held so dear. It was now a tribute "to the memory of a great man," not an individual but an immortal hero. Napoleon was not forgotten, however. When he died 17 years later, Beethoven is supposed to have said, with reference to the second movement *Funeral March*, "I have already composed the proper music for the occasion."

(Also record side 4 band 5)

LUDWIG VAN BEETHOVEN

Beethoven was, in a very real sense, the end of the Viennese classic period and also the beginning of the romantic age.

References

Deutsch, Otto Erich. *Mozart: A Documentary Biography.* Palo Alto: Stanford University Press, 1966.

Geiringer, Karl. *Haydn: A Creative Life in Music.* Berkeley: University of California Press, 1968.

Pauly, Reinhard G. *Music in the Classic Period.* 2d ed. Englewood Cliffs: Prentice-Hall, 1973.

Thayer, Alexander W. *The Life of Beethoven.* Edited by Elliot Forbes. Princeton: Princeton University Press, 1964.

Wellesz, Egon and Sternfeld, Frederick, eds. *The Age of Enlightenment, 1745–1790.* New York: Oxford University Press, 1973.

Chronology

Born	Composer	Died
1797	Schubert	1828
1803	Berlioz	1869
1809	Mendelssohn	1847
1810	Chopin	1849
1810	Schumann	1856
1811	Liszt	1886
1813	Wagner	1883
1813	Verdi	1901
1822	Franck	1890
1823	Lalo	1892
1824	Bruckner	1896
1825	J. Strauss	1899
1833	Brahms	1897
1835	Saint-Saens	1921
1836	Delibes	1891
1838	Bizet	1875
1838	Bruch	1920
1840	Tchaikovsky	1893
1841	Dvorak	1904
1843	Grieg	1907
1844	Rimsky-Korsakov	1908
1845	Fauré	1924
1854	Sousa	1932
1858	Leoncavallo	1919
1858	Puccini	1924
1860	Wolf	1903
1860	Mahler	1911
1863	Mascagni	1945
1864	R. Strauss	1949
1865	Dukas	1935
1865	Sibelius	1957
1873	Rachmaninoff	1943

(Records side 5 band 2 to side 6 band 4)

The Romantic Age (1825-1900)

20

The romantic movement in the arts is concerned with the assertion of imagination and sentiment as opposed to logic, emphasis on the personal as opposed to the universal, stress of the subjective as opposed to the objective, and preeminence of spontaneous freedom over deliberate formality. The romantic movement in music trailed a similar movement in literature but eventually surpassed it in opulence. Music is an ideal medium for romantic utterances, and it has been referred to as *the* romantic art. In spirit, romanticism is the opposite of classicism. The pendulum swings back and forth between the two, with first one and then the other in ascendency. Music, however, is never completely lacking in either. It is simply a question of emphasis.

Romantic composers continued to use the forms and mediums perfected in the classic era, but in a freer and more personal manner. To these they made contributions of their own. The tone or symphonic poem, the character piece, and the art song are innovations of the romantic period molded to conform to its precepts. Music drama is a romantic version of opera.

There are no clear-cut dividing lines between periods in music. The transition from classic to romantic is no exception. Romantic elements are detected readily in works of Beethoven. Carl Maria von Weber (1786–1826) who died a year before him and Franz Schubert (1797–1828) who died a year after, generally are considered to be the first champions of the new movement. Full realization of the romantic impulse probably was delayed by their untimely deaths. Even so, their contributions to the romantic movement were substantial.

C. M. von Weber

Weber anticipated many romantic developments. He was among the first to write a large programmatic work *(Konzertstuck in F minor, op. 79)*, a concert waltz *(Invitation to the Dance, op. 65)*, patriotic songs, and occasional pieces for the piano. He broke with the classic Italian opera traditions exemplified by Rossini (1792–1868) and founded German romantic opera, strongly influencing the ensuing music dramas of Wagner (1813–1883). *Oberon,* Weber's last opera, is replete with romantic elements, many of which are evident in the overture.

C. M. von Weber: *Oberon* (1826)
(1786–1826) Overture 9:30

> On the basis of previous triumphs, Weber was commissioned to provide music for an opera to be premiered at Covent Garden in London. *Oberon,* a fairy opera in 21 spectacular scenes, was the result. Weber supervised the rehearsals and conducted the first 12 performances before his death. The opera played 19 more times that season and then slipped into virtual oblivion except for the overture and an aria or two.

Schubert's symphonies and chamber music are perhaps no more romantic than Beethoven's, but his art songs (see index) and his character pieces for piano are truly romantic expressions. It was a time of extremes—of gigantic works and miniatures. The "Great" *Symphony no. 9 in C* by Schubert is one of the former, and his little *Moments Musicaux* are examples of the latter.

FRANZ SCHUBERT

FRANZ SCHUBERT: *Moments Musicaux, op. 94* (1827)
(1797–1828) No. 3 in F minor 2:00

Musical Moment was one of the designations Schubert used for short piano pieces of a lyrical or improvisatory nature. The third is the most familiar of the six comprising the group.

The decade between 1803 and 1813 saw the birth of the first generation of full-fledged romantic composers: Hector Berlioz, Felix Mendelssohn, Robert Schumann, Frederic Chopin, Franz Liszt, Richard Wagner, and Giuseppi Verdi.

HECTOR BERLIOZ (1803–1869) had a stormy career befitting his romantic nature. He defied convention and tradition. He was ever an experimenter and innovator, so much so that most of his works were slow to win favor. His personal life was as hectic as his artistic life. He fell madly in love with an English actress and in the romantic tradition was equally unhappy at first when she rejected him and later when she finally accepted him and they were married. Though Berlioz played only the guitar and the flageolet (a flute-type instrument but never a standard orchestral instrument), he was a master of orchestration. His treatise on instrumentation is the earliest orchestration text still in print. His considerable literary talent was put to use in his position as music critic for a Paris newspaper. When he toured Germany and Italy, he reported his activities in two volumes of *Musical Travels,* and he penned the texts for his dramatic works. If he was a less complete musician than the masters of the previous periods, his interests ranged further afield. Two of his most famous works have already been discussed, the *Symphony Fantastique* (see p. 189) and the *Requiem* (see p. 74). To these should be added the *Roman Carnival Overture.*

Hector Berlioz

Hector Berlioz: *Le Carnaval Romain, op. 9* (1838) 8:40
(1803–1869)

> This music originally was the prelude to the second act of the opera *Benvenuto Cellini.* Berlioz adapted it for independent concert performance several years after the first performance of the opera. The concert version is usually classified as an overture.

Felix Mendelssohn (1809–1847) was born into a wealthy and influential family. The proverbial picture of a struggling artist does not apply in his case. He was afforded every advantage and grew up in a stimulating intellectual environment. His remarkable talents were evident at an early age. His compositions never surpassed the quality of his *Midsummer Night's Dream Overture* which he wrote at the age of seventeen. He was

Felix Mendelssohn

a brilliant pianist, organist, and conductor. He toured extensively and occupied several important posts. One of Mendelssohn's greatest contributions to music was initiating and fostering the Bach revival which has been gaining momentum ever since. It was he who instigated the first performance of Bach's *St. Matthew Passion* subsequent to the composer's death, and it is a tribute to his perception to have recognized the value of this neglected masterpiece. His compositions include oratorios on the order of Handel (see p. 120), concertos for violin and for piano, symphonies, and a quantity of piano and chamber music. His *Songs Without Words* are not his greatest works, but they are among his best known. Unlike some of his compositions, which are rather akin to those of the baroque and classic composers, these character pieces clearly reflect the romantic spirit of his times.

Felix Mendelssohn: *Songs Without Words, op. 67* (1844)
(1809–1847) 4. Spinning Song 1:55

> Mendelssohn created a new genre of piano composition with these slight, lyric piano pieces. He wrote eight volumes of them between 1830 and 1845, of which opus 67 is the sixth. These sketches are drawn with a sure hand and with infinite charm, grace, and sensitivity.

Robert Schumann (1810–1856) is another romanticist whose talents were both literary and musical. His career as a pianist ended abruptly when a device he was using to develop finger independence permanently injured his hand. Thenceforth he concentrated on composition and literary activities. He was a founder of the music periodical *Neue Zeitschrift für Musik* and was its editor from 1835 to 1844. The publication ardently championed liberal and progressive tendencies. Chopin and Brahms, among many others, benefited from Schumann's perceptive and knowledgeable essays and criticisms. His writings were potent, beneficial forces in music and laudable examples of music journalism. The first 23 published compositions of Schumann are for piano. Only later did he turn to songs, chamber music, and works for orchestra. Though all four of his symphonies and several of his large works remain in the repertory, he seems to have been most at home writing in the smaller forms and for piano and voice.

Because of his literary inclination, it was only natural that Schumann should be attracted to the great lyric poets and the art song. An awareness of his personal plight provides added insight to the romantic outpouring of his songs. Schumann and Clara Wieck carried on a tempestuous courtship for several years against the strenuous objections of her father. Their love prevailed against every insidious strategy, but their marriage was delayed. The consummation of their romance opened the floodgates of his inspiration. He turned from the composition of piano music to songs and wrote about 140 within the year to inaugurate his most productive period. The 16 songs of the *Dichterliebe* cycle are included in that total.

Robert Schumann: *Dichterliebe* (Poet's Love), *op. 48* (1840)
(1810–1856) 7. Ich grolle nicht (I'll not complain) 1:50

This is the most familiar song of the cycle, but *Im wunderschönen Monat Mai* (no. 1) follows as a close second.

(Record side 5 band 7)

Frederic Chopin (1810–1849) was the most highly specialized of the first-rank composers. He wrote almost exclusively in small forms for piano, but in this limited area he is supreme. His relationship to the piano character piece is similar to that of Handel to the oratorio, Mozart to the concerto, Beethoven to the symphony, and Schubert to the art song. Each made a definitive contribution to the particular medium. Chopin's brief character pieces exploit a mode of expression and an instrument which came into vogue with the romantics. Both Mozart and Beethoven played and wrote for the piano, but for the most part in a manner also suited to the harpsichord. A truly distinctive style of writing for the piano utilizing its full capabilities was born with Chopin.

Colorplate 3. EUGENE DELACROIX: The Arab Tax

The romantic painter Delacroix (1790–1863) was a contemporary and friend of Chopin. His paintings, like the music of the period, broke with the traditions of classicism to express and evoke intense emotions in new and distinctive ways.

Courtesy The National Gallery of Art, Washington, D.C.
Chester Dale Fund

Colorplate 4. EDGAR DEGAS: Four Dancers

Degas (1834–1917) is classified as an impressionist, but not really as an orthodox or even a typical representative of the style, if indeed one exists. He shared with impressionist composers an interest in ballet and its performers.

Courtesy The National Gallery of Art, Washington, D.C.
Chester Dale Collection

ROBERT SCHUMANN

Chopin's fame as a composer rests on a variety of small piano pieces of types designated with fanciful titles: ballades, etudes, mazurkas, polonaises, waltzes, preludes, and nocturnes. The ballades, of which there are four, borrow their name and to an extent their spirit from the poetic form. Chopin published two books of twelve *Etudes* (studies) each, plus a collection of three. They are studies in the sense that they include all the pianistic difficulties and harmonic effects of a revolutionary piano style, but they never degenerate into mere pedantic exercises. On the contrary, they include some of Chopin's most inspired passages. Chopin left his native Poland permanently at the age of twenty, but his Slavic origin and his romantic patriotism inspired a quantity of music. His fifty-six *Mazurkas* and twelve *Polonaises* use Polish dance rhythms. He used waltz rhythm for fourteen famous pieces. Perhaps his most popular creations are included in the cameo-like *24 Preludes.* The very name *nocturne* (night piece) is fraught with romantic suggestions, and Chopin's poetic musical language gave eloquent voice to these suggestions in nineteen pieces with that title. The *Nocturne op. 9 no. 2* is a celebrated gem from this collection.

FREDERIC CHOPIN

FREDERIC CHOPIN: *Nocturnes, op. 9* (1831)
(1810–1849) No. 2 in E-flat 4:20

(Also record side 5 band 6)[1]

FRANZ LISZT (1811–1886) was without a doubt one of the most influential figures of his time. His career was as long and varied as it was spectacular. It began in his native Hungary when he was only nine with a public performance of a difficult piano concerto and extended to his death 66 years later in Bayreuth. His triumphs as a pianist were rivaled by his achievements as a composer, conductor, and teacher. His tours as the greatest piano virtuoso of the 19th century took him to the music capitals of Europe where he circulated in the highest circles with the famous, rich, and titled. Aspiring young musicians flocked to him, and deserving ones could count on him for instruction and assistance. During his 11-year tenure as court conductor at Weimar, it became a center for the new romantic music to which Liszt contributed prolifically as a composer. Only a few of his numerous works are still programed, and his popular reputation is secured by the relatively trivial *Liebestraum*. He deserves a better fate, for he has a long list of worthy compositions to his credit. His piano music is brilliant, though sometimes bombastic. His 19 *Hungarian Rhapsodies* for piano, some of which he transcribed for orchestra, popularized

1. See fn. p. 16.

Franz Liszt

rhapsody as a designation for musical works (see p. 181). The 12 symphonic (tone) poems inaugurated a new form (see p. 188). In these extended works for orchestra the form and content, liberated from classic restraints, are dictated in large measure by the literary programs which inspired them. The third and best known of the symphonic poems, *Les Preludes,* is Liszt's musical interpretation of philosophical concepts expressed in one of Lamartine's *New Poetic Meditations.*

Franz Liszt: *Les Preludes, Symphonic Poem no. 3* (1854) 16:00
(1811–1886)

The following quotation from Lamartine is printed in the score:

> What is our life but a series of preludes to that unknown song, the first solemn note of which is sounded by death? Love forms the enchanted daybreak of every life; but what is the destiny where the first delights of happiness are not interrupted by some storm, whose fatal breath dissipates its fair illusions, whose fell lightning consumes its altar? And what wounded spirit, when one of its tempests is over, does not seek to rest its memories in the sweet calm of country life? Yet man does not resign himself long to enjoy the beneficent tepidity which first charmed him on nature's bosom; when the trumpet's loud clangor has called him to arms, he rushes to the post of danger, whatever may be the war that calls him to the ranks, to find in battle the full consciousness of himself and the complete possession of his strength.

Richard Wagner and Giuseppi Verdi complete the list of first-generation romantic composers. Their contributions were primarily in the field of opera where their contributions are more properly discussed (see Chapter 14). Following Wagner and Verdi, Georges Bizet (1838–1875) and Giacomo Puccini (1858–1924) are the big names in romantic opera.

César Franck (1822–1890) was temperamentally more of an ascetic and mystic than a romantic, but he adopted and expanded the musical materials and procedures of his immediate predecessors. In spite of early promise as a concert artist on the piano and organ, he elected to follow an unspectacular career as a church organist, teacher, and composer. He lived and died in comparative obscurity, yet he exerted a powerful influence on French music. Young composers at the Paris conservatory who objected to the dominance of opera in French music turned to Franck, who was professor of organ, for their training rather than to the regular composition classes. Many of the big names in French instrumental music received guidance from Franck, and they in turn perpetuated his ideas. Of his compositions only a small number, mostly written when he was in his sixties, are well known. His cyclic *Symphony in D minor* is one of the most played works in the symphonic literature. His lone sonata for violin, also cyclic in form, occupies a similar position in that literature. The exquisite *Symphonic Variations* for solo piano and orchestra amply demonstrate his extraordinary mastery of musical organization and the eloquence of his highly personal harmonic idiom.

César Franck: *Symphonic Variations* (1885) 13:50
(1822–1890)

> This unique work contains brilliant and gratifying music for both the solo piano and the orchestra. The solo and accompaniment are beautifully balanced and integrated. It is one of the earliest and most successful concerto-like pieces in variation form. The treatment of variation form, however, is by no means traditional. It is played without pauses, and it lacks a well-defined theme. Instead it has three distinctive ideas which are amalgamated, fused, transformed, and developed in the continuous unfolding of the variations.
>
> (Also record side 6 band 1)

Johannes Brahms (1833–1897) is sometimes referred to as the classic romanticist. His temperament was romantic to the roots, but he opposed in principle and practice the unbridled fervor and the uncritical sentimentality of the ultraromantics. His romanticism was always restrained and disciplined. His musical utterances, no matter how im-

Johannes Brahms

passioned, are confined to classic patterns. Brahms was the antipode of the extravagant Liszt-Wagner type of romanticism, and as such was championed by and champion of a rabid anti-Wagner clique. Brahms, to his credit, took no part in this and openly admired works of Wagner, particularly the opera *Die Meistersinger*. It was quite against his will that he found himself in the center of the Wagner controversy, and he was neither deterred by his adversaries nor deflected by his advocates. More than most composers, Brahms was free to compose according to his own dictates. He toured as a pianist and accompanist and did some conducting, but most of his life was devoted to composition without sponsorship and consequently without restriction. He eschewed program and dramatic music but wrote magnificently in all the absolute forms for voices, piano, various chamber groups, and orchestra. The quality of his music is of such uniform excellence that it is virtually impossible to choose between works except on the basis of personal preference. He wrote quantities of vocal music, both solo and ensemble, and a *German Requiem* in seven large sections using passages from the German Bible for the text. He is one of the few composers of the romantic period seriously and consistently concerned with chamber music. He wrote numerous sets of variations continuing and elaborating on the traditions of Haydn, Mozart, and Beethoven. His works involving orchestra, generally conceded to be his best, include two overtures, two piano concertos, a violin concerto, a double concerto for violin and cello, and four symphonies. In the realm of the symphony, Brahms inherited the mantle of Beethoven.

Johannes Brahms: *Symphony no. 4 in E minor, op. 98* (1885)
(1833–1897)

1.	Allegro non troppo	10:45
2.	Andante moderato	10:15
3.	Allegro giocoso	6:00
4.	Allegro energico e passionato	9:00

The epic grandeur of Brahms's symphonies requires no explanation for those who have assimilated the symphonies of Beethoven. They continue the same traditions but clothe them in the raiment of the 19th century. It seems inconceivable now that this profoundly emotional music ever could have been considered austere, as it was by early auditors. Adjectives like sombre, meditative, elegiac, now seem more appropriate for the first two movements. Their songfulness, tinged with a dark, melancholy romanticism, is anything but austere. The third movement finds the staid Brahms in an unusually boisterous mood. It contains a remarkable example of invertible counterpoint. As the movement progresses, what was the melody in the opening becomes the bass, and the previous bass line becomes the melody. The finale is a set of 31 variations on the theme announced in the first eight measures.

If any composer of symphonic music requires no introduction to the general listener, it is Peter Ilich Tchaikovsky (1840–1893). It is inconceivable that anyone has not heard some of his music, if not in the original at least in a popular version. Biographers have bared intimate details of his personal life. Tchaikovsky began the study of music very early, but none of his teachers detected signs of genius in their charge. He was trained in law and for a time worked as a clerk in the Ministry of Justice in St. Petersburg, meanwhile continuing his musical studies. He resigned his post to devote himself to music. He taught private lessons to augment his meager financial resources until he was appointed professor of harmony in the Moscow Conservatory. He traveled throughout Europe while still on the staff at the conservatory but nevertheless found the position irksome. A curious arrangement with a wealthy widow, Nadejada von Meck, eventually enabled him to resign it. She settled on him a generous annuity, but by mutual consent they never met (except once by accident). Their communication was by correspondence exclusively. The Czar granted Tchaikovsky a pension which, added to his annuity, left him free to travel and compose. He spent much time abroad and in 1891 came to America where he conducted concerts in New York, Philadelphia, and Baltimore.

Tchaikovsky is the most cosmopolitan of the 19th-century Russian composers and, with the possible exception of Rimsky-Korsakov, the most polished technically. The emotion of Tchaikovsky's music is more intense than profound. Consequently its appeal is more immediate than enduring. It must be that two new listeners arise to take the place of every one satiated with his music, for its popularity shows no signs of diminishing. Tchaikovsky's music was not sufficiently "Russian" for him to be grouped with the nationalistic composers of his time, but it abounds in Russian characteristics—folk songs and folk-like melodies, traditional rhythms, violent and sudden contrasts of mood. He composed for all mediums, but orchestra was his forte. He was a brilliant orchestrator and fecund melodist. These virtues overbalance a rather mechanical application of structural formulas. He wrote operas, ballets, tone poems, concertos, and six symphonies of which the last three are performed profusely. Like most of the late romantic composers, he was inclined toward the classic forms. The overture-fantasy *Romeo and Juliet* is an interesting blend of classic form and romantic content.

PETER ILICH TCHAIKOVSKY

P. I. Tchaikovsky: *Romeo and Juliet* (1870) 19:45
(1840–1893)

This overture-fantasy has a regular sonata form with introduction, exposition, development, recapitulation, and coda. The themes and sections of the sonata form can be related to the characters and situations of the Shakespeare drama from which the work takes its name. The chorale-like introduction is descriptive of Friar Lawrence. The fiery principal theme portrays the feud between the houses of Montague and Capulet, and the subordinate theme is tender love music.

Romeo and Juliet is the earliest work of Tchaikovsky to find a permanent place in the orchestral literature. He revised it twice, and the version invariably heard is the final one.

Several composers who were born in the 19th century but lived well into the 20th century continued to write in an essentially romantic style to the end of their creative lives. Two of these were Richard Strauss (1864–1949) and Sergei Rachmaninoff (1873–1943). Rachmaninoff was perhaps better known during his lifetime as a concert pianist than as a composer. He composed for orchestra and for voices, but the works which secure his position in the ranks of composers are the ones involving piano (see page 57). Strauss, born into a musical family, scored spectacular successes with a series of tone poems written while he was still in his twenties. Then he turned his talent for dramatic music to opera, for which it was equally adept. His later years (after 1910) were less productive, and he never again matched his early triumphs. *Till Eulenspiegel* was composed while his creative powers were at their peak.

Richard Strauss: *Till Eulenspiegel, op. 28* (1895) 13:45
(1864–1949)

The complete title of this tone poem is *Till Eulenspiegel's Merry Pranks,* to which Strauss added the annotation, "After the old-fashioned roguish manner—in rondo form." Till is a puckish character in German folklore. The composer did not provide a detailed account of the adventures portrayed in the music, but others have. Wilhelm Mauke describes it this way:

> Once upon a time there was a prankish rogue, ever up to new tricks, named Till Eulenspiegel. Now he jumps on his horse and gallops into the midst of a crowd of market women, overturning their wares with a prodigious clatter. Now he lights out with seven-league boots; now conceals himself in a mousehole. Disguised as a priest, he 'drips with unction and morals,' yet out of his toe peeps the scamp. As a cavalier he makes love, at first in jest, but soon in earnest, and is rebuffed. He is furious, and swears vengeance on all mankind, but,

RICHARD STRAUSS

meeting some 'philistines' he forgets his wrath and mocks them. At length his hoaxes fail. He is tried in a Court of Justice and is condemned to hang for his misdeeds; but he still whistles defiantly as he ascends the ladder. Even on the scaffold he jests. Now he swings; now he gasps for air; a last convulsion. Till is dead.

The "once upon a time" music with which the piece begins, serves as a coda and brings it to a close. The rondo form is far from typical.

In the works of Anton Bruckner (1824–1896) and Gustav Mahler (1860–1911) romanticism was already a little overripe. Reverting to classic forms was not enough to stem the tide against it. Widespread nationalism was to revitalize romanticism for a while, but the movement which began so lustily ran its course and expended its energy like the classic period before it in the span of a lifetime. Of the late romantic compositions those by Mahler are currently most in vogue.

GUSTAV MAHLER: *Symphony no. 4 in G* (1900)

(1860–1911)	1.	Deliberately, unhurried	17:55
	2.	Leisurely, without haste	10:00
	3.	Peacefully	18:10
	4.	Very leisurely	8:50

This is the lightest, brightest, and shortest of Mahler's symphonies, though it is by no means small or trivial. A solo soprano voice introduced in the fourth movement sings a text describing the delights of heaven in childlike terms. English equivalents are given for Mahler's German tempo indications for the movements.

The composers of the period could point to solid achievements. Romantic music accounts for a large part of the current repertory, its popularity unchallenged. Its composers invented new forms, modified old ones, enlarged the orchestra, enriched the harmonic resources, and expanded the emotional range of music. Audiences increased in size. Composers were freed from bondage and obtained if not a more secure at least a more honored position in society. The romantic period was, in its own way, another golden age of music.

References

Barzun, Jacques. *Berlioz and the Romantic Century.* 3rd ed. New York: Columbia University Press, 1969.

Klaus, Kenneth B. *The Romantic Period in Music.* Boston: Allyn and Bacon, 1970.

Longyear, Rey M. *Nineteenth Century Romanticism in Music.* 2d. ed. Englewood Cliffs: Prentice-Hall, 1973.

CESAR FRANCK

Photo courtesy of Brown Brothers

Photo courtesy of
Brown Brothers

GUSTAV MAHLER

Chronology

Born	Composer	Died
1804	Glinka	1857
1811	Liszt	1886
1824	Smetana	1884
1833	Borodin	1887
1835	Cui	1918
1837	Balakirev	1910
1839	Mussorgsky	1881
1840	Tchaikovsky	1893
1841	Chabrier	1894
1841	Dvorak	1904
1843	Grieg	1907
1844	Rimsky-Korsakov	1908
1844	Sarasate	1908
1860	Albeniz	1909
1861	MacDowell	1908
1862	Debussy	1918
1862	Delius	1934
1865	Sibelius	1957
1867	Granados	1916
1874	Ives	1954
1875	Ravel	1937
1876	Falla	1946
1880	Bloch	1959
1881	Bartok	1945
1881	Enesco	1955
1882	Kodaly	1967
1884	Griffes	1920
1887	Villa-Lobos	1959
1896	Weinberger	1967
1898	Harris	
1899	Chavez	
1900	Copland	

(Record side 6 bands 5–7)

Nationalism and Impressionism

21

Nationalism and impressionism are musical styles which bridge the 19th and 20th centuries. Both began in the 19th century and lasted into the 20th. Nationalism is one aspect of romanticism, but a rather distinct aspect. Impressionism represents a break with romantic notions and foreshadows the more radical changes in music that were to follow.

Nationalism

Rebounding from Napoleon's grandiose schemes of subjugation and domination, a wave of nationalism swept over the various ethnic groups of Europe. Small groups struggling for identification and independence and large ones responding to the surge of expansion were equally enveloped. Nationalism is a sort of group romanticism. Composers were quick to seize the banner of the new movement, active in extolling the virtues of their particular patriotism. A certain amount of geographic and political influence in the arts is almost inevitable, but the conscious cultivation of nationalistic elements was a feature of the romantic and postromantic periods.

Nationalism in music took manifold forms. It was expressed by deliberately incorporating in the musical fabric melodic and rhythmic peculiarities of a particular region. These features usually are established by and derived from the folk songs and dances of the people. The borrowing sometimes was direct, with complete folk melodies appearing intact in composed works. The process had the effect of bringing art music closer to the common man, another facet of the romantic movement.

National heroes, folk characters, legends, epics, and myths—all were grist in the mill of patriotism. They were glorified in songs and symphonic poems. Operas were based on them. Some composers achieved enviable reputations solely on the basis of works with nationalistic pretentions. Even those not identified with the movement were not immune to its influences.

Nationalism fared better in music than in the other arts. Expressions which in prose or poetry would be blatant propaganda were interestingly exotic in music. Music dedicated to opposing ideologies was not explicit enough to be offensive. The fervent emotions of a piece like Sibelius's *Finlandia,* which might be banned in a subjugated country for inciting the people to revolt, could be appreciated by persons not partisans in the conflict. Strongly nationalistic music, far more than literature and painting, transcends geographic, political, and ethnic borders. The widespread acceptance of pieces written with avowed patriotic intent attests to this. So does the adoption of foreign dialects for specific works, as in the Spanish and Italian caprices of the Russian composers Rimsky-Korsakov and Tchaikovsky respectively.

A significant effect of nationalism in music was to neutralize the world-wide domination of music by German musicians and to hasten the demise of Germanic romanticism. In this way nationalism paved the way for impressionism and the modern era, both of which contain residual traces of nationalism.

The list of composers associated with the nationalistic movement contains many familiar names. It will be observed that most of them are from smaller countries and racial groups or from countries previously lacking a thriving indigenous musical tradition, not from Germany, Italy, France, or England.

One of the first countries to turn consciously to nationalism was Russia. Michael Glinka's opera *A Life for the Czar* (1836) was an early example. Around 1875 a group of Russian composers, subsequently known as *The Five,* banded together in a united effort to build a national musical tradition. Alexander Borodin (1833–1887), Cesar Cui (1835–1918), Modest Mussorgsky (1839–1881), Mily Balakirev (1837–1910), and Nikolai Rimsky-Korsakov (1844–1908) were members of the group. Borodin is best known for his opera *Prince Igor* which contains the famous *Polovtsian Dances* and is the source of the Broadway musical show *Kismet.* Cui and Balakirev are rarely played now. Mussorgsky's masterpiece is the opera *Boris Godounov* (see p. 19), but his *Pictures at an Exhibition* (see p. 186), his symphonic poem *Night on Bald Mountain,* and some of his songs are more familiar. Rimsky-Korsakov was the least nationalistic, the most highly trained, and the most successful of the group, with a number of concert favorites to his credit including the colorful *Capriccio Espagnol* (see p. 109). Tchaikovsky was excluded from the group, because his music was not sufficiently "Russian," though it was permeated with Russian qualities.

Bedrich Smetana (1824–1884), the great Czech nationalist, is remembered for his comic opera *The Bartered Bride* and for his manifestly nationalistic cycle of six symphonic poems *My Fatherland (Ma Vlast)* of which *The Moldau* depicting the route of that river through Bohemia is most famous. Antonin Dvorak (1841–1904) is also a Czech nationalist, but two of his most popular works, the *New World Symphony* (see p. 170) and the *American Quartet,* are impregnated with American influences occasioned by his three-year stay in this country.

Hungarian elements lend an authentic ring to the Hungarian Rhapsodies of Franz Liszt (1811–1886) and more recently to the works of Bela Bartok (1881–1945) and Zoltan Kodaly (1882–1967).

Spanish dance rhythms are particularly infectious, and they figure prominently in the music of Spanish composers Isaac Albeniz (1860–1909), Enrique Granados (1867–1916), and Manuel de Falla (1876–1946). Iberian rhythms have also attracted non-Spanish composers Emmanuel Chabrier (1841–1894), Rimsky-Korsakov, Debussy, and Ravel. Composers Heitor Villa-Lobos (1887–1959) of Brazil and Carlos Chavez (1899–) of Mexico are exponents of Latin-American nationalism.

The stirrings of nationalism reached into the Scandinavian countries, and several composers of local importance imparted the flavor of the northland to their music. Edvard Grieg (1843–1907) is the name invariably associated with Scandinavian nationalism. The music of another northerner, Jean Sibelius (1865–1957), *is* the music of Finland as far as the outside world is concerned. Supposedly he did not use actual folk material, but his music is saturated with the moods and sounds regarded as typical of Finland, though it is he alone who made them so.

Confusion exists as to just what America's indigenous music is and just what constitutes "Americanism" in music. As soon as our musical traditions were sufficiently mature to resent the yoke of European influence, composers' interest in native resources roused. Negro music, Indian music, folk music (especially Western), and jazz were explored. Elements of all four have found their way into worthy compositions, but none has seemed to be ideally suited to a continuing tradition. Obvious folk and traditional elements have been included in serious American music only sporadically. Nationalism has been a peripheral rather than a central aspect of music in the United States, but American composers of late have declared their independence from Europe. It is no longer considered essential, as it was a couple of generations ago, for an American composer to complete his training abroad. It isn't even the fashion. With increasing numbers of American musicians being trained on their native soil, an autogenous musical tradition is emerging. Music is being composed which has an American sound. The American sound is still too elusive to be defined precisely, but it is heard and recognized increasingly in the music of this country. American music is achieving identity without obvious devices, and this perhaps is the best kind of nationalism. Edward MacDowell (1861–1908) used Indian themes but never outgrew his Germanic training. Though Roy Harris (1898–) and Aaron Copland (1900–) both studied in France, they are regarded as two of the more "American" composers of their generation. The young, domestically-trained composers are not as a rule consciously nationalistic in orientation.

The distinctive characteristics of each nation's music are most apparent when selections from various geographic regions are heard in succession. The suggested examples provide a panoramic view of nationalism in music.

ALEXANDER BORODIN: *Prince Igor* (1890)
(1833–1887) Polovtsian Dances 11:35

Borodin worked on his opera for many years but never completed it. It was finished by Rimsky-Korsakov and Glazunov and given its first performance three years after the composer's death. Borodin said, "*Prince Igor* is essentially a national opera which can be of interest only to us Russians who like to refresh ourselves at the fountainhead of our history, and to see the origins of our nationality revived upon the stage." The setting of the opera is in Central Asia during the 12th century. The Polovtsi, a Tartar race, have captured Prince Igor in the second act, and the Polovtsian maidens dance in his honor. The music for this most famous scene of the opera compounds savagery, passion, and power in music which belies Borodin's modest estimate of its worth. There are voice parts in the original, but the dances are often played in concerts with instruments taking the vocal lines.

BEDRICH SMETANA: *The Bartered Bride* (1866)
(1824–1884) Overture 6:05

Bohemia, an area of modern Czechoslovakia, gained a measure of political independence from Austria in 1860. Two years later a National Theater dedicated to the performance of Bohemian opera was founded by public subscription. Smetana began immediately to compose operas imbued with the nationalistic spirit and in the Bohemian language for performance there. After the enthusiastic reception of *The Bartered Bride,* the second of his eight operas, Smetana was appointed first conductor of the Opera. Excerpts from

The Bartered Bride, and the opera itself in translation, have become international favorites. The mood of the overture and the opera is that of a festive Bohemian village.

MANUEL DE FALLA: *El Amor Brujo (Love, the Sorcerer)* (1915) 15:50
(1876–1946)

Introduction
Dance of Terror
The Magic Circle
Ritual Fire Dance*
Pantomime
Finale

When Falla returned to Spain at the beginning of World War I after seven years in Paris, his countrymen suspected him of having diluted his Spanish blood with French wine. After a brief period drenching himself in the songs and dances of his native land, he silenced their doubts by composing the thoroughly Spanish ballet *El Amor Brujo* for the Andalusian gypsy dancer Pastora Impero.

The story of the ballet concerns a gypsy girl who is haunted by her dead lover. His appearance whenever she is about to kiss her new lover is frustrating the romance. The dead man, unable to resist a pretty face in life or death, is distracted during a rendezvous by a girl friend of his ex-sweetheart. The new lovers kiss; the spell is broken; the spectre disappears; and all ends happily.

The *Ritual Fire Dance* from this work is one of Falla's most popular creations. In addition to the numbers listed, two numbers with a part for contralto voice are included in the complete ballet and in concert and recorded performances when a singer is used.

*(Record side 6 band 7)

JEAN SIBELIUS: *Finlandia, op. 26 no. 7* (1899) 8:45
(1865–1957)

This work was written while Finland was oppressed by the iron rule of Imperial Russia. Its effect on the Finns was so inflammatory that its performance was banned throughout the country. When eventually they gained concessions and finally independence, *Finlandia* became a symbol of triumphant struggle and freedom.

AARON COPLAND: *Billy the Kid* (1938) 20:00
(1900–)

The Open Prairie
Street in Frontier Town
Card Game at Night
Gun Battle
Celebration after Billy's Capture
The Open Prairie Again

JEAN SIBELIUS

The sections listed are included in an orchestral suite taken from the ballet commissioned by Lincoln Kirstein, director of the Ballet Caravan. It is as American as apple pie. Not only is the ballet set in the old West with a legendary figure as its central character, but cowboy tunes are dexterously woven into the musical fabric. Among those included are: *Get Along Little Dogies, The Old Chisholm Trail, Old Paint,* and *The Dying Cowboy.*

(Also record side 6 band 6)[1]

Impressionism

Impressionism began as an art movement. Edouard Manet was using impressionist techniques as early as 1863, but the term was first used in a derisive commentary on a painting by Claude Monet. A group of painters which included Renoir and Degas adopted the term officially for their exhibitions starting in 1877. The impressionists, reacting negatively to the prevailing style of painting classical and sentimental subjects, used primary colors in juxtaposition to achieve greater brilliance and luminosity than was possible with the customary blended pigments. Their representation of the effects of natural sunlight blurred outlines. Minor details tended to disappear, and forms were suggested rather than defined. Spontaneous impressions were captured on canvas, not studied renderings.

The symbolist poets Stéphane Mallarmé and Paul Verlaine were kindred spirits with the impressionist painters, and like the impressionist painters they preceded and set the stage for the corresponding style in music.

1. See fn. p. 16.

Impressionism in music and the name Claude Debussy (1862–1918) are inseparable. He was the first impressionist composer and almost the only one whose works are regarded as exclusively and purely impressionistic, but perhaps this is because his music sets the standards by which impressionism in music is measured. Debussy drew inspiration from the impressionist painters and the symbolist poets. His music, like their pictures and poems, is subtle and suggestive rather than bold and exuberant. It is sensuous but not passionate, picturesque but not graphic. Color and mood take precedence over line and structure. He was not prolific, but every page of his music is finely wrought. It includes two books of *Preludes* and numerous small works for piano, an opera *Pelleas and Melisande,* song cycles and cantatas, a small quantity of chamber music, and a few exquisitely colored orchestral works. The quintessence of impressionism is embodied in his *Clouds.*

Claude Debussy: *Nocturnes* (1899)
(1862–1918) 1. Nuages (Clouds) 7:20

Nuages is the first of three *Nocturnes* for which Debussy provided the following program notes:

> The title *Nocturnes* is intended to have here a more general and, above all, a more decorative meaning. We, then, are not concerned with the form of the Nocturne, but with everything that this word includes in the way of diversified impression and special lights.
>
> Clouds: The unchangeable appearance of the sky, with the slow and solemn march of clouds dissolving in a gray agony tinted with white.

(Also record side 6 band 5)

Debussy was not a nationalist in the usual sense, but he did regard impressionism as a French reaction to German romanticism. A clue to his thinking is provided by the way he signed his name: "Claude Debussy, French musician."

Maurice Ravel (1875–1937) is invariably linked with Debussy as an impressionist composer. He was influenced by Debussy and impressionism, but he was no slavish imitator. His music is less fragmentary than that of Debussy, more lyric and dynamic. Precision and clarity are characteristics of his art, as it is of the French language and literature. He wrote brilliant music for piano and made equally brilliant transcriptions of some of it for orchestra, in addition to his original orchestral compositions. Among his best-known works are: *Alborada del gracioso, Bolero,* two piano concertos, a string quartet, the ballet suites *Daphnis and Chloe* and *Mother Goose, La Valse,* and the unforgettable *Pavane.*

Maurice Ravel: *Pavane pour une infante défunte* (1899) 5:20
(1875–1937)

> This is one of Ravel's compositions which exists in versions for both piano and orchestra. Annotators disagree as to whether this is a "Pavane for a Dead Princess" or a "Pavane for a Dead Infant." Whichever, the pavane which started out as a stately dance in 16th-century Spain became a tender elegy in late 19th-century France. The style is not really typical of impressionism, but it is typical of Ravel.

Impressionism was almost, but not quite, a French monopoly. The Germans were not receptive to the new style, as would be expected since it was a reaction to their romanticism, but impressionist influences can be detected in many English, Italian, Spanish, and American works written during the first third of the century. Though several non-French com-

Claude Debussy

Maurice Ravel

posers were influenced by impressionism, about the only ones classified as impressionists, and these not consistently, are Frederick Delius (1862–1934) and Charles Tomlinson Griffes (1884–1920). Delius lived in France after the age of 26, so he scarcely qualified as non-French, though he was born in England of German parentage and studied music in the United States and Germany. This leaves Griffes as the one composer without French connections who can be regarded as an impressionist. The first of his *Roman Sketches* is the best known, and the fourth makes an interesting comparison with Debussy's *Nocturne* of the same title.

CHARLES GRIFFES:	*Roman Sketches, op. 7* (1917)	
(1884–1920)	1. The White Peacock	5:20
	4. Clouds	4:20

The four *Roman Sketches* originally were for piano. Griffes scored the first and last for orchestra before his untimely death. A quotation from the mystic poet William Sharp prefaces each of the sketches. The one preceding *The White Peacock* begins:

Here where the sunlight
Floodeth the garden,
Where the pomegranate
Reareth its glory
Where the oleanders
Dream through the noontides;

and ends:

Pale, pale as the breath of blue
smoke in far woodlands,
Here, as the breath, as the soul of this beauty,
Moves the White Peacock.

The lines quoted in the score of *Clouds* are:

Mountainous glories,
They move superbly;
Crumbling so slowly,
That none perceives when
The golden domes
Are sunk in the valleys
Of fathomless snows.

References

Demuth, Norman. *Ravel.* New York: Collier-Macmillan International, 1962.
Lockspeiser, Edward. *Debussy.* 4th ed. New York: McGraw-Hill, 1972.
Orenstein, Arbie. *Ravel: Man and Musician.* New York: Columbia University Press, 1975.

Chronology

1872	Vaughan Williams	1958
1874	Schoenberg	1951
1874	Ives	1954
1876	Falla	1946
1880	Bloch	1959
1881	Bartok	1945
1882	Kodaly	1967
1882	Stravinsky	1971
1883	Webern	1945
1883	Varèse	1965
1885	Berg	1935
1887	Villa-Lobos	1959
1890	Ibert	1962
1891	Prokofiev	1953
1892	Honegger	1955
1892	Milhaud	1974
1895	Hindemith	1963
1896	Sessions	
1896	Weinberger	1967
1897	Cowell	1965
1898	Gershwin	1937
1898	Harris	
1899	Chavez	
1899	Thompson	
1900	Weill	1950
1900	Copland	
1902	Walton	
1903	Khachaturian	
1906	Shostakovich	1975
1908	Carter	
1908	Messiaen	
1910	Barber	
1911	Hovhaness	
1911	Menotti	
1912	Cage	
1913	Britten	
1914	Kleinsinger	
1917	Ward	
1918	Bernstein	

(Records side 6 band 6 to side 8 band 5)

Modern Music to 1950

22

It is a curious state of affairs when the music of the 20th century requires special explanation, even justification. That this is so is perhaps understandable if indefensible. A more natural situation would be for the people of any age to be most receptive to the arts and crafts of their own time, which is essentially the case in literature, drama, and architecture. There is little chance that a novel by Dickens will turn up as a book-of-the-month selection, that Shakespeare will force Edward Albee off Broadway, or that Gothic-style architecture will be revived. Unhappily, the parallel does not extend to serious music. Reasons for the neglect of contemporary music are worthy of investigation.

Conductors are inclined to place the blame on audiences, who presumably demand familiar music, without conceding that the familiarity of old music is the result of its having been programed to the exclusion of the new. With the masterpieces of the past being played because they are familiar and being familiar because they are played, contemporary works have little chance of breaking into the charmed circle. Established patterns are slow to change, and in music practical considerations retard the process.

Modern music on the whole is difficult to play. It is technically demanding and unfamiliar to the players. Readying a new work for performance requires more rehearsal time than the quick review needed for the standard repertory, and rehearsal time at union scale is expensive. Performance fees for copyrighted works are small, but there are no performance fees for works in public domain. The compositions of all of the masters of the past are in direct competition for performances with the works of living composers. These aggravating details are but a prelude to the main problem—the basic lack of understanding of the musical idioms of our time.

Performers and listeners conditioned to sweet concords, singable melodies, and symmetric rhythmic patterns are bewildered by the complexities and irregularities of contemporary music. Often their first impression is that new music has forsaken tradition and that radical innovation has replaced reason. Actually, the development of musical materials has always proceeded in a logical and orderly fashion, but the pace has accelerated tremendously in the past 75 years. The rapidity with which musical resources have expanded in recent times has made it difficult for performers and listeners alike to keep abreast of the latest developments. Though the disparity between the old and the new was more apparent than real for the first half of the century, musical taste has lagged farther and farther behind the conceptions of avant-garde composers, and the gulf between them and the listening public continues to widen. It was not always thus!

Before 1800 most composers were attached to a court or a church which provided a ready market for their latest creations. Auspicious occasions of church and state were commemorated with special compositions. As a result of their institutional connections, composers had both the time and the incentive to produce voluminous amounts of music and in the process to become masters of their craft. That some of their works are enduring masterpieces is a purely gratuitous circumstance. A natural corollary of placing a premium on new works was that old ones were short-lived. The repetition of familiar favorites season after season was unknown in that period. Many compositions since revived were discarded in their own time after a few performances. *The Art of Fugue* by Bach, now universally regarded as a monument of musical art, sold only 30 copies in the 18th century, and the plates for it were melted for their metal by Bach's sons, themselves reputable composers.

How different the situation is now. The geniuses of the past are regarded with reverence. Even their inferior works are programed as a sort of holy obligation, while contemporary composers are denied the opportunities which made possible the achievements of their predecessors. Music students are indoctrinated so thoroughly in the musical language of the past that they adopt an archaic dialect as their own. Music listeners are subjected to the same influences. It is small wonder under these conditions that we speak most fluently and understand most readily a musical language which dates from the time of the American Revolution.

It would be folly to suggest the elimination of the old, but bringing the performance of the new into balance with it is not only a desirable but a necessary objective if music is to remain a vital cultural force. Not all contemporary music measures up to the quality of masterpieces sifted from the prodigious production of past ages, but currency and freshness compensate. Besides, the expressions of qualified artists deserve hearings, and in no other way can new masterpieces be created and discovered.

Persons steeped in the musical traditions of the past, and few escape, may be prejudiced against innovation. One who is conditioned to regard the style of Bach, Mozart, or Beethoven as the ideal by which all other musical expressions are to be measured is apt to view with disdain the styles of Schoenberg, Stravinsky, and their contemporaries, not to mention the more recent composers. It is strange and unfortunate that our listening experiences are concentrated on the music of the 18th and 19th centuries. Relating current practices to those of the past is one way of bridging the gap between them, but in the final analysis listening to the music of our time is the best way to become attuned to it.

Now as always, each composer has a distinctive musical personality, but beneath the surface a common heritage provides bonds between contemporaries and links with the masters of preceding generations. Many features of 20th-century music which appear to be new are merely the latest manifestations of practices rooted in tradition. Viewed in this light they are immediately more intelligible.

The rhythmic limitations observed in music conforming to fixed metric patterns and in which constant pulses are divided in prescribed ways must be regarded as arbitrary. That these limitations were honored for so long is more amazing than that they were abandoned early in this century. With rhythm exploited for its own sake, as it has been increasingly during the past 75 years, it was inevitable that rhythmic possibilities would be expanded to include asymmetric meters, shifted accents, and complex and irregular divisions of rhythmic units. The existence of duple and triple meters and pulses divided in regular fractions ultimately suggests alternating and combining duple and triple meters in various ways and dividing pulses irregularly, standard features of modern music. Accents displaced in relation to the metric organization of the music have been used for centuries, but are now more conspicuous. The organization of durations according to serial procedures, found in some post-Webern (1883–1945) compositions, traces its origins back to the isorhythm (see p. 239) of the 14th century. The principles of augmentation and diminution (increasing and decreasing rhythmic values) practiced for centuries have been expanded, updated, and systematized by Olivier Messiaen (1908–). He writes music with no fixed metric scheme in which certain notes in a succession of more or less uniform values are prolonged or reduced by a fraction, often by adding a dot to or withdrawing a dot from the note symbol, which increases or decreases its value by half. In the music of Elliott Carter (1908–) there are passages in which the tempo (pace) is systematically changed by precise degrees at small time intervals. This concept adds a new dimension to the old idea of ritardando (gradually decreasing the tempo) and accelerando (gradually increasing the tempo). Though ties between rhythmic practices present and past are readily established, learning to accept the unexpected along with the expected is the only requirement for responding to the rhythms of 20th-century music.

Learning to appreciate contemporary melody is more of a problem. The concept of melody has evolved over the centuries, but in the minds of music lovers generally the word implies a succession of tones which is singable and easily remembered. Such a description is valid for most of the melodies of the past and for the popular and familiar music of the day, but it is a narrow view of melody. Melodies that are singable by untrained voices of necessity have a restricted compass and predominantly conjunct motion. Melodies are more easily remembered when they are based on familiar scale, chord, and rhythm patterns, but limitations of this sort artificially inhibit creativity in an age of freedom and unlimited resources. Composers who give free rein to their imaginations or apply advanced principles in the creation of wide-ranging, angular, disjunct, instrumental lines free of traditional scale and chord influences are accused of writing music which is tuneless. Such accusations should not be leveled at music containing lines of inherent logic and beauty which do not conform to traditional concepts of melody. The definition of melody rather should be broadened to embrace all tonal successions of inherent logic and beauty. The problem is that the perception of beauty is largely in the eye of the beholder, and complex logic may be incomprehensible to all but the most avid scholars. Casual listeners therefore should approach contemporary music with an open mind regarding the essential attributes of melody, and when they find none should look elsewhere in the sound spectrum for the essence of the particular work.

Counterpoint, the art of combining melodies, has been renovated, but the results have been less startling than the melodies themselves. The melodies used in contrapuntal associations display the same characteristics as other melodies, but the old ideal of fitting them together in a happy blend is replaced by one in which combined melodies pursue conflicting paths with obstinate independence. When the ear is conditioned to follow the lines of contrapuntal music, clashes between them whether momentary or perpetual do not attract much attention.

Harmony evolved slowly and systematically from the time pitches were first sounded together up to the end of the 19th century, by which time the most complex harmonies in common use were seventh chords consisting of four alternate scale tones. The ratios of their vibrations were relatively simple, and they blended into thoroughly agreeable sounds.

Then the evolutionary process exploded. Within 25 years harmonic materials were expanded to include chords of seven and more tones and the most complex relationships possible between the twelve available notes. The suddenness of the expansion eliminated the possibility of gradual adjustment. Before the first of these new dissonant chords had been assimilated, newer and more strident ones were introduced. Traditional concepts of consonance and dissonance were upended. Though the dissonant harmonies of the 20th century are the logical culmination of evolutionary processes set in motion when two tones were first sounded together, most listeners were unprepared for the burst of speed at the finish. Much antagonism toward new music stems from a reluctance to accept the more complex tonal relationships as legitimate sonorities. If consonance is equated with beauty and dissonance with ugliness, then certainly modern music is not very pretty. However, if consonance is equated with repose and dissonance with tension, which is more valid, the high-powered music of this century makes that of the past seem tranquil to the point of immobility. There is no reluctance on the part of contemporary composers to use any conceivable combination of tones, but most vertically conceived combinations of tones can be analyzed in terms of their relationship to conventional arrangements. Some are conventional chord structures with notes omitted or with foreign tones added. Some combine two conventional structures, and some build chords from intervals other than those found in traditional harmonies. An infinite number of sonorities are available to contemporary composers compared with a mere handful in use less than a hundred years ago. The composer's art has become more involved and the listener's art more exciting with the harmonic innovations in the first half of this century.

In the matter of harmonic progression, too, recent composers have explored new possibilities. They eschew the stereotyped harmonic formulas which abound in conventional music. Freedom of chord relationship as well as structure is constantly exploited. Dissonant chords are treated as functionally independent entities, not bound by archaic principles of resolution and progression. Beyond this, simultaneous sounds are unordered—the product of independent linear motion, systematic procedures not primarily concerned with harmonic considerations, or coincidence. To appreciate music in the newer idioms, the composer's premises, which may reject all traditional concepts of harmony, must be accepted.

Contemporary concepts of melody and harmony inevitably weaken the bonds of tonality. Whereas traditional music gravitates to a well-defined tonal center, tonal centers in modern music are usually vague and often nonexistent. When tonality vanishes, a primary orienting device for listeners is sacrificed. For this reason the 20th-century styles in which some semblance of tonality is retained are more accessible. Those

Arnold Schoenberg

in which serial (twelve-tone) procedures or abstract logic is substituted for tonality present problems that can be surmounted only by familiarity with the particular idiom.

Most phases of contemporary music have been the center of controversy at one time or another. The one aspect of modern music that has received unanimous acclaim has been reserved for last. The severest critics of contemporary music are lavish in their praise of 20th-century orchestration. The exploitation of instrumental color in the present century is unprecedented. Modern instruments and orchestras have reached a pinnacle of perfection, and composers are taking full advantage of newly discovered and developed instrumental resources. In this respect at least, the composers of our time have never been excelled.

New music is as complex and unpredictable as the times in which we live. Creative artists sublimate the impulses and aspirations of their time and place. Their creations, therefore, should receive the most sympathetic reception from their contemporaries and countrymen. We may admire the masterpieces of the past and find escape in the rustic simplicity of a Haydn, for certainly great art is timeless and universal, but the ultimate emotional responses should be evoked by artistic creations intimately reflecting the moods of our own frantic age. When the opposite is true, the only plausible explanation would seem to be that either the producers or the consumers of the art are out of step with the times. If we can believe history, the critics are more apt to be wrong than the creators.

A point in time has now been reached when the works produced during the first half of this century can be viewed with a degree of perspective and objectivity. Some winnowing of the significant and enduring from the trivial and transient has taken place. In retrospect the evidence

SERGE PROKOFIEV

is convincing that the United States has become the center of world music. Whereas the history of music prior to 1900 could have been written with barely a mention of this country, a high percentage of the important musicians since then have lived, worked, or visited here. This premise is supported by the composers and works selected to illustrate the styles of music that flourished between 1900 and 1950.

ARNOLD SCHOENBERG was born in Vienna in 1874. Following a distinguished if controversial musical career in Europe, he came to this country in 1933. He taught a master class at the Malkin Conservatory in Boston before settling permanently in southern California, where he acquired U.S. citizenship and Americanized the spelling of his name. In 1935 he was appointed professor of music at the University of Southern California in Los Angeles, and the next year he moved across town to a similar position at the University of California. He retired from the university in 1944 at the age of 70 but continued to compose and to teach a select group of private pupils during the remaining seven years of his life.

To Schoenberg must be attributed one of the most profound innovations in the annals of music. He devised a system of "composition with 12 tones related only to one another" in which conventional principles of harmony, counterpoint, and tonality are replaced by new precepts of tonal organization. Schoenberg's method is based on a *series* of 12 different notes in a prescribed order which establishes a pattern of intervals. This series and its resulting sequence of intervals is the total basis for a strict *serial* composition. Within the limits imposed by the series in its various guises, the composer is free to distribute the pitches and to regulate the rhythm, texture, instrumentation and form according to his musical instincts. The freedom is disciplined, however, for every note from beginning to end appears only in relation to its assigned position in the original series. This approach seems like a radical departure from conventional practices, but Schoenberg claimed historical precedents for it and staunchly defended it as a logical and necessary forward step in the evolution of music. In composing his *String Quartet no. 4* (see p. 106) Schoenberg stringently observed his own principles of serial organization. Serial procedures prevail in *A Survivor from Warsaw,* but they do not control the pitch inflections in the part of the narrator.

ARNOLD SCHOENBERG: *A Survivor from Warsaw, op. 46* (1947) 6:15
(1874–1951)

> Schoenberg, whose gifts were literary and artistic as well as musical, wrote the text in English for this dramatic cantata for narrator, men's chorus, and orchestra. The narration is a first person recounting of the horrors experienced by a Jew during the occupation of Warsaw by the Nazis. The rhythm of the narration is notated precisely, but in lieu of exact pitches only rising and falling vocal inflections are indicated. At the climax of the narrative the chorus sings a traditional Hebrew prayer in unison while the orchestra provides an elaborate setting.

Serial music, being difficult to play and to comprehend, has never attracted a wide audience, but a host of disciples has been converted to serial composition. ALBAN BERG (1885–1935) was one of the first and most distinguished composers to come under Schoenberg's influence. His mature works are atonal, but he did not follow serial procedures as consistently or rigidly as Schoenberg. An irrepressible lyricism and romanticism broaden the appeal of his music. The opera *Wozzeck,* and the *Violin Concerto* commissioned and premiered by the American violinist Louis Krasner are recognized masterpieces.

ALBAN BERG: *Violin Concerto* (1935)
(1885–1935) 1. Andante—Allegretto 10:20
2. Allegro—Adagio 13:20

> Berg agreed to write a violin concerto early in 1934 but did not begin work on it until a beautiful young girl to whom he was deeply attached died unexpectedly. His reaction to the tragic event was to compose this monument "to the memory of an angel" in three months of feverish creativity. It was a requiem for her and for him. He did not live to hear the first performance the following year.
>
> After an introduction of approximately one minute's duration, the solo violin clearly announces the 12 notes of the series in their original order starting on the lowest pitch and ascending in an unbroken line to the last note of the series in a very high register. The flavor of the series permeates the work and provides an effective

if subconscious unifying element. It is not necessary or even desirable to search for evidence of the series when listening to serial music for pleasure.

Expressionism is the name for the style of Schoenberg and his school. The term, like impressionism, was borrowed from painting and as in painting, the two styles are antithetical. Where the impressionists used ultrarefined techniques in naturalistic portrayals of the external world as perceived by the senses, the expressionists (Picasso, Kandinsky, Klee) expressed the subconscious, inner self in grotesque abstractions with utter disregard for reality and the traditional principles of beauty and design. Expressionism in music is characterized by fragmentation of thematic material, disjunct lines, discordant harmony, and a high degree of abstract organization.

ANTON WEBERN (1883–1945), a composer closely associated with Schoenberg and Berg in the early development of twelve-tone composition, was the ultimate expressionist. His music is not as accessible as that of Berg, but it has had a greater direct influence on the younger generation of serialists. Composers like Pierre Boulez (1925–) and Karlheinz Stockhausen (1928–), who have extended serial procedures to parameters of music other than pitch (such as rhythm, dynamics, and tone color), pay particular homage to Webern. Webern's contact with Americans was brief and tragic. His son was killed in a World War II air raid, and he was shot fatally when he violated a curfew imposed by U.S. occupation troops. The University of Washington in Seattle acquired his manuscripts, which are the object of much scholarly study. The 10-minute *Symphony, op. 21* is probably the best example of Webern's mature style, but the *Three Songs, op. 18* provide a more ingratiating introduction to his music.

ANTON WEBERN: *Three Songs, op. 18* (1925)
(1883–1945)

1.	Schatzerl klein (Sweetheart, Dear)	:48
2.	Erlösung (Redemption)	1:00
3.	Ave, Regina	1:23

These songs demonstrate Webern's penchant for brevity and economy of means. His music gives the impression of having been distilled to the point where only the essence remains. His texture is sparse and transparent. No masses of sound or multiplicity of lines compete with each other for attention. The problem is to perceive the thread of continuity which forges the disjointed fragments into a unified whole. When Webern conceived these songs, the principles of twelve-tone composition were newly formulated. In this, his second opus using the method, he already handles it with assurance and imagination.

(Record side 8 bands 2–4)

If the expressionist movement emanating from Vienna exemplifies the break with musical tradition, the prevailing style of Russian music represents its continuation. Listening to a work of Dmitri Shostakovich, born in St. Petersburg, immediately after hearing examples of expressionist music places these contemporaneous styles in sharp relief. Visits to this country by Shostakovich in 1949 as a delegate to the Cultural and Scientific World Peace Conference and again in 1959 on the cultural exchange program between the Soviet Union and the U.S. have had no noticeable effect on his music or ours. Many of his compositions are too closely tied to communist ideology to sustain interest abroad. He quickly repudiated his sporadic ventures into "decadent modernism" and did penance with the production of works strictly in accordance with the dogma of "socialist realism." The premiere of his *Fifth Symphony* in Leningrad was praised as "an example of true Soviet art, classical in formal design, lucid in its melodic and harmonic procedures, and optimistic in its philosophical connotations."

Dmitri Shostakovich: *Symphony no. 5 in D minor, op. 47* (1937)
(1906–1975)

1.	Moderato	17:17
2.	Allegretto	4:55
3.	Largo	15:55
4.	Allegro non troppo	9:32

Shostakovich was catapulted to instant fame by his *First Symphony* written while he was still in his teens. A series of more progressive works aroused the ire of Soviet officialdom and put him in a position of disrepute. The *Fourth Symphony* was rehearsed but withdrawn and never performed after its modernism was criticized. Shostakovich's preeminence was reestablished with his *Fifth Symphony* which remains, along with the *First*, as the most successful of his 15 works in the form.

Serge Prokofiev (1891–1953), though more progressive and cosmopolitan than Shostakovich, was influential and admired in Soviet musical circles. From 1918 until he established Soviet citizenship in 1933, he lived principally in the United States and France. His reputation was spread by international tours as a pianist, frequently playing his own compositions. His stature as a composer is predicated at least partially upon the breadth of his endeavors. He wrote in all of the conventional forms—symphonies, suites, concertos, ballets, operas, symphonic poems, piano music, and chamber music, and in addition he composed film scores and music for children. One of his most famous works, if not his greatest, is in the latter category.

Colorplate 5. WASSILY KANDINSKY: Composition Number Three (1914)

Kandinsky and his nonrepresentational art were rejected by both Soviet Russia and Nazi Germany before he found sanctuary in France. Parallels are readily perceived between 20th-century music and his nonobjective paintings with their complex line and color relationships.

Courtesy The Museum of Modern Art, New York
Mrs. Simon Guggenheim Fund

Colorplate 6. JOSÉ OROZCO: Zapatistas

Many paintings and murals of Orozco (1883–1949) are nationalistic in the sense that they glorify the common people and causes of an emerging nation, Mexico. His vivid colors, strong lines, and insistent repetition of bold patterns have direct counterparts in the music of Spain and Latin America.

Courtesy The Museum of Modern Art, New York

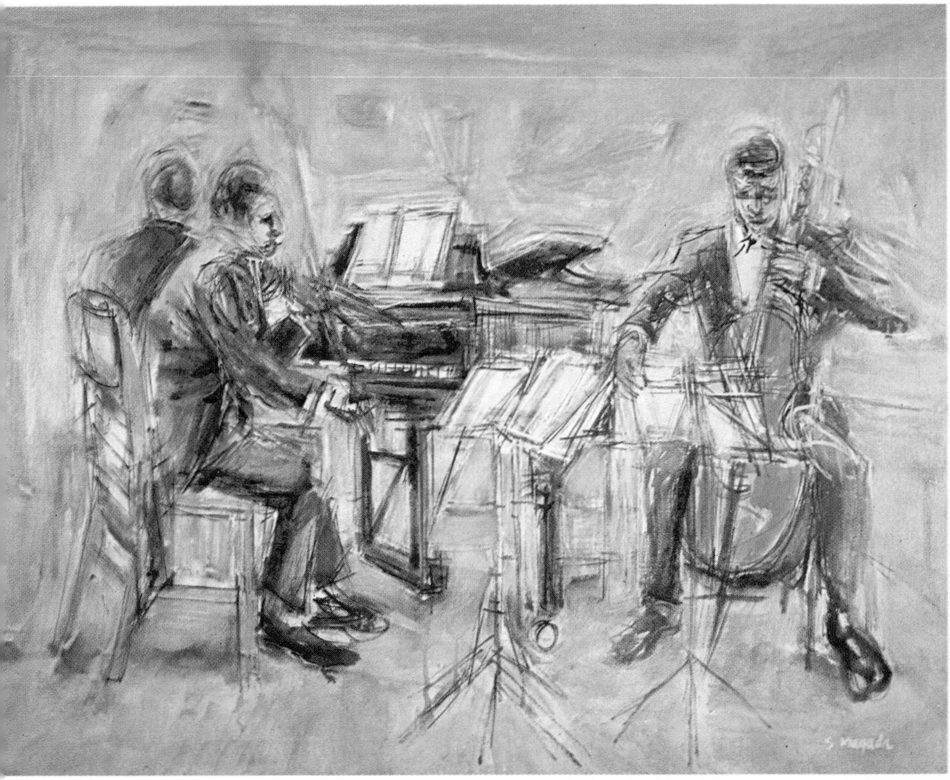

Colorplate 7. STEVE MAGADA: Trio

Musicians and musical instruments have been favorite subjects for artists of all periods and styles. Steve Magada is a contemporary painter who continues this tradition.

Courtesy Steve Magada

Colorplate 8. AGAM: Double Metamorphosis II

"Op" art, of which Agam (Yaacov Gipstein) is an exponent, emerged as a significant movement in the early 1960s concurrently with similar developments in electronic and computer music.

Collection The Museum of Modern Art, New York
Gift of Mr. and Mrs. George Jaffin

DMITRI SHOSTAKOVICH

SERGE PROKOFIEV: *Peter and the Wolf, op. 67* (1936) 22:15
(1891–1953)

> Though intended for children, Prokofiev's basic compositional techniques, somewhat simplified, are embodied in this delightful fable for narrator and orchestra. Its appeal is not limited to children. Like youth, it is almost a shame to waste it on them.

PAUL HINDEMITH (1895–1963) was a complete and practical musician. He played several instruments—the violin, viola, and piano professionally. He was a composer, conductor, teacher, theorist, and author. His impact on 20th-century music through his students, his writings, and his personal appearances has been enormous. As a composer he would be classified by contemporary standards as a traditionalist, but his music is not old-fashioned by any stretch of the imagination. His youthful works were regarded as radical, as are the works of most young composers, but he is known as the champion of *Gebrauchsmusik* (music for practical use) and *Hausmusik* (music to be played at home). The practicality of his approach can be gathered from the fact that there are 59 entries, some for multiple works, under his name in the current *Schwann-1 Record and Tape Guide*. He regarded composition as a craft, and he was a master craftsman. He was against atonality and serialism but not against dissonance or complexity. Critics detect in his music classic, romantic, baroque, archaic, and modern influences, which is to say that he wrote in the style that suited his purpose at the moment. His friendship with Jewish musicians brought him into conflict with the Nazi regime, and he left his native Germany the year after *Mathis der Maler* was composed. He concertized in this country during the late 1930s and settled here in 1940, teaching at Yale and Harvard before retiring and moving to Zurich in 1953.

PAUL HINDEMITH

PAUL HINDEMITH: *Mathis der Maler (Matthias the Painter)* (1934)
(1895–1963)

1.	Angelic Concert	8:00
2.	Entombment*	4:08
3.	The Temptation of Saint Anthony	13:30

The symphony *Mathis der Maler* is taken from the semihistorical opera of the same name. The opera depicts episodes in the life of painter Mathis Gothart Nithart, known as Mathis Grünewald, and the symphony relates specifically to three facets of the Isenheim altarpiece which he painted. The title of each movement of the symphony is taken from the subject shown in one panel of the painting (see colorplate 1).

*(Record side 8 band 5. Themes p. 375)

Bela Bartok (1881–1945), one of the titans of 20th-century music, developed a dynamic, personal style which is not easily categorized. He is connected with no "ism" unless it be that of modernism. He did extensive research and publication in the field of folk music but except for a few articles did not write about art music. He taught piano but not composition. His works until near the end of his career were problematical. These factors contributed to the delay in recognizing the magnitude of his genius. He first toured the United States in 1927 as a concert pianist. In 1940 he came to New York where he lived in relative poverty and obscurity until his death. Though not unknown during his lifetime, fame and remuneration commensurate with the worth of his music came posthumously. Bartok's output, just short of 100 works, includes many arrangements of folk songs and dances, and folk influences of his native Hungary abound in the other works. Practically all forms and mediums were included in his production, with piano music and chamber music especially abundant. The one form that he never attempted was a symphony, but his *Concerto for Orchestra* is very close to a symphony in concept.

Bela Bartok: *Concerto for Orchestra* (1943)
(1881–1945)

1.	Introduction: Andante non troppo—Allegro vivace	9:48
2.	Game of Pairs: Allegretto scherzando	6:17
3.	Elegy: Andante, non troppo	7:11
4.	Interrupted Intermezzo: Allegretto	4:08
5.	Finale: Presto	8:52

This work was written for the Koussevitzky Music Foundation in memory of Mrs. Natalie Koussevitzky, wife of the then conductor of the Boston Symphony Orchestra. It is not a problematic or experimental composition but a solid artistic achievement in the eloquent musical language of our time. Bartok provided the following program notes for the first performance:

> The general mood of the work represents, apart from the jesting second movement, a gradual transition from the sternness of the first movement and the lugubrious death-song of the third, to the life-assertion of the last one . . . The title of this symphony-like orchestral work is explained by its tendency to treat the single orchestral instruments in a *concertant* or soloistic manner. The 'virtuoso' treatment appears, for instance, in the fugato sections of the development of the first movement (brass instruments), or in the *perpetuum mobile-like* passage of the principal theme in the last movement

Bela Bartok

> (strings), and especially in the second movement, in which pairs of instruments consecutively appear with brilliant passages . . .

The "interruption" in the *Interrupted Intermezzo* is a parody of an insipid theme from the Shostakovich *Seventh Symphony*. Written in Leningrad while that city was under siege by the Nazis during World War II, the symphony enjoyed a spectacular if short-lived success.

(Also record side 7 band 1)[1]

Igor Stravinsky (1882–1971) made his first big splash in the musical world with his ballet *The Firebird* in 1910 when impressionism was still a controversial style. *The Firebird* (see p. 202) shows definite traces of impressionist influence, but within three years Stravinsky was blazing new trials. The style of *The Rite of Spring* (see p. 100) is anything but impressionistic. The usual label is *primitivism* or *barbarism*. The elemental force of *The Rite's* throbbing rhythms and strident harmonies, not to mention its sensual choreography, shocked the staid audience at the pre-

1. See fn. p. 16.

IGOR STRAVINSKY

miere and provoked a near riot. Not content to capitalize on the sensation he had created, Stravinsky turned immediately to new modes of expression, exploring unusual small instrumental combinations. These pioneering efforts paved the way for another 20th-century style, *neoclassicism*. Where other composers of his generation have been caught in the wake of changing styles, he has been at the forefront spearheading the changes. His creativity did not diminish or stagnate with advancing years. At the age of 70 he turned to a new (for him) style of composition employing serial procedures in a distinctly personal way. During an incredibly active and varied musical career spanning more than six decades he composed for virtually every conventional medium and invented new ones. There is no doubt that his influence on 20th-century music has been greater than that of any other composer. Each of his many styles has attracted a legion of imitators. Like a prophet, he was without honor only in his own country, Russia, which he left in 1911. His many extended trips took him around the world, but he resided principally in France until 1939 when he moved to Hollywood. His death in 1971 brought to a close not only a spectacular career but a significant epoch in the history of music.

No single work by Stravinsky can be regarded as typical or representative, but the *Octet* is a perennial favorite and, after the ballets, one of his most influential works.

IGOR STRAVINSKY: *Octet for Wind Instruments* (1923, revised 1952) 16:00
(1882–1971)

1. Sinfonia
2. Theme with variations
3. Finale

The *Octet* for flute, clarinet, 2 bassoons, 2 trumpets, and 2 trombones illustrates Stravinsky's preoccupation with unusual instrumental combinations. The original version in 1923 was one of the first works in this century to revert to classic ideals, a philosophy which subsequently was embraced by many composers. Stravinsky provided the following program notes for a 1952 performance:

> Composition, structure, form, here all are in the line of the 18th-century masters. Sonority has not been my first concern, and indeed, must be considered only as a result. The introduction is comparable—has an importance in the whole scheme—to the introductions in late Haydn symphonies. The *Allegro* (1) is a typical two-theme *sonata-allegro* (form) in the key of E-flat. The second movement is a theme with variations, a form which has occupied me in many works from *Pulcinella* and the *Concerto for Two Pianos, Jeu de Cartes,* to *Danses Concertantes* and the two-piano *Sonata.* In the *Octet,* however, it is the first variation which recurs rather than the theme in its original state. The final variation is a *fugato* (with added—nonstrictly *fugato*—notes) with, as subject, the intervals of the theme inverted. A measured flute cadenza modulates to the finale in C major, a kind of rondo with coda.

Unlike the composers discussed in this chapter who were *in* but not *of* the United States, CHARLES IVES (1874–1954) was a 24-carat American. He traced his lineage back to Captain William Ives who came to Boston on the "Truelove" in 1635. His father, after service in the Civil War as a Union Army bandmaster, became the leading musician in Danbury, Connecticut, where Charles was born. Young Ives learned to play the drums, cornet, piano, violin, and organ and became a member of his father's band. He listened with interest as his father had the band play with sections stationed in various locations around the town and as he dabbled with experimental tunings of a many-stringed contrivance. These effects and the sounds of rural New England were absorbed and reflected in his music. "Virtually every work he wrote," according to Nicolas Slonimsky, "bears relation to American life, not only by literary association, but through actual quotation of American music sources, from church anthems to popular dances and marches." Most of the innovations of 20th-century music—atonality, polytonality, polymeters, microtones, and tone clusters—were anticipated in his music early in the century when Schoenberg and Stravinsky were just severing their ties

Photo courtesy of The Bettmann Archive

CHARLES IVES

with romanticism. One can only imagine what his influence would have been if his music had become known as soon as it was written instead of suffering tragic neglect. His music was too far ahead of its time from the beginning, and he was too isolated from the mainstreams of musical activity to promote it. Between 1896 and 1920 he produced a profusion of works, few of which were performed until years later. He was not, however, a starving musician. After graduating from Yale in 1898 he went into business and became a partner in a prosperous insurance agency which gave him freedom to compose without concern for financial returns. He published his *Concord Sonata* for piano and 114 songs at his own expense and distributed copies gratis. His manuscript scores are now in the Yale library where they are attracting the attention they should have had 50 years ago. The first work of his to be issued by a commercial publisher was *Three Places in New England* in 1935, 21 years after it was completed and 15 years after he had virtually stopped composing.

CHARLES IVES: *Three Places in New England* (1903–1914)
(1874–1954)

1.	The "St. Gaudens" in Boston Common	8:55
2.	Putnam's Camp, Redding, Connecticut*	5:37
3.	The Housatonic at Stockbridge	3:45

Each of the movements is vividly descriptive of the place in New England specified in the title. The first movement, subtitled *Col. Shaw and his Colored Regiment,* is prefaced by a poem (probably by Ives) which contains the lines, "Moving—Marching—Faces of Souls! . . . Slowly, restlessly—swaying us on with you Towards other Freedom!" As fragments of Civil War melodies are projected against a hauntingly dissonant background, one can easily visualize a spectral procession marching to the beat of the drum.

The second movement is a musical fantasy depicting a child's Fourth of July outing at the Revolutionary Memorial located at the site of General Israel Putnam's winter quarters. Snatches of familiar tunes are heard as two bands playing different marches approach from opposite directions, pass each other, and depart.

The summer after they were married, Ives and his wife took a walk through the meadows along the Housatonic river near Stockbridge. This walk and a poem by Robert Underwood Johnson which begins, "Contented river! in the dreamy realm . . . ." inspired the third movement of this "New England Symphony."

The music of Ives is not suave or sophisticated. He had no opportunity, and perhaps no inclination, to polish and perfect his technique through repeated hearings of his own works and those of his European contemporaries. Music for him was a primordial means of expression. The approach is always simple and direct, even when the means are extremely complex. Like the New England countryside, his music has a peculiar rough-hewn beauty which is sometimes sentimental, sometimes crude, but always filled with vitality.

*(Record side 6 band 6)

The composers discussed in this chapter are recognized giants of 20th-century music. They reached their maturity relatively early in the century. The quantity and quality of their music and innumerable performances have earned them international reputations, and their influence on the mainstreams of recent music has been enormous. The works cited are but an infinitessimal sampling of the brilliantly conceived and executed works by a host of composers writing in these contemporary styles. Care has been exercised to assure that such works are amply represented in preceding chapters. The composers are listed in the chronology on page 294. The styles prevalent prior to 1950, while still current, can no longer be regarded as radical. That distinction has passed to a new generation of composers whose fascinating explorations are considered in the next chapter.

References

Austin, William. *Music in the Twentieth Century.* New York: W. W. Norton, 1966.

Dallin, Leon. *Techniques of Twentieth Century Composition.* 3d. ed. Dubuque: Wm. C. Brown Company Publishers, 1974.

Deri, Otto. *Exploring Twentieth-Century Music.* New York: Holt, Rinehart and Winston, 1968.

Hansen, Peter S. *Introduction to Twentieth Century Music.* 3d. ed. Boston: Allyn & Bacon, 1971.

Salzman, Eric. *Twentieth Century Music: An Introduction.* 2d. ed. New York: Prentice-Hall, 1974.

Twelve Tone Composition. Recorded lecture-demonstration. Folkways 3612.

Chronology

1883	Varèse	1965
1900	Krenek	
1900	Luening	
1901	Partch	1974
1908	Messiaen	
1911	Ussachevsky	
1912	Cage	
1916	Babbitt	
1922	Foss	
1922	Xenakis	
1923	Kraft	
1924	Hiller	
1925	Berio	
1925	Boulez	
1925	Schuller	
1926	Gaburo	
1928	Stockhausen	
1929	Randall	
1933	Penderecki	

(Record side 8 band 6)

The New Music

23

Summarizing the trends in music since 1950 is complicated by the lack of perspective. Inherent in the writing of history while it is still being made is the risk of overlooking something of importance or of glorifying a transient fad, but the time is past when the musical events in the second half of this century can be ignored. The methods and materials of the present and the compositions being created right now constitute the legacy our generation will pass on to posterity. From them will emerge the masterpieces of our time and the foundations of the future. Perhaps some composer currently struggling for recognition will eventually merit a place beside Bach, Mozart, and Beethoven. He may come from the ranks of composers continuing along the now well-marked paths discussed in the preceding chapter, or he may be from the vanguard exploring new ways and means or carrying old ones to new extremes. What is certain is that today's music is as provocative and unpredictable as tomorrow's headlines.

Certain basic trends in new music are apparent. Pitches are no longer limited to those which can be written in traditional notation and played on conventional instruments. New sound sources are being exploited, and familiar sounds are being modified in new ways. In the matter of musical organization two divergent trends can be detected. One is moving toward the systematic organization and absolute control of musical elements according to preconceived rational procedures. The other, striving for spontaneous expression and unlimited freedom, invokes the vagaries of chance, random selection, and improvisation. These contrasting approaches to musical organization are sometimes linked together as *system and chance music*. The new music and its pioneers are surveyed in this chapter. The categories and participants overlap and sometimes, as in system and chance music, start in opposite directions but meet on the other side of the circle.

Total Organization

The total organization concept and the ultimate control of musical elements by predetermined procedures is an outgrowth of the twelve-tone method, but where only the pitches are governed by serial order in the "classical" twelve-tone system of the first half of the century, the new serialism extends to other aspects of music. The other parameters—as they are now called, borrowing a term from mathematics—include rhythm (durations), tempo (speed levels), dynamics (degrees of loudness), articulation (modes of attack), density (number of parts), and octave distribution (spacing). As a rule the initial pitch series is transformed by some rational method into an order of values applicable to the other serially controlled elements. The procedures vary from composer to composer and work to work, but the possibilities which have been used include deriving the values of the other series from the notes, intervals, and frequencies of the pitch series. To avoid the excessive uniformity of configuration that might otherwise result from the strict ordering of several parameters concurrently, the order within a given series is sometimes subjected to systematic and progressive rotation. The rotation plan and the choice and arrangement of components can be serially controlled to produce music in which the sound events are essentially predetermined by a system conceived and set in motion by the composer.

The roots of the new serialism can be traced back to Schoenberg (1874–1951), Webern (1883–1945), and Messiaen (1908–). Ernst Krenek (1900–) is an active composer and lucid apologist for totally organized music, and his *Sestina* (1957) for voice and instrumental ensemble is a perfect example of ultimate serialization. Unfortunately, the recording of this work is out of print, but the notes by the composer on the record jacket provide authentic insights to the philosophy and techniques of the idiom.

According to Krenek his *Sestina* is based on a series of twelve tones divided in two sets of six each. The tones of each set rotate in a pattern identical with that of key words at the end of each line in the six stanzas of the poem he wrote as a text for the work. Durations are derived by a formula from the relative magnitude of the intervals between tones of the pitch set and additional factors. Other parameters regulated serially are: density, spacing, speed, dynamics, and "other details too complex to be described here." Krenek concludes his analysis with the following statement:

> It is obvious that so complete a determination by serial rule of a sufficient number of parameters will make control of the remaining ones impossible. In an exact mathematical sense they already are ordered, as a result of the determination of the other parameters. But what happens in this remaining sector is well-nigh unpredictable (except perhaps by electronic computation), and although intentionally brought about by the composer, it is not consciously planned by him as the sector analyzed above. Therefore these happenings may be considered chance results. The paradox of ultimate necessity's causing unpredictable chance is the topic of the *Sestina.*

PIERRE BOULEZ (1925–   ) studied music and higher mathematics at Saint Étienne in Lyon before entering the Paris Conservatory and devoting his full energies to music. His subsequent preoccupation with total serialization and abstract organization may be reflections of his earlier training as a mathematician, but there is no question that he made the right choice when he decided on music as a career. He is preeminent among musicians of his generation, not only as a composer but as a conductor, spokesman, and champion of new music. He has followed parallel careers in composition and conducting since his student years. He made worldwide tours as musical director of a theater company and was founder-conductor of an annual series of concerts in Paris devoted to avant-garde music. Resounding successes as a guest conductor of major orchestras led to his appointment as music director of the New York Philharmonic, succeeding Leonard Bernstein. He has tried his hand at most of the post-1950 approaches to composition. His music is performed as frequently as any of the difficult and problematical music of our time. It never fails to attract attention, and it receives its share of critical acclaim. The work which has contributed more than any other to his reputation as a composer and one of his most felicitous is *Le Marteau sans Maître* (the hammer without a master) based on three surrealist poems by René Char. It consists of nine interrelated movements for alto voice and six instruments. His *Structure Ia* for two pianos is an example of exceptionally strict and all-encompassing serialism for which a detailed analysis[1] is available. A prepared analysis is a practical necessity when the complexity makes the constructional plan virtually undecipherable without prior knowledge of the procedures employed. The serial operations in Boulez's *Structure Ia* are representative of the ways serial control is extended to parameters of music other than pitch. According to Ligeti the

1. Gyorgy Ligeti, "Pierre Boulez, Decision and Automatism in Structure Ia" Die Reihe No. 4, 1958 (English edition, 1960).

first stage in the composition of such works is to make decisions regarding the selection, arrangement, and mutual relationships of elements and the choice of operations to be carried out. The second stage is to execute these decisions. The third and final stage is to make decisions regarding those dimensions of the music not automatically predetermined in the preceding stages.

PIERRE BOULEZ: *Structures—Ia* (1952) 2:35
(1925–)

> The twelve-tone pitch series of *Structure Ia* is derived from a 1949 piano composition, *Modes de valeurs et d'intensités,* by Boulez's teacher, Messiaen. The durations are produced by multiplying a basic unit by factors from 1 to 12. The permutations of the duration series are derived from the notes of the pitch series. There are 12 degrees of loudness and 12 modes of attack, both serially ordered and systematically related to the initial pitch series. There are 48 possible permutations of the pitch series. Each one is used once and only once, and each is associated with the appropriate form of the duration series to form a serial thread. The 48 serial threads are distributed in 14 sections with from one to six threads beginning and ending simultaneously in each section. At this writing the recording of *Structure Ia* is out of print, hopefully only temporarily.

When ultimate control in composition is coupled with absolute precision in performance, the end result is predetermined at the moment of conception, but the nature and complexity of the procedures make the outcome and, even more significantly, the effect unpredictable. The fact that the only recordings of two of the most representative examples of totally organized music have gone out of print is perhaps an indication that the tide of the future is flowing in the opposite direction. Unpredictable outcomes can also be produced by the reverse approach—reducing or eliminating controls and introducing elements of chance, possibilities explored in the next section.

Indeterminacy and Aleatory

The antithesis of total organization is *indeterminacy* or *aleatory,* terms applied to concepts of composition which delegate de facto control of substantive musical events to the performers and/or to chance. The absence of prescribed controls results in a high degree of freedom. Where complete control produces a highly structured sequence of musical events, absolute freedom is most apt to result in a chaotic jumble which does not conform to the definition of music as "organized sound." Where music ends, *antimusic* begins, but consensus is lacking on the placement of the dividing line. The air is always full of sound, but is it music? The following work suggests that John Cage thinks it is.

JOHN CAGE: 4:33 (1952)
(1912–) 1. :33
2. 2:40
3. 1:20

> According to the score this piece may be performed by any instrumentalist or combination of instrumentalists and last any length of time, but it is invariably known by the total duration of its three movements as first performed by pianist David Tudor on August 29, 1952 in Woodstock, New York. No sounds are produced intentionally. The only function of the performer(s) is to indicate in some way the beginnings and endings of the movements. Tudor did it by closing the lid over the keyboard for the beginnings and opening it for the endings. There is no recording, but Tudor's activities can be duplicated by anyone with a stopwatch. The sounds of the piece, however, are any that occur spontaneously during the performance, and they are different on every occasion.

Granting the validity of the premise that random sounds are or can be music means that the definition of music must be broadened to include sound events in which any and all parameters are indeterminate. John Cage is the high priest and leading expounder of this philosophy. A sampling of quotations from the descriptive notes in the catalog of his works (Henmar Press Inc., 1962) will give some idea of his *modus operandi* and provide an introduction to indeterminacy as a trend in new music.

> *Music for Piano I* (1952) is written entirely in whole notes, their duration being indeterminate. Each system is seven seconds. Dynamics are given but piano tone production on the keyboard or strings is free. The notes correspond to imperfections in the paper upon which the piece was written.

> *TV Koeln* (1958) uses noises produced either on the interior of the piano construction or on the exterior, together with auxiliary instruments and keyboard aggregates specified only as to the number of tones in them.

> *Imaginary Landscape no. 4* (1951) for 12 radios, 24 players and conductor. Kilocycle, amplitude and timbre changes are notated. Two players are required for each radio. (The sounds are those produced by the radios as the players rotate the tuning and volume dials.)

> The *Concert for Piano and Orchestra* (1957–58) is without a master score, but each part is written in detail in a notation where space is relative to time determined by the performer and later

> altered by a conductor. Both specific directives and specific freedoms are given to each player including the conductor. Notes are of three sizes referring ambiguously to duration or amplitude. . . . The pianist's part is a "book" containing 84 different kinds of composition, some, varieties of the same species, others, altogether different. The pianist is free to play any elements of his choice, wholly or in part in any sequence.

Cage suggests combining certain of his indeterminate works, compounding the indeterminacy. His *Aria,* for example, can be performed alone or with *Fontana Mix* or with any part of *Concert.* There is a recording of *Aria* with *Fontana Mix.*

JOHN CAGE: *Aria* with *Fontana Mix* (1958) 10:00
(1912–)

> In the notation of *Aria* time is represented horizontally, pitch vertically, but roughly suggested rather than accurately described. Dotted lines in various colors indicate ten singing styles established by the singer. Black squares are any unmusical uses of the voice or auxiliary devices. The text employs vowels and consonants and words from five languages. Elements which are not notated, such as dynamics, are freely determined by the singer. The score of *Fontana Mix* gives directions for the production of any number of tracks of magnetic tape or parts for any number of players of any kind of instruments. The version on the record is, of course, only one of the infinite ways of realizing the two scores.

In the indeterminate works of Cage compositional decisions are sometimes made by tossing coins and similar chance operations, and procedures differing markedly in conception and realization release the ensuing events from the conscious control of the composer. The notation is unconventional and rarely provides more than loose guidelines for the activities of the executants. The degree of license delegated to performers can result in renditions of the same work which have little in common except the title. A work is less a product than a process renewed with each performance. Compositions in this genre assume a definite form only when they are recorded, and there is a certain incongruity in a recording of an indeterminate work.

The element of indeterminacy is more circumscribed in some works by other composers. The following is representative of a number of works involving controlled chance, or *aleatory* to use the current term.

KARLHEINZ STOCKHAUSEN: *Zyklus (Cycle) for Percussion* (1959) 11:36
(1928–)

> One player stands in the center of more than 20 percussion instruments arranged in a circle. He turns clockwise or counterclockwise,

> as he chooses, playing the instruments that come before him during one complete rotation. The 16-page, spiral-bound score has no beginning and no end. The player starts wherever he wishes, plays through the remaining pages in order, and completes the cycle by returning to the initial point and repeating the first sound. In place of formal notation specially conceived symbols are arranged in "time fields" on the pages of the score.

In aleatoric and indeterminate music the shape and sound are determined in large measure by the performers, but with extents and limits prescribed by the composer. Performers are guided by the composer's directions through some sort of score however vague and permissive its symbols may be. In these styles projecting their own creativity is not a primary concern of performers, as it is in improvisation.

Improvisation

Improvisation is defined as "the art of performing music spontaneously, without the aid of manuscript, sketches, or memory." Improvisation has existed in music since its beginnings. Bach, Handel, Mozart, and Beethoven were renowned improvisors, and improvising is the stock-in-trade of every jazz musician. The affinity between indeterminacy and improvisation is obvious, as are the differences. In both, the work materializes at the moment of performance, but performers are guided in the former by preconceived elements or processes. In the latter, performers follow their own creative instincts and utilize their full technical and musical resources in a unified composer-performer role. Predetermined elements may serve as points of departure for improvisation. In jazz, for example, the spontaneously improvised melodic lines are usually based on the form and harmonic progressions of a familiar song. The type of improvisation that attracts avant-garde musicians is that in which preexistent elements are minimal. Improvisation in its purest state has no composer, and there is no composition independent of the performance. Each beginning and ending frames a new work which has never existed before and never will again. Permanency is achieved only when an improvised performance is captured on a recording.

The Improvisation Chamber Ensemble founded by Lukas Foss in 1957 practiced a type of improvisation which, as the name implies, was more akin to classical chamber music than to jazz. Their approach was to chart a formal or textural plan from which individual guide-sheets for the four instruments of the ensemble (piano, clarinet, percussion, and cello) were extracted. Any predetermined pitch patterns were notated on the guide-sheets, and at designated points the role of each performer—such as to lead, respond, or support—was assigned.

The members rehearsed as a group to improve their improvisational skills and their ability to interact effectively with each other in joint creative ventures. Repeated improvisations from the same chart tended to evolve and stabilize but never became mere rote repetitions. Serendipitous moments, invented by the players but not planned, were highlights of the performances. The Improvisation Chamber Ensemble is no longer active, but it can still be heard in the interludes of the *Time Cycle* recording.

LUKAS FOSS: *Time Cycle* (1960)		
(1922–)	1. We're Late	3:50
	Improvised Interlude No. 1	2:20
	2. When the Bells Justle	5:00
	Improvised Interlude No. 2	4:50
	3. Sechzehnter Jänur (January 16)	5:45
	Improvised Interlude No. 3	3:05
	4. O Mensch, gib Acht (O Man! Take Heed!)	5:40

Sections for the improvisation ensemble alternate with sections for soprano and orchestra. The two groups never play together. The improvised interludes contrast with the composed movements in which serial devices are combined with complex contrapuntal procedures in a highly organized but transparent texture. The four composed movements are unified by a common chord (C-sharp, A, B, D-sharp) and by a common literary theme (time, clocks, bells) but otherwise are unrelated.

Improvisation, one of the older but still viable approaches to music making, is essentially an instinctive and irrational art. One of the newest approaches to composition, conversely, is predicated entirely upon logic and reason.

Formalized Music

Music produced by compositional processes governed by abstract logic is classified by IANNIS XENAKIS (1922–) as *formalized music.* In his book *Formalized Music: Thought and Mathematics in Composition* (Indiana University Press, 1971) he describes his revolutionary theories in detail. His investigations have lead to a sort of abstraction and formalization of compositional processes. He explains in mathematical terms the logical causes of sound sensations and their uses in wanted constructions and attempts to give the art of music a reasoned support less perishable than the impulse of the moment. For his purposes the qualifications "beautiful" and "ugly" are irrelevant. The quantity of intelligence conveyed by the sounds are the true criterion of their validity. He denounces linear thought (polyphony) and perceives contradictions in serial music. In their place he proposes "a world of sound-masses, vast groups of sound-events, clouds, and galaxies governed by new characteristics such as density, degree of order, and rate of change, which require definitions and realizations using probability theory."

In his music Xenakis utilizes sounds from all sources or, in his words, all classes of sonic elements—vocal, instrumental, concrete (microphone collected), electronic (synthesized), and digital (computer generated). When writing for conventional instruments, his usual procedure is to represent the mathematical operations graphically and then to transcribe the graphs into staff notation.

Xenakis is of the opinion that existing concert halls are unsuitable for present-day music and that a new kind of architecture, a field in which he has worked, should be devised. In the meantime he suggests performing works like his symbolic *Terretektorh* in a large ballroom from which all possible aural and visual obstructions have been removed and where the listeners are free to move about or sit on portable stools. According to his directions the 90 members of the orchestra are to be scattered quasi-stochastically throughout the hall, each seated on an individual dais. This distribution of the players brings a radically new kinetic conception to music and, in his opinion, combined with the mobility of the audience enriches the composition in both spatial dimension and movement. Variable speeds and accelerations of sound movement are realized. The composition is thus a "sonotron," to quote Xenakis, "an accelerator of sonorous particles, a disintegrator of sonorous masses, a synthesizer. It puts the sound and the music all around the listener and close up to him. It tears down the psychological and auditive curtain that separates him from the players when positioned far off and on a pedestal, itself frequently enough placed inside a box." It is obvious that the spatial concepts of Xenakis cannot be adequately recorded or reproduced by existing means, but opportunities to hear his orchestral works in live performances that comply with his directions are rare. For the foreseeable future most listeners will experience them only in their recorded versions.

IANNIS XENAKIS: *Terretektorh* (1966) 14:49
(1922–)

The sound spectrum exploited in *Terretektorh* is essentially dry and noisy. The orchestral resources are augmented in this direction by having each musician play, in addition to his normal string or wind instrument, wood block, maracas, whip, and siren-whistle.

The theoretical treatises and compositions of Xenakis exert a profound and growing influence on contemporary musical thought. Their impact would be even greater, no doubt, if more musicians had the necessary command of higher mathematics to comprehend fully his philosophic concepts and to apply his compositional methods. The problems of microtonal music are equally intriguing and vexing, but in a very different way.

Microtonal Music

Microtones, intervals smaller than those accommodated by conventional notation and instruments, have existed since the beginning of music theory, and their inclusion in music would seem to be the next logical step in its evolution. The barriers to this seemingly logical development have, until recently, discouraged all but a few hardy individualists. Existing notation, instruments, and players are ill suited to the increased complexity of true microtonal music. Devising a new system of notation, designing and constructing new instruments or adapting old ones, and training performers are formidable tasks. HARRY PARTCH was one of few who accepted the challenge on all counts. After formulating a convincing rationale for a scale of 43 unequal intervals (in place of 12 equal intervals), he proceeded to develop a notational system, build instruments, and teach performers for the single purpose of playing his music. If recognition was meagre and slow in coming, it was perhaps because so much of his time and energy was consumed in these peripheral activities without which his music would not have been heard at all. His flair for words and visual effects adds to the impact of his dramatic works, where he is at his best. Regrettably, there is little opportunity to see them on stage. Next best is seeing the film *Windsong*,[2] a modern rendering of the ancient myth of Daphne and Apollo, for which he did the music. Ten Partch instruments are heard on the sound track playing music based, like all he has written, on the 43-tone scale.

HARRY PARTCH: *Windsong (Daphne of the Dunes)* (1958) 11:00
(1901–1974)

An excerpted version of the *Windsong* sound track is available on Composers Recordings record CRI 193 (monaural). The record jacket and a 4-page insert contain photographs and descriptions of Partch's instruments and a brief summary of his musical career. Retitled *Daphne of the Dunes* and recorded in stereo, this music is included on Columbia record MS–7207.

A simpler but more limited and theoretically less valid type of microtonal music than that of Partch is possible if the only microtonal

2. Available through Cinema 16, New York.

intervals used are equal quarter tones exactly half as large as the smallest intervals in traditional music. There are 24 tones in a quarter-tone scale, half of which coincide with conventional pitches. Quarter-tone music can be notated on a conventional staff with the addition of a few new symbols and can be played on several conventional instruments with relatively minor adaptations in the playing techniques and mechanisms. Penderecki's *Threnody for the Victims of Hiroshima* (see p. 101) and Don Ellis's *House in the Country* (see p. 353) illustrate this type of microtonal music.

The problems that impede the progress of microtonal music are of no concern to composers making electronic music. They have at their command the full range of audible frequencies, and working directly on magnetic tape they have no need for notation or performers.

Electronic Music

Any recording or transmission of sound involves electronic equipment, but the designation *electronic music*[3] is reserved for music with sounds modified or generated electronically. Early experiments with electrical instruments date back to the last century, but the electronic age really arrived in music with the invention of the magnetic tape recorder.

The tape recorder provides not only a highly efficient means of sound recording and reproduction but also several simple and practical ways of modifying sounds. For example, by increasing or decreasing the speed at which the tape travels over the playback head, the pitch is raised or lowered. When the direction of the tape is reversed, the sounds are heard backwards. A tape loop fashioned by joining the two ends of a piece of tape repeats a sound pattern endlessly. Sounds can be fragmented and rearranged by cutting and splicing the tape on which they are recorded, and any number of sound tracks can be combined. Starting in 1952 Vladimir Ussachevsky (1911–) and Otto Luening (1900–) produced electronic music using tape manipulations of this sort. Tape manipulations can, of course, be used on recorded sounds from any source.

Electronic sounds are produced by audio oscillators and generators. Oscillators produce a simple wave form with a single frequency (no overtones) and a sound like a test tone or a tuning fork. Generators produce more complex wave forms and various tone qualities. *White noise* is a common component of electronic music. White noise, analogous

3. Record side 8 band 6 is a recorded introduction to electronic music (see Additional Examples p. 332).

with white light, is considered to contain all frequencies with random amplitudes. The audible effect is rather like that of escaping steam.

Electronic music constructed from nonelectronic sounds is called *musique concrète.* In musique concrète sounds from natural sources—voices, instruments, or any other vibrating medium—are modified electronically or by tape manipulation.

The electronic devices used to modify both concrète and electronic sounds include amplifiers, filters, modulators, equalizers, and reverberation units. Processed sounds are recorded on one or more tapes. Multiple tapes are synchronized and their signals passed through a mixer where they are balanced and combined for recording on a final composite tape. The tape recording *is* the work. It may be transferred to discs for commercial distribution, and some graphic representation of its content may be prepared, but the actual composition, in both the general and the specific sense, takes place in the sound studio on the tape. *Poème Electronique* by Edgard Varèse is, to use the composer's words, an example of "organized sound" created directly on magnetic tape. Oscillator, generator, voice, bell, and percussion instrument sounds, though modified and reshaped, are recognizable in this landmark electronic composition.

EDGARD VARÈSE: *Poème Electronique* (1958) 8:05
(1883–1965)

> This work was first heard in the Philips Corporation pavilion at the Brussels World's Fair. The interior shape of the building designed by the architect Le Corbusier in collaboration with Iannis Xenakis provided a series of hyperbolic and parabolic curves along which 425 loudspeakers were meticulously placed. Visitors passing through the building were engulfed in continuous arcs of sound while viewing unrelated, diverse images projected on the ceiling. A simple recording gives only a glimpse of the total aural and visual experience conceived by Varèse, Le Corbusier, and Xenakis.

In the early days of electronic music makeshift devices intended for other functions were used to generate and modify the sound materials. Widespread interest in electronic music and advances in electronic technology led to the development of music *synthesizers,* integrated systems of electronic components designed expressly for the production and control of musical sounds, or at least sounds that are used musically, a distinction that is perhaps necessary until electronic instruments gain universal acceptance. That day may not be far off. Where the cost of early prototypes was prohibitive, several standardized makes and models now on the market are in a practical price range for educational institutions and affluent individuals. Versatility and simplicity of operation are continually improving. A growing number of college music departments have fully equipped electronic studios and routinely include the study of electronic music in the curriculum. Even in the more adventuresome public schools students are introduced to electronic music and music making. These developments have taken place in a remarkably brief span of time.

The unique RCA Mark II synthesizer acquired by the Columbia-Princeton Electronic Music Center in 1959 was built at a cost variously reported from $250,000 to $500,000. The most advanced music synthesizer of its time and still one of the most sophisticated, it has the capacity to create any sound that can be adequately specified and transmitted by a loudspeaker. Milton Babbitt is one of the few composers to have mastered its complexities. His *Ensembles for Synthesizer*, like all of his electronic compositions to date, was realized on the RCA synthesizer. The input for this particular synthesizer is coded on punched tape. Every parameter of the sound is specified. Nothing is left to chance. Babbitt does not splice the magnetic tape or alter the signal after it is recorded. His predilection for conventional pitch relationships survives in *Ensembles* even though the pitch successions move at rates surpassing the limits of human performance and approaching the thresholds of perception.

MILTON BABBITT: *Ensembles for Synthesizer* (1964) 10:38
(1916–)

The following notes by the composer prepared for a New York performance of the piece are quoted on the jacket of the Columbia recording:

> The title *Ensembles* refers to the multiple characteristics of the work. In both its customary meaning and its more general one signifying "collections," the term refers most immediately to the different pitch, rhythmic, registral, textural, and timbral "ensembles" associated with each of the many delineated sections of the composition, no two of which are identical, and no one of which is of more than a few seconds duration in this ten-minute work. . . . Also, in its meaning of "set," the word "ensemble" relevantly suggests the, I trust, familiar (serial) principles of tonal and temporal organization which are employed in this as in other of my compositions.

An obvious disadvantage of pure electronic music is that there is nothing to watch during a performance, a disadvantage shared by all music heard via recordings. The deficiency is remedied in concert performances when live performers are used in conjunction with electronic tapes. Many of the composers who have worked extensively in the electronic medium have explored the possibilities of combining prerecorded and live sound. Live performers supply an intrinsic visual element and at the same time provide a desirable link with more conventional music.

No two works for prerecorded tape and live performers are alike, but *Antiphony IV* by Kenneth Gaburo is representative of the type. It is an intriguing example of new music, because it employs so many of the techniques and materials discussed in this chapter. In addition it exhibits the composer's special interest in *compositional linguistics*, a term he has coined meaning, in general, "language as music, and music as language."

KENNETH GABURO: *Antiphony IV (Poised)* (1967) 9:24
(1926–)

> This work is for piccolo, bass trombone, double bass, and two-channel tape recorder operated by a fourth performer. In a live performance the piccolo and double bass are amplified but not otherwise modified. The players produce normal sounds and many special effects on the instruments. The piccolo and trombone play quarter tones—pitch differences only half as large as the smallest in conventional music. The right tape channel consists exclusively of electronically generated sounds: noise bands, high-frequency square wave clusters, low modulated pulse trains, clangorous signals, and percussive, synthesized "bass" modulated signals. The left tape channel is composed of vocal sounds derived from a phonetic transcription of the following poem[4] by Virginia Hommel.
>
> Poised above the sea as if to drop
> Tense.
>
> heavy, hot
>
> Waits
> Gaining strength
>
> And pours forth in soaring chill illusion!
>
> On the tape each phoneme is heard first with the normal voice identity retained and then in progressively more complex electromechanical transformations.

The next step in the evolution of electronic music leads from synthesizers to computers.

Music by Computers

Computer music is still in its infancy. In their 1959 book *Experimental Music* (McGraw-Hill), Hiller and Isaacson could report only six

4. Used by permission of Lingua Press, La Jolla, California 92037.

experiments besides their own in which computers had been used to produce music. In the first experiments simple melodies were computer-composed utilizing elementary probability tables for selecting successive notes. Hiller and Isaacson programed a computer to create music consistent with certain technical and stylistic principles. Pitch, duration, dynamics, and playing instructions determined by the computer were represented on a Teletype printout by numbers, letters, and symbols which were transcribed into conventional notation for live performance. Experiments in this vein using an Illiac computer culminated in their *Illiac Suite* for string quartet. Attempts to link a computer with a Musicwriter for direct production of musical notation were fraught with mechanical problems. This type of computer composition was superseded by that in which computer-generated sounds are recorded directly on magnetic tape, rendering notation of any sort superfluous except for copyright purposes or for cuing prerecorded sound to live sound.

The modern computer may be regarded as the ultimate electronic music synthesizer. A complete system for the production of computer music requires a digital computer, an appropriate computer program, a digital-to-analog converter, and a loudspeaker. Basically the characteristics of a sound wave are defined numerically in a language acceptable to the computer, and the sequence of numbers is stored in the computer memory. The numbers in the memory are transferred in succession to a digital-to-analog converter which generates a pulse of voltage corresponding to each number. The resultant pattern of fluctuating voltages smoothed by a filter constitutes an electronic signal that can be recorded on magnetic tape, amplified, and converted into sound by a loudspeaker.

The creation of sound by means of a computer is not as simple as might be presumed from this superficial explanation. Part of the difficulty stems from the innate complexity of the musical sounds that must be represented numerically and the infinite ways they may begin and end. Every parameter of a tone—its pitch, quality, duration, attack, decay, and intensity—must be specified in computer language. Another problem is that for high-fidelity sound the numbers from the digital computer must be processed and converted to voltages at the rate of 30,000 or more per second of music.

A prerequisite for sound synthesis is a very fast and efficient program. Computer programs designed specifically for musical composition have been developed and are being improved constantly. These specialized programs facilitate the encoding of the requisite information and reduce the amount of time and effort the composer must expend on the mechanics of computer programing. One such program, Music V, was developed at the Bell Telephone Laboratories, principally by Max V. Matthews. In Music V the subprogram "instruments" can play any number of notes at the same time. The program adds and automatically synchronizes all parts and puts out the combined sound. MUSIC V is written in a general-purpose computer language, FORTRAN IV. Development of the first full-fledged special-purpose computer language for music, TEMPO (Transformational Electronic Music Process Organizer), was started by John L. Clough and his associates at Oberlin College in 1968 and completed at the University of Michigan, where the language was initially implemented in 1973. An adjunct program, PLAY, controls the digital-to-analog conversion process. A special feature of the system is MUTILS, a set of routines for real-time sound synthesis, that is, a one-to-one ratio between computer time and sound output. The great advantage of real-time synthesis is that the sound can be monitored as it is generated by the computer, eliminating the customary delay imposed by the high sampling rate required for high-fidelity sound. The availability of a special computer language for music will undoubtedly stimulate the production of computer music in the years to come.

A promising new way of describing sound sequences to computers is to represent them graphically using a light pen to draw on a cathode-ray tube attached to a small computer. The small computer reads the graphs and transmits the information digitally to a larger computer, after which the synthesizing process is the same as for other input modes.

The full range of audible frequencies is available in computer music, but the pitches can be limited to those of conventional scales, a twelve-tone scale, or any arbitrary set of pitch relationships. Computers can be programed to produce strict serial music or to make random selections within prescribed limits and in a sense to "compose" in accordance with instructions provided by the programer. Computer music in which a significant portion of the compositional decisions are made by the computer is another type of indeterminate music. A computer controlled by a program which defines general extents rather than details and directs random selection for unspecified parameters of sound will produce many variants of the same composition.

The exploration of the computer as a musical instrument has really just begun. Present limitations are more in the operators than in the machines. Scientists skilled in computer technology are rarely disciplined in the art of music, and few composers have sufficient knowledge of mathematics, acoustics, and programing to cope effectively with the complexities of modern computers. These deficiencies are apparent in some of the early computer music, but contemplating the computer's potential in the production and control of sound boggles the mind. The suggested listening example is one of the most ambitious and successful computer pieces of the past decade. Newer examples should be added as they become available.

J. K. Randall: *Lyric Variations for Violin and Computer* (1968) 20:18
(1929–)

J. K. Randall is a thoroughly trained musician on the faculty of Princeton University and, judging by these variations, a master of computer composition. They were produced over a period of three years in collaboration with the violinist who commissioned them (Paul Zukofsky) and a sound engineer using a Music 4B program and an IBM 7094 computer. Information about the piece was provided by the composer for the Vanguard recording (VCS–10057).

Variations 1–5 for violin alone are structurally analogous to variations 6–10 in reverse order for computer alone. The two-minute "jungle" of variable rates of change in variation 10 for computer (which took nine hours to compute) corresponds to the two-minute violin melody of the opening variation 1. Variations 11–20 for violin and computer together are a transformation of variations 1–10, with variation 20 presenting in a quite direct way the total pitch-time configuration which the variations vary.

The computer functions solely as an instrument in this piece, not as a composer-surrogate. Every parameter of sound is specified in complete detail, including such peripheral aspects as vibrato, tremolo, and reverberation. The computer-generated sounds are synchronized and combined with multiple tracks of natural violin sounds on the final composite recording.

Multimedia

Multimedia and *mixed media* are terms applied to contemporary works in which two or more distinct art forms are combined. Technically, a composite art form such as opera or ballet qualifies for the category, but in current usage the terms generally imply a combination of avant-garde music with spectacular visual effects. The visual elements may be supplied by live musicians, actors, or dancers; they may be still or moving projected images or merely a display of lights within the hall, a so-called *light show*. Senses other than hearing and sight may be involved and sensory stimulation outside the performance area regarded as relevant to the artistic experience. Aleatory is the rule rather than the exception. When significant elements of the production are left to chance, the result is a *happening*. Audience participation is often encouraged. More extreme multimedia concepts lead to *total theater* in which distinctions between composer, performer, and spectator are obscured. Philosophically and aesthetically the multimedia protagonists are heading in a direction that ultimately leads to embracing all sensual experience as art and in which distinctions between art and life approach the vanishing point.

Meaningful illustrations of multimedia works are not practical in a classroom situation, and therefore none are suggested. The Varèse *Poème Electronique* cited as an example of electronic music was a multimedia work as initially presented at the Brussels World's Fair (see p. 326).

What will the music of the future be like? No one knows, of course, but one thing is certain—the styles of music will continue to evolve as each generation assimilates some innovations of the past and discards others. Composers will persist in their quest for new methods and materials, and each succeeding period will have its own "new music."

Additional Examples

Electronic Music

Karlheinz Stockhausen: *Gesang der Junglinge* (DGG 138811)

Music of Our Time: A Guide to the Electronic Revolution in Music (Record side 8 band 6)

Nonesuch Guide to Electronic Music (HC–73018)

Music by Computers

John Cage & Lejaren Hiller: HPSCHD for Harpsichords and Computer-Generated Sound Tapes with KNOBS, a computer printout for playback control by the listener.

Miscellaneous

Sounds of New Music (Folkways 6160)

References

Cope, David. *New Directions in Music*. 2d ed. Dubuque: Wm. C. Brown Company Publishers, 1976.

Mathews, Max V. *The Technology of Computer Music*. Cambridge: M.I.T. Press, 1969.

Schwartz, Elliott, and Childs, Barney, eds. *Contemporary Composers on Contemporary Music*. New York: Holt, Rinehart and Winston, 1967.

Strange, Allen. *Electronic Music*. Dubuque: Wm. C. Brown Company Publishers, 1972.

Trythall, Gilbert. *Principles and Practice of Electronic Music*. New York: Grosset and Dunlap, 1973. (with record)

Von Foerster, Heinz, and Beauchamp, James W., eds. *Music by Computers*. New York: John Wiley and Sons, 1969. (with records)

Courtesy of B.M.I. Archives

EDGARD VARÉSE

IANNIS XENAKIS

Photo courtesy of
Indiana University

Chronology*

1868	Joplin	1917
1870	Lehar	1948
1873	Handy	1958
1887	Romberg	1951
1888	Berlin	
1892	Porter	1964
1898	Gershwin	1937
1899	Ellington	1974
1900	Weill	1958
1902	Rodgers	
1904	Loewe	
1918	Bernstein	
1920	Lewis	
1925	Schuller	
1928	Bacharach	
1928	Bock	
1930	Cacavas	
1932	Ellis	
1944	Hamlisch	
1948	Webber	
1950	Wonder	

(Record side 10 bands 1–8)

* Composers of popular music and jazz.

Folk and Popular Music

24

Folk music is the expression of a group of kindred people bound together by ties of race, language, religion, or custom. It has existed since the first spontaneous stamping of rhythm and chanting of melody. It includes all the songs and dances originated or used among the common people. The words of the songs generally are artless poems dealing with mundane phases of everyday life, but texts of genuine charm, wit, and pathos are not foreign to the genre. The mores and folkways of the people are reflected in the lines. Tales of romantic and tragic love, patriotism, moral lessons, legendary figures, bits of philosophy and history, all are suitable subjects. Any thought or emotion which touches the lives and fancies of an ethnic group may find expression in song and dance.

The songs, requiring only the voice for performance, greatly exceed the number of dance tunes. The latter are inconsequential by comparison but make a fascinating study, partially because of their association with distinctive instruments such as bagpipes, zithers, guitars, and fiddles and with distinctive manners of playing. The folk instruments and playing styles are also used in song accompaniments.

A traditional view that folk songs develop anonymously as the result of concerted action and that folk dance music springs from unpremeditated accompaniments for rustic entertainments is valid only for aboriginal peoples in primitive societies. The folk music of Europe and the Americas is too sophisticated to have originated in deliberate joint ventures. The initial spark in folk music, as in art music, must come from an individual intellect. The will of the people is manifest in the selection and modification of its folk art. Acceptance is a more cogent reason for the classification than origin. Applying this criterion, the songs of Stephen Foster (1826–1864) and Irving Berlin's *White Christmas* (1942) are as much a part of our folk heritage as the songs of anonymous origin handed down through generations. Anonymity of authorship, often cited as a characteristic of folk music, is increasingly rare in these days of copyrights and publication. Most of the songs whose composers are unknown date from earlier times.

Few folk songs, if any, however, date back to ancient times. If any do, they have been so transformed through the years it has been impossible to trace them. Of course it is difficult to verify the lineage of a song which has been sung for generations in innumerable variations before it assumed definitive, written form. Modifications occur even after a song is notated and published. Community sings always turn up slightly discrepant versions of familiar songs. Tracing a folk song back to its origin is complicated by the fact that the text is as prone to change as the music. Not only do folk melodies exist in several versions (a traditional song learned by word of mouth is almost never sung in exactly the same way by two singers), but each locale may have a different set of words. The earliest authenticated secular folk songs date from the 13th century. Several are preserved from the 15th and 16th centuries, but living folk songs are mostly of more recent origin, predominantly from the 18th and 19th centuries.

Everyone agrees that folk music possesses certain national traits, but objective descriptions of these traits are not easily formulated. Short notes occurring on the beat *(Scotch snaps)* sometimes are pointed out as characteristics of Scotch music. Certain cadence formulas (approaching the tonic note from a third above or below) are mentioned as characteristics of American music. While it is true that these features appear in the literatures indicated, they also appear elsewhere. Obvious similarities are observable in the folk music of widely separated cultures. A person attuned to the dialects of folk music can identify the sources of tunes and styles with which he is intimately acquainted, just as one recognizes dialects in his native tongue, though he may have difficulty in describing them. It can only be deduced that the composite sound somehow reflects the national personality. The locality from which a folk song comes can be pinpointed more accurately by its text and the manner of performance than by its musical traits.

Folk melodies have a proven ability to attract and to communicate with listeners. In the folk song literature composers have a tested treasury of thematic material. As early as the 15th century they started taking advantage of it. A French folk song, *L'homme armé,* was used in at least thirty polyphonic masses between the 15th and 17th centuries. The practice of using thematic elements of folk origin in art music continues unabated. It was and is particularly prevalent in the music of nationalistic composers.

Borrowing between folk music and art music is not a one-way street. Individually composed and published songs are assimilated directly into the folk song literature. Dozens of Stephen Foster songs have acquired folk song status during the last century. In addition to outright adoption of composed songs in the folk repertory, songs of anonymous origin show evidence of art music's rational procedures in their forms and melodic contours. Continuous interaction between folk and art music is an established practice.

The United States has one of the largest and most varied folk song literatures. Immigrants from all over the world brought the songs and dances of their native lands with them. The ethnic groups that contributed to this musical melting pot have tended, with some exceptions, to lose their identity. In the process of Americanization, their native tongues and customs have been forgotten and their musical traditions transformed and assimilated. Each has made a contribution to the total body of American folk music and then adopted it as its own. To these imported influences, styles of essentially indigenous origin were added: American Indian and Negro music, our own patriotic songs, cowboy songs, revivalist hymns, and spirituals. An incomparable treasury of recorded folk music is deposited in the Library of Congress, and recordings of authentic folk music are being issued commercially in increasing numbers.

Until recently traditional folk music was not much in evidence in urban America, but the situation has changed dramatically. Authentic folk music and newly composed songs in folk style are now all the rage. Some of the most popular and prosperous TV stars and groups specialize in folk and folklike music. A network television studio may seem a strange place to practice folk art, but this is only one of the ways folk music has adapted to changing times and tastes. The protest, peace, and freedom movements inspired a whole new body of music in the folk tradition. Gospel songs are heard by millions of noncommunicants, and some radio stations program country and western music exclusively.

The most exciting aspect of the new folk movement is that Americans are again becoming a singing people. Teenagers and college students particularly are active participants, not just observers, in the burgeoning folk music revival. Folk music is not something to read about, and much of the fun is missed when it is heard from recordings and broadcasts. To really experience the joy of folk music, get together with a few friends, a collection of folk songs if necessary, and a guitar. It will not be difficult to find a guitarist. According to a recent survey there are more than ten million nonprofessional guitar players in the country, which gives some measure of the current boom in amateur music making.

The distinctions between folk music and popular music are by no means as clear as they once were, and popular music cannot be entirely disassociated from jazz. The blurring of the dividing lines between current musical styles was dramatized in the 1975 Newport Jazz Festival when such disparate types as gospel, ragtime, blues, swing, Afro-Latin, soul, pop-rock, Dixieland, bebop, cool, and electronic jazz-rock were all heard in the same series of concerts.

The critical difference between folk music and popular music is longevity. A song becomes a true folk song only after it has survived for a generation or more and has become a part of a folk tradition. A popular song, almost by definition, is one with broad, immediate, and implicitly transient appeal. A pop tune rarely remains in the top forty for more than a season. Even so, the two categories are not mutually exclusive. Genuine folk songs have become popular hits, and some popular songs of past eras have acquired folk status.

The degree of sophistication distinguishes popular music from jazz, more so now than when jazz was in its infancy. Popular music tends to be simple, direct, and uncomplicated. Jazz styles all exhibit some degree of complexity, at least in their rhythms. The nature of the differences between popular music and jazz make it possible for the same piece to be a simple popular song and also the basis for highly sophisticated jazz improvisation.

The type of popular music most akin to folk music is *country*. Country music is not far from its bluegrass and hillbilly roots. It could quite logically be regarded as a kind of folk music if it were not for its phenomenal popular and commercial success. Commercial exploitation of country music began on November 28, 1925 when the first WSM Barn Dance program was broadcast over radio station WSM in Nashville. The early programs, by all accounts, were not too different from the rustic entertainments that could be heard in real barns around the countryside. When the show followed a Metropolitan Opera broadcast, the announcer's introduction was, "Well, folks, you've been up in the clouds with grand opera; now get down to earth with us in a four-hour shindig of Grand Ole Opry." The name caught on; Grand Ole Opry became a national institution; and Nashville became the mecca of country music.

Practically every country music personality has been associated with the Grand Ole Opry at one time or another, and it has made stars of many of them. Loretta Lynn is one. Without it she might still be singing folk music for a few friends in Van Lear, Kentucky where she grew up. As it is, she has found fame and fortune as an award-winning country singer.

Loretta Lynn: *Back to the Country* (1975) 2:19

This is the title song of the Loretta Lynn album MCA 471. It could survive and become a folk song, but for the present it is a popular song in country style. It was written by Tracey Lee.[1]

One reason cited for the popularity of country music is that it came along at a time when jazz was becoming more sophisticated and losing its mass appeal. The same thing could be said of *rock.* Where rock might have been dismissed a couple of decades ago as a transient fad, it has shown unexpected signs of survival and of becoming an enduring style.

Rock music is not easily described, but its sound is unmistakable. The most obvious characteristic is the consistently high dynamic level. In live performances the instruments and voices are amplified to the point where the music can almost be felt as well as heard, and listeners are inclined to adjust the volume controls to achieve the same effect from radios and record players. The impact of the music apparently is dependent to some extent on a sound intensity approaching the threshold of pain, though there is evidence that overexposure to such sounds permanently impairs hearing. The rhythm of rock features fast, heavy, even divisions of the beat. The melodies are declamatory rather than lyric. They typically have many repeated notes and figures within a narrow range. The static harmonies of pure rock are in revolt against the musical conventions of the establishment. Three or four basic chords (triads) alternate in the most primitive way, and the standard progressions of jazz and classical music are shunned. In both the melodies and the harmonies strong folk and modal influences can be detected. The forms of folk music and jazz are also the forms of rock, but there are many irregularities.

Rock 'n' roll, as it was called initially, emerged as a distinct musical type in the early 1950s. Its immediate ancestors were rhythm and blues music and country and western music, which were themselves products of composite influences. Basic rock 'n' roll is now sometimes called *hard rock* to distinguish it from subsequent developments. Hard rock is simple, direct, gut-level music suitable for dancing. The inventiveness of the Rolling Stones led to complexities and improvisational elements beyond the basic rock style and to a brand of rock known as *acid rock,* the LSD connotation no doubt deliberate. *Psychedelic rock,* a contribution of the now defunct Beatles, is less energetic and more sophisticated in its themes and instrumentation (including electronic instruments) than hard or acid rock. Its subtle and symbolic homage to the drug culture is manifest in its lyrics and in the psychedelic visual effects sometimes associated with it.

1. Popular songs are often identified by the name of the performer rather than the composer when they are not the same.

Soul music, also known as *black rock,* expresses the yearning, anxiety, spirit, pride, and passion of the black community and is the special province of black musicians. It might have remained an esoteric branch of rock except for the commercial exploitation by Motown Records. The Motown company of Detroit recruited a roster of artists and developed a formula for soul music that gained acceptance by local radio stations around the country featuring the top forty tunes. This brought black rock to a universal audience, placed it in the mainstream of popular music, and made stars of its performers. Motown promotion launched the spectacular careers of Diana Ross and the Supremes, who epitomized the Motown style. Stevie Wonder is the biggest talent and current superstar of the Motown stable. He writes his own material, sings, and on his recordings plays multiple instruments—electric and acoustic pianos, Arp and Moog synthesizers, and drums. In 1975 he received Grammy Awards in five different categories from the National Academy of Recording Arts and Sciences.

STEVIE WONDER: *Higher Ground* (1973) 3:54
(1950–)

This is one of the recordings in which Stevie, as he is called on the record jacket, is the whole show. He wrote the music, lyrics, and arrangement, sang the song, played all of the instruments, and produced the record album containing it (*Innervisions*—Tamla T 326L).

With age, rock is showing signs of mellowing. The ear-splitting intensity which was its trademark in the early years now at times yields to a more restrained and expressive *soft rock* style. Soft rock's deviations from the original premises of rock may well be pointing in the direction of important future developments.

The diversity and vitality of rock music after more than two decades proves that it is no passing fancy. Whether it will continue to progress within a basic rock framework, gradually evolve into a new style, or be replaced by an essentially different kind of popular music is, at this time, anybody's guess. Trends in popular music are as changeable and unpredictable as the weather. The following is an atypical example of rock, but it shows how far the style has come since its raucous beginnings.

ANDREW LLOYD WEBBER: *Jesus Christ Superstar* (1970) 87:16
(1948–)

This is a rock opera with the scope and all the ingredients of traditional opera. The lyrics by Tim Rice retell events in the last week of Christ's life using contemporary language and portraying the characters as real people. Both the words and music are wrenchingly modern, but not irreverent, and very much in tune with the tastes of the times. Written by two young Englishmen, *Superstar* was an instantaneous hit around the world. In the first year of its release 3.5 million copies of the recording and tapes were sold for a gross of $40 million.

With the emergence of country and rock music Nashville and Detroit became popular music centers. The influence of New York's Tin Pan Alley and Broadway and Hollywood's musicals on the popular music scene diminished correspondingly, but did not disappear. Marvin Hamlisch is still writing songs in the mold of George Gershwin and Oscar Hammerstein and for the same outlets. His music for the 1974 film *The Way We Were* won Motion Picture Academy Oscars for the best original song and the best original score. The hit song *What I Did for Love* and the featured number *One* are from his Broadway musical *A Chorus Line.*

MARVIN HAMLISCH: *A Chorus Line* (1975)		
(1944–)	What I Did for Love	3:45
	One—Finale	5:02

In the show, *One* precedes *What I Did for Love* and returns in the finale. The former features the entire company; the latter is a solo for Diana, one of the members of the chorus line.

A cross section of folk and popular music can be heard by listening to a selection or two broadcast by each music station on the radio band, and all of the styles and star performers are abundantly represented on recordings.

References

Belz, Carl. *The Story of Rock.* 2d ed. New York: Oxford University Press, 1972.

Cohn, Nik. *Rock Dreams.* New York: Popular Library, 1974.

Eisen, Jonathan, ed. *The Age of Rock: Sounds of the American Cultural Revolution.* New York: Random House, 1969. (Also Vintage paperback edition)

Gentry, Linnell. *A History and Encyclopedia of Country, Western, and Gospel Music.* 2d ed. Nashville: Clairmont, 1969.

Price, Steven D. *Take Me Home: The Rise of Country and Western Music.* New York: Praeger, 1974.

Roxon, Lillian. *Rock Encyclopedia.* New York: Grosset and Dunlap, 1974.

Shaw, Arnold. *The World of Soul: The Black Contribution to Pop Music.* Chicago: Henry Regnery, 1970.

Stambler, Irwin. *Encyclopedia of Pop, Rock and Soul.* New York: St. Martin's Press, 1975.

Stambler, Irwin, and Landon, Grelun. *Encyclopedia of Folk, Country and Western Music.* New York: St. Martin's Press, 1975.

Jazz

25

There are no adequate designations for broad musical types. Classical, folk, popular, and jazz are used so loosely as to be almost meaningless. Devotees are inclined to develop precise terminology for music in their particular spheres of interest and to label other types with some general or condescending term. The types of music and subcategories listed in a 1976 RCA Music Service (record club) brochure were: easy listening (instrumental/vocal), country, today's sound (rock/soul/folk), Broadway-Hollywood-TV, and classical. The American Society of Composers, Authors and Publishers (ASCAP) classifies composers as *popular* or *standard.* ASCAP's popular category includes pop-rock, country and western, rhythm and blues, musical theater, jazz, and film music. The standard category encompasses the so-called serious music: symphonic, chamber, and educational. In jazz circles the music considered up to this point is regarded as classical (longhair), folk, or popular. The subject of this chapter is the remaining kind of music, jazz.

True jazz, as opposed to the popular music with which it is sometimes grouped, attracts a following fully as informed and dedicated as any symphony or chamber music audience. Critical reviews of performances and recordings appear in general interest periodicals. Without becoming totally disassociated from dance elements, jazz is increasingly conceived as an abstract art form intended for concentrated listening independent of overt physical responses.

Jazz and popular music cannot be completely divorced. The more durable popular tunes of yesteryear have been and continue to be played in the current jazz styles and to serve as a basis for jazz improvisation.

The same cannot be said of the pop-rock tunes which have dominated the popular field in recent years. During this period original jazz creations have grown in number and importance. Jazz musicians as a rule are highly proficient instrumentalists, and many are academically trained. No great technical demands are made on performers in the popular field, and attitudes toward their music is not so different from the attitudes toward jazz 50 years ago.

Jazz, once regarded by some as a destructive influence whose sudden appearance on the musical scene would be matched by an equally sudden and welcome demise, is now an established and accepted mode of musical expression. The classics, regarded by others as remnants of the past outliving their usefulness but refusing to die, continue to flourish if not to prosper. If history repeats itself, different kinds of music will exist side by side in the future as they have since the cults of Apollo and Dionysus cultivated contrasting musical styles in ancient Greece. Classic and jazz styles occupy parallel positions in contemporary culture. The esteemed traditions of the classics are matched by the brief but colorful history of jazz which began around the turn of the century in the Storyville section of New Orleans. The year 1897, when the first piano rag was published, is often used as a point of departure by jazz historians, though the term was not widespread until 1917 when the first jazz recordings were made by the Original Dixieland Jazz Band.

The origins of jazz have been attributed to a wide range of forces and influences. Rags, hymns, spirituals, blues, work songs, quadrilles, marches, waltzes, minstrels, Spanish and French music, all have been suggested as ancestors of jazz. Whatever its forebears, the miracle that is jazz was synthesized from diverse elements by a people in a foreign environment without any ready-made, adequate and appropriate means of musical expression. In the beginning jazz was uniquely a product of black Americans. Residual elements retained from their African heritage and influences absorbed from their New World surroundings were fused into an essentially new musical language.

Some obvious features of earlier music, such as syncopation and the pentatonic (five-tone) scale which exist in primitive African music and several other traditions, were appropriated by jazz for its own use. Outright borrowing of tunes from other styles, a practice which continues today, started at once. Early rag pieces like *High Society* and *I Wish I Could Shimmy Like My Sister Kate* were being played in quite different versions by the brass bands of the town. The still popular *Tiger Rag* was based on the quadrille *Get Out of Here.* In spite of this borrowing, jazz was definitely something new, something more than the sum of its parts.

Though its genesis may be earlier, the documented story of jazz commences with the piano rags played in New Orleans during the final decade of the last century. Ragtime piano playing was mostly improvisatory in a percussive style with little use of pedal. The absence of a text was conducive to nonlyric, instrumental melodies. Harmony was basically the primary chords of conventional music. Rhythm, the most distinctive feature of ragtime, was characterized by elaborate syncopations, sometimes created by short notes in accented portions of the measure (and conversely, longer notes in unaccented portions) and sometimes by cross rhythms between melodic groupings of three and six notes in conjunction with underlying beat patterns of two and four. Other rhythmic devices included placing accents just before and after the normal pulse and using rests where accents normally fall. These rhythmic characteristics are the common denominators of jazz.

Though elements of ragtime had been heard earlier, apparently no example of the style appeared in print before 1897 when *Harlem Rag* by Tom Turpin (1873–1922) was published. That same year a piano method book, *Ragtime Instructor,* by Ben Harney (1871–1938) came out. Harney was a white song writer and pianist playing in New York. At this early date jazz had already crossed the color line and the boundaries of the South, but it was to remain for some time essentially if not exclusively a product of southern Negro culture.

The ragtime craze reached its zenith around the turn of the century. The most famous rag composer then, as now, was Scott Joplin. The theme music for the Academy Award-winning motion picture *The Sting* was from Joplin's rag *The Entertainer.* The film sparked an instantaneous rag and Joplin revival. His *Maple Leaf Rag* is universally regarded as a classic in the style.

SCOTT JOPLIN: *Maple Leaf Rag* (1899) 3:14
(1868–1917)

> *Maple Leaf Rag* takes its name from the Maple Leaf Club in Sedalia, Missouri where Joplin played. It has a clear sectional structure—AA BB A CC DD—in which each strain, except the return of A, is repeated immediately. A performance by Joplin taken from a piano roll is included in the *Smithsonian Collection of Classic Jazz.* The *Listeners Guide* recording is by Joshua Rifkin.
>
> (Record side 9 band 1)

During the ragtime piano era small miscellaneous groups of instrumentalists, many of whom could not read music, collectively improvised for popular entertainments, parades, and dances. The results could not have been other than wildly contrapuntal and shockingly dissonant.

Free improvisation, however, was to become a continuing feature of the infant art.

The publication in 1912 and 1914 respectively of the *Memphis Blues* and the *St. Louis Blues* by W. C. Handy ushered in the next jazz epoch. The blues, stemming more or less directly from spirituals and work songs, introduced several characteristics of subsequent jazz. They were different from rags in several respects. As songs, their melodies are vocal in style rather than instrumental. The texts, usually lamenting the absence or loss of a lover, typically are sung in a declamatory manner over a steady pulsating accompaniment. The tempo generally is slow, though faster blues are not unknown. Whereas ragtime harmonies are mostly triads, blues traditionally are based on a standard chord progression which includes seventh chords. Like most popular music, blues are predominantly major, but notes approximating the third and seventh scale degrees of natural minor are featured melodically, sometimes while the corresponding major note is in the accompaniment. These *blue notes* take their name from the style. Blues singers often slide into notes and hover in the vicinity of but not exactly on the notated pitch.

The words, melody, and harmony in blues generally conform to a standard 12-bar pattern. The words most often consist of three lines, the second of which is a repetition or slightly altered version of the first. The third line completes the thought and ends with a terminal rhyme. The poetic meter is predominantly iambic pentameter (U — U — U — U — U —) or a rough approximation of it. Each line of the text is set as a musical phrase with a distinctive melodic and harmonic content, which is to say that the repetition in the words is not reflected in the music. Frequently the singer has a long note or a rest at the end of a phrase during which a brief instrumental improvisation, called a *break*, is interpolated. All of these features are illustrated in the first strain of Handy's *St. Louis Blues.*

W. C. HANDY: *St. Louis Blues* (1914) 3:08
(1873–1958)

The *St. Louis Blues* is not a simple blues but an extended composition of three distinct strains. The first and third strains, each of which is repeated in the printed version, are perfect examples of 12-bar blues form. The unrepeated middle strain is a less typical 16-bar blues. On the 1925 Bessie Smith recording, reproduced in the *Smithsonian Collection of Classic Jazz* and in the *Listeners Guide* record album, the third strain is not repeated. Louis Armstrong, playing cornet, provides the instrumental breaks.

(Record side 9 band 2)

The styles of ragtime and the blues coalesced in jazz, a term of unsavory origin which did not appear in print before the second decade of the century. By this time jazz bands had migrated from New Orleans and were appearing regularly in Chicago, New York, and San Francisco. Chicago was the new mecca.

With the entrance into the field of white and trained musicians, a refining, and in a sense, a corrupting process began. The crude virility of primitive jazz was mellowed by the intrusion of European elements—sentimental melodies of the ballad and Viennese operetta type and impressionist harmonies. The lusty blues singers were largely replaced by crooners. The bands grew to sizes which made improvisation impractical, and written arrangements became the rule. With the addition of strings the bands became so large and the arrangements so pretentious that the anomalous name *symphonic jazz* was coined for the style. What must have appeared to Paul Whiteman, his admirers and imitators as a great elevation of jazz style and a popularization of classic values, in retrospect seems to have been a rather unfortunate compromise for both. Before the roaring 20s were over, there were three distinct branches of jazz: *symphonic, sweet* (popular), and *hot* (Dixieland). Symphonic and sweet popular music retained some of the superficial aspects of jazz and were appropriate for dancing all the varied steps of the fox trot, but only hot Dixieland was true to the original traditions.

Small groups, mainly black, continued to play hot jazz all through this period, not only preserving its traditions but enhancing them. Vocalists with these groups often improvised in an instrumental style using nonsense syllables, a contribution of hot jazz known as *scat singing.* Louis Armstrong was an illustrious scat singer and hot jazz performer on the cornet. He is heard in both roles on the suggested recording. Jazz pieces are often more closely identified with a performer or group than with a composer. In such instances, like the following, the performers are named in place of the composers.

LOUIS ARMSTRONG AND HIS HOT FIVE: *Hotter Than That* (1927) 2:59

> This performance is included in the *Listeners Guide* record album and in the *Smithsonian Collection of Classic Jazz.* Lil Hardin Armstrong, who married Louis in 1924, wrote the piece and played piano in the group.
>
> (Record side 9 band 3)

Boogie-woogie and *Kansas City* are jazz styles that developed in the 20s and carried over into the 30s. Boogie characteristically is a piano style in blues form with an insistently repeated bass figure played by the left hand while a totally independent improvisation is played by the right hand. Short fragments were sometimes repeated in the right-hand part. When similar repeated fragments—which were always rhythmic and could be either melodic or harmonic—appeared in the instrumental Kansas City style, they were called *riffs*. Kansas City jazz featured a heavy, four-beat rhythm in contrast to the two-beat rhythm prevalent in preceding styles. Bennie Moten's band, which later became Count Basie's, was the most famous in the area. The contributions of southwestern groups to the development of jazz have been receiving added attention in recent books on the subject. Kansas City style, according to some authorities, led directly into the big band era and the birth of *swing* in the mid-30s. The swinging big band of Duke Ellington was one of the best. In conception and performance his *Old King Dooji* has a propulsive four-beat rhythm and the use of riffs in common with Kansas City style plus the subtleties and refinements that make it swing.

DUKE ELLINGTON: *Old King Dooji* (1938) 2:29
(1899–1974)

This is a sterling example of post-Kansas-City style and of pre-World-War-II swing. King Dooji must have been a mythical king of a mythical kingdom, because composer Ellington provided no clue to his identity.

(Record side 9 band 4)

Swing was much closer to the spirit of jazz than the sweet and commercial music that was still being played, but the very nature of the big bands required that the emphasis be shifted from individual improvisation to precise group performance of written arrangements. The arrangements, however, incorporated many features of jazz rhythm and made provision on occasion for improvisation in breaks and hot choruses and over riffs and subdued backgrounds. In addition, the tradition of improvising was kept alive by smaller groups comprised of members and associates of the big bands. Benny Goodman had a 15-piece orchestra and was called the King of Swing, but there was also a Benny Goodman Trio, Quartet, Quintet, and Sextet. There were some regulars in the Benny Goodman small groups—Teddy Wilson, piano; Gene Krupa, drums; and Lionel Hampton, vibraphone; all of whom became leaders—but the personnel varied. The following example is played by the four regulars.

BENNY GOODMAN QUARTET: *Dizzy Spells* (1938) 5:47

Benny Goodman and his band made history on January 16, 1938 when they played a jazz concert in New York's prestigious Carnegie Hall. The Trio and the Quartet were represented on the program, and the performance of *Dizzy Spells* that night is the one reproduced in the *Listeners Guide* record album.

(Record side 9 band 5)

Many of the musicians in the swing bands were real jazz enthusiasts, and often after engagements with the band they congregated in small clubs for impromptu *jam sessions.* The jam sessions were completely unwritten, unrehearsed, and unstandardized. Any number could play. For patrons who found inspired, uninhibited improvisation more appealing than the studied perfection of formal performances and listening more enjoyable than dancing, staged jam sessions became a regular form of entertainment.

With the end of World War II the curtain rang down on the swing era. The power and discipline of its full-throated sections were muffled and the very foundation of jazz was assailed by a disturbing upheaval known as *bebop* or merely *bop.* Bop shunned time-honored formulas to experiment with exciting new rhythmic, melodic, and harmonic materials. As is often the case with experimenters, their music was sometimes pointlessly eccentric and sometimes just misunderstood. The players still committed to swing and Dixie were united in their resistance to the inroads of bop. Its frenzied repetition of trivial melodic tidbits was a threat to the traditions for which they stood. This iconoclastic upstart temporarily split jazzmen into factions and alienated them from their fans, but from the rubble of the conflict arose a rejuvenated art which is contemporary jazz. The older styles survive in modified forms, and new ones have been added.

Dixieland is a durable style that spans the history of jazz. The first white jazz band, one instrumental in introducing the new style of music north of the Mason-Dixon line, was the Original Dixieland Jazz Band. Early Dixieland was coarse and undisciplined. Vigor and abandon were its trademarks. Studied perfection was foreign to its nature, and a certain crudeness of tone and technique were part of the bargain. Dixieland may very well be the purest form of jazz, and after a series of recessions it is again riding a crest of popularity. Dixieland is still heard in the French Quarter of New Orleans and throughout the land. Over the years Dixieland style has become somewhat more restrained, refined and, for purists, tainted by influences of newer jazz styles, but its basic traditions have been preserved. The following is an example of 1955 vintage Dixieland.

TURK MURPHY AND HIS BAND: *High Society* (1955) 3:01

High Society is a perennial favorite. This version was recorded during a performance at the New Orleans Jazz Festival before a live audience. The clarinet solo has a ring of authenticity, though the clarinetist (Bill Carter) was only 20 years old and a newcomer in the band at the time.

(Record side 9 band 6)

Ferdinand "Jelly Roll" Morton (1885–1941) was a first-generation jazzman from New Orleans. On his calling card he listed himself as the originator of jazz, and certainly he contributed significantly to its history. In a 1939 recording of *Oh, Didn't He Ramble* Jelly Roll and his New Orleans Jazzmen re-created a scene from the archaic period when jazz was heard mainly in street parades and funeral processions. In the corteges going to the cemetery the early bands played in a reverent slow and mournful style. They switched to the fast pace and syncopated rhythms of jazz when the cemetery gates were behind them, and the recent mourners strutted and jigged their way home to this music. The same tune was sometimes played going to and returning from the cemetery. Morton's recording of the old cemetery tune has both versions. The Morton recording on the Bluebird label is long since out of print, but the same piece played the same two ways can be heard on a 1975 recording by Al Hirt, which graphically demonstrates the persistence of the Dixieland style. Hirt's commentary on the record describes the jazz funeral tradition.

Al Hirt: *Jazz Funeral—Oh, Didn't He Ramble* (1975) 10:10

> Dixieland greats Al Hirt and Pete Fountain play in their own neighboring clubs on New Orlean's Bourbon Street. They joined forces to entertain football fans who were in town for Super Bowl IX. The concert, which included this selection, was recorded live and released as *Super Jazz I* (Monument PZG 33485).

The swing style and big band concept which were mainstream jazz in the 30s and 40s are kept alive and essentially intact in the *stage bands* which now flourish in high schools and colleges. Among the pros, *progressive jazz* with Stan Kenton as its leading exponent was the successor to symphonic jazz and swing. Kenton formerly played for dances, but his ideas are more dramatically embodied in recordings and concert performances which are quite undanceable. He often abandons rigid, conventional rhythmic patterns, prime requisites of dance music, in favor of fluid pulses and asymmetric meters. The instrumentation is large and lavish, including on occasion strings and such unlikely jazz instruments as flutes, oboes, and French horns. Symphonic materials and techniques are borrowed freely—not insipid romantic melodies but the heady harmonies and dissonant counterpoint of the 20th century. The term *neophonic* was used by Kenton for one phase of his progressive jazz, one that he was instrumental in introducing in many educational institutions. Whether or not progressive jazz is really jazz depends upon the point of view, but there is no denying that it is a style with logical antecedents cultivated by a legion of dedicated musicians. Progressive jazz in its various guises has been a remarkably durable style. Kenton's first band was organized in 1941. The suggested listening is from an album recorded live in London during his 1972 European tour.

STAN KENTON AND HIS ORCHESTRA: *Malaga* (1972) 8:15

This Bill Holman composition has a decided Spanish flavor, an extended form, and a sound thoroughly representative of Kenton progressive jazz. It is included in the *Stan Kenton Today* album (London BP 44179–80).

The small combo counterpart of progressive jazz is *modern jazz* under which might be listed such subclassifications as *cool, West Coast, funky,* and *free.* Cool style is characterized by the relaxed understatement and elegant transparency epitomized in the playing of Lester Young (1909–1959) during the last decade of his career. West Coast is the brand of cool cultivated mainly by white musicians in the Los Angeles area. Gerry Mulligan was a charter member of this school. In funky jazz the feeling of bop is revived. It is more direct and rhythmic than cool. Any type of jazz that abandons the traditional restraints of harmony and form can be labeled free jazz. Ornette Coleman's *Free Jazz* (Atlantic S–1364) is a 36-minute free improvisation by Coleman and seven other musicians.

Modern jazz in both the general and the specific sense, descends directly from the improvisations of small groups in the 30s and early 40s and particularly from Charlie Parker (1920–1955) and bop. The size and instrumentation of the groups vary. All of the usual instruments of jazz are used, along with some newly converted such as flute and French horn and of recent vintage such as vibes and electric guitar. The players of modern jazz tend to be thoroughly knowledgeable musicians with solid academic training and virtuoso techniques. Versed in both the classics and jazz, they achieve a highly polished style even in spontaneous performances. In their hands the traditional elements of jazz become suave and sophisticated. Modern jazz is not so much something new as it is a new perfection of old methods. It is the type of jazz most generally admired by nonjazz musicians and a type which seems to proffer great potential for future development. It is doubtful that any modern jazz selection can be regarded as typical, but the following are representative. The first is closer to traditional jazz in that it uses a Gershwin popular tune of yesteryear as a point of departure.

George Gershwin/Modern Jazz Quartet: *But Not for Me* (1965) 3:41
(1898–1937)

The Benny Goodman Quartet and the Modern Jazz Quartet have three instruments in common—piano, vibraphone, and drums. The use of the bass in the MJQ in place of Goodman's clarinet is only one of the reasons for the great difference in the sound of the two groups. The flavor of the MJQ improvisation is definitely cool, though clearly in the mainstream jazz tradition.

(Record side 9 band 7)

In the second example of modern jazz the combination of instruments (trumpet, 2 saxophones, piano, bass, and drums) is more traditional than in the Modern Jazz Quartet, but the style of playing is farther out. Miles Davis is both the composer and the leader of the group. The piece evolves from a germ motive introduced at the beginning. The motive and crux of the piece is a two-chord progression in a long-short rhythm that sounds like an emphatic musical setting of the title words, "so what!"

Miles Davis Sextet: *So What* (1959) 9:05

This Miles Davis group is remarkable in that both saxophone players, John Coltraine and Julian "Cannonball" Adderly, went on to form their own groups and to make impressive contributions to jazz before their untimely deaths in 1967 and 1975 respectively. Miles Davis's *So What* is on Columbia PC 8163 and in the *Smithsonian Collection of Classic Jazz.*

Third stream is a term first used circa 1960 by Gunther Schuller (1925–) to denote a special kind of modern jazz which is a synthesis of jazz and recent "classical" elements. Creators of third stream music must, of course, be well grounded in jazz and the other contemporary idioms. The synthesis is accomplished in several ways. For example, two performing mediums may be combined as they are in Schuller's *Conversations* for jazz quartet and string quartet (on Atlantic S–1345), or a twelve-tone row may be used as the basis for jazz improvisation as in *Improvisational Suite No. 1* by Don Ellis (1932–). The Modern Jazz Quartet was an active force in third stream music until it disbanded in 1974. John Lewis, MJQ musical director and pianist, composed several works for jazz quartet and orchestra and commissioned others. His *In Memoriam* is the last recording of the MJQ with orchestra.

John Lewis: *In Memoriam* (1973)
(1920–) First Movement 8:40
Second Movement 9:03

In Memoriam is more symphonic than jazz-like in orientation, a fact confirmed by its division into two movements. The first movement was written in memory of one of Lewis's piano teachers. The second movement is a tribute to other musicians from Stravinsky to Armstrong whom he admired.

In their book *A Study of Jazz* (see p. 357) Tanner and Gerow call the most recent period of jazz the "eclectic era" and detect in it traces of all the preceding styles of jazz plus influences of classic, ethnic, and electronic music. Unless eclecticism can be regarded as a style, there really is no predominant trend discernable in today's jazz or any name for it.

The broad spectrum of current jazz is vividly demonstrated in recent festival programs. For example, the 1975 Newport Jazz Festival in New York included such diverse styles and performers as pianists Earl "Fatha" Hines, longtime associate of Louis Armstrong, and John Lewis, late of the Modern Jazz Quartet; the intimate improvisation of the Red Norvo Trio and the explosive big bands of Harry James, Count Basie, Buddy Rich, Lionel Hampton, and Stan Kenton; the J. C. White gospel singers and soul competition winner Oliver Canidy; the revolutionary experiments of the Miles Davis ensemble and the old-time Dixieland of Bob Crosby and his Bobcats and Papa French and the Original Tuxedo Jazz Band from New Orleans. All were regarded by the producer as proper representatives of the contemporary jazz scene.

Eclecticism is apparent in the stylistic diversity of performances by different groups and within the performances of a single group. Ideas from every conceivable source are absorbed and given a jazz interpretation. This process is amply illustrated in the album *The New Don Ellis Band Goes Underground* (Columbia CS 9889). The massive sound of the big swing bands can be heard in places, sometimes playing rock progressions. Other passages echo the cool style. Some of the rhythms can be traced back to sources in Mexico or Spain, Bulgaria, and India. Riffs of Kansas City origin are much in evidence, as are blues influences, which now might more aptly be called soul.

The instrumentation of the New Don Ellis Band is as eclectic as its performance style. It includes all of the usual jazz instruments in profusion plus voices, but that is only the beginning. The saxophone players double on flute, oboe, and bass clarinet. The trumpet players double on quarter-tone trumpets and fluegel horns, which are like oversized cornets. The piano player doubles on the harpsichord and the clavinet, the latter an electronic keyboard instrument. The most striking feature of the instrumentation, however, is the use of electronics to generate and modify the sounds. Don Ellis plays an electrophonic trumpet, and Pete Robinson plays an electronic Fender-Rhodes piano. A ring modulator specially built for the band and a Conn Multivider, both electronic devices used to modify tones, are also listed in the instrumentation. The electronic sounds are most prominent in the suggested selection, but the whole album should be heard to appreciate fully its eclecticism.

THE NEW DON ELLIS BAND: *House in the Country* (1969) 2:46
(Record side 9 band 8)

By the time these words reach print, some of the suggested recordings will be out of print. New ones will have taken their place, and they should be substituted. What will the new jazz be like? As of now the future course of jazz is an enigma, but perhaps from today's multiplicity of styles a new style will emerge and dominate the field for a time. Since its inception jazz has demonstrated a pronounced tendency to restyle itself almost every decade. Advances in electronic technology have added a new dimension to the jazz of the 60s and 70s. Amplification through conventional and contact microphones facilitates balancing otherwise impractical instrumental combinations. Electronic devices are now in use that drastically modify the range and quality of conventional instruments and provide reverberation and echo effects in live performances. Despite all the changes in styles over the years a thread of continuity runs through the history of jazz, and consistent elements preserve its identity as a coherent body of music.

Traditional jazz structures are rudimentary and relatively stereotyped. They consist of the 12-bar blues form (see p. 130) and the 32-bar song form. The 32-bar song form has four parts of equal length in an A A B A (ternary) pattern. B is the *bridge* in popular terminology. It connects (and separates) repetitions of A, which invariably contains the more cogent ideas. The brevity and simplicity of popular lyrics dictate small, regular forms. Dimensions are extended by repeating the entire pattern. Arrangements typically change key for the second chorus. Except for isolated examples and in progressive and third stream jazz, the developmental procedures and extended forms of concert music have not been used.

Harmonically, jazz started with and periodically reverts to the most elemental materials. In between it has borrowed heavily from other styles, particularly impressionism. Certain chord structures and progressions which have become jazz clichés originated elsewhere. Jazz is more imitative than creative in this respect. Real innovation is rare. Sonorities attributed to jazz composers usually were only popularized by them, but in this they are rendering a service to concert music. Listeners conditioned to the sounds of Kenton and Ellis are not easily shocked by Stravinsky or Bartok. The fact that the *St. Louis Blues* and *The Rite of Spring* are contemporaneous should dispel the rather prevalent notion that symphonists appropriate harmonic materials from jazz. The best claim jazz can make to harmonic innovation may be the blue notes which are more properly a melodic phenomenon. Even these appeared early in other mediums (Bartok *String Quartet no. 2, op. 17,* 1915–1917). Influence either way is improbable since it is unlikely that Bartok or early blues singers ever heard of each other.

Jazz melody must be approached from two points of view. The published tunes have unpretentious contours that the man in the street can sing, whistle, and identify with. The improvisations based on these tunes and their settings are unique inventions that vary with every realization. Versions in which simple melodies are intricately ornamented beyond recognition are the delight of jazz buffs. As a result, jazz more than any other form of music is an art of performers and performances rather than of composers and compositions. The few composers like George Gershwin (1898–1937) and Duke Ellington (1899–1974) who have made reputations in jazz are the exception. The luminaries of jazz are the performers whose virtuoso improvisations are the essence of jazz melody. Improvisation per se is one of the most persistent features of jazz.

Rhythm is the realm of undisputed jazz originality. The rhythmic devices of ragtime have endured without interruption through all the changing styles of jazz from early New Orleans to the present. Rhythm more than any other element makes jazz stand apart as a distinctive, homogeneous body of music. Cataloging its obvious features—syncopation, displaced accents, and nonsynchronous melodic-accompaniment groupings—does little to explain its vitality or originality. All of these devices occur in other music, but the effect is not the same. One reason is that the subtle effects of jazz rhythm defy precise notation. They must be felt.

Jazz rhythms, in spite of their attractiveness, have exerted comparatively little influence on other musical styles due to one peculiarity. They are completely meaningful only in terms of a prominent underlying beat. In the big bands the beat is supplied by a rhythm section, a section not to be confused with the percussion of a symphony orchestra. The rhythm section is fully as important and almost as large, not to mention as loud, as the other sections. Pianos, string bass, guitar, and traps are typical members of the rhythm section. The traps are not a single instrument but a whole set of drums, cymbals, and other percussion instruments played by one player using both hands and both feet. When necessary for balance the guitar and bass are amplified. In the smaller jazz ensembles the rhythm, melody, and harmony duties are usually shared by the various instruments. With the piano as a solo instrument the left hand ordinarily plays on the beat while the right hand exercises characteristic freedom. Whatever the medium, a pronounced regular beat provides a foil for syncopation and shifted accents in the other parts. Lacking the equivalent of a jazz beat, the other elements of jazz rhythm occur only incidentally in classic idioms.

Interaction between jazz and classical music has been and probably will continue to be limited. The absence of techniques in either immediately accessible to the other precludes the danger of assimilation. It also assures the healthy preservation of these two distinct types of music.

Though jazz is a newcomer in the field of the arts, it is the logical inheritor of honorable traditions. Some of the most venerable musical practices are preserved only in jazz and popular music. Playing keyboard instruments from symbols other than notation was an indispensable accomplishment for musicians of the baroque period. This practice, a lost art as far as other musicians are concerned, flourishes with the players of jazz and popular music. The symbols have changed from numbers below the staff to letters and numbers above the staff, but the principles are the same. Improvisation, another lost art for academic musicians, is revived in jazz. Bach, whose prowess in playing from symbols and in improvising was legendary, probably would be disenchanted with colleagues less ably endowed and delighted with the fresh new turn these ancient arts have taken in the hands of jazz musicians.

Jazz, though in a state of flux during its entire existence, still represents a continuous and more important a growing tradition. Record and tape sales are soaring. Juke boxes dispense jazz along with all the varieties of popular music. Radio and television stations fill the air waves with music, predominantly the top forty tunes to be sure, but with a sprinkling of jazz and classics. Popular music might engulf the other kinds, but they are capturing a fair share of the mature listening public. While the demand for the classics and the more progressive styles of jazz may not be keeping pace with that for popular music, at least it is moving in the same direction. The net result is that more people are hearing and making more music than ever before in the history of mankind. There is no real competition between the various types of music, because the approaches and aims are different.

The performers of the standard literature strive for faithful renditions of precisely notated compositions of enduring value worthy to pass on to posterity, while jazz musicians improvise according to their inspiration at the moment with no thought of the future. Their intent is not to create an immortal masterpiece, but to give spontaneous and eloquent voice to a fleeting mood. An improvised piece is short-lived. It is born in the heads and fingers of the players and lingers only in the memory of the listeners unless it is recorded. It catches the spirit of the times and reflects kaleidoscopic changes of taste the way a newspaper reports the events of the day. A newspaper is not a novel, and a jazz performance is not a symphony or a string quartet, but jazz is an eminently viable style of music.

Records

Decade of Jazz, Vol. 1, 1939–49. Blue Note LA158–G2
Decade of Jazz, Vol. 2, 1949–59. Blue Note LA159–G2
Decade of Jazz, Vol. 3, 1959–69. Blue Note LA160–G2
Definitive Jazz Scene, Vols. 1–3. Impulse S–99, S–100, S–9101
Encyclopedia of Jazz on Records, Vols. 1–5. MCA 4061–4063
Jazz, Vols. 1–11. Folkways 2801–2811
A Jazz Piano Anthology. Columbia KG–32355
The Smithsonian Collection of Classic Jazz. Available through the Smithsonian Associates. Distributed by W. W. Norton & Co.
The Story of Jazz. Folkways 7312 (Langston Hughes narration with examples)
What Is Jazz? Columbia CL 919 (Leonard Bernstein lecture with examples)

References

Berendt, Joachim. *Jazz Book: From New Orleans to Rock and Free Jazz.* New York: Lawrence Hill, 1974.
Gammond, Peter. *Scott Joplin and the Ragtime Era.* New York: St. Martin's Press, 1975.
Hentoff, Nat, and McCarthy, Albert J., eds. *Jazz.* New York: Da Capo Press, 1975.
Russell, Ross. *Jazz Style in Kansas City and the Southwest.* Berkeley: University of California Press, 1971.
Sargeant, Winthrop. *Jazz, Hot and Hybrid.* 3d ed., enl. New York: Da Capo Press, 1975.
Schuller, Gunther: *Early Jazz: Its Roots and Musical Development.* New York: Oxford University Press, 1968.
Simon, George. *The Big Bands.* Rev. ed., enl. New York: Macmillan, 1974.
Southern, Eileen. *The Music of Black Americans.* New York: W. W. Norton, 1971.

Tanner, Paul, and Gerow, Maurice. *A Study of Jazz.* 3d ed., with record. Dubuque: Wm. C. Brown Company Publishers, 1977.

Williams, Martin, general ed. *The Macmillan Jazz Masters Series.* New York: Macmillan.

Gitler, Ira. *Jazz Masters of the Forties.* 1966, paper 1974.

Goldberg, Joe. *Jazz Masters of the Fifties.* 1965.

Hadlock, Richard. *Jazz Masters of the Twenties.* 1965, paper 1974.

Stewart, Rex. *Jazz Masters of the Thirties.* 1972.

Williams, Martin. *Jazz Masters in Transition, 1957–1969.* 1970.

———. *Jazz Masters of New Orleans.* 1967.

The Music of Other Cultures

26

The body of music discussed in the preceding chapters, though vast and varied, is representative of a miniscule portion of the world's music. Each geographic region and ethnic group has its own distinctive music, instruments, and traditions. Ethnomusicology is a thriving new branch of music scholarship devoted to the study of regional and non-Western music. Recordings and films made by ethnomusicologists have made it possible to become familiar with music from the far corners of the earth, and worldwide travel has exposed millions of people to the music of foreign lands. Some music of other cultures has meaning only for the members of the community which created it and for the scholars who examine it scientifically, but some has universal appeal. A sampling of the latter type of ethnic music is presented in this chapter. The purpose is neither scholarly nor scientific but to expand the range of listening experiences and to entertain. Since recordings of the music of other cultures are not always readily available, all of the suggested examples are included in the record album which accompanies the *Listeners Guide* (fourth edition).

A special affinity exists between the music of black Africa and the American people. Large numbers of the population are of African descent, and African influences were decisive in the formulation of the jazz idiom. The music of the black tribes and nations of Africa is remarkably homogeneous considering the diversity of their languages, physical features, cultural traits, and life-styles. Throughout central Africa a strong predilection for percussion-type instruments sounded by striking or shaking and its corollary, a preoccupation with the rhythmic aspect of music, are evident. An acute sense of rhythm seems to be innate. In African music multiple rhythms are combined in such complex relationships that the high degree of organization in the patterns may not be perceived by the uninitiated, but the catchy polyrhythms rarely fail to evoke an emotional response. Africans, whether participating or observing, become emotionally involved in their music, and it is an inherent part of their daily lives from birth to death.

The first example of African music is from Senegal, the westernmost country in Africa. The inhabitants are principally Wolofs and Mandingos. Their dress and dietary customs reflect their Moslem religion, but their intricate drumming is distinctly West African in style. In a favorite form of entertainment, drummers and spectators gather in a circle. An individual from among the spectators moves to the center of the group where he or she dances impromptu, alone or with a partner, until exhausted or displaced by another dancer. Meanwhile, the complex rhythms of the drums continue without interruption. Drum sounds predominate in *Greetings from Podor,* but individual voices, group singing, and handclapping can also be heard.

SENEGAL: *Greetings from Podor* 1:29

> This recording was made during a 1969 transafrica expedition by hovercraft. Podor is a town of some 4,000 inhabitants on the Senegal river which marks the border between Senegal and Mauritania to the north.

(Record side 10 band 1)

From Dakar, the capital of Senegal, it is about 1,300 miles southeast as the crow flies to Accra, the capital of Ghana. The distance between the two countries must have been a formidable barrier to cultural exchanges in the time before modern means of transportation and communication, but the music of both countries belongs to the same West African tradition. The people and music of Ghana are better known in the United States. Probable reasons are that Ghana is more populous, Christian missionaries were active there, and many Ghanaians speak and write English.

The Ashanti (also spelled Asante) people inhabit the inland plateau region of Ghana. The ceremonial drums of the Asantehene, paramount chief of the Ashanti, heard in the next example are used in pairs, one tuned to a relatively low pitch, the other to a higher pitch. One is regarded as male, the other as female. A piece of metal attached to the head of the male drum sounds when it is played. The drums are made of wood and shaped like a bowl on top of a cylinder. The drum head, which goes on the bowl end, is made from the skin of elephant ears.

GHANA: *The Ceremonial Drums of the Asantehene* 1:01

This is another example of authentic African music recorded in the field. It is important to record and preserve the ceremonial music of the paramount hereditary chief (Asantehene) while it is still possible, because his authority and the reasons for the music's existence are diminishing since Ghana gained its independence and formed a central government.

(Record side 10 band 2)

Japanese music throughout its history has been closely associated with drama and dance. Kabuki, more spectacle than drama, incorporates traditional themes, acting, and dancing in theatrical performances designed for the tastes of the common people. It emerged as a distinct dramatic type before the beginning of the 16th century. It is not the most venerable Japanese dramatic genre, but since the 18th century it has been the most popular.

In 1954 the Azuma Kabuki Musicians toured this country and gave American audiences their initial exposure to the music and dance traditions of the Orient. The following example is from a recording of the troupe made at that time. The high-pitched, nasal voice quality which characterizes Japanese singing can be heard in the part of the narrators. The string instruments included in the ensemble are shamisens (samisens). The shamisen has a long neck, three silk strings, and a square sound box made of wood and covered top and bottom with skin. It is played with a fan-shaped ivory pick and is the popular instrument used in Japan by street singers and geishas.

JAPAN/KABUKI: *O-Matsuribayashi* (Festival Music) 1:55

In addition to the singing narrators, the ensemble includes shamisens, drum and bass drum, bell, flute, and gong. The music is a modern arrangement of older classics.

(Record side 10 band 3)

Strangely, it is not the traditional music of Japan that is taught in the Japanese public schools, but mainly Western music. This practice was instituted by Emperor Mutsuhito (reigned 1868–1912) and continues to the present time. As a result modern Japan has excellent symphony orchestras and opera companies that perform occidental music and composers who write in European styles.

Western music has made no inroads in Bali, one of some 3,000 islands comprising the Southeast Asian Republic of Indonesia. Though the island is small (93 miles long and at most 50 miles wide) and has a population under two million, it is justly world famous for its indigenous music and dance, which are inseparable. Music is an integral part of the Balinese way of life. No temple ceremony or village festival, and there are many, is complete without a program of dances and plays. Many villagers spend their nights practicing the intricate movements of the ritual dances and rehearsing the musical accompaniments. Except in certain plays and temple ceremonies, the music of Bali and Java, its larger neighbor to the west, is almost purely instrumental. In both countries the instrumental ensembles are known as *gamelans,* orchestras consisting principally of gongs, metallophones, drums, and cymbals.

The 25-piece gamelan heard on the recorded example is reputed to be the foremost in Bali. It is from the village of Pliatan, where it plays ceremonial temple music and accompanies both traditional and modern forms of the dance. The *Kapi Radja* serves as an overture to a dance program *Dancers of Bali* recorded on Columbia ML 4618.

BALI/GAMELAN: *Overture—Kapi Radja* 2:58

> *Kapi Radja* is a composition in modern style based on a melody from North Bali. The musicians of that region have introduced bold innovations within the framework of native musical idioms.
>
> (Record side 10 band 4)

The music of Bali is community centered. The gamelans are large ensembles that produce a composite sound, and there are no individual star performers. In contrast, the music of India is performed exclusively by small groups and individuals who have dedicated their lives to perfecting their art. The procedures of Indian music, which have their foundation in religion and philosophy, are fantastically complicated. To master them requires intense and prolonged mental and physical discipline. The nature of the complexity lies in the requirement that the performers must create seemingly free and spontaneous improvisations that conform strictly to interrelated melodic, rhythmic, and structural patterns.

Ravi Shankar, the *sitar* player on the recorded example, is the greatest and most renowned of India's musicians. The sitar is a plucked string instrument with a long neck and six tone-producing strings. The sound is resonated by 19 sympathetic strings and two seasoned gourds, one at the base of the instrument and the other at the upper end of the neck. Twenty frets on the neck are moved to adjust the tuning, which varies from piece to piece. Smaller (microtonal) pitch deviations are made by pulling the strings sideways on the fingerboard. The sitar is accompanied by *tabla* and *tamboura.* The tabla is a pair of hand drums tuned to the main tones of the pitch pattern upon which the improvised melody is based. The tamboura is another plucked string instrument with four or five strings, each tuned to a tone of the melodic pitch pattern, which are always played open providing a continuous drone accompaniment.

INDIA/RAVI SHANKAR: *Thumri* 5:25

> *Thumri* denotes a type of Indian music which is less orthodox in style than most of the music played by Ravi Shankar. In Thumri style the inclusion of folk themes and changing from one underlying pitch pattern to another are permissible. The melodies are lyrical but highly ornamented. The mood is light and capricious.
>
> (Record side 10 band 5)

The ancient Bulgars began their westward migration from the Far East and by the 8th century had occupied the territory at the junction between East and West which is now Bulgaria. Traces of oriental influence which some detect in Bulgarian music can be ascribed to the Eastern origin of the people or to the Turkish occupation of the country which began in the 14th century and lasted until 1878. It was during the period of subjugation and comparative isolation that the music traditions, which thrive to the present time, developed among the common people. Bulgarian folk music is functional. There are songs and dances for every occasion—Sundays, feast days, fairs, weddings, work, and worship.

It can be generalized that Bulgarian tunes have a limited range and that the songs are mostly homophonic, but these features are not distinguishing. The striking feature of Bulgarian music is its rhythm. A high percentage of the meters in Bulgarian music are asymmetric (see p. 82), many involving unequal divisions of seven-beat measures. Similar metric patterns occur in the folk music of Rumania, Greece, Yugoslavia, Albania, and Turkey. One view is that the meters which divide 3+2+2 and 2+2+3 are triple meters that have the first or third beat elongated. Curiously, the pattern with an elongated second beat (2+3+2) is unknown in the folk music of Eastern and Southern Europe. The following round-and-chain dance is a brilliant example of 2+2+3 Bulgarian rhythm.

BULGARIA: *Tsone Mile Chedo/Eleno Mome* (Dance) 2:01

> The performers on the recording are peasant virtuosos recruited from various parts of Bulgaria by the State Folk Dance Ensemble. They are heard playing, in addition to a drum, four pairs of native instruments: 2 gaidas—medium-sized bagpipes with one drone and a chanter with eight holes; 2 gudulkas—string instruments played

in an upright position with a primitive bow; 2 tamburas—plucked string instruments with a long, fretted neck (compare the tamboura of India); and 2 kavals—shepherd pipes about 30 inches long with seven holes and no mouthpiece. As is customary, this dance piece has two distinct tunes, the second in this instance introduced by the kavals near midpoint in the performance.

(Record side 10 band 6)

The guitar is the national instrument of Spain. It came to the Iberian peninsula from the Orient by way of the invading Arabs, but when one thinks of the guitar, one thinks of Spanish music and more particularly *flamenco*. Flamenco is not a single, well-defined style, but a group of related styles that belong to a common tradition. Arabic, Moorish, Byzantine, and Jewish influences are detected in flamenco, but it is really the music of the Spanish Gypsies.

Flamenco encompasses all of the styles of guitar playing, but its trademark is the rapid, rhythmic strumming of full-bodied chords. Singing, dancing, and spectator interjections (clapping, stamping, heel-tapping, finger-snapping, and cries of *Ole*!) are also part and parcel of the flamenco tradition. The atmosphere of flamenco in its natural habitat, the cantinas of southern Spain, is captured and all of its elements are vividly displayed in the first flamenco example.

SPAIN/FLAMENCO: *En la Cueva* (*Bulerias*) 2:46

En la cueva means "in the cave," an allusion to the caves on Sacre Monte, a hill in Granada inhabited by the early gypsies where tourists are now entertained. *Bulerias* is a comparatively recent song style, though its rhythmic characteristics are of traditional derivation, which originated in the city of Jerez in southern Spain. The performing group is the Cuadro Flamenco.

(Record side 10 band 7)

A folk art with the potential for mass appeal is apt to be cultivated, refined, commercialized, and transported to the concert stage and recording studio. This phenomenon was observed in the evolution of country music and jazz. It has also occurred in flamenco. This (perhaps final) stage in the evolution of flamenco guitar is demonstrated in the following 1975 recording by the young Spanish guitar virtuoso Manolo Sanlucar. He has the impeccable technique of a modern concert artist, but he has also immersed himself in flamenco traditions, feels them deeply, and expresses them eloquently. The mood he projects is authentic, but distilled to the point where extraneous elements are eliminated. The melodies and chord progressions are derived from the flamenco (Phrygian) scale, but the aloof atmosphere is that of a distant stage or remote recording studio, not that of an intimate cantina. Something is gained and something is lost in the transformation.

SPAIN/FLAMENCO GUITAR: *Viva Jerez* (Long Live Jerez) 4:02

> Jerez de la Frontera, a city in the South of Spain where the Arab influence was most persistent, was and is one of the centers of flamenco music. This selection is from the album *Manolo Sanlucar: King of Flamenco Guitar* (Columbia M 33365).
>
> (Record side 10 band 8)

The preceding example illustrates a type of regional folk music in the process of becoming a kind of international art music. The following example reverses the process and shows a typical American popular song converted to a folk idiom. The popular song *Fire Down Below* (not to be confused with the chantey of the same name) was the title song of a 1957 Columbia motion picture starring Rita Hayworth, Jack Lemmon, and Robert Mitchum. The song was created especially for the motion picture by Ned Washington and Lester Lee and was released independently on two major record labels, but the Native Steel Drum Band of the West Indies treats it like an anonymous folk tune.

Steel drums are true folk instruments of recent origin. In the late 1930s "Spree" Simon discovered that different pitches could be produced by striking the head of an oil barrel in different places, and the concept of the steel drum was born. Steel drums are made by hand out of discarded oil barrels of various sizes which became plentiful in the West Indies during World War II. Designs and shapes are hammered into the heads of the barrels so that each area produces a definite pitch when it is struck. The steel drums are played with large mallets producing a powerful dynamic sound. A steel drum band consists of about 18 drums plus an assortment of untuned percussion instruments such as maracas, claves, and bells.

WEST INDIES/STEEL DRUM BAND: *Fire Down Below* 3:26

> This performance by the Native Steel Drum Band was recorded on location in the West Indies by a recording crew for Everest Records. The performers, who are black, possess the same rhythmic drive and predilection for percussion instruments as their African ancestors.
>
> (Record side 10 band 9)

This brief and highly selective survey of the music of other cultures provides only a glimpse into the treasury of the world's music. It does, however, confirm the fact that not just Western art music but all of the modes of human expression using rhythm and pitch—ethnic, folk, popular, jazz, modern, and ultramodern music included—are essential elements in the tonal universe. Each makes its own special contribution to the glorious art of music.

References

Holroyde, Peggy. *The Music of India.* New York: Praeger, 1972.

Hood, Mantle. *The Ethnomusicologist.* New York: McGraw-Hill, 1971. (with records)

Malm, William P. *Music Cultures of the Pacific, the Near East, and Asia.* Englewood Cliffs: Prentice-Hall, 1966.

Nettl, Bruno. *Folk and Traditional Music of the Western Continents.* 2d. ed. Englewood Cliffs: Prentice-Hall, 1973.

Nketia, J. H. Kwabena. *The Music of Africa.* New York: W. W. Norton, 1974.

Shankar, Ravi. *My Music, My Life.* New York: Simon and Schuster, 1968.

General References

Appendix I

Apel, Willi. *Harvard Dictionary of Music,* 2d. ed. Cambridge: Harvard University Press, 1969.

Baker's Biographical Dictionary of Musicians, 5th ed., revision and 1971 supplement by Nicolas Slonimsky. New York: G. Schrimer.

Grout, Donald J. *A History of Western Music.* Rev. ed. New York: W. W. Norton, 1973.

Grove's Dictionary of Music and Musicians. 5th ed. edited by Eric Blom with 1961 supplement by Denis Stevens, 10 vols. New York: St. Martin's Press, paper 1970.

Lang, Paul Henry. *Music in Western Civilization.* New York: W. W. Norton, 1941.

Scholes, Percy A. *The Oxford Companion to Music.* 10th ed. edited by John O. Ward. New York: Oxford University Press, 1970.

Schwann-1 Record & Tape Guide. Issued monthly. Available at record dealers.

Schwann-2 Record & Tape Guide. Issued in February and August. Available at record dealers.

Musical Examples

Appendix II

BARBER: *Symphony no. 1* (p. 71)[1], large orchestra

1. Page of text where the example is cited for the purpose indicated.

SCHUBERT: *Who Is Sylvia* (p. 90–92), melodic contour

GREGORIAN CHANT: *Alleluia, Vidimus stellam* (p. 111), monophonic texture

Source: *Liber Usualis,* Copyright 1934 by Desclee & Cie., Tournai, Belgium. Reprinted from *Masterpieces of Music Before 1750,* An Anthology of Musical Examples Compiled and Edited by Carl Parrish and John F. Ohl. Copyright 1951 by W. W. Norton & Company, Inc., and used with the permission of the publishers.

BACH: *Two-Part Invention no. 3* (p. 114), polyphonic texture

WAGNER: *Die Meistersinger Vorspiel* (p. 116), polyphonic texture

MENDELSSOHN: *Elijah, no. 15* (p. 120), homophonic texture

BEETHOVEN: *Symphony no. 5* (p. 126), motive

BACH: *French Suite no. 4* (p. 132), binary form

CHOPIN: *Mazurka no. 24* (p. 132), ternary form

CHOPIN: *Nocturne no. 4* (p. 133), ternary form

2. Identifying letters and numbers above the theme correspond with the form diagram in the text.

SCHUMANN: *Scenes from Childhood, no. 7* (p. 134), ternary form

SCHUMANN: *Scenes from Childhood, no. 1* (p. 135), ternary form

TCHAIKOVSKY: *Nutcracker Suite* (p. 135), ternary form

HINDEMITH: *Mathis der Maler* (p. 136), ternary form

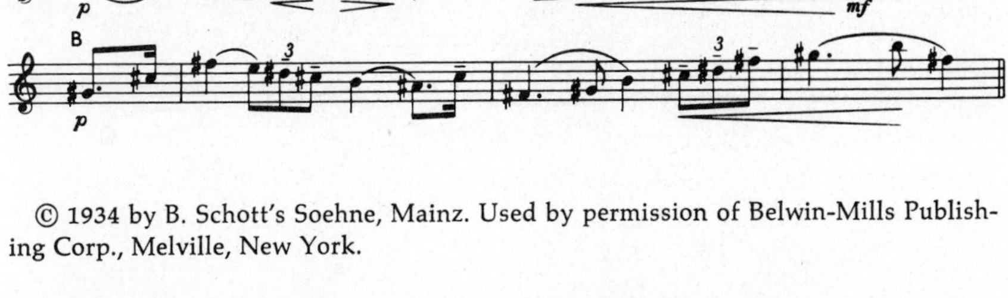

Sousa: *Hands Across the Sea* (p. 137), compound binary form

Introduction March-A

March-B

Trio-A

Trio-B

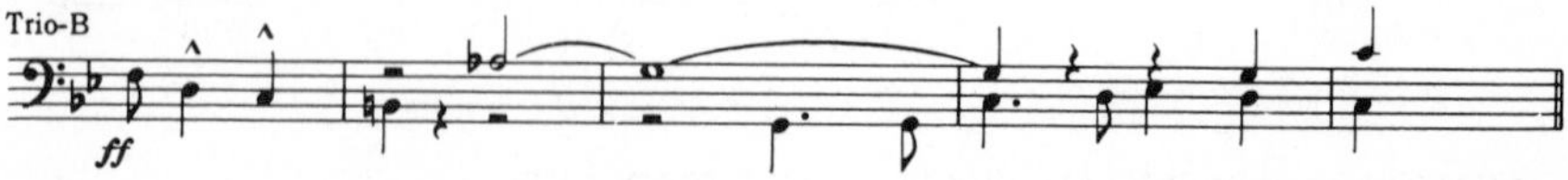

Mozart: *Symphony no. 35* (p. 139), compound ternary form

Minuet – A

Minuet – B

Trio – A

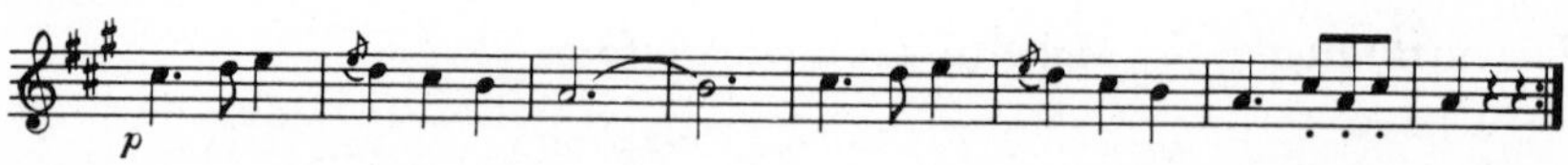

Trio – B

Beethoven: *Violin Sonata no. 5* (p. 140), compound ternary form

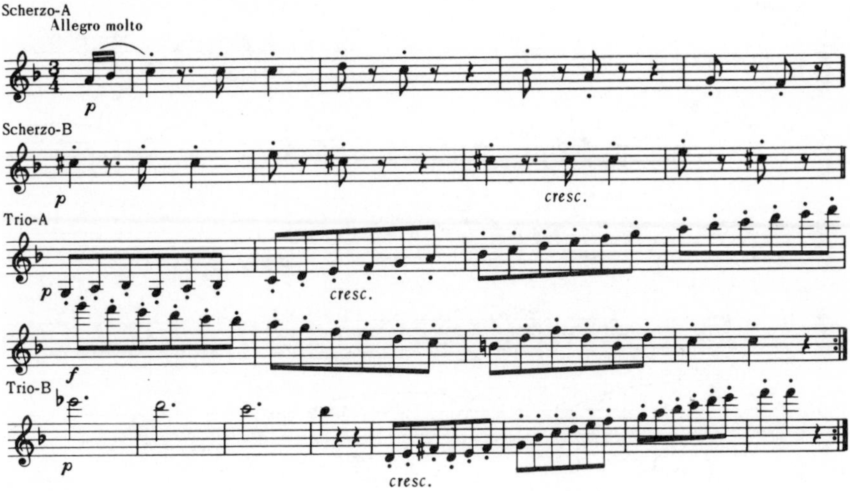
Scherzo-A
Allegro molto
p
Scherzo-B
p
cresc.
Trio-A
p
cresc.
f
Trio-B
p
cresc.

Handel: *Messiah* (p. 141), compound ternary form

Part I-A
Largo
He was des - pis-ed, des - pis - ed and re - ject-ed,
Part I-B
He was des - pis - ed, re - ject - ed,
Part II-A
He gave his back to the smit - ers, He gave his back to the smit - ers,
Part II-B
He hid not his face from shame and spit - ting.

Bach: *Partita no. 3 for Violin* (p. 145), old rondo form

Rondo Theme
tr

MOZART: *Serenade "Eine Kleine Nachtmusik"* (p. 146), rondo form, five-part

BEETHOVEN: *Piano Sonata no. 2* (p. 147), rondo form, seven-part

BEETHOVEN: *Piano Sonata no. 8* (p. 150), sonata form

BACH: *Musical Offering* (p. 157), canon

BACH: *Well-Tempered Clavier vol. I, no. 16* (p. 159), fugue

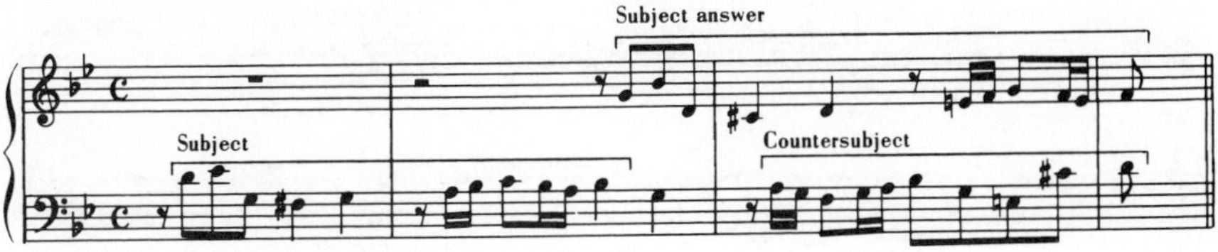

HAYDN: *String Quartet, "Emperor"* (p. 161), theme and variations

BEETHOVEN: *Piano Sonata no. 12* (p. 162), theme and variations

Brahms: *Variations on a Theme of Haydn* (p. 162), theme and variations

Haydn theme

Paganini: *Caprice no. 24* (p. 163), theme and variations

Theme

Purcell: *Dido and Aeneas* (p. 165), continuous variations

Ground

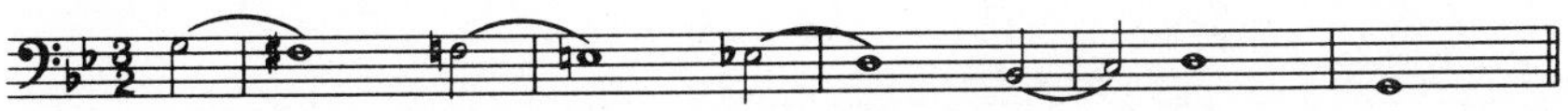

Bach: *Passacaglia and Fugue* (p. 165), continuous variations

Theme

Dvorak: *Symphony no. 9(5)* (p. 170), cyclic form

Motto theme

VIVALDI: *Violin Concerto in A minor* (p. 178), ritornello form

Ritornello theme

BACH: *Schübler Chorale Prelude no. 1* (p. 180), chorale prelude

Chorale melody

MUSSORGSKY: *Pictures at an Exhibition* (p. 186), program music

Promenade theme

BERLIOZ: *Symphonie Fantasique* (p. 189), program symphony

Idée fixe

BACH: *Wie schön leuchtet der Morgenstern* (p. 227), cantata

Chorale melody

Glossary and Index of Terms

Absolute music—abstract music with no extramusical implications. 184
A cappella—in the church style, that is, without accompaniment.
Accelerando—accelerating; gradually faster.
Adagio—comfortable, easy; a slow tempo.
Ad libitum (ad. lib.)—at will.
Affettuoso—with feeling.
Agitato—agitated.
Agnus Dei—a part of the Mass. 220
Air—a simple melody.
Alborada—morning song.
Aleatory—318
Allegretto—somewhat slower than allegro.
Allegro—cheerful; a lively, brisk tempo.
Allemande—171
Alto—low female voice. 17
—the second highest part in four-part music.
Andante—going along, walking; the median tempo.
Andantino—somewhat faster or slower than andante. 86
Animato—animated.
Antimusic—318
Antiphonal—responsorial singing or related instrumental effects.
Appassionata—with passion.
Arch form—152
Aria—a lyric song with instrumental accompaniment.
Articulation—11
Art song—an independent song for solo voice and piano. 58
Assai—very.
Atonal, atonality—without tonality; not in a key. 105
Attack—11
Augmentation—increased rhythmic values, usually doubled.
Augmented interval—an interval a semitone larger than the corresponding major or perfect interval.
Avant-garde—at the forefront; in the newest style.

Bagatelle—a trifle; a piece of modest pretensions.
Ballade—a word of varied meanings now usually applied to lyric or dramatic pieces. 182
Ballet—201
Band—65
Bar—a measure. 76
Bar lines—the lines between measures in musical notation. 84
Baritone—the male voice range between tenor and bass. 18
Baritone horn—42
Baroque binary form—131
Bass—low male voice. 19
—the largest string instrument. 24
—the lowest part in multipart music.
Bass clarinet—31
Bass trombone—42

Basso continuo—246
Basso ostinato—164
Bassoon—33
Battery—the percussion section.
Beat—the pulse of music; the unit of time marked by conductors. 76
Bebop, bop—348
Bell—the flared end of wind instruments.
Bell-lyra—42
Bells—43
Benedictus—a part of the Mass. 220
Binary form—131
  Compound—136
Blue notes—345
Blues—345
  Form—130
Boogie-woogie—346
Bourée—a dance of French origin frequently included in suites.
Bow—20
Bow form—152
Break—345
Bridge—135, 353
Brillante—brilliant.
Brio—spirit.
Buffo—comic.

Cadence—a closing effect associated with the ends of phrases. 127
Cadenza—an improvisatory passage typically found in concertos. 152
Camerata—193
Canon—155
Cantabile—singing style.
Cantata—226
Cantus planus—see Gregorian chant.
Capriccioso—capricious.
Caprice, capriccio—an instrumental composition in a free or whimsical style.
Cassation—174
Celesta—51
Cello—23
Cembalo—harpsichord.
Chaconne—165
Chamber music—59
Chance music—316
Chant—monophonic, liturgical music.
Chimes—43
Choir—a group that sings sacred music; a section of related instruments. 63
Choral—pertaining to a chorus or choir.
Chorale—a Protestant hymn tune.
Chorale prelude—a type of organ composition based on a chorale. 180
Chord—three or more tones sounding together.
Chords—97
  Cluster—99
  Eleventh—99
  Ninth—98
  Seventh—98
  Thirteenth—99
  Triad—97
Choreography—the composition and arrangement of dance movements, as for a ballet.
Chromatic—denoting a note or chord foreign to the tonality.
Chromatic scale—101
Church (ecclesiastical) modes—102
Clarinet—30
Classicism—257
Clavecin—harpsichord.
Claves—a pair of cylindrical hardwood sticks; Latin-American percussion instruments.
Clavier—keyboard.
Clicktrack—206
Coda—a concluding section added to a musical form. 136
Codetta—a small coda added to a principal part within a form. 136
Coloratura—colorful, florid; applied to highly ornamented passages in vocal music and to the voices that sing them.
Combo—a small jazz ensemble.
Compositional linguistics—328
Compound binary form—136
Compound ternary form—139
Computer music—328
Con—with.
Concertino—a small concerto; the solo group in a concerto grosso.
Concertmaster—the leader of the first violins in an orchestra.
Concerto—a composition for a solo instrument with orchestra.
Concerto grosso—178
Continuo—the figured bass part or its realization. 246
Contrabass—24
Contrabassoon—36
Contralto—alto voice.
Contrapuntal—employing counterpoint; polyphonic.
Cornet—36
Countermelody—a secondary melody associated with a principal melody.
Counterpoint—the art of combining melodies and the melodies thus combined. 113

Countersubject—a thematic counterpoint, especially to the subject of a fugue. 158
Country music—338
Courante—172
Credo—a part of the Mass. 220
Crescendo—gradually louder.
Cyclic form—169
Cymbals—44

Da capo (D.C.)—repeat from the beginning. 141
Da capo aria—141
Damper—a mechanism that stops the vibration of a sound source, such as a piano string.
Dance band—67
Decay—11
Decibel—the smallest unit of perceived loudness. 9
Deciso—with decision.
Decrescendo—gradually softer.
Development—a section, particularly in sonata form, in which the themes are worked out. 149
Di—of.
Dies irae—day of wrath; a section of the Requiem Mass and the plainsong melody associated with it.
Diminution—decreased rhythmic values, usually halved.
Divertimento—a multimovement instrumental form. 174
Dixieland—348
Dominant—the fifth degree of the scale and the chord and key associated with it.
Double bass—24
Doux—sweet.
Downbeat—84
Drums—43
  Bass—43
  Side—43
  Snare—43
  Tenor—43
Duet, duo—a composition for two performers. 59
Duration—11
Dynamics—107

E, ed—and.
Electronic instruments—52
Electronic music—325
Elegy—a composition in the mood of a lament.
Embouchure—the formation of the lips and tongue in relation to the mouthpiece of a wind instrument. 26
Energico—energetic.
English horn—33
Ensemble—a small group of performers; the art of playing together.
Episode—a passage between themes or statements of the subject, especially in a fugue. 158, 177
Eroica—heroic.
Espagnol(e)—Spanish.
Espressivo—expressively.
Ethnologist—one who studies the races of man, their origins, arts, and crafts.
Ethnomusicology—the study of regional and non-Western music. 358
Etude—a study.
Euphonium—42
Exposition—the section of a composition in which the themes are stated. 149
  Double—151
Expressionism—303

Fandango—a Spanish dance, possibly of South American origin.
Fantasia—181
Figured bass—a bass line with number and symbol notation for chords. 246
Finale—a final movement or section.
Fine—end. 141
Flamenco—363
Fluegel horn—38
Flute—27
Folk music—335
Foreign keys—keys with fewer than five tones in common. 106
Formalized music—322
Free part form—142
French horn—38
Frequency—the number of sound-producing vibrations per second.
Frets—thin strips of material fixed across the fingerboard of certain string instruments where the strings are stopped.
Fugato, fughetta—a fugal passage in a more extended form. 159
Fugue—115, 158
Funebre—funereal.
Fuoco—fire.

Gallant style—257
Gamelan—361
Gavotte—a dance of French origin frequently included in suites.
Gebrauchsmusik—music for practical use.

Gigue—172
Giocoso—playful.
Giojoso—joyful.
Giusto—just, strict, proper.
Glissando—sliding between tones sounding the intervening pitches.
Glockenspiel—42
Gloria—a part of the Mass. 220
Gong—a broad, slightly convex metal disc; an oriental percussion instrument.
Grave—slow, solemn.
Grazia, grazioso—grace, graceful.
Greek music—236
Gregorian chant—the monophonic liturgical music of the Roman Catholic Church. 111, 237
Ground, ground bass—a bass theme which is repeated continuously. 164

Habanera—a dance of Cuban origin popular in Spain.
Half step—a minor second; a semitone.
Happening—331
Harmony—the sounding together of different tones, especially in chord progressions. 95
Harp—45
Harpsichord—51
Hausmusik—music to be played at home.
Heterophony—112
Homophonic texture, homophony—116
Horn—38
Hydraulis—237

Imitation—repetition in another part after a short time lapse. 113
Impressario—an agent, manager, or producer.
Impressionism—290
Impromptu—a casual character piece, usually for piano. 182
Improvisation—321
Incidental music—204
Indeterminacy—318
Instrumentation—the writing of music for particular instruments or the instruments written for.
Intensity—the physical characteristic of sound that produces loudness.
Intermezzo—a digression interposed between parts of a more profound work.
Interval—the difference in pitch between two tones.
Intervals—95
Introduction—a passage or section preceding the main body of a form. 137
Invention—a term used by Bach for two-part contrapuntal compositions.
Inversion—contrary motion, ascending intervals becoming equivalent descending intervals and vice versa, or the reversal of the above-below relationship between two melodic lines.
Isorhythm—a principle of organization involving repetitions of a rhythmic pattern.

Jam session—a spontaneous jazz performance.
Jazz—343
Jazz styles—346
  Bebop, bop—348
  Boogie-woogie—346
  Cool—350
  Dixieland—348
  Eclectic—352
  Funky—350
  Kansas City—346
  Modern—350
  Neophonic—349
  Progressive—349
  Swing—347
  Symphonic—346
  Third stream—351
  West Coast—350

K., Koechel catalog—source of the identifying numbers for Mozart works.
Kabuki—360
Kettledrums—42
Key—the tonal center of a work or passage, identified by a letter name. 101
Key relationships—101
Keyboard instruments—47
Keynote—the central note of the key; the first degree of the scale in tonal music; the tonic note.
Konzertstuck—concert piece.
Kyrie—a part of the Mass. 219

L., Longo edition—source of the identifying numbers for Domenico Scarlatti works.
Larghetto—not quite as slow as largo.
Largo—broad, large; a very slow tempo.
Leitmotiv—194
Lent, lento—slow.
Libretto—the story and words of a dramatic musical work.
Lied—song.
Lieder—songs; plural of lied. 58
Light show—331

Linear—pertaining to lines, emphasizing the horizontal (contrapuntal) aspect of music as opposed to the vertical (harmonic).

Lyric—songlike, expressing intimate rather than epic or heroic ideas.

M.M., Maelzel metronome—numbers following the abbreviation indicate the number of beats per minute.
Ma—but.

Maestoso—majestically.
Magnificat—canticle of the Virgin Mary. 229
Major—a term denoting a quality of interval, scale, chord, key, tonality, or mode.
Manual—one of the keyboards of an organ or harpsichord.
Maraca—a Latin-American percussion instrument made of a gourd or gourdlike shell containing seeds or pebbles.
Marcato—marked.

Marcia, marciale—march, marchlike.
Mass—the solemn rite of the Roman Catholic Church commemorating the sacrifice of Christ. 219
Measure—a metric unit in music consisting of a specified number and pattern of beats. 76
Mediant—the third degree of the scale and the chord and key associated with it; the relative major of a minor key.
Medley—a hodgepodge of loosely connected tunes.

Menuet, menuetto—minuet.
Metallophones—percussion instruments of definite pitch consisting of a graduated set of metal bars.
Meter—the number and pattern of beats in a measure of music. 75
Meter signature—the numerical representation of the meter. 84
Metronome—a mechanical device used to establish tempos in music. 85
Mezzo-soprano—the female voice range between soprano and alto. 15
Microtones—intervals smaller than a semitone. 324
Mikrokosmos—microcosm (Bartok).

Minor—a term denoting a quality of interval, scale, chord, key, tonality, or mode.
Minuet—a French dance of rustic origin but courtly style in a moderately fast triple meter.

Miserere—Vulgate Psalm 50. 261

Mode—pertaining to major or minor or to one of the scale patterns of early church music. 101
Moderato, modéré—moderate.
Modulation—change of key. 106
Molto—very, much.
Monophonic texture, monophony—music consisting of a single unaccompanied line. 110
Mosso—motion.

Motive—the smallest recognizable structural unit of music. 126
Moto—motion.
Motto theme—a theme of special significance in a multimovement or programmatic work.
Movement—a complete and relatively independent part of an extended composition.
Moviola—a machine used for individual viewing of a motion picture for editing and scoring purposes.

Music drama—a special type of opera written by Wagner. 194

Musicologist—one devoted to the scientific study of music, particularly its history and literature.

Mute—a device used to soften and modify the tone of instruments.

Nocturne—a night piece. 182
Non—not.
Non troppo—not too much.

O—or.

Octave—a very consonant interval formed by two closely related tones which span eight scale degrees.

Opus (op.)—work; opus numbers ordinarily are assigned to the works of a composer in order of publication.
Oratorio—227
Orchestra—68
Orchestration—the art of writing and arranging music for orchestra.
Ordinary—the unchanging parts of the Mass.
Ordre—a suitelike collection of pieces.
Organs—50
Organum—237
Orgelbüchlein—little organ book (Bach).
Overtones—9
Overture—175

Parallel keys—the major key and the minor key with the same keynote. 106
Partita—a group of movements, mostly dances, like a suite. 174
Passacaglia—165
Passion—229
Passionato—impassioned.
Pasticcio—an operatic work pieced together from various sources. 194
Pastorale—a simple piece in an idyllic or rustic mood. 182
Pathetique—pathetic.
Pavane—292
Pedalboard—the keyboard of an organ played with the feet.
Percussion instruments—42
Period—127
Perpetuum mobile—perpetual motion.
Phrase—126
Phrasing—11
Piano—49
  Prepared—49
Piccolo—30
Pitch—7
Piu—more.
Piu tosto—rather.
Pizzicato—plucked.
Plainchant, plainsong—see Gregorian chant.
Poco—little.
Polka—a dance of Bohemian origin.
Polonaise—a dance of Polish origin.
Polyphonic texture, polyphony—music conceived as a combination of two or more melodies. 113
Polytonality—the presence of two or more tonalities (keys) at the same time. 104
Popular music—338

Potpourri—a medley of tunes from another source.
Prelude—179
Premiere—first performance.
Prestissimo—faster than presto; the fastest tempo marking.
Presto—very fast, rapid.
Program music—music with literary or pictorial associations. 184

Quadrille—a dance of 19th-century French origin.
Quarter tones—intervals half as large as semitones (minor seconds).
Quartet—a composition for four performers. 60
Quintet—a composition for five performers. 62

Rags, ragtime—344
Recapitulation—the section of a form in which the thematic material of the exposition returns. 149
Recitative—a passage in declamatory style for solo voice with a simple harmonic accompaniment. 246
Reed—the vibrating member of woodwind instruments. 25
Register—a portion of the pitch range of an instrument or voice.
Related keys—keys with five or more notes in common. 106
Relative keys—pairs of keys, one major and one minor, that have all seven notes in common but different keynotes; see also Mediant and Submediant. 106
Religioso—religiously.
Remote keys—keys with fewer than five notes in common. 106
Repeat signs—134
Repertoire, repertory—a treasury, collection, or list of works ready or available for performance.
Requiem—a Mass for the dead. 223
Rest—a symbol representing silence in music or such a period of silence.
Retrograde—backwards, from the end to the beginning.
Retrograde inversion—a combination of retrograde and inversion.
Rhapsody—181
Rhythm—75
Riff—347
Ritardando—gradually slower.
Ritornello form—177
Rock, rock 'n' roll—339

Rococo—257
Roman music—237
Romanticism—267
Rondeau—rondo.
Rondo—a piece or movement in rondo form.
Rondo form—144
  Five-part (simple)—145
  Old—144
  Seven-part (rondo-sonata)—147
Rondo sonata form—147
Rota—a round canon. 155
Round, round canon—a canon in which the end leads back to the beginning. 155
Rubato—a term suggesting freedom in rhythm and tempo.

S., Schmieder catalog—source of the identifying numbers of Bach works.
Sanctus—a part of the Mass. 220
Sarabande—172
Saxophones—31
Scale—a stepwise arrangement of the notes of a given key and/or mode.
Scat singing—346
Scherzando—playful, sportive.
Scherzo—joke, jest; a piece or movement characterized by vivacious rhythm or humor. 140
Score—a composite of all the parts of a composition.
Section—an instrumental choir. 65
  —a part of a large form.
Seguidilla—a Spanish dance.
Semitone—a minor second, the smallest conventional interval.
Sempre—always.
Sentence—127
Sequence—a type of liturgical chant.
  —the immediate repetition of a musical segment at a different pitch level.
Serenade—evening music, particularly a lover's song or a multimovement instrumental composition. 174
Serial music—105, 301
Sinfonia—an instrumental composition, often with an introductory function.
Sitar—361
Solo—alone; a piece or passage for one instrument or voice alone or predominant. 57
Sonata—a multimovement composition for one or two instruments.
Sonata form—148
  Complete—167
Sonata-rondo form—147
Song cycle—213
Song without words—a songlike instrumental piece. 182, 271
Sonority—sound; used as a more inclusive term than chord or harmony.
Soprano—high female or unchanged voice. 15
  —the highest part.
Sostenuto—sustained.
Soul music—340
Sousaphone—39
Spiccato—separated.
Spirito, spiritoso—spirited.
Stabat Mater—229
Stage band—349
Steel drums—364
Stop—a control device on an organ.
  —the act of depressing an instrumental string with the finger.
Stopped notes—notes produced on a French horn with the player's hand tightly inserted in the bell.
Stradivarius—one of the extremely valuable string instruments made by Antonio Stradivari (1644–1737).
Strain—a short well-defined subdivision of a composition.
Stretto—in a fugue, overlapping statements of the subject; elsewhere, a faster tempo.
String bass—24
String instruments—20
Strophic form—210
Subdominant—the fourth degree of the scale and the chord and key associated with it.
Subject—the main theme of a fugue. 115, 158
Submediant—the sixth degree of the scale and the chord and key associated with it; the relative minor of a major key.
Subtonic (leading tone)—the seventh degree of the scale and the chord and key associated with it.
Suite—171
Supertonic—the second degree of the scale and the chord and key associated with it.
Swing—347
Symphonic poem—188
Symphony—a complete sonata (multimovement) form for orchestra.

Synthesizers—52, 326
System and chance music—316

Tabla—361
Tambourine—a small one-headed drum that has metal jingle discs inserted in the rim.
Tambura—361
Tarantella—a fast Italian dance.
Te Deum—229
Tempo—the rate of speed in music. 85
Tenor—high male voice. 17
—the second lowest part in four-part music.
Ternary form—132
Compound—139
Theme—a musical idea of structural significance.
Theme and variation form—160
Third stream music—351
Thorough bass—see Figured bass.
Three-part form—132
Through-composed form—211
Timbre—tone color or quality. 9, 108
Time signature—the numerical representation of the meter. 84
Timpani—42
Toccata—a brilliant, freely constructed composition. 182
Tonality—101
Tone color—9, 108
Tone poem—188
Tone row—a series of all twelve tones in a specific order with none repeated.
Tonic—the first degree of the scale and the chord and key associated with it; the keynote.
Top forty—the forty most popular songs as established by various surveys.
Tosto—nearly.
Total organization—316
Total theater—331
Tract—a type of liturgical chant.
Transition—a connecting passage between structural elements of a musical form. 135
Transpose—to change to another pitch level and key.
Traps—the percussion instruments, collectively, used in jazz and popular music.
Très—very.
Triads—97
Triangle—44
Trio—a composition for three performers. 60
—the contrasting section in marches, minuets, and scherzos. 137, 139
Trombone—42
Troubadours—238
Trouvères—238
Trumpet—36
Tuba—38
Tuba mirum—a section of the Dies irae.
Tubular bells—43
Twelve-tone system—a technique of composition based on a series or tone row. 105, 301
Two-part form—131

Un—a, an.
Unison—the same pitch.
Upbeat—85

Valse—waltz.
Variation form—160
Continuous—164
Sectional—160
Variazioni—variations.
Vibraphone, vibraharp, vibes—a definite pitch percussion instrument consisting of a graduated set of metal bars with motordriven resonators that produce a vibrato effect.
Vibrato—slight, rapid fluctuations in pitch used, especially on string instruments, to intensify the emotional quality of sustained tones.
Vielle—238
Vif—lively.
Viola—22
Violin—21
Violoncello—23
Vivace—lively, quick.
Voices—15
Vorspiel—prelude. 180

Waltz—a perennially popular dance in triple meter that originated about 1800.
White noise—325
Whole step—a major second.
Whole tone scale—103
Wind instruments—25

Xylophone—43

Index of Composers, Performers, and Works

* Throughout this index an asterisk preceding an entry means a work or complete selection included in the *Listeners Guide Record Album.*